HOUGHTON MIFFLIN
SOCIAL STUDIES

★ WESTERN HEMISPHERE & EUROPE ★

GEOGRAPHY AND CULTURE

Visit
www.eduplace.com/kids

HOUGHTON MIFFLIN   BOSTON

★ AUTHORS ★

Dr. Sarah Witham Bednarz
Associate Professor, Geography
Texas A&M University

Dr. Mark C. Schug
Professor and Director
Center for Economic Education
University of Wisconsin, Milwaukee

Dr. Inés M. Miyares
Associate Professor, Geography
Hunter College
City University of New York

Dr. Charles S. White
Associate Professor
School of Education
Boston University

The United States has honored the Louisiana Purchase and the Lewis and Clark expedition in a new nickel series. The first nickel of the series features a rendition of the Jefferson Peace Medal. Thomas Jefferson commissioned this medal for Lewis and Clark's historic trip, which began in 1804.

Louisiana Purchase/Peace Medal nickel circulating coin images courtesy United States Mint. Used with permission.

HOUGHTON MIFFLIN
SOCIAL STUDIES

★ WESTERN HEMISPHERE & EUROPE ★

GEOGRAPHY AND CULTURE

HOUGHTON MIFFLIN

BOSTON

Consultants

Dr. Munir Bashshur
Education Department
American University of
 Beirut, Lebanon

Charmarie Blaisdell
Department of History
Northeastern University
Boston, Massachusetts

David Buck
Department of History
University of Wisconsin—
 Milwaukee
Milwaukee, Wisconsin

Stephen Fugita
Ethnic Studies Program
Santa Clara University
Santa Clara, California

Erich Gruen
Departments of Classics
 and History
University of California,
 Berkeley
Berkeley, California

Sharon Harley
Afro-American Studies
 Program
University of Maryland at
 College Park
College Park, Maryland

Charles Haynes
Senior Scholar for Religious
 Freedom
The Freedom Forum First
 Amendment Center
Arlington, Virginia

Alusine Jalloh
The Africa Program
University of Texas at
 Arlington
Arlington, Texas

Shabbir Mansuri
Council on Islamic
 Education
Fountain Valley, California

Michelle Maskiell
Department of History
Montana State University
Bozeman, Montana

Doug Monroy
Department of Southwest
 Studies
Colorado College
Colorado Springs, Colorado

Vasudha Narayanan
Department of Religion
University of Florida
Gainesville, Florida

Amanda Porterfield
Department of Religious
 Studies
University of Wyoming
Laramie, Wyoming

Cliff Trafzer
Departments of History and
 Ethnic Studies
University of California,
 Riverside
Riverside, California

Mark Wasserman
Department of History
Rutgers University
New Brunswick, New Jersey

Printed in the U.S.A.

ISBN: 0-618-47770-5

123456789-DW-13 12 11 10 09 08 07 06 05 04

Contents

Bringing the world to your classroom!

Resources

Extend Lessons

Features

Skill Lessons

Visual Learning

Become skilled at reading visuals. Graphs, maps, and timelines help you put all the information together.

Charts and Graphs

Diagrams and Infographics

Timelines

Fine Art

About Your Textbook

① How It's Organized

Units The major sections of your book are units.

Each unit starts with a big idea.

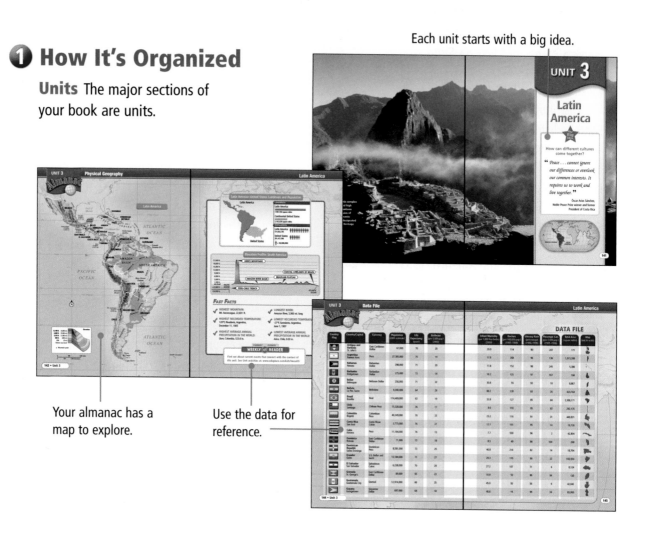

Your almanac has a map to explore.

Use the data for reference.

Chapters Units are divided into chapters, and each opens with a vocabulary preview.

Get ready for reading.

Four important concepts get you started.

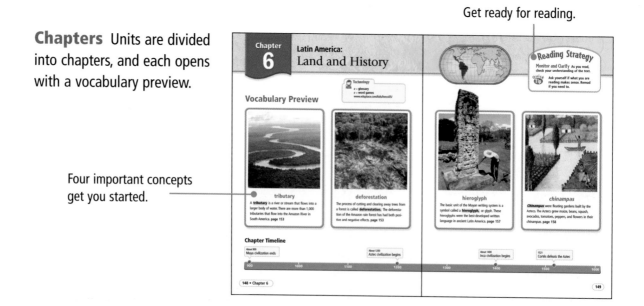

② Core and Extend

Lessons Each chapter is divided into core lessons. Each chapter also has an extend lesson.

Core Lessons

Lessons bring the events of history to life and help you meet your state's standards.

Core Lesson 3

Extend Lessons

These go deeper into an important topic.

Extend Lesson
Geography

Core Lesson

Vocabulary strategies help with word meanings.

Before you read, use your prior knowledge.

Reading skills support your understanding of the text.

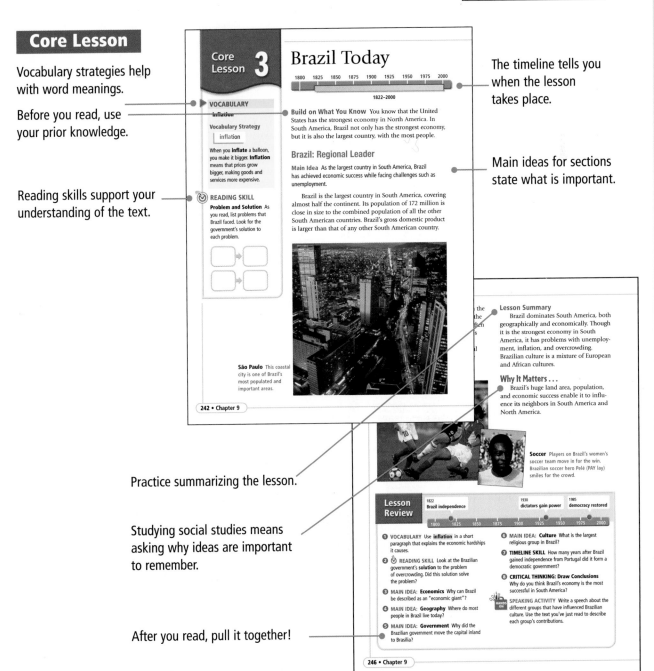

Core Lesson 3

Brazil Today

1800 1825 1850 1875 1900 1925 1950 1975 2000

1822–2000

VOCABULARY
inflation

Vocabulary Strategy
inflation

When you **inflate** a balloon, you make it bigger. **Inflation** means that prices grow bigger, making goods and services more expensive.

READING SKILL
Problem and Solution As you read, list problems that Brazil faced. Look for the government's solution to each problem.

Build on What You Know You know that the United States has the strongest economy in North America. In South America, Brazil not only has the strongest economy, but it is also the largest country, with the most people.

Brazil: Regional Leader

Main Idea As the largest country in South America, Brazil has achieved economic success while facing challenges such as unemployment.

Brazil is the largest country in South America, covering almost half the continent. Its population of 172 million is close in size to the combined population of all the other South American countries. Brazil's gross domestic product is larger than that of any other South American country.

São Paulo This coastal city is one of Brazil's most populated and important areas.

242 • Chapter 9

The timeline tells you when the lesson takes place.

Main ideas for sections state what is important.

Lesson Summary

Brazil dominates South America, both geographically and economically. Though it is the strongest economy in South America, it has problems with unemployment, inflation, and overcrowding. Brazilian culture is a mixture of European and African cultures.

Why It Matters . . .

Brazil's huge land area, population, and economic success enable it to influence its neighbors in South America and North America.

Soccer Players on Brazil's women's soccer team move in for the win. Brazilian soccer hero Pelé (PAY lay) smiles for the crowd.

Practice summarizing the lesson.

Studying social studies means asking why ideas are important to remember.

Lesson Review

1822 **Brazil independence**
1930 **dictators gain power**
1985 **democracy restored**

1800 1825 1850 1875 1900 1925 1950 1975 2000

❶ **VOCABULARY** Use **inflation** in a short paragraph that explains the economic hardships it causes.

❷ **READING SKILL** Look at the Brazilian government's **solution** to the problem of overcrowding. Did this solution solve the problem?

❸ **MAIN IDEA: Economics** Why can Brazil be described as an "economic giant"?

❹ **MAIN IDEA: Geography** Where do most people in Brazil live today?

❺ **MAIN IDEA: Government** Why did the Brazilian government move the capital inland to Brasília?

❻ **MAIN IDEA: Culture** What is the largest religious group in Brazil?

❼ **TIMELINE SKILL** How many years after Brazil gained independence from Portugal did it form a democratic government?

❽ **CRITICAL THINKING: Draw Conclusions** Why do you think Brazil's economy is the most successful in South America?

SPEAKING ACTIVITY Write a speech about the different groups that have influenced Brazilian culture. Use the text you've just read to describe each group's contributions.

246 • Chapter 9

After you read, pull it together!

Extend Lesson

Learn more about an important topic from one of the core lessons in each chapter.

Dig in and extend your knowledge.

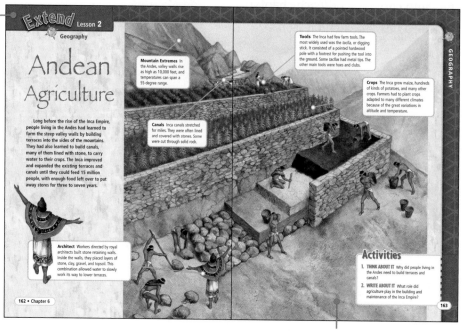

Look closely. Connect the past to the present.

Look for literature, readers' theater, geography, economics—and more.

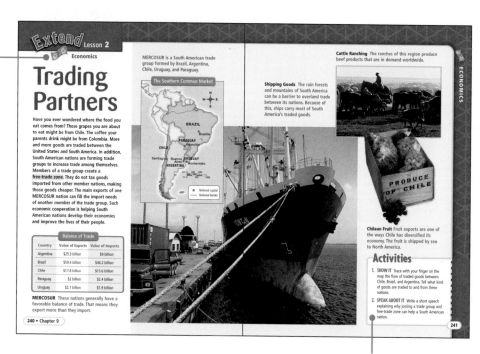

Write, talk, draw, and debate!

③ Skills

Skill Building

Learn map, graph, and study skills, as well as critical thinking skills for life.

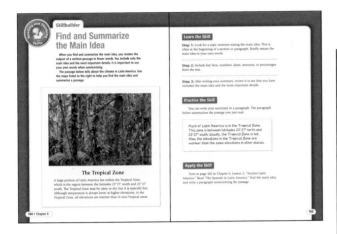

Each Skillbuilder lesson steps it out.

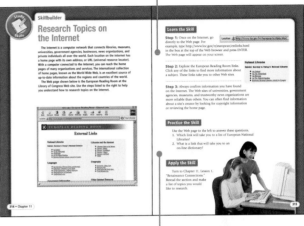

Practice and apply social studies skills.

④ References

Skillbuilder Handbook

The back of your book includes sections you'll refer to again and again.

Resources

Look for atlas maps, a glossary of social studies terms, and an index.

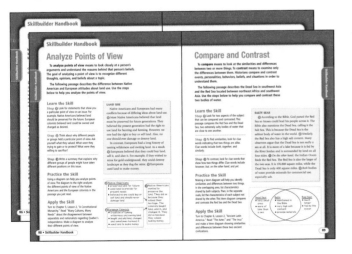

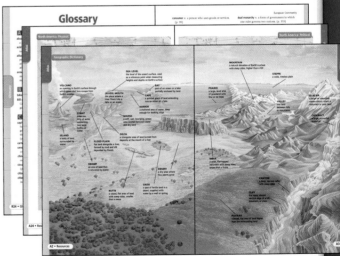

Reading Social Studies

Your book includes many features to help you be a successful reader. Here's what you will find:

VOCABULARY SUPPORT

Every chapter and lesson helps you with social studies terms. You'll build your vocabulary through strategies you're learning in language arts.

Preview
Get a jump start on four important words from the chapter.

Vocabulary Strategies
Focus on word roots, prefixes, suffixes, or compound words, for example.

Vocabulary Practice
Reuse words in the reviews, skills, and extends. Show that you know your vocabulary.

READING STRATEGIES

Look for the reading strategy and quick tip at the beginning of each chapter.

Predict and Infer
Before you read, think about what you'll learn.

Monitor and Clarify
Check your understanding. Could you explain what you just read to someone else?

Question
Stop and ask yourself a question. Did you understand what you read?

Summarize
After you read, think about the most important ideas of the lesson.

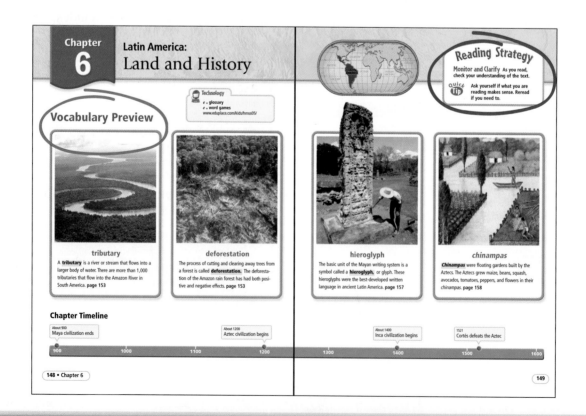

Chapter 6 — Latin America: **Land and History**

Technology
e • glossary
e • word games
www.eduplace.com/kids/hmss05/

Reading Strategy

Monitor and Clarify As you read, check your understanding of the text.

quick Tip Ask yourself if what you are reading makes sense. Reread if you need to.

Vocabulary Preview

tributary
A **tributary** is a river or stream that flows into a larger body of water. There are more than 1,000 tributaries that flow into the Amazon River in South America. page 153

deforestation
The process of cutting and clearing away trees from a forest is called **deforestation.** The deforestation of the Amazon rain forest has had both positive and negative effects. page 153

hieroglyph
The basic unit of the Mayan writing system is a symbol called a **hieroglyph,** or glyph. These hieroglyphs were the best-developed written language in ancient Latin America. page 157

chinampas
Chinampas were floating gardens built by the Aztecs. The Aztecs grew maize, beans, squash, avocados, tomatoes, peppers, and flowers in their *chinampas.* page 158

Chapter Timeline

About 900
Maya civilization ends

About 1200
Aztec civilization begins

About 1400
Inca civilization begins

1521
Cortés defeats the Aztec

900   1000   1100   1200   1300   1400   1500   1600

148 • Chapter 6

149

Physical Geography

Build on What You Know The United States is geographically diverse, with mountains and plains, forests and deserts. Latin America is physically diverse as well, but common language and culture tie this large region together.

VOCABULARY
tributary
deforestation
Tropical Zone
El Niño

Vocabulary Strategy

deforestation

The prefix **de-** means "remove." **Deforestation** means to remove a forest.

READING SKILL
Compare and Contrast
Take notes on the different landforms in Mexico and South America.

Defining Latin America

Main Idea Latin America is a vast land of varied geography united by a common language.

Latin America includes Mexico, Central America, the Caribbean, and South America. Because the languages of most of its colonizers—Spanish and Portuguese—are derived from Latin, Europeans later referred to the region's colonies as *Latin America*. Because the region is defined by a cultural connection, in this case language, it is called a culture region.

Mexico is the farthest north of the Latin American countries. You can see that Mexico's major physical features include mountains, plateaus, and plains.

Mexico's two major mountain ranges share the name Sierra Madre (see EHR uh MAH dray). Between the two ranges sits Mexico's large central plateau. The vast northern stretches of the central plateau are desert.

Volcanoes Latin America has many active volcanoes. This volcano, named Mount Popocatépetl (poh puh KAT uh peht uhl) is located near Mexico City.

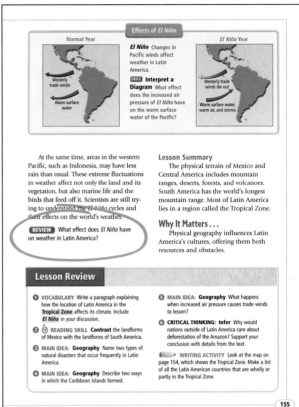

Effects of *El Niño*

Normal Year

El Niño Changes in Pacific winds affect weather in Latin America.

SKILL **Interpret a Diagram** What effect does the increased air pressure of *El Niño* have on the warm surface water of the Pacific?

El Niño Year

Westerly trade winds

Warm surface water

Westerly trade winds die out

Warm surface water, warm air, and storms

At the same time, areas in the western Pacific, such as Indonesia, may have less rain than usual. These extreme fluctuations in weather affect not only the land and its vegetation, but also marine life and the birds that feed off it. Scientists are still trying to understand the *El Niño* cycles and their effects on the world's weather.

REVIEW What effect does *El Niño* have on weather in Latin America?

Lesson Summary

The physical terrain of Mexico and Central America includes mountain ranges, deserts, forests, and volcanoes. South America has the world's longest mountain range. Most of Latin America lies in a region called the Tropical Zone.

Why It Matters . . .

Physical geography influences Latin America's cultures, offering them both resources and obstacles.

Lesson Review

1 **VOCABULARY** Write a paragraph explaining how the location of Latin America in the **Tropical Zone** affects its climate. Include *El Niño* in your discussion.

2 **READING SKILL** **Contrast** the landforms of Mexico with the landforms of South America.

3 **MAIN IDEA: Geography** Name two types of natural disasters that occur frequently in Latin America.

4 **MAIN IDEA: Geography** Describe two ways in which the Caribbean Islands formed.

5 **MAIN IDEA: Geography** What happens when increased air pressure causes trade winds to lessen?

6 **CRITICAL THINKING: Infer** Why would nations outside of Latin America care about deforestation of the Amazon? Support your conclusion with details from the text.

WRITING ACTIVITY Look at the map on page 154, which shows the Tropical Zone. Make a list of all the Latin American countries that are wholly or partly in the Tropical Zone.

READING SKILLS

As you read, organize the information. These reading skills will help you:

Sequence

Cause and Effect

Compare and Contrast

Problem and Solution

Draw Conclusions

Predict Outcomes

Categorize (or) Classify

Main Idea and Details

COMPREHENSION SUPPORT

Build on What You Know
Check your prior knowledge. You may already know a lot!

Review Questions
Connect with the text. Did you understand what you just read?

Summaries
Look for three ways to summarize—a list, an organizer, or a paragraph.

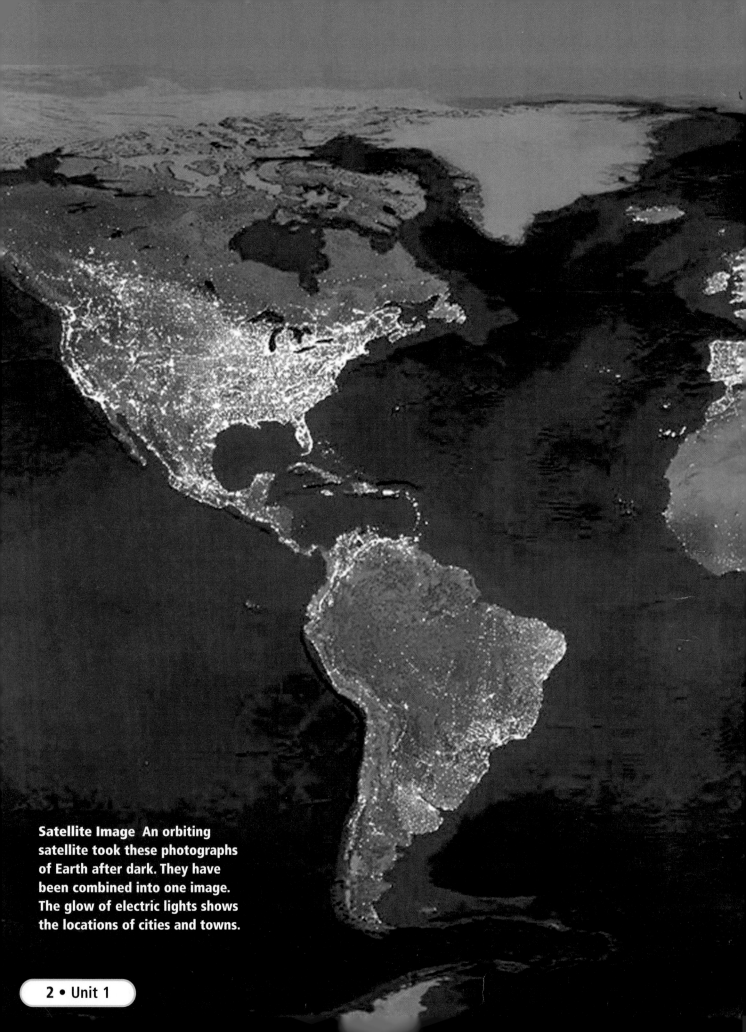

Satellite Image An orbiting satellite took these photographs of Earth after dark. They have been combined into one image. The glow of electric lights shows the locations of cities and towns.

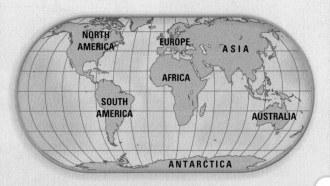

Introduction to World Cultures and Geography

The Big Idea

What makes a place special?

" *The land was ours before we were the land's.* "

Robert Frost,
poet

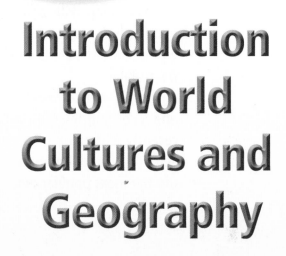

NORTH AMERICA

EUROPE

ASIA

AFRICA

SOUTH AMERICA

AUSTRALIA

ANTARCTICA

3

Geography Skills Handbook

Map Basics

Maps are an important tool for studying the use of space on Earth. This handbook covers the basic map skills and information that geographers rely on as they investigate the world—and the skills you will need as you study geography.

Mapmaking depends on surveying, or measuring and recording the features of Earth's surface. Until recently, this could be undertaken only on land or sea. Today, aerial photography and satellite imaging are the most popular ways to gather data.

Compasses Magnetic compasses, introduced by the Chinese in the 1100s, help people accurately determine directions.

Sextant Determining a ship's location at sea was the purpose of this 1750 instrument, called a sextant.

Grid An early example of a three-dimensional geographic grid.

Theodolite Nigerian surveyors use a theodolite, which measures angles and distances on Earth.

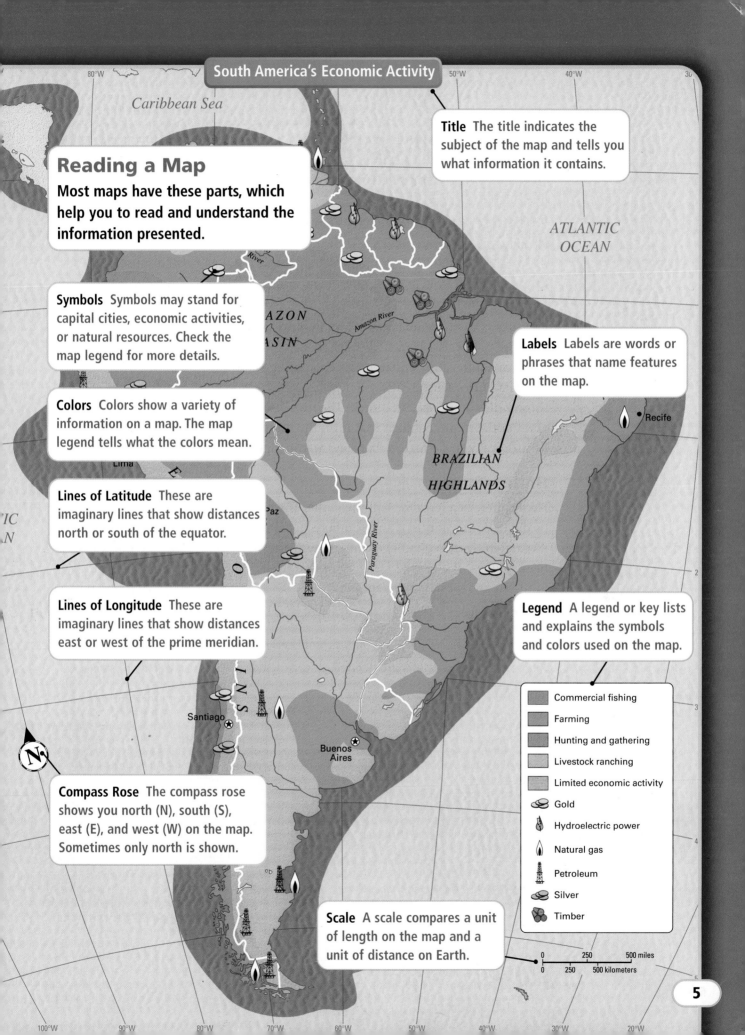

Reading a Map

Most maps have these parts, which help you to read and understand the information presented.

Title The title indicates the subject of the map and tells you what information it contains.

Symbols Symbols may stand for capital cities, economic activities, or natural resources. Check the map legend for more details.

Labels Labels are words or phrases that name features on the map.

Colors Colors show a variety of information on a map. The map legend tells what the colors mean.

Lines of Latitude These are imaginary lines that show distances north or south of the equator.

Lines of Longitude These are imaginary lines that show distances east or west of the prime meridian.

Legend A legend or key lists and explains the symbols and colors used on the map.

Compass Rose The compass rose shows you north (N), south (S), east (E), and west (W) on the map. Sometimes only north is shown.

Scale A scale compares a unit of length on the map and a unit of distance on Earth.

Caribbean Sea

ATLANTIC OCEAN

AMAZON BASIN

Amazon River

BRAZILIAN HIGHLANDS

Recife

Lima

Paz

Paraguay River

ANDES

Santiago

Buenos Aires

Legend:
- Commercial fishing
- Farming
- Hunting and gathering
- Livestock ranching
- Limited economic activity
- Gold
- Hydroelectric power
- Natural gas
- Petroleum
- Silver
- Timber

0   250   500 miles
0   250   500 kilometers

5

Longitude and Latitude Lines

Longitude and latitude lines appear together on a map and allow you to pinpoint the absolute locations of cities and other geographic features. You express these locations as coordinates of intersecting lines. These are measured in degrees.

Longitude lines are imaginary lines that run north and south; they are also known as meridians. They show distances in degrees east or west of the prime meridian. The prime meridian is a longitude line that runs from the North Pole to the South Pole through Greenwich, England. It marks 0° longitude.

Longitude Lines (Meridians)

Latitude lines are imaginary lines that run east to west around the globe; they are also known as parallels. They show distances in degrees north or south of the equator. The equator is a latitude line that circles Earth halfway between the north and south poles. It marks 0° latitude. The tropics of Cancer and Capricorn are parallels that form the boundaries of the tropical zone, a region that stays warm all year.

Latitude Lines (Parallels)
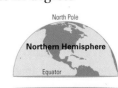

Hemisphere

Hemisphere is a term for half the globe. The globe can be divided into northern and southern hemispheres (separated by the equator) or into eastern and western hemispheres. The United States is located in the northern and western hemispheres.

Scale

A geographer decides what scale to use by determining how much detail to show. If many details are needed, a large scale is used. If fewer details are needed, a small scale is used.

Washington D.C. Metro Area
Scale: 1:4,500,000
1 inch= 70 miles

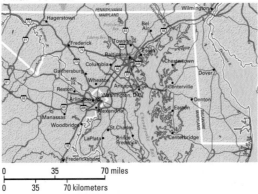

Small scale used, without a lot of detail.

Washington D.C.
Scale: 1:88,700
1 inch= 1.4 miles

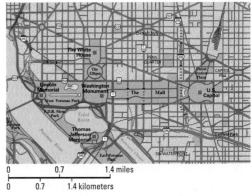

Larger scale used, with a lot of detail.

Projections

A projection is a way of showing the curved surface of Earth on a flat map. Flat maps cannot show sizes, shapes, and directions with total accuracy. As a result, all projections distort some aspect of Earth's surface. Below are four projections.

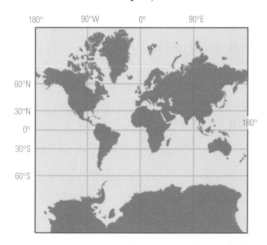

Mercator Projection The Mercator projection shows most of the continents as they look on a globe. However, the projection stretches out the lands near the north and south poles. The Mercator projection is used for all kinds of navigation.

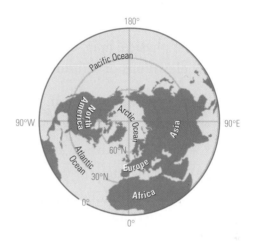

Azimuthal Projection An azimuthal projection shows Earth so that a straight line from the central point to any other point on the map corresponds to the shortest distance between the two points. Sizes and shapes of the continents are distorted.

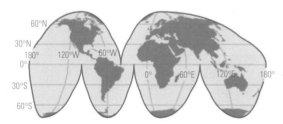

Homolosine Projection This projection shows landmasses' shapes and sizes accurately, but distances are not correct.

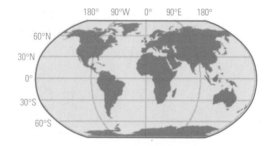

Robinson Projection For textbook maps, the Robinson projection is commonly used. It shows the entire Earth, with continents and oceans having nearly their true sizes and shapes. However, the landmasses near the poles appear flattened.

Practice the Skill

1. What are the longitude and latitude of your city or town?

2. What information is provided by the legend in the map on page 5?

3. What is a projection? Compare and contrast the depictions of Antarctica in the Mercator and Robinson projections.

Apply the Skill

1. **Make Inferences** Why do you think latitude and longitude are important to sailors?

Geography Skills Handbook

Different Types of Maps

Physical Maps

Physical maps help you see the landforms and bodies of water in specific areas. By studying a physical map, you can learn the relative locations and characteristics of places in a region.

On a physical map, color, shading, or contour lines are used to show elevations or altitudes, also called relief.

Ask these questions about the physical features shown on a physical map:

- Where on Earth's surface is this area located?
- What is its relative location?
- What is the shape of the region?
- In which directions do the rivers flow? How might the directions of flow affect travel and transportation in the region?
- Are there mountains or deserts? How might they affect the people living in the area?

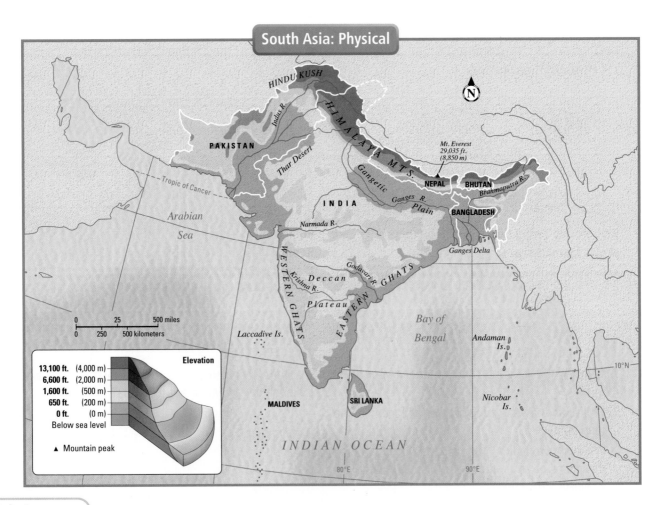

Political Maps

Political maps show features that humans have created on Earth's surface. Included on a political map may be cities, states, provinces, territories, and countries.

Ask these questions about the political features shown on a political map:

- Where on Earth's surface is this area located?

- What is its relative location? How might a country's location affect its economy and its relationships with other countries?

- What is the shape and size of the country? How might its shape and size affect the people living in the country?

- Who are the region's, country's, state's, or city's neighbors?

- How populated does the area seem to be? How might that affect activities there?

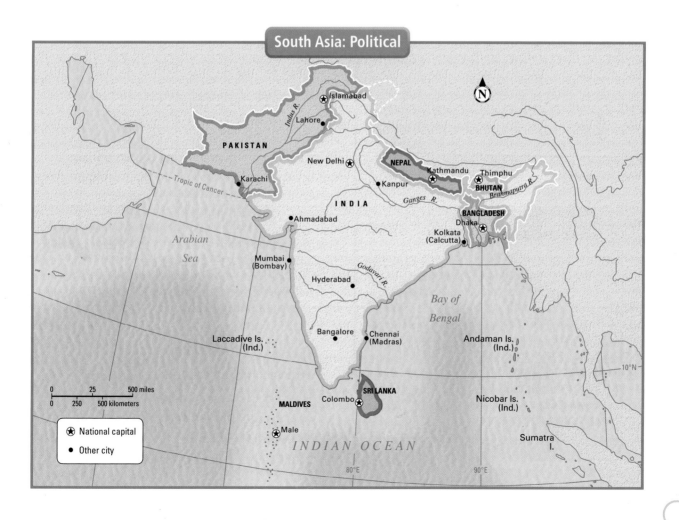

South Asia: Political

Thematic Maps

Geographers also rely on thematic maps, which focus on specific ideas. For example, in this textbook you will see thematic maps that show climates, types of vegetation, natural resources, population densities, and economic activities. Some thematic maps show historical trends; others may focus on movements of people or ideas. Thematic maps may be presented in a variety of ways.

Qualitative Maps On a qualitative map, colors, symbols, dots, or lines are used to help you see patterns related to a specific idea. The map shown here depicts the influence of the Roman Empire on Europe, North Africa, and Southwest Asia.

Cultural Legacy of the Roman Empire

Christian areas around A.D. 500

Romance language spoken, present day

Boundary of Roman Empire, A.D. 395

0   500   1,000 miles
0   500   1,000 kilometers
Azimuthal Equidistant Projection

Use the suggestions below to help you interpret the map.

- Check the title to identify the theme and the data being presented.
- Carefully study the legend to understand the theme and the information presented.
- Look at the physical or political features of the area. How might the theme of the map affect them?
- What are the relationships among the data?

Cartograms A cartogram presents information about countries other than their shapes and sizes. The size of each country is determined by the data being presented, and not by its actual land size. On the cartogram shown here, the countries' sizes show the amounts of their oil reserves.

Use the suggestions below to help you interpret the map.

- Check the title and the legend to identify the data being presented.
- Look at the relative sizes of the countries shown. Which is the largest?
- Which countries are smallest?
- How do the sizes of these countries on a physical map differ from their sizes in the cartogram?
- What are the relationships among the data?

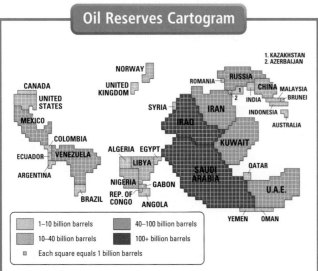

Oil Reserves Cartogram

1. KAZAKHSTAN
2. AZERBAIJAN

1–10 billion barrels
10–40 billion barrels
40–100 billion barrels
100+ billion barrels

Each square equals 1 billion barrels

Flow-Line Maps Flow-line maps illustrate movements of people, goods, or ideas. The movements are usually shown by a series of arrows. Locations, directions, and scopes of movement can be seen. The width of an arrow may show how extensive a flow is. Often the information is related to a period of time. The map shown here portrays the movement of the Bantu peoples in Africa.

Use the suggestions below to help you interpret the map.

- Check the title and the legend to identify the data being presented.
- Over what period of time did the movement occur?
- In what directions did the movement occur?
- How extensive was the movement?

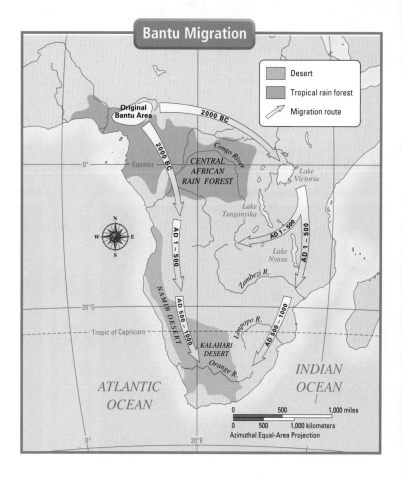

Practice the Skill

1. In what direction does the Ganges River flow?
2. Kathmandu is the capital of which South Asian nation?
3. Which city is closer to the Thar Desert—Lahore, Pakistan, or New Delhi, India?
4. Why are only a few nations shown in the cartogram on page 10?
5. Which kind of thematic map would be best for showing the locations of climate zones?

Apply the Skill

Obtain a physical-political map of your state. Use the data on it to create two separate maps. One should show physical features only, and the other map should show political features only.

Chapter 1

Welcome to the World

Technology

e • **glossary**
e • **word games**
www.eduplace.com/kids/hmss05/

Vocabulary Preview

history

History is a record of the people and events of the past. Knowledge of what happened in the past helps us understand the world today.
page 15

government

The people and laws that run a country are its **government.** The headquarters of the United States government are located in Washington, D.C.
page 16

Reading Strategy

Summarize As you read, use this strategy to focus on important ideas.

Quick Tip Use the main ideas to get started. Then look for important details that explain those ideas.

economics

Economics is the study of how people manage resources to produce, exchange, and use goods and services. A region's economics affects its people, culture, and government.

page 17

culture region

South Asia is a **culture region** of the world. Many of the people there share a history, a language, beliefs, and other ways of life.

page 19

The World at Your Fingertips

VOCABULARY

history
geography
government
citizen
economics
scarcity
culture

Vocabulary Strategy

scarcity

Scarcity comes from the word **scarce**. The suffix "ity" makes a word a noun. Scarcity occurs when there is not enough of an item that people want.

READING SKILL

Categorize Categorize the kind of information about the world you can learn from each of the five fields of social studies.

Build on What You Know If you found something new and wanted to learn about it, what would you do? You wouldn't just look at one small part of it. You would probably examine the object from all different angles. That is how social studies examines the world—from different angles.

Learning About the World

Main Idea Social studies, including history and geography, gives us information that helps us understand the world and its peoples.

For centuries, people in different parts of the world have been trying to get along with one another, not always with success. Part of the problem is a lack of understanding of other people's ways of life. Certain advances in communication and transportation, such as the Internet and high-speed planes, have brought people closer together. So have increased international trade and immigration. Knowledge of other societies can be a key to understanding them.

Social studies is a way to learn about the world. It draws on information from five fields of learning—geography, history, economics, government, and culture. Each field looks at the world from a different angle. Consider the approaches you might use if you were starting at a new school. Figuring out how to get around would be learning your school's geography. Asking other students where they come from is learning their history. Making choices about which school supplies you can afford to buy is economics. Learning the school rules is learning about its government. Clubs, teams, styles of clothing, holidays, and even ways of saying things are part of the school's culture.

History

Knowing history and geography helps orient you in time and space. **History** is a record of the past. The people and events of the past shaped the world as it is today. Historians such as David McCullough search for primary sources, such as newspapers, letters, journals, and other documents, to find out about past events. As he explains,

> 66 **How can we know who we are and where we are going if we don't know anything about where we have come from and what we have been through, the courage shown, the costs paid, to be where we are?** 99

Geography

Geography is the study of people, places, and the environment. Geography deals with the world in spatial terms. The study of geography focuses on five themes: **location, region, place, movement,** and **human-environment interaction.**

Location tells where a place is. Several countries that have features in common form a region. Place considers an area's distinguishing characteristics. Movement is a study of the migrations of people, animals, and even plants. Human-environment interaction considers how people change and are changed by the natural features of Earth.

REVIEW Explain the difference between the study of history and geography.

Five Themes of Geography

❶ Location Israel is on the southeast shore of the Mediterranean.

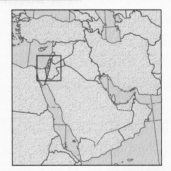

❷ Region Israel is part of Southwest Asia.

❸ Place Israel has a dry climate in the south, and a wetter climate in the north, with prosperous farms and thriving cities.

❹ Movement Immigrants arrive in Israel.

❺ Human-Environment Interaction Irrigation systems supply Israel's dry climate with water.

Amartya Sen (b. 1933) Amartya Sen (ah MART yah sen) was born in India. As a professor at Trinity College in Cambridge, England, he taught and studied economics. An important part of his research was to look at catastrophes, such as famine, that happen to the world's poorest people. By showing governments that food shortages are often caused by social and economic conditions, he hoped to prevent famines in the future. In 1998, Sen won the Nobel Prize in Economic Sciences for his research in welfare economics.

Government, Economics, and Culture

Main Idea Government, economics, and culture look at different aspects of the world's people.

Every country has laws and a way to govern itself. Laws are the rules by which people live. **Government** is the people and groups within a society that have the authority to make laws, to make sure they are carried out, and to settle disagreements about them. The kind of government determines who has the authority to make the laws and see that they are carried out.

In certain kinds of governments, everyone, including those in charge, must obey the laws. Some of the laws tell the government what it cannot do. People may have the authority to make laws directly or they may make laws through elected representatives. The governments of the United States, Mexico, and India are examples of this kind of government.

Rulers in other governments can do whatever they want without regard to the law. For example, in a totalitarian government the people have no say. Rulers have total control.

A **citizen** is a legal member of a country. Citizens have rights, such as the right to vote in elections, and duties, such as paying taxes. Being born in a country can make you a citizen. Another way is to move to a country, complete certain requirements, and take part in a naturalization ceremony.

Naturalization The process for becoming a citizen is called naturalization. The last step of the process is a ceremony where people swear to support and defend the Constitution and laws of the land.

Economics

Looking at the long list of flavors at the ice cream store, you have a decision to make. You have only enough money for one cone. Will it be mint chip or bubble gum flavor? You will have to choose. **Economics** is the study of how people manage their resources by producing, exchanging, and using goods and services. Economics is about choice.

Some economists claim that people's desires are unlimited. Resources to satisfy these desires, however, are limited. These economists refer to the conflict between people's desires and their limited resources as **scarcity.**

Economists identify three types of resources: natural, human, and capital. Natural resources are gifts of nature, such as forests, fertile soil, and water. Human resources are skills people have to produce goods and services. Capital resources are the things people make, such as machines and equipment, to produce goods and services.

Kinds of Economics

Blue jeans are a product. Who decides whether to make them and how many to make and what price to charge? In a command economy, the government decides. In a market economy, individual businesses decide, based on what they think consumers want.

Different countries and regions have different levels of economic development. In a country with a high level of development, most people are well educated, have good health, and earn decent salaries. Services such as clean running water, electricity, and transportation are plentiful. Technology is advanced, and businesses flourish.

A country with a low level of development is marked by few jobs in industry, poor services, and low literacy rates. Life expectancy is low. These countries are often called developing countries.

REVIEW How does a market economy differ from a command economy?

Citizenship IN ACTION

High Tech for the Developing World Mae Jemison is a former astronaut and the first African American woman to orbit Earth. In 1993, she left the space program and set up the Jemison Institute for Advancing Technology in Developing Countries. This organization uses space program technology to help developing countries.

One project uses a satellite-based telecommunication system to improve health care in West Africa. Another project is an international science camp for students aged 12 to 16.

Culture

Some people wear saris. Others wear T-shirts. Some people eat cereal and milk for breakfast. Others eat pickled fish. Some people go to church on Sunday morning. Others kneel and pray to Allah five times a day. All these differences are expressions of **culture.** Culture consists of the beliefs, customs, laws, art, and ways of living that a group of people share.

Religion is part of most cultures; so is a shared language. The ways people express themselves through music, dance, literature, and the visual arts are important parts of every culture; so are the technology and tools they use to accomplish various tasks. Each kind of food, clothing, or technology, each belief, language, or tool shared by a culture is called a culture trait. Taken together, the culture traits of a people shape their way of life.

Lesson Summary

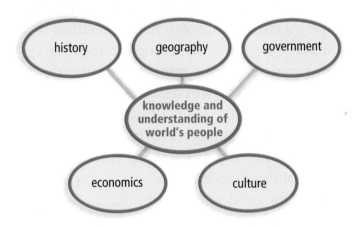

Why It Matters . . .

Understanding your world is essential if you are to be an informed citizen of a global society.

Lesson Review

1 VOCABULARY Match each word with its definition.

> culture geography history

(a) the study of people, places, and the environment
(b) the beliefs, customs, laws, and art that a people share
(c) a record of the past

2 READING SKILL Into what **category** would you put knowledge of a people's art and music?

3 MAIN IDEA What five areas of learning does social studies include?

4 MAIN IDEA: History What resources do people use to find out about the past?

5 MAIN IDEA: Economics What are the three main kinds of resources, and how is each one defined?

6 FACTS TO KNOW What are the **five themes of geography**?

7 CRITICAL THINKING: Infer Do people in the United States share a culture? Explain your answer.

ART ACTIVITY Reread the section on citizenship. Make a poster showing the rights and responsibilities of a citizen.

Many Regions, Many Cultures

Build on What You Know Have you ever seen a movie or read a book about people in another country? You probably noticed that the food they ate, the homes they lived in, or even the language they spoke was different from your own. The world has many different cultures because it has many different regions.

Different Places, Different Cultures

Main Idea The world can be divided into regions according to culture.

A **culture region** is an area of the world in which many people share similar beliefs, history, and languages. The people in a culture region may have religion, technology, and ways of earning a living in common as well. They may grow and eat similar foods, wear similar kinds of clothes, and build houses in similar styles.

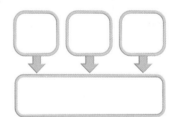
Culture Region The people of a culture region often share common food and drink. These women from Tamilnadu, India, are picking tea, which people throughout South Asia use to make hot beverages.

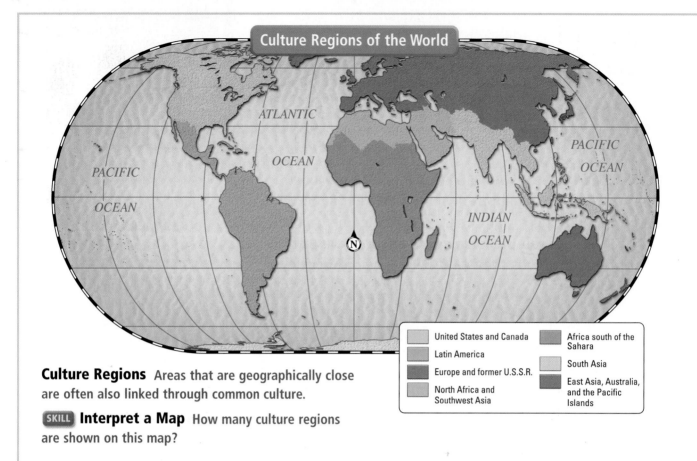

ATLANTIC

OCEAN

PACIFIC

OCEAN

PACIFIC

OCEAN

INDIAN

OCEAN

N

United States and Canada

Latin America

Europe and former U.S.S.R.

North Africa and
Southwest Asia

Africa south of the
Sahara

South Asia

East Asia, Australia,
and the Pacific
Islands

Culture Regions Areas that are geographically close
are often also linked through common culture.

SKILL **Interpret a Map** How many culture regions
are shown on this map?

The World's Culture Regions

The map above shows the major culture regions of the world. Latin America is
one culture region. The Spanish and
Portuguese languages help to tie its people together. So does its common history.

Southwest Asia and North Africa is
another culture region. Most countries
in this region share a common desert
climate and landscape. People have
adapted to the desert in similar ways, thus
creating a common culture. Islam, which
is the major religion in this region, also
helps shape a common culture.

Usually, not every person in a region
belongs to the dominant, or mainstream,
culture. Some regions are multicultural.
For example, the United States and
Canada contain other cultures besides the
dominant one.

Although most people in this region
speak English, many people in eastern
Canada speak French. Many people in the
United States speak Spanish, especially in
the Southwest. Some people even speak a
simplified combination, or pidgin, of several languages.

In both Canada and the United States,
Catholics, Protestants, Jews, Muslims,
Buddhists, and members of other religions
are free to worship.

For thousands of years, culture regions
have changed and evolved as they have
borrowed culture traits from one another.
They have also come to depend upon
each other economically. Decisions and
events in one part of the world affect
other parts. Advances in transportation
and communication have increased this
interdependence.

Different Homes Home life can differ greatly in different culture regions, sometimes depending on a region's climate or natural resources.

When oil-producing nations in the Middle East raise the price of oil, for example, the price of gasoline at the neighborhood gas station is likely to rise. If there is an especially abundant banana crop in parts of Latin America, the price of bananas may drop at the local grocery store. More and more, people of different countries are becoming part of one world.

REVIEW Name two characteristics that make the United States multicultural.

Lesson Summary

- People in a culture region share similar beliefs, history, and languages.
- There are seven major culture regions in the world.
- Culture regions change, borrow from each other, and depend on each other.

Why It Matters...

Understanding other cultures can help you understand how people in other regions live and think.

Lesson Review

1 VOCABULARY Write a short paragraph about world cultures, using **culture region** and **interdependence.**

2 READING SKILL What can you **conclude** are some of the factors that have led to the development of different culture regions?

3 MAIN IDEA: Culture List at least three things people in a culture region may have in common.

4 MAIN IDEA: Geography Which continents have more than one culture region?

5 MAIN IDEA: Economics What is one cause of cultural change?

6 PLACES TO KNOW Name three culture regions in the world.

7 CRITICAL THINKING: Cause and Effect How might a poor crop of Brazilian coffee beans affect the cost of coffee at a local supermarket?

SPEAKING ACTIVITY With a partner, prepare and present a dialogue between two people from different countries, explaining what makes their culture regions different.

The Giant Kuafu Chases the Sun

Folklore of CHINA

From the earliest times, people have created myths and legends to explain the natural world. Some stories explain why earthquakes occur or lightning strikes. Others tell how rivers, deserts, canyons, and other landforms came to be. This ancient Chinese myth, dating back at least 2,500 years, comes from the area of northern China where Chinese civilization first began. The myth explains how the province of Shaanxi got its mountains.

Shaanxi, also known as Shensi, is in northern China. The southern part of the province contains the high and rugged Qinling Range, also called the Tsinling Mountains, where the average peak is 8,000 feet high and some are over 12,000 feet high.

Long ago, soon after time began, giants roamed the flat and fertile Earth. One of the largest, bravest, and fastest of them all was named Kuafu—and his strength knew no bounds.

Every day, Kuafu watched the sun rise in the east and set in the west. When night came, he became greatly saddened. He thought, "I do not like the darkness. All life falls into a silent slumber. If I could catch the sun, then I could keep night as bright as day. The plants could grow forever, and it would always be warm. I would never have to sleep again."

The next day, Kuafu stretched his legs and started to race after the sun. He ran like the wind over several thousand miles without rest. Finally, he chased the sun to the Yu Valley where it came to rest every day but Kuafu was thirsty and very, very tired. His thirst grew, and soon it became overwhelming. He had never known a thirst like this, and his body seemed to be drying up like mud bricks in an oven.

Kuafu found the nearest stream and drank it dry. It was not enough. With a giant's stride, he quickly reached the mighty Yellow River. He drank it dry, but again, it was not enough. He continued toward the Great Sea—surely it held water enough to quench his thirst.

On his journey, he drank dry every well and every stream and every lake he came across. His thirst became overpowering, and Kuafu fell to the ground before he reached the Sea. In a fit of anger, with a branch of a peach tree, he made a final swing at the sun. But before the branch reached the sun, Kuafu died of thirst.

The sun set in the Yu Valley, and night came. When the sun rose again, Kuafu's body had been transformed into a mountain range. The peach tree branch extended from his side and formed a peach tree grove. To this day, the peaches in this grove are sweet and moist, always ready to relieve the thirst of those who would choose to chase the sun.

Activities

1. **THINK ABOUT IT** Contests involving the sun, as well as efforts to reach the sun, are common in the myths and legends of many societies. Why do you think stories about the sun are told in so many cultures?

2. **WRITE ABOUT IT** Although Kuafu was not a real person, his myth has survived for thousands of years. Write a short essay explaining why you think myths and legends are an important part of many cultures.

Skillbuilder

Read a Time Zone Map

A time zone map shows the 24 time zones of the world. The prime meridian runs through Greenwich (GREHN ich), England. Each zone east of Greenwich is one hour later than the zone before. Each zone west of Greenwich is one hour earlier. The International Date Line runs through the Pacific Ocean. It is the location where each day begins. If it is Saturday to the east of the International Date Line, then it is Sunday to the west of it.

World Time Zones

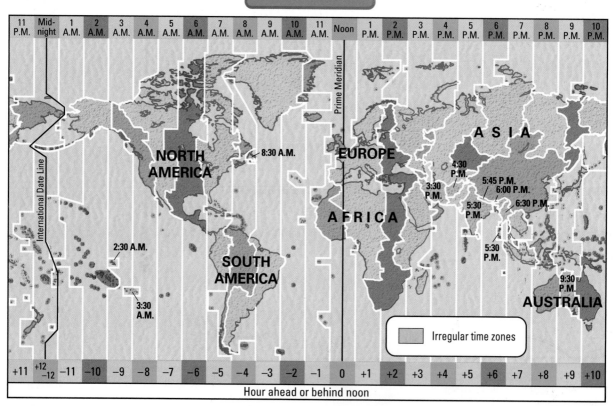

Step 1: Read the title. It tells you what the map is intended to show.

Step 2: Read the labels at the top of the map. They show the hours across the world when it is noon in Greenwich. The labels at the bottom show the number of hours earlier or later than the time in Greenwich.

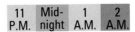

Step 3: Locate a place whose time you know. Locate the place where you want to know the time. Count the number of time zones between them. Then add or subtract that number of hours. For example, if it is noontime on the west coast of Africa, you can see that it is 7:00 A.M. on the east coast of the United States. That is a difference of five hours.

Practice the Skill

Practice determining the difference in hours between various time zones. For example, if you select the yellow zone in western Asia and you live in Chicago, you will have a time difference of 11 hours. Now select one time zone in Africa, one in Europe, and one in Australia. For each location, determine the number of hours' difference with the time zone in which you live.

Apply the Skill

Use the steps listed to help you find times and time differences on a time zone map.

Visual Summary

1–2. ✏️ Write a description for each concept shown below.

The World at Your Fingertips

_____

_____

_____

Many Regions, Many Cultures

_____

_____

_____

Facts and Main Ideas

Answer the following questions

3. **Citizenship** How can someone become a citizen of a country?

4. **Culture** What are some characteristics of a culture?

5. **Geography** How can decisions made in one part of the world affect people in another part of the world?

6. **Culture** What aspects of daily life might people in the same culture region share?

7. **Culture** What makes the United States and Canada a multicultural region?

Vocabulary

Choose a word from the list to complete each sentence below.

citizen, p. 16
scarcity, p. 17
interdependence, p. 20

8. As a legal member of a country, a _____ has both rights and duties in that country.

9. Economic trade, transportation, and communication have led to _____ among the nations of the world.

10. When people's desire for a resource such as water is greater than the amount of available water, there is a _____.

TEST PREP Read a Time Zone Map

Study the map and apply what you learned about time zones to answer each question.

11. What is the time difference between Los Angeles and New York City?

    A. one hour

    B. two hours

    C. three hours

    D. four hours

12. If it is 2 P.M. in Houston, what time would it be in Chicago?

    A. 1 P.M.

    B. 2 P.M.

    C. 3 P.M.

    D. 4 P.M.

13. What area of the country always has the earliest time?

    A. north

    B. south

    C. east

    D. west

 TEST PREP Write a short paragraph to answer each question below.

14. **Infer** Why might life expectancy—the average number of years people live—be low in a country with a low level of development?

15. **Cause and Effect** If countries in the Middle East stopped producing oil, how might that affect the people and the economy of the United States?

Activities

 DRAMA ACTIVITY Prepare and present a one-act play in which a person from another culture region visits an American family, experiencing the culture of the United States for the first time. Focus on unique aspects of language, technology, food, and clothing that a person from another culture might find surprising or strange.

WRITING ACTIVITY Make a list of food and other products in your home that have come from other nations. Include music, clothing, and other cultural traits. Compare your list with classmates.

 Technology

Writing Process Tips
Get help with your list at
www.eduplace.com/kids/hmss05/

Vocabulary Preview

Technology

e • **glossary**
e • **word games**
www.eduplace.com/kids/hmss05/

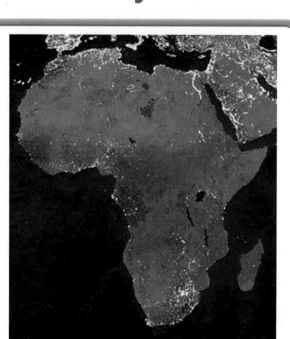

continent

The **continent** of Africa is one of seven such huge landmasses on Earth. Other continents are North America, South America, Europe, Asia, Australia, and Antarctica.

page 30

migrate

For thousands of years, people have moved from one area of Earth to another. They **migrate** for various reasons, as problems push them out of one place or advantages pull them to another.

page 33

Reading Strategy

Predict and Infer Use this strategy before you read each lesson in this chapter.

 Quick Tip Look at the pictures in each lesson to predict what it will be about.

cartographer

In the past, a **cartographer,** or mapmaker, often had limited information about the places shown on maps. Today's technology allows cartographers to make much more detailed and more accurate maps for geographers and other people to use. **page 38**

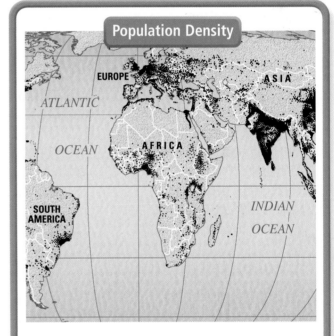

Population Density

thematic map

When you want to find out a specific kind of geographical information about a place, a **thematic map** can help. It focuses on one theme, such as population density or the income of people. **page 40**

The Five Themes of Geography

Build on What You Know Where do you live? You might answer that question with your street address, or with the town you live in, or with "the United States." You might also say you live in the mountains or in the desert or by the ocean. These are some of the ways a geographer would describe a place too.

Location and Place

Main Idea Where a place is and what it is like are important themes in geography.

Millions of years ago, all land on Earth was joined together into one big landmass. Scientists call this landmass *Pangaea* (pan GEE uh), which means "all land." Pieces of Pangaea broke away and drifted apart, forming the seven continents that Earth has today. A **continent** is a large continuous mass of land.

Natural forces that are still active today caused Pangaea to break apart. Scientists discovered that giant slabs of Earth's surface, called tectonic plates, move, causing the continents to drift. This creates earthquakes, volcanoes, and mountains. Geographers study the processes that cause changes like these. To help you understand how geographers think about the world, consider geography's five themes—location, place, region, movement, and human-environment interaction.

Often, the first thing you want to know about a place is where it is located. Geography helps you think about things spatially—where they are located and how they got there. Location allows you to discuss places in the world in terms everyone can understand.

Pangaea Seven continents were once one continent.

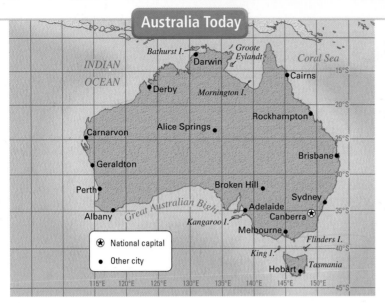

Absolute Location Maps with latitude and longitude lines show exactly where a place is located.

SKILL **Interpret a Map** What is the latitude of Adelaide? What island is almost entirely enclosed by the lines 40° and 45° south latitude and 145° and 150° east longitude?

Location

If someone asks you where your school is, you might say, "On Fifth Street." Ask a geographer where Melbourne, Australia, is located, and you may get the answer "38° south latitude, 145° east longitude." This is its absolute location. **Absolute location** is the exact spot on Earth where a place can be found.

Using a system of imaginary lines drawn on its surface, geographers can locate any place on Earth. Lines that run parallel to the equator are called **latitude** lines. They show distance north and south of the equator. Lines that run between the North and South Poles are called **longitude** lines. They show distance east and west of the prime meridian.

Another way to define the location of a place is to describe its relation to other places. You might say your school is "near the fire station" or "two blocks west of the pet store." If someone asks you where Canada is, you might say, "North of the United States." The location of one place in relation to other places is called its **relative location.**

Place

Another useful theme of geography is place. If you go to a new place, the first thing you want to know is what it is like. Is it crowded or is there a lot of open space? How is the climate? What language do people speak? Every place on Earth has a distinct group of physical features, such as its climate, landforms and bodies of water, and plant and animal life. Places can also have human characteristics, or features that human beings have created, such as cities and towns, governments, and cultural traditions.

If you could go back to the days when dinosaurs roamed Earth, you would see a world much different from the one you know. Much of Earth had a moist, warm climate, and the continents were not located where they are today. Rivers, forests, wetlands, glaciers, oceans—the physical features of Earth—continue to change. Some changes are dramatic, caused by erupting volcanoes, earthquakes, and hurricanes. Others happen slowly, such as the formation of a canyon.

REVIEW Give an example of a physical feature and an example of a human characteristic where you live.

Region	Climate	Plant Life
Tropical Rain Forest	Hot and wet all year	Thick trees, broad leaves Trees stay green all year
Tropical Grassland	Hot all year Wet and dry seasons	Tall grasses Some trees
Mediterranean	Hot, dry summers Cool-to-mild winters	Open forests, some clumps of trees Many shrubs, herbs, grasses
Temperate Forest	Warm summers Cold-to-cool winters	Mixed forests; some trees lose leaves in winter, others stay green all year
Cool Forest	Cool-to-mild summers Long, cold winters	Mostly trees with needles; stay green all year; some trees lose leaves in winter
Cool Grassland	Warm summers Cool winters Drier than forest regions	Prairies: Tall, thick grass Higher lands: Shorter grass
Desert	Hot all year Very little rain	Sand or bare soil, few plants May have cactus, some grass and bushes
Tundra	Short, cool summers Long, cold winters Little rain or snow	Rolling plains: No trees, some patches of moss, short grass, flowering plants
Arctic	Very cold Covered in ice all year	None
High Mountain	Varies, depending on altitude	Varies, depending on altitude

Natural Regions The land and climate affect plant life in different physical regions. **SKILL Interpret a Chart** In which types of climates are trees most likely to stay green all year?

Region and Movement

Main Idea The world can be divided into human and physical regions, and both people and physical features on Earth move.

Geographers group places into regions. A region is a group of places that have physical features or human characteristics, or both, in common. A geographer interested in languages, for example, might divide the world into language regions. All the countries where Spanish is the major language would form one Spanish-speaking language region. Geographers compare regions to understand the differences and similarities among them.

Tundra The tundra, where these grizzly bears live, is one of the ten natural regions of the world.

The world can be divided into ten natural regions. A natural region has its own unique combination of plant and animal life and climate. Tropical rain forest regions are in Central and South America, Africa south of the Sahara, Southeast Asia, Australia, and the Pacific Islands. What is their climate like?

Movement

People, goods, and ideas move from one place to another. So do animals, plants, and other physical features of Earth. Movement is the fourth geographic theme. The Internet is a good tool for the movement of ideas. Sometimes people move within a country. For example, vast numbers of people have migrated from farms to cities. **Migrate** means to move from one area to settle in another. You may have ancestors who immigrated to the United States—perhaps from Africa, Europe, Latin America, or Asia. When people emigrate, or leave an area, they take their ideas and customs with them. They may also adopt new ideas from their new home.

Migration is a result of push and pull factors. Problems in one place push people out. Advantages in another place pull people in. Poverty, overcrowding, lack of jobs and schooling, prejudice, war, and political oppression are push factors. Pull factors include a higher standard of living, employment and educational opportunities, rights, freedom, peace, and safety.

Natural barriers, such as mountain ranges, canyons, and raging rivers, can make migration difficult. Oceans, lakes, navigable rivers, and flat land can make it easier. Modern forms of transportation have made it easier than ever for people to move back and forth between countries.

REVIEW How do push and pull factors work together to explain migration?

Migration As you can see, people have been on the move for at least 90,000 years.

SKILL **Interpret a Map** About how many years ago did humans migrate to North America?

Land Bridge During the last Ice Age, the oceans shrank and uncovered a land bridge between Asia and North America. Humans in Asia crossed this land bridge and were the first people in North America.

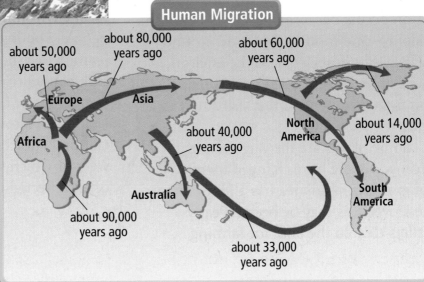

Human Migration

about 50,000 years ago

about 80,000 years ago

about 60,000 years ago

Europe

Asia

Africa

about 40,000 years ago

North America

about 14,000 years ago

Australia

South America

about 90,000 years ago

about 33,000 years ago

Saving Special Places Many of the most wonderful and special places on Earth may be destroyed or ruined over time unless they are protected. To prevent this, UNESCO (the United Nations Educational, Scientific, and Cultural Organization) set up the World Heritage Committee in 1972. This group identifies human-made and natural wonders all over the world and looks for ways to protect them for the benefit of the world community. So far, the list of World Heritage Sites numbers more than 690. The Grand Canyon (see photograph at right), the Galápagos Islands, the Roman Colosseum, and the Pyramids of Giza are just a few of the places protected for future generations.

Human-Environment Interaction

Main Idea Human society is shaped by the environment, and the environment is shaped by humans.

Interaction between human beings and their environment is the fifth theme of geography. Human-environment interaction occurs because humans depend on, adapt to, and modify the world around them. Human society and the environment cannot be separated. Each shapes and is shaped by the other. Earth is a unified system.

Some places are the way they are because people have changed them. For example, if an area has a lot of open meadows, this may be because early settlers cleared the land for farming.

Human changes may help or hurt the environment. Pollution is an example of a harmful effect. The environment can also harm people. For example, hurricanes wash away beaches and houses along the shore; earthquakes cause fire and destruction.

Humans have often adapted their way of life to the natural resources that their local environment provided. In the past, people who lived near teeming oceans learned to fish. Those who lived near rich soil learned to farm. People built their homes out of local materials and ate the food easily grown in their surroundings. Cultural choices, such as what clothes to wear or which sports to participate in, often reflected the environment.

Adaptation and Interaction

Because of technology, this close adaptation to the environment is not as common as it once was. Airplanes, for example, can quickly fly frozen fish from the coast to towns far inland. Even so, there are many more ice skaters in Canada and surfers in California than the other way around.

People and the environment continually interact. For example, when thousands of people in a city choose to use public transportation or ride bicycles rather than drive, less gasoline is burned. When less gasoline is burned, there is less air pollution. In other words, when the environment is healthy, the people who live in it are able to lead healthier lives.

REVIEW Name one way in which humans affect the environment and one way the environment affects humans.

Lesson Summary

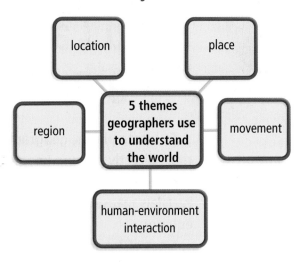

Why It Matters...

The five themes enable you to discuss and explain people, places, and environments of the past and present.

Lesson Review

1 VOCABULARY Choose the correct word to complete each sentence.

continent   migrate

One of seven large landmasses on Earth is called a _____.

To move from one area to another is to _____.

2 🕐 READING SKILL Use your chart to list one way that humans affect the environment and one way that natural disasters affect the environment.

3 MAIN IDEA: Geography What physical processes can cause places to change over time?

4 MAIN IDEA: Geography How do push and pull factors cause migration?

5 MAIN IDEA: Geography What are some ways people have adapted to their environment?

6 PLACES TO KNOW Where are **tropical rain forest regions** located?

7 CRITICAL THINKING: Infer What factors make your part of the United States a region?

ART ACTIVITY Write and illustrate a magazine article about why people moved to your region of the country. Include several pull factors in your article.

Skillbuilder

Read Latitude and Longitude

To locate places, geographers use a global grid system (see the chart directly below). Imaginary lines of latitude, called parallels, circle the globe. The equator circles the middle of the globe at 0°. Parallels measure distance in degrees north and south of the equator.

Lines of longitude, called meridians, circle the globe from pole to pole. Meridians measure distance in degrees east and west of the prime meridian. The prime meridian is at 0°. It passes through Greenwich, England.

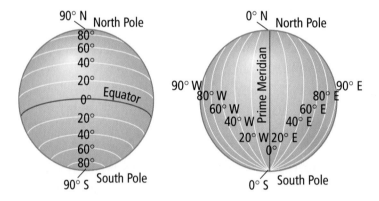

The world map below shows lines of latitude and longitude. Use the steps listed to the right to help you locate places on Earth.

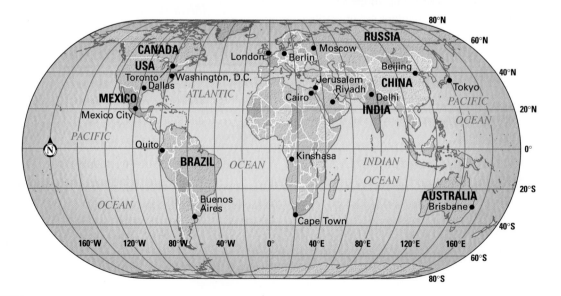

Learn the Skill

Step 1: Place a finger on the place you want to locate. With a finger from your other hand, find the nearest parallel. Write down its number. Be sure to include north or south. (You may have to guesstimate the actual number.)

Step 2: Keep your finger on the place you want to locate. Now find the nearest meridian. Write down its number. Be sure to include east or west. (You may have to guesstimate the actual number.)

Step 3: If you know the longitude and latitude of a place and want to find it on a map, put one finger on the line of longitude and another on the line of latitude. Bring your fingers together until they meet.

Practice the Skill

Writing a summary will help you understand latitude and longitude. The paragraph below summarizes the information you have learned.

> Use latitude and longitude to locate a place on a globe or map. Lines of latitude circle Earth. Lines of longitude run through the poles. The numbers of the lines at the place where two lines cross is the location of that place.

Apply the Skill

Turn to page 31 in Chapter 2, Lesson 1, "The Five Themes of Geography." Look at the map of Australia and write a paragraph summarizing how you located the city of Adelaide.

The Geographer's Tools

VOCABULARY

cartographer
map projection
thematic map

Vocabulary Strategy

cartographer

Just as a photo**grapher** makes pictures of people, a **cartographer** makes a kind of picture of Earth and its features. A synonym for cartographer is mapmaker.

READING SKILL

Problem and Solution
Note the problems that geographers have drawing features of the Earth. Then note some of the solutions they have invented to solve these problems.

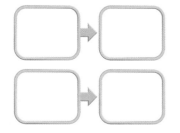

Build on What You Know How have you used maps? Perhaps you've drawn a map to show a friend the way to your home or looked at a street map to locate a soccer field. Your family might have used a road atlas on a car trip. Maps are basic tools for geographers.

Maps and Globes

Main Idea Geographers use maps and globes to learn about and display the features of Earth.

Both maps and globes represent Earth and its features. A globe is an accurate model of the world because it has three dimensions and can show its actual shape. Globes are difficult to carry around, however. Maps are more practical. They can be folded, carried, hung on a wall, or printed in a book or magazine. However, because maps show the world in only two dimensions, they are not perfectly accurate. Look at the pictures below to see why. When the orange peel is flattened out, the picture on the orange is distorted, or twisted out of shape. Cartographers, or mapmakers, have the same problem with maps.

Map Distortion Draw a picture on the entire surface of an orange and then peel the orange in one continuous piece. After you lay the peel flat, your image will be distorted.

Projections

The different ways of showing Earth's curved surface on a flat map are called **map projections.** All projections distort Earth, but different projections distort it in different ways. Some make places look bigger or smaller than they really are in relation to other places. Other projections distort shapes. For more than 400 years, the Mercator projection was most often shown on maps of the world. Recently, the Robinson projection has come into common use because it gives a fairer and more accurate picture of the shapes and sizes of the continents.

Maps, Charts, and Graphs

Main Idea Maps, charts, and graphs are clear ways to present much data.

Displaying Information

Along with maps, geographers use charts and graphs to display and compare information. The graphs and maps on page 41 contain related information about the world's population. Notice how each quickly and clearly presents facts that would otherwise take up many paragraphs of text.

REVIEW What are the main problems faced by cartographers?

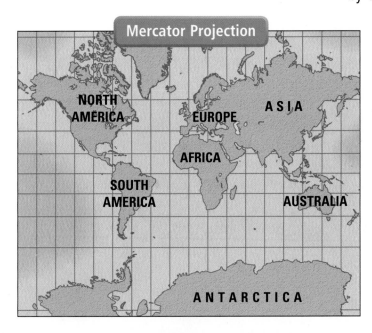

Mercator Projection This map projection distorts the sizes of the continents.

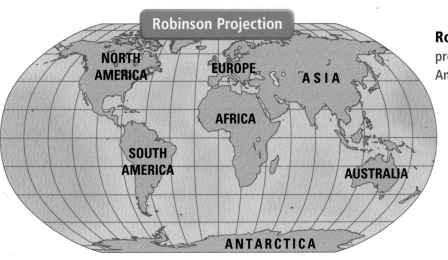

Robinson Projection This map projection is more accurate, but Antarctica is still distorted.

SKILL Interpret a Map Compare the size of Africa in relation to other continents on the two projections. How do they differ?

Reference Maps

General reference maps, which show natural and human-made features, are used to locate a place. **Thematic maps** focus on one specific idea or theme. The population map on page 41 is an example of a thematic map. Pilots and sailors use nautical maps to find their way through air and over water. A nautical map is sometimes called a chart.

REVIEW How do maps, charts, and graphs differ from words in explaining geographical information?

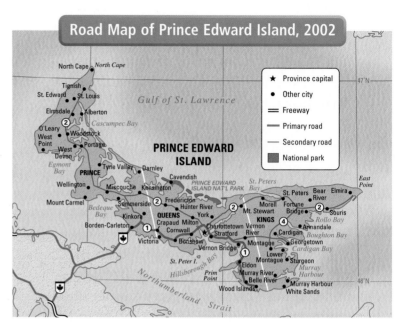

Road Map This road map is a reference map that shows how to get from one place to another.

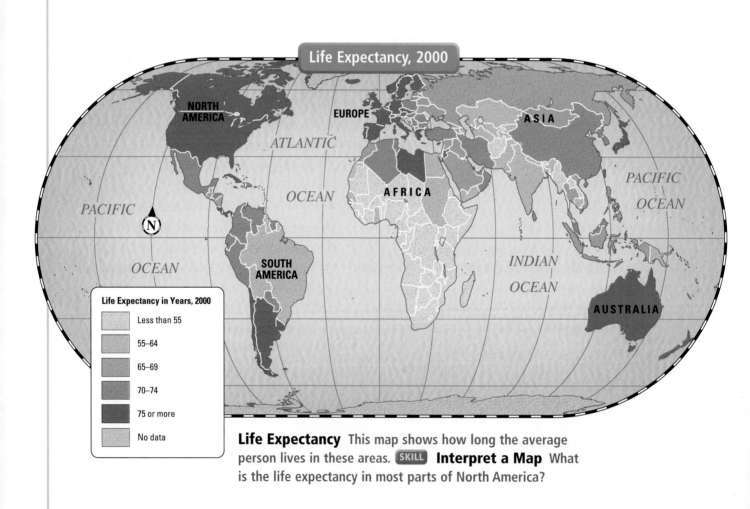

Life Expectancy This map shows how long the average person lives in these areas. **SKILL** **Interpret a Map** What is the life expectancy in most parts of North America?

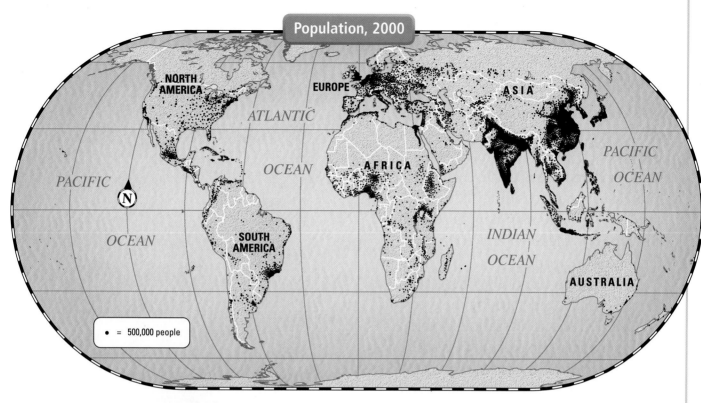

Population, 2000

• = 500,000 people

Population The black dots on this map show population density.

SKILL **Interpret a Map** Which continent shown on this map has the largest population? the smallest?

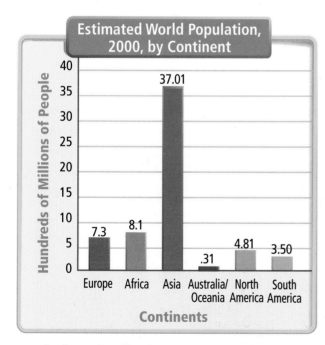

Estimated World Population, 2000, by Continent

Hundreds of Millions of People

- Europe: 7.3
- Africa: 8.1
- Asia: 37.01
- Australia/Oceania: .31
- North America: 4.81
- South America: 3.50

Continents

Population Distribution A continent's population is affected by its size and geography.

SKILL **Read a Graph** How many people live in Europe? Which continent has the smallest population?

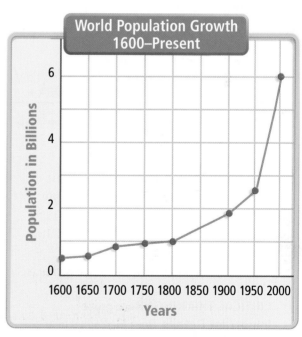

World Population Growth 1600–Present

Population in Billions

Years: 1600 1650 1700 1750 1800 1850 1900 1950 2000

Growth The world's population has grown rapidly over the last few decades.

SKILL **Read a Graph** How much did the world's population increase between 1600 and 1900? between 1900 and 2000?

Mapmaker's Tools

Main Idea Technological advances have made mapmaking easier.

People have been drawing maps of their world for thousands of years. Geographers today have many tools to help them represent Earth. Increased knowledge and technology allow a cartographer to construct maps that give a much more detailed and accurate picture of the world.

Advances in technology have also helped people to determine their position on Earth. In the 1100s, sailors developed the magnetic compass, which is still used today to determine direction. In the 1730s, the sextant began to be used in navigation. It measures the angle between the horizon and the sun, moon, or a star in order to calculate latitude. Thirty years later, John Harrison developed the chronometer. This device helps sailors find their ship's longitude.

Early Map This Babylonian world map was drawn on a clay tablet thousands of years ago.

Mercator Map This map of the Arctic was drawn in 1595 by Gerardus Mercator (1512–1594), the famous mapmaker for whom the map projection was named. It is one of many old maps that are rare, beautiful, and important historical artifacts.

CRITICAL THINKING   Recognize Important Details Does Mercator's map show more land or more water?
Identify Problems What types of problems might Mercator have faced when he created this map?

Global Positioning System

In the 1970s, the U.S. Department of Defense developed the Global Positioning System (GPS). GPS allows people on land, at sea, or in the air to pinpoint their location or to track moving objects in any weather. A network of 24 satellites that orbit Earth beam down data to palm-sized receivers, aiding the military in maneuvers. Civilians use them for hiking or finding shorter travel routes.

REVIEW What are some of the technological advances that have been made in determining location?

Lesson Summary

- Maps, globes, charts, and graphs help geographers learn and show facts about Earth.
- Different map projections help geographers show the curved surface of Earth on a flat paper.

Why It Matters...

Knowing how to use the tools of geography adds to your ability to understand the world.

Satellite Network Satellites such as this are part of the GPS orbiting network. A GPS device on Earth, which receives these satellite signals, can locate its exact position on Earth.

GPS This small gadget receives satellite signals to show its exact position on Earth.

Lesson Review

1. **VOCABULARY** Why do **cartographers** use **map projections?**

2. **READING SKILL** Explain the **solution** Robinson developed for the problem of showing Earth's continents on paper.

3. **MAIN IDEA: Geography** What are the differences among the three main kinds of maps?

4. **MAIN IDEA: Geography** How have new tools and knowledge helped cartographers?

5. **MAIN IDEA: Geography** What kinds of information can be displayed on maps and graphs?

6. **FACTS TO KNOW** What is the major problem with the **Mercator Projection?**

7. **CRITICAL THINKING: Classify** What kind of map would show how many students are in each school in your school district?

HANDS ON

MAP ACTIVITY Draw a map of the route you take to school or some other familiar destination. Include the names of streets, landmarks such as shops and other buildings, and any other useful information.

A Map of Earth in 3-D

On February 11, 2000, the space shuttle *Endeavour* was launched into space on an 11-day mission to complete the most in-depth mapping project in history. The Shuttle Radar Topography Mission (SRTM) collected data on 80 percent of Earth's surface. This information was gathered by beaming radar waves at Earth and converting the echoes into images through a process known as interferometry (ihn tuhr fuh RAHM ih tree).

With the aid of computers, the resulting information can be used to produce almost limitless numbers of three-dimensional (3-D) maps. These maps show the topography—rivers, forests, mountains, and valleys—of Earth's surface. It took one year to process the data into 3-D maps. These maps, the most accurate topographical maps ever, will help scientists to better study Earth's surface. The data will also be useful to the general public; for example, it can be used to find new locations for cellular-phone towers and to create maps for hikers.

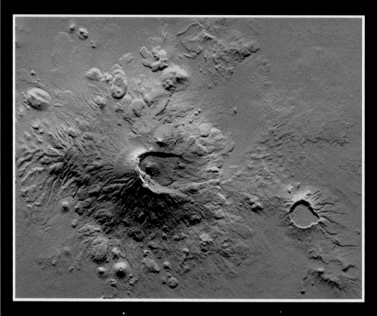

Mountain This image was taken by the SRTM of a mountain in Tanzania, Africa. Note how the color gets bluer as elevation increases at the top of the mountain.

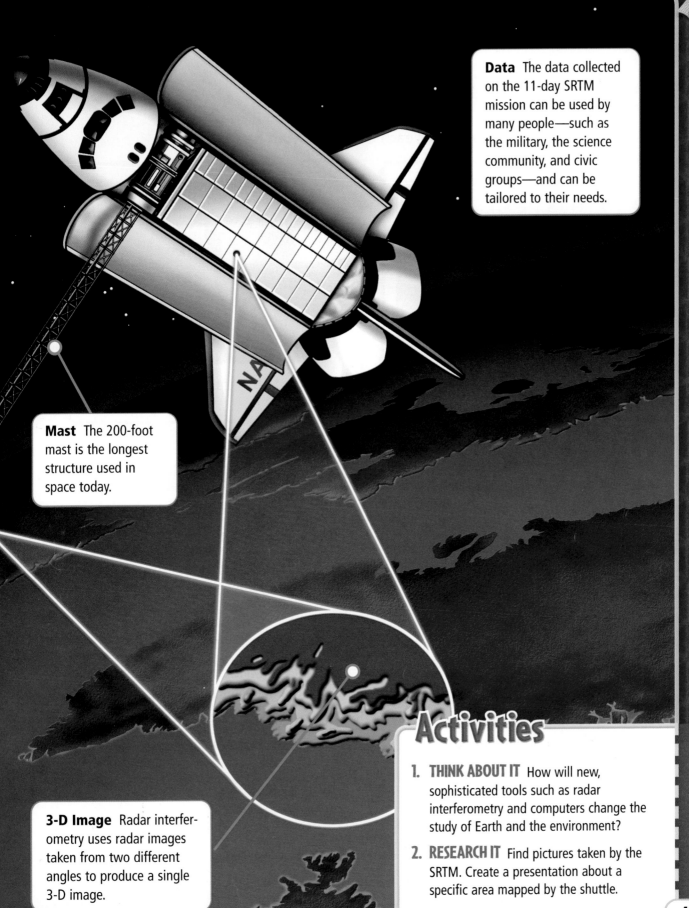

Data The data collected on the 11-day SRTM mission can be used by many people—such as the military, the science community, and civic groups—and can be tailored to their needs.

Mast The 200-foot mast is the longest structure used in space today.

3-D Image Radar interferometry uses radar images taken from two different angles to produce a single 3-D image.

Activities

1. **THINK ABOUT IT** How will new, sophisticated tools such as radar interferometry and computers change the study of Earth and the environment?

2. **RESEARCH IT** Find pictures taken by the SRTM. Create a presentation about a specific area mapped by the shuttle.

Review and Test Prep

Visual Summary

1–2.  Write a description for each concept shown below.

> **The Five Themes of Geography**
>
> **The Geographer's Tools**

Facts and Main Ideas

Answer the following questions

3. **Geography** What system do geographers use to determine absolute location?

4. **Geography** How is relative location different from absolute location?

5. **History** What are some of the natural barriers that made migration difficult in the past?

6. **Geography** Why is a globe an accurate representation of the world?

7. **Geography** Why do most modern cartographers prefer the Robinson projection to the Mercator projection?

Vocabulary

Choose a word from the list to complete each sentence below.

> latitude, p. 31
> cartographer, p. 38
> thematic map, p. 40

8. A mapmaker is also called a _____.

9. If you wanted to study the population in a country, you might look at a _____.

10. A line that runs parallel to the equator and shows distance north or south is a line of _____.

Apply Skills

 TEST PREP **Read Latitude and Longitude** Study the map and apply what you learned about latitude and longitude to answer each question.

11. Which states have their northern borders near latitude 35°N?

    A. Arkansas, Tennessee, North Carolina

    B. Louisiana, Mississippi, Alabama

    C. Mississippi, Alabama, Georgia

    D. Missouri, Kentucky, Virginia

12. Which state extends south to about latitude 25°N?

    A. Florida

    B. Mississippi

    C. North Carolina

    D. South Carolina

Critical Thinking

 TEST PREP Write a short paragraph to answer each question below.

13. **Contrast** Maps and globes both represent Earth and its features. Contrast the advantages of a map with the advantages of a globe.

14. **Evaluate** Why would the leaders of a country find a population density map of their country useful?

Activities

 MAP ACTIVITY Work with a partner using a world map or globe. Take turns asking questions such as, "I'm a city at _____ latitude and _____ longitude. What city am I?" and "I'm a city _____ longitude east of Los Angeles. What city am I?"

 WRITING ACTIVITY Choose your own community or another and use the five themes of geography to describe it. Answer these questions: Where is the community located? (location) What are its physical and human characteristics? (place) In what type of region is it? (region) What movement has occurred into and out of the community? (movement) How have the people adapted to the environment? (human-environment interaction) Arrange your work in a five-page booklet with a title page.

 Technology

Writing Process Tips
Get help with your booklet at
www.eduplace.com/kids/hmss05/

Vocabulary and Main Ideas

Answer each of the following questions.

1. What does the study of **government** tell us about the world and its people?

2. What does the study of **economics** tell us about the world and its people?

3. What is a **culture region?**

4. Why do people **migrate?**

5. What do **latitude** and **longitude** tell about the location of a place?

6. What does a **thematic map** show?

7. Why do **cartographers** use different **map projections** when presenting Earth?

Critical Thinking

 TEST PREP Write a short paragraph to answer each question below.

8. **Cause and Effect** What effect would a shortage of oil production in the Middle East have on the United States, and why?

9. **Compare and Contrast** Compare and contrast maps and globes. What similar features do they have? How are they different?

Apply Skills

 TEST PREP Use the map below and what you have learned about time zones to answer each question.

10. Which of these two states are in the same time zone?

    A. California and Washington
    B. Colorado and Kansas
    C. Illinois and Indiana
    D. Georgia and Alabama

11. If you are in Chicago and making a phone call to Los Angeles at 3:00 P.M. your time, what time is it in Los Angeles?

    A. 4:00 P.M.
    B. 3:00 P.M.
    C. 1:00 P.M.
    D. 12:00 noon

12. Which of the following states is in two different time zones?

    A. California
    B. Nebraska
    C. Texas
    D. Florida

Unit Activity

Make a "Special Place" Brochure

- Choose a place you want to know more about. It could be your home community or some other place in the world you would like to visit someday.

- Research to find out about this place: its location, what physical region it is in, what culture region it is in, and so on.

- Create a brochure that gives the information you found out. Include illustrations and, if you like, maps.

At the Library

You may find these books at your school or public library.

The Longitude Prize, by Joan Dash
In the eighteenth century, carpenter John Harrison won a prize for being the first person to invent a way to measure longitude at sea.

The Kingfisher Young People's Atlas of the World, by Philip Steele
This atlas includes maps, fun facts about places around the world, and a section on mapmaking.

Connect to Today

Create a bulletin board about a place in the world.

- Choose a place that is in the news headlines today.

- Show the location of the place on a map. Give its latitude and longitude.

- List information about the culture region it is in. Draw or find pictures to illustrate the place.

- List information about the physical region it is in. Draw or find pictures to illustrate the place.

- Write a brief summary about why the place is in the news.

Technology

Get your information for the bulletin board from the Weekly Reader at **www.eduplace.com/kids/hmss05/**

Read About It

Look for these Social Studies books in your classroom.

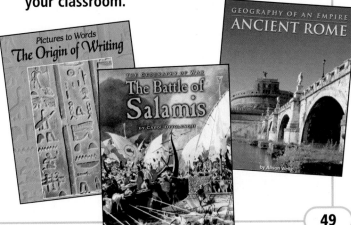

Mount Rushmore This monument is located in the Black Hills of South Dakota. The 60-foot likenesses of (from left to right) George Washington, Thomas Jefferson, Theodore Roosevelt, and Abraham Lincoln took 14 years to carve into the granite cliff.

UNIT 2

The United States and Canada

The Big Idea

What makes a good citizen?

" *We hold these truths to be self-evident: that all men are created equal.* "

Declaration of Independence

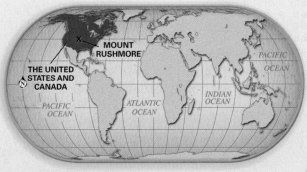

Almanac

The United States and Canada

N

ARCTIC OCEAN

Ellesmere Island

Queen Elizabeth Islands

Baffin Bay

Beaufort Sea

Chukchi Sea

BROOKS RANGE

Yukon R.

MACKENZIE MTS.

Mackenzie R.

Great Bear Lake

Victoria Island

Baffin Island

Davis Strait

ALASKA RANGE

Mt. McKinley ▲
20,320 ft.
(6,194 m)

Bering Strait

Bering Sea

Mt. Logan
19,551 ft.
(5,959 m)

COAST MOUNTAINS

Great Slave Lake

Lake Athabasca

CANADIAN SHIELD

Hudson Bay

Kodiak Is.

Aleutian Islands

Gulf of Alaska

Queen Charlotte Is.

CANADA

Lake Winnipeg

James Bay

Gulf of St. Lawrence

Newfoundland and Labrador

Vancouver I.

COAST RANGES

Columbia R.

CASCADES

ROCKY MOUNTAINS

GREAT PLAINS

Missouri R.

Mississippi R.

Great L.

St. Lawrence R.

GREAT BASIN

SIERRA NEVADA

Mt. Whitney ▲
14,494 ft.
(4,421 m)

Death Valley
-282 ft.
(-86 m)

Colorado R.

UNITED STATES

Ohio R.

APPALACHIAN MTS.

Channel Is.

Rio Grande

Mississippi R.

COASTAL PLAIN

Gulf of Mexico

ATLANTIC OCEAN

PACIFIC OCEAN

Hawaiian Islands

22°N
Niihau *Kauai*
Oahu
Molokai
Lanai *Maui*
Kahoolawe

HAWAII

20°N

| 0 | 75 | 150 miles |
| 0 | 75 | 150 kilometers |

Hawaii

160°W   158°W   156°W   154°W

Tropic of Cancer

Caribbean Sea

| 0 | 600 | 1,200 miles |
| 0 | 600 | 1,200 kilometers |

Equator

PACIFIC OCEAN

Elevation

13,100 ft.	(4,000 m)
6,600 ft.	(2,000 m)
3,275 ft.	(1,000 m)
650 ft.	(200 m)
0 ft.	(0 m)
Below sea level	

▲ Mountain peak

Tropic of Capricorn

180°W   160°W   140°W   120°W   100°W   80°W

Natural Hazards of the United States and Canada

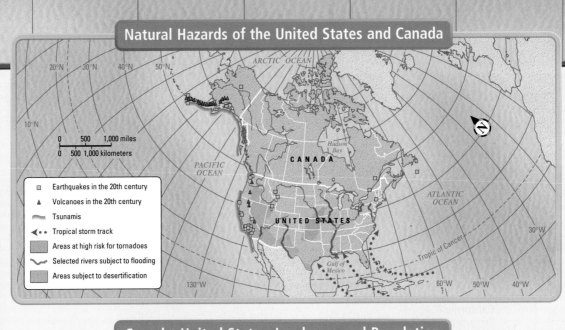

- ☐ Earthquakes in the 20th century
- ▲ Volcanoes in the 20th century
- ⌒ Tsunamis
- ◀•• Tropical storm track
- ▮ Areas at high risk for tornadoes
- ⌄ Selected rivers subject to flooding
- ▮ Areas subject to desertification

Canada–United States: Landmass and Population

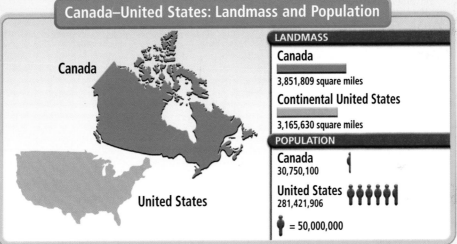

Canada

United States

LANDMASS

Canada
3,851,809 square miles

Continental United States
3,165,630 square miles

POPULATION

Canada
30,750,100

United States
281,421,906

🚶 = 50,000,000

FAST FACTS

 HIGHEST TIDE:
The Bay of Fundy, between New Brunswick and Nova Scotia in Canada, has the highest tides in the world, sometimes running as high as 70 feet.

 HIGHEST MOUNTAIN:
Mt. McKinley, 20,320 ft.

 LONGEST RIVER:
Missouri River, 2,466 mi.

 HIGHEST RECORDED TEMPERATURE:
134°F, Death Valley, California, July 10, 1913

 LOWEST RECORDED TEMPERATURE:
–81.4°F, Snag, Yukon, February 3, 1947

CURRENT EVENTS
WEEKLY (WR) READER

Find out about current events that connect with the content of this unit. See Unit activities at: www.eduplace.com/kids/hmss05/

State Flag	State/ Capital	Population (2000)	Population Rank (2000)	Infant Mortality (per 1,000 live births) (1998)	Doctors (per 100,000 pop.) (1998–1999)
	Alabama (AL) Montgomery	4,447,100	23	10.2	198
	Alaska (AK) Juneau	626,900	48	5.9	167
	Arizona (AZ) Phoenix	5,130,600	20	7.5	202
	Arkansas (AR) Little Rock	2,673,400	33	8.9	190
	California (CA) Sacramento	33,871,600	1	5.8	247
	Colorado (CO) Denver	4,301,300	24	6.7	238
	Connecticut (CT) Hartford	3,405,600	29	7.0	354
	Delaware (DE) Dover	783,600	45	9.6	234
	*District of Columbia (DC)	572,100	—	12.5	737
	Florida (FL) Tallahassee	15,982,400	4	7.2	238
	Georgia (GA) Atlanta	8,186,500	10	8.5	211
	Hawaii (HI) Honolulu	1,211,500	42	6.9	265
	Idaho (ID) Boise	1,294,000	39	7.2	154
	Illinois (IL) Springfield	12,419,300	5	8.4	260
	Indiana (IN) Indianapolis	6,080,500	14	7.6	195
	Iowa (IA) Des Moines	2,926,300	30	6.6	173
	Kansas (KS) Topeka	2,688,400	32	7.0	203

*The federal district of Washington, D.C., is the capital city of the United States.

DATA FILE

Population Density (per square mile)	Per Capita Income ($) (1999)	High School Graduates (%) (1998)	Area Rank (2000)	Total Area (square miles)	Map (not to scale)
85.1	21,941	78.8	30	52,237	
1.0	27,274	90.6	1	615,230	
45.0	24,199	81.9	6	114,006	
50.3	21,146	76.8	28	53,182	
213.2	28,513	80.1	3	158,869	
41.3	30,291	89.6	8	104,100	
614.3	37,452	83.7	48	5,544	
327.0	29,341	85.2	49	2,396	
8,412.6	36,554	83.8	51	68	
266.7	26,796	81.9	23	59,928	
138.8	26,007	80.0	24	58,977	
187.6	26,623	84.6	47	6,459	
15.5	22,418	82.7	14	83,574	
214.4	29,908	84.2	25	57,918	
167.0	24,949	83.5	38	36,420	
51.9	24,600	87.7	26	56,276	
32.7	25,467	89.2	15	82,282	

State Flag	State/Capital	Population (2000)	Population Rank (2000)	Infant Mortality (per 1,000 live births) (1998)	Doctors (per 100,000 pop.) (1998–1999)
	Kentucky (KY) Frankfort	4,041,800	25	7.5	209
	Louisiana (LA) Baton Rouge	4,469,000	22	9.1	246
	Maine (ME) Augusta	1,274,900	40	6.3	223
	Maryland (MD) Annapolis	5,296,500	19	8.6	374
	Massachusetts (MA) Boston	6,349,100	13	5.1	412
	Michigan (MI) Lansing	9,938,400	8	8.2	224
	Minnesota (MN) St. Paul	4,919,500	21	5.9	249
	Mississippi (MS) Jackson	2,844,700	31	10.1	163
	Missouri (MO) Jefferson City	5,595,200	17	7.7	230
	Montana (MT) Helena	902,200	44	7.4	190
	Nebraska (NE) Lincoln	1,711,300	38	7.3	218
	Nevada (NV) Carson City	1,998,300	35	7.0	173
	New Hampshire (NH) Concord	1,235,800	41	4.4	237
	New Jersey (NJ) Trenton	8,414,400	9	6.4	295
	New Mexico (NM) Santa Fe	1,819,000	36	7.2	212
	New York (NY) Albany	18,976,500	3	6.3	387
	North Carolina (NC) Raleigh	8,049,300	11	9.3	232

DATA FILE

Population Density (per square mile)	Per Capita Income ($) (1999)	High School Graduates (%) (1998)	Area Rank (2000)	Total Area (square miles)	Map (not to scale)
100.0	22,147	77.9	37	40,411	
90.0	21,794	78.6	31	49,651	
37.8	23,867	86.7	39	33,741	
430.7	30,757	84.7	42	12,297	
687.1	34,168	85.6	45	9,241	
102.8	26,625	85.4	11	96,705	
56.6	29,281	89.4	12	86,943	
58.9	19,608	77.3	32	48,286	
80.3	25,040	82.9	21	69,709	
6.1	21,337	89.1	4	147,046	
22.1	26,235	87.7	16	77,358	
18.1	29,022	89.1	7	110,567	
133.1	29,552	84.0	44	9,283	
1,024.3	34,525	86.5	46	8,215	
15.0	21,097	79.6	5	121,598	
351.5	32,459	81.5	27	53,989	
153.0	25,072	81.4	29	52,672	

State Flag	State/ Capital	Population (2000)	Population Rank (2000)	Infant Mortality (per 1,000 live births) (1998)	Doctors (per 100,000 pop.) (1998–1999)	
	North Dakota (ND) Bismarck	642,200	47	8.6	222	
	Ohio (OH) Columbus	11,353,100	7	8.0	235	
	Oklahoma (OK) Oklahoma City	3,450,700	27	8.5	169	
	Oregon (OR) Salem	3,421,400	28	5.4	225	
	Pennsylvania (PA) Harrisburg	12,281,100	6	7.1	291	
	Rhode Island (RI) Providence	1,048,300	43	7.0	338	
	South Carolina (SC) Columbia	4,012,000	26	9.6	207	
	South Dakota (SD) Pierre	754,800	46	9.1	184	
	Tennessee (TN) Nashville	5,689,300	16	8.2	246	
	Texas (TX) Austin	20,851,800	2	6.4	203	
	Utah (UT) Salt Lake City	2,233,200	34	5.6	200	
	Vermont (VT) Montpelier	608,800	49	7.0	305	
	Virginia (VA) Richmond	7,078,500	12	7.7	241	
	Washington (WA) Olympia	5,894,100	15	5.7	235	
	West Virginia (WV) Charleston	1,808,300	37	8.0	215	
	Wisconsin (WI) Madison	5,363,700	18	7.2	227	
	Wyoming (WY) Cheyenne	493,800	50	7.2	171	
	United States Washington, D.C.	281,422,000	3	7.0	251	

DATA FILE

Population Density (per square mile)	Per Capita Income ($) (1999)	High School Graduates (%) (1998)	Area Rank (2000)	Total Area (square miles)	Map (not to scale)
9.1	22,488	84.3	18	70,704	
253.3	25,895	86.2	34	44,828	
49.4	21,802	84.6	20	69,903	
35.2	25,947	85.5	10	97,132	
266.6	27,420	84.1	33	46,058	
851.6	24,418	80.7	50	1,231	
128.6	22,467	78.6	40	31,189	
9.8	24,007	86.3	17	77,121	
135.0	24,461	76.9	36	42,146	
78.0	25,363	78.3	2	267,277	
26.3	22,333	89.3	13	84,904	
63.3	24,758	86.7	43	9,615	
167.2	28,193	82.6	35	42,326	
83.4	28,968	92.0	19	70,637	
74.6	19,973	76.4	41	24,231	
82.0	26,212	88.0	22	65,499	
5.0	24,864	90.0	9	97,818	
74.3	33,900	83.0	4	3,787,319	

Province or Territory Flag	Province or Territory/ Capital	Population (2000)	Population Rank (2000)	Infant Mortality (per 1,000 live births) (1998)	Doctors (per 100,000 pop.) (1998–1999)
	Alberta (AB) Edmonton	2,997,200	4	4.8	162
	British Columbia (BC) Victoria	4,063,800	3	4.7	193
	Manitoba (MB) Winnipeg	1,147,900	5	7.5	177
	New Brunswick (NB) Fredericton	756,600	8	5.7	153
	Newfoundland and Labrador (NF) St. John's	538,800	9	5.2	171
	Northwest Territories (NT) Yellowknife	42,100	11	10.9	92
	Nova Scotia (NS) Halifax	941,000	7	4.4	196
	Nunavut (NU) Iqaluit	27,700	13	N/A	N/A
	Ontario (ON) Toronto	11,669,300	1	5.5	178
	Prince Edward Island (PE) Charlottetown	138,900	10	4.4	128
	Quebec (QC) Quebec City	7,372,400	2	5.6	211
	Saskatchewan (SK) Regina	1,023,600	6	8.9	149
	Yukon Territory (YT) Whitehorse	30,700	12	8.4	149
	Canada Ottawa, Ontario	30,750,000	36	5.5	185

DATA FILE

Population Density (per square mile)	Per Capita Income ($) (1999)	High School Graduates (%) (1998)	Area Rank (2000)	Total Area (square miles)	Map (not to scale)
11.7	30,038	86	6	255,285	
11.1	31,592	87	5	366,255	
4.6	26,829	79	8	250,934	
26.7	26,607	78	11	28,345	
3.4	27,692	71	10	156,649	
0.08	33,738 (1994)	64 (1996)	3	503,951	
44.0	25,712	78	12	21,425	
0.03	27,421 (1994)	N/A	1	818,959	
28.3	32,537	84	4	412,582	
49.4	25,534	74	13	2,814	
12.4	28,826	78	2	594,860	
4.1	26,463	82	7	251,700	
0.2	36,130	67 (1996)	9	186,661	
8.0	23,000	82	3	3,850,420	

Chapter 3

Physical Geography:
United States and Canada

Technology

e • glossary
e • word games
www.eduplace.com/kids/hmss05/

Vocabulary Preview

glacier

A **glacier** is a thick sheet of ice that moves slowly across land. Thousands of years ago, glaciers covered much of North America.
page 66

erosion

Erosion is a process where wind, rivers, and rain wear away soil and stone. The Grand Canyon was largely formed by river erosion.
page 67

THE UNITED
STATES
AND
CANADA

ATLANTIC
OCEAN

PACIFIC
OCEAN

OCEAN

INDIAN
OCEAN

PACIFIC
OCEAN

Reading Strategy

Monitor and Clarify As you read, check to make sure that you understand the text.

Quick Tip Ask yourself if what you are reading makes sense. Reread if you need to.

river system

A **river system** is a network of rivers and streams. North America's rivers empty into bays, oceans, seas, gulfs, lakes, and other rivers. **page 67**

vegetation

Trees, shrubs, grasses, and other plants are **vegetation.** The vegetation found in a region of North America is determined by the climate and physical geography of the area. **page 74**

From Coast to Coast

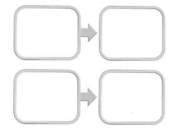
Build on What You Know Do you have to cross a river or climb a hill where you live? Think about the land near your school and home. It affects what you do every day.

North America

Main Idea The North American continent includes Canada, the United States, Greenland, Mexico, the Central American countries, and the Caribbean Islands.

Earth's geography changes continually. Sometimes change happens violently, as in the eruption of a volcano or the jolt of an earthquake. At other times, change occurs very slowly, as when rain washes away soil, or weather wears down a mountain. All these natural processes affect the physical geography of North America.

North America's huge landmass is home to several large countries and many smaller ones. Find Canada and the United States on the Unit Almanac map on page 52. Canada is the second largest country in area in the world. The United States is almost as great in area. North America also includes the Danish dependency Greenland, which is the world's largest island.

Varied Landscape North America is a vast area with varied physical features and climate. Mountain ranges, such as this, run parallel to each coastline.

Countries on the Continent

Mexico, the Central American countries, and the Caribbean island nations, such as Cuba, the Dominican Republic, and Haiti, are part of the continent of North America. These countries, along with the South American nations, make up what is considered Latin America. Find these countries on the Unit 3 Almanac map on page 142. Their heritage differs from that of the United States and Canada. Historically, Latin America owes much of its culture to Spain and Portugal. The United States and Canada were greatly influenced by the British and French. Because of these different cultural heritages, geographers study the United States and Canada separately from Latin America.

Most of the United States and Canada is located in the middle latitudes of the northern hemisphere of Earth. This area between the Arctic Circle and the Tropic of Cancer has a temperate climate. It is not as hot as land closer to the equator. It is not as cold as regions near the North or South Poles. Many plants and animals thrive in this climate. Productive farming enables countries in the middle latitudes to feed large populations.

The Middle Latitudes

Northern Hemisphere The United States and Canada are mostly located between the Arctic Circle and the Tropic of Cancer.

SKILL **Interpret a Map** Do you think Canada or the United States has the colder climate? Why?

An Isolated Continent

North America is almost completely surrounded by water. Its landmass stretches from the Arctic Ocean to the Gulf of Mexico and from the Pacific Ocean to the Atlantic Ocean. Find these bodies of water on page 52 of the Unit Almanac.

At one time, these waters isolated North America, or kept it separate from the rest of the world. Unique plants, such as the giant sequoia and the saguaro cactus, and animals, such as the bald eagle and the American alligator, developed in North America.

The oceans and seas were also a barrier to people. The earliest settlers arrived 12,000 to 35,000 years ago. No other people reached this continent until thousands of years later.

REVIEW Why do the middle latitudes have a moderate climate?

Crossing the Barriers

As people learned more about ship-building and navigation, the oceans became a hazardous but passable travel route. Settlers arrived in North America with plants and animals from their home countries. Many of these plants and animals were new to the continent. In some places, these replaced the native plants and animals.

In the 20th century, the distance from other countries helped protect Canada and the United States mainland from attack during the two World Wars. Today, satellites, the Internet, modern transportation, and other technologies link people everywhere.

Physical Processes That Shaped the Land

Natural processes have shaped North America. Some of the continent's most dramatic landforms were created by the action of wind, water, ice, and moving slabs of Earth's crust. **Landforms** are features of Earth's surface, such as mountains, valleys, and plateaus.

A **glacier** is a thick sheet of ice that moves slowly across land. Thousands of years ago, when Earth was much colder, glaciers covered much of North America. As they flowed across the land, they smoothed out rough surfaces, carved depressions and deep trenches, and piled up rock and dirt. When the ice melted, North America had new valleys, lakes, and hills.

Biography

Sacagawea Sacagawea (sak uh guh WEE uh) was a Shoshone woman who had a vital role in the exploration of what is now the northwestern United States. She guided explorers Meriwether Lewis and William Clark from what is now North Dakota into the Pacific Northwest. They had been sent to explore the newly purchased Louisiana Territory. Sacagawea's husband, French Canadian trapper Toussaint Charbonneau, and their baby son were also on the journey, which lasted from 1804 to 1806.

Sacagawea identified fruits and vegetables for the group to eat and helped the explorers communicate with the Native Americans whom they met along the trail. Historians believe that she was born around 1786 and probably died in 1812.

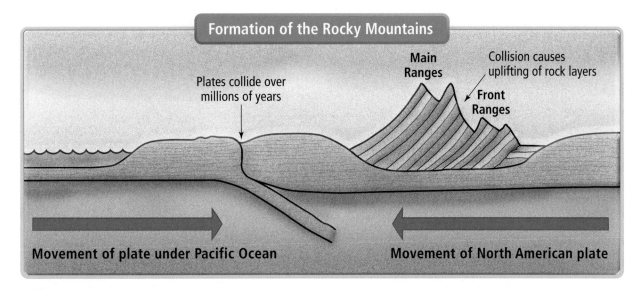

Formation of the Rocky Mountains

Plates collide over millions of years

Main Ranges

Collision causes uplifting of rock layers

Front Ranges

Movement of plate under Pacific Ocean

Movement of North American plate

Tectonic Plates The Rocky Mountains were formed 40 to 70 million years ago as a result of a collision between the tectonic plate under the Pacific Ocean and the North American plate.

Erosion

Wind, rivers, and rain wear away soil and stone in a process called **erosion.** Erosion can create magnificent landforms. The Grand Canyon is at least partly the result of millions of years of erosion by the Colorado River. Volcanoes, such as Mount St. Helens, and earthquakes are other natural forces that change the land. All these mighty forces have created landforms across North America.

Waterways

North America has an extensive **river system,** or network of major rivers and streams. The longest rivers are the Mississippi and Missouri rivers in the United States and the Mackenzie River in Canada. Find these rivers on the Unit Almanac map on page 52. When snow melts and rain falls, the water runs down into creeks that collect more water, becoming rivers. North America's rivers empty into bays, oceans, seas, gulfs, lakes, and other rivers.

REVIEW What are some natural processes that shaped the land in North America?

St. Lawrence Seaway This water route connects the Atlantic Ocean and the Great Lakes.

Regions of the United States and Canada

Main Idea The United States and Canada share many common geographic regions.

The United States and Canada share many geographic regions. Find these regions on the Unit Almanac map on page 52.

Atlantic Coastal Plain This region runs along the Gulf of Mexico and the east coast of North America. The region has much rich farmland and some swamps and wetlands.

Appalachian Mountains This 400-million-year-old mountain range lies west of the Atlantic Coastal Plain. These forest-covered mountains have weathered, or worn down, over time.

Central Lowlands West of the Appalachians are the Central Lowlands. They extend west to the Great Plains and are generally flat. The soil is rich, and many farms are located here.

Great Plains The Great Plains have grasslands and few trees. The land gradually rises from the Central Lowlands to the Rocky Mountains. Farmers grow crops and ranchers raise cattle in some areas.

The Rocky Mountains and Coastal Ranges North America's highest mountain ranges lie in the west. They include the Rocky Mountains, the Sierra Nevada and the Cascade ranges of the United States, and the Coast Mountains of Canada. These high, rugged, and heavily forested mountain ranges run along the western part of the continent from Mexico to Alaska.

Canadian Rocky Mountains These are part of the rugged range that reaches from Mexico to Alaska in western North America.

Grand Canyon This Arizona landform is one of the natural wonders of the world. It was formed by millions of years of erosion.

Intermountain Region Located between the Rocky Mountains and the western coastal mountains, this region is dry and contains plateaus, basins, and deserts. Ranchers raise cattle and sheep in some areas. The Grand Canyon is found here.

Canadian Shield The Canadian Shield includes most of Greenland, curves around the Hudson Bay, and reaches into the United States along the Great Lakes. The central and northwestern part of this huge rocky region has flat plains with hills and lakes. The northeast has high mountains, and the south is covered with forests. The shield is rich in minerals, such as iron, gold, copper, and uranium. Most of the land is not farmable and is sparsely populated.

REVIEW Which regions of Canada and the United States have productive farmland?

Lesson Summary

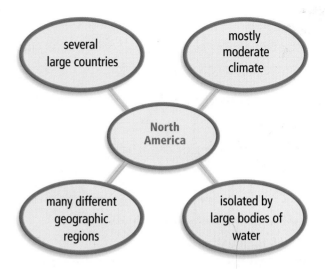

Why It Matters...

North America's geography contributes to the prosperity of the people who live there.

Lesson Review

1 VOCABULARY Write a paragraph explaining how **landforms** were formed in North America. Use these words in your paragraph: **glacier, erosion, river system.**

2 READING SKILL What do you think **caused** the landforms in your region of the country?

3 MAIN IDEA: Geography Describe North America's location on Earth and tell how this affects its climate and plant and animal life.

4 MAIN IDEA: History What barriers prevented plants, animals, and people from reaching North America? How were the barriers overcome?

5 MAIN IDEA: Geography What processes of nature help to shape the land?

6 PLACES TO KNOW Compare and contrast the **Appalachian Mountains** and the **Rocky Mountains.**

7 CRITICAL THINKING: Infer What natural features of North America attracted people from other lands? Support your conclusion with details from the text.

WRITING ACTIVITY List two regions of North America. Describe in a few words the kinds of plants, animals, and jobs that are found in each.

Earth-Surveying Satellite

Satellites supply scientists with data about Earth's surface, the atmosphere, and the ocean floor. They carry instruments to analyze weather conditions and survey the ozone layer. Satellites measure heat radiation, plant growth, ocean conditions, and other features of our environment. They relay phone calls and TV programs.

Satellite There are different types of satellites and different kinds of orbits to give scientists the specific data and services they need.

Sun-synchronous Polar Orbit
This kind of satellite passes over the north and south poles, circling the globe north to south and south to north in a 24-hour day. As a result, the satellite always crosses the equator at the same local times—say, 2:00 A.M. and 2:00 P.M. As it circles Earth, it makes observations of lands at every latitude.

Engineers These technicians and other scientists are needed to work on the satellites, designing instruments and measuring data.

Activities

1. **THINK ABOUT IT** Identify the two continents shown on this satellite picture of Earth.

2. **CALCULATE IT** Your sun-synchronous satellite passes over the equator twice a day—at 10:00 A.M. traveling north to south, at 10:00 P.M. traveling south to north. At what time will the satellite pass over the North Pole? Make a diagram to illustrate the satellite's movement around Earth.

Climate and Resources

VOCABULARY

weather
precipitation
climate
vegetation
economy

Vocabulary Strategy

vege**ta**tion

Think of the word **vegetable** when you see **vegetation.** Both vegetable and vegetation come from the same root word that means something that lives and grows.

READING SKILL

Compare and Contrast As you read, take notes to compare the natural resources of the United States and Canada.

Build on What You Know When you want to make something, you use what you have around you. North Americans also use the many natural resources available to them to build their economy.

Natural Wealth

Main Idea Both Canada and the United States are rich in natural resources that help their economies flourish.

The United States and Canada are rich in natural resources. This wealth has influenced their economic development.

The farmlands of the midwestern United States and the prairies in the central provinces of Canada have rich soil. Forests are found in western Canada and the northwestern, northeastern, and southeastern United States. There are oil fields in Alberta, Canada; in Texas, California, Louisiana, Oklahoma, and Alaska; and in the Gulf of Mexico. Coal is found in Canada's western provinces; in the Appalachian Mountains; and in Illinois, Indiana, and Wyoming.

Wheat Fields Crops raised in the United States and Canada feed the people of these countries and are exported to other countries all over the world.

Water Routes

Water routes affect where people and industry are located. Settlers in North America followed rivers to areas where freshwater and good soil permitted farming and raising cattle. Businesses grew in new communities. People still use rivers to ship natural resources, such as timber and coal, and as trade and travel routes. Fishing is a food source and an industry. Rivers and lakes supply water and power, and offer recreational activities.

REVIEW List some important natural resources of the United States and Canada.

Mississippi River This is one of the largest rivers in North America. It flows for 2,350 miles from its source at Lake Itasca in Minnesota to the Gulf of Mexico. The name *Mississippi* is from the Native American Algonquian language and means "Big River."

Citizenship IN ACTION

The Nature Conservancy The Conservancy works with communities to protect natural areas, plants, and animals. It has safeguarded 12 million acres and 1,400 land preserves, such as this one, in the United States. In its Great Lakes Program, and in Minnesota, the Conservancy is working with Canadian and U.S. groups to protect wildlife and 10,000 acres of the last tallgrass prairie on the U.S.-Canadian border.

Climate and Vegetation

Main Idea A region's climate and physical geography determine the vegetation that grows there.

Weather is the state of the atmosphere near Earth at a given time and place. It includes temperature, wind, and precipitation, or moisture such as rain or snow that falls to Earth. Climate is the typical weather in a region over a long period of time. A region's climate helps determine what types of vegetation—trees, shrubs, grasses, and other plants—will grow there.

North America's vegetation zones are determined by the climate and physical geography of each area. It is usually warmer in the south and colder in the north, but physical features such as mountains and oceans also affect the climate.

Polar and Tundra Northern Canada and Alaska have cool summers and very cold winters. It is usually above freezing (32°F/0°C) there for only two months each year. Precipitation varies from 4 to 20 inches a year. Much of the ground is frozen all year except for the surface, which thaws in summer.

Forest Forests of conifer (evergreen) and broadleaf trees cover much of Canada and the northwestern, northeastern, and southeastern United States. Precipitation averages between 10 and 80 inches annually. Temperatures vary from mild to cold in different forested areas.

Mountain Vegetation At higher altitudes, such as this mountainside, the plants that grow must be able to survive severe cold weather.

Rain Forest Along the Pacific Coast, precipitation can reach 167 inches each year. Rain forests with trees 300 feet tall grow in these areas. The ground is covered in bushes, small trees, and other plants. Moss and lichen are the smallest vegetation. One acre of rain forest might have 6,000 pounds of these tiny plants. The temperature is moderate even in the north, seldom falling below 32°F in winter.

Grassland The center of North America is covered by grasslands. The prairie in the Mississippi Valley may get 30 inches or more of precipitation each year. Grasses are tall and thick. Farther west, the land gets less rainfall—as little as 15 inches in Alberta, Canada—and the grass is shorter. People grow grain and raise cattle in these areas.

Desert The deserts of the American Southwest get less than 10 inches of precipitation a year. Plants in the deserts must be able to endure harsh sun, high temperatures, and little rain. Only the hardiest bushes, shrubs, a few small trees, and cacti survive there.

REVIEW How do climate and geography influence why people move to an area?

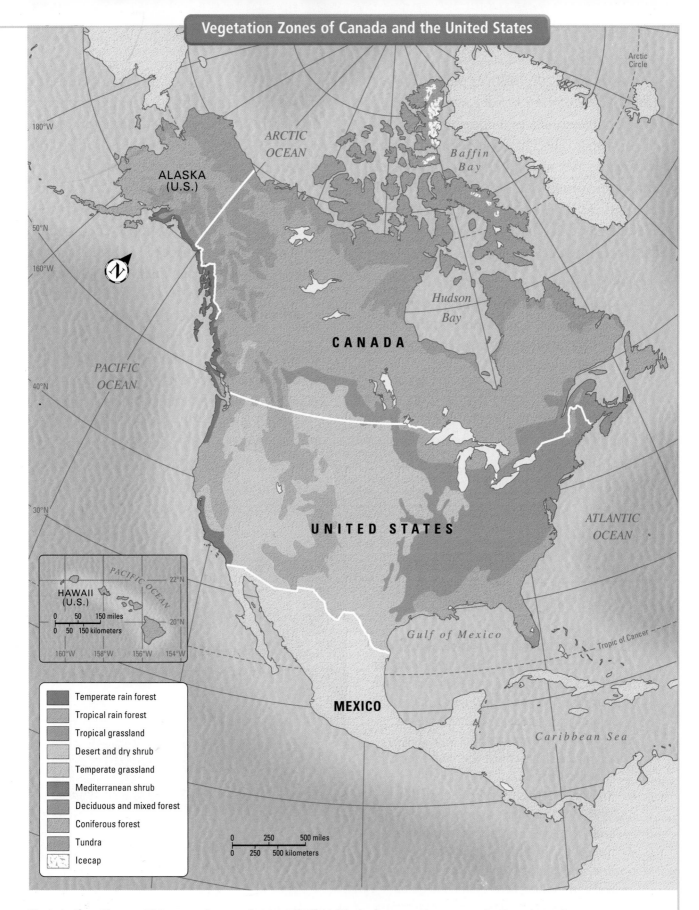

Vegetation Zones of Canada and the United States

ALASKA
(U.S.)

ARCTIC
OCEAN

Baffin
Bay

Arctic
Circle

CANADA

Hudson
Bay

PACIFIC
OCEAN

UNITED STATES

ATLANTIC
OCEAN

HAWAII
(U.S.)

PACIFIC OCEAN

Gulf of Mexico

Tropic of Cancer

MEXICO

Caribbean Sea

Legend
- Temperate rain forest
- Tropical rain forest
- Tropical grassland
- Desert and dry shrub
- Temperate grassland
- Mediterranean shrub
- Deciduous and mixed forest
- Coniferous forest
- Tundra
- Icecap

0   250   500 miles
0   250   500 kilometers

Vegetation Zones This map shows where and what kind of vegetation grows in Canada and the United States. **SKILL Interpret a Map** What kind of vegetation zone covers most of Canada? What part of the United States is covered by temperate grassland?

Neighbors and Leaders

More than 200 million people cross the U.S.–Canadian border every year. Trade between the two countries exceeds $1 billion a day. They cooperate on issues as diverse as national security and defense, the environment, air traffic, and fishing regulations. United States President John F. Kennedy described the relationship between these countries:

> 66 **Geography has made us neighbors, history has made us friends, economics has made us partners, and necessity has made us allies.** 99

Both countries have strong economies and are leaders in world trade. An **economy** is the way that business owners use resources to provide the goods and services that people want.

NAFTA

In 1992, the leaders of Canada and the United States, along with Mexico, signed the North American Free Trade Agreement, or NAFTA. The goal was to eliminate trade barriers between these countries.

Before NAFTA was signed into law, no one knew how free trade would affect the U.S. economy. Plenty of people had opinions, though. Some people warned that Americans would lose jobs if trade became freer. They predicted that more companies would move their factories to Mexico.

Most economists believed NAFTA would be good for each country. They believed free trade helps businesses and keeps prices low for consumers.

Years after NAFTA passed, it is clear that North American trade has grown. Between 1993 and 2001, total trade between Canada, Mexico, and the United States more than doubled.

Spotlight on CULTURE

The Cajuns: Americans with Canadian Roots The French settled in Acadia, which is now Nova Scotia, Canada, in 1604. The British gained control of much of Nova Scotia, and in 1755, they expelled most French Acadians. Many of the displaced settlers relocated to southern Louisiana, which was under the rule of France at that time.

Known as Cajuns, the descendants of those French Canadians share a special cultural heritage. Their language has French, English, Spanish, German, and Native American influences. Their unique music is played with fiddles, accordions, and guitars. The man shown here plays the accordion at a Cajun music festival in Louisiana.

CRITICAL THINKING Recognize Effects What effect did Britain's rule over Nova Scotia have on the French in Acadia?

Recognize Important Details What are some features of the Cajun culture?

Most leaders in Canada, Mexico, and the United States have been pleased by the increase in trade. However, some report that NAFTA has not helped to create enough jobs. Other nations will watch NAFTA's effects carefully. If free trade works in North America, they may want similar agreements with the United States.

REVIEW What common interests make the United States and Canada allies and partners?

U.S. – Canada Trade
1993–2001

Dollars (in Billions)

240
200
160
120
80
40
0

1993   1995   1997   1999   2001
Year

Exports to Canada
Imports from Canada

Lesson Summary

The United States and Canada are similar in many ways. The climate tends to be cold in the north and warm in the south. The vegetation ranges from polar tundra to grassland and from forest to desert. Both countries' rich natural resources have helped make them leaders in world trade.

Why It Matters . . .

The prosperity of people living in the United States and Canada affects the prosperity of the modern global economy.

Trade Canada is our nation's biggest trading partner. Since NAFTA was passed, trade with Canada has more than doubled.

SKILL **Interpret a Graph** What was the value of imports from Canada in 1999?

Lesson Review

1 VOCABULARY Write a paragraph describing how a region's **climate** and **vegetation** can have an effect on a country's **economy.**

2 READING SKILL **Compare** the natural resources of Canada with the resources of the United States.

3 MAIN IDEA: Geography How do climate and geography affect vegetation?

4 MAIN IDEA: Economics What natural resources are found in North America?

5 MAIN IDEA: Geography How have waterways affected settlement and development in the United States and Canada?

6 PLACES TO KNOW Describe the **grassland zone** of North America.

7 CRITICAL THINKING: Draw Conclusions How does the variety of vegetation zones affect the economies of the United States and Canada?

HANDS ON

ART ACTIVITY Choose one of the vegetation zones discussed in the lesson. Draw a picture showing what the land looks like.

Skillbuilder

Read a Physical Map

Physical maps show the natural features of Earth's surface. These include landforms such as mountains, hills, and plains; and bodies of water such as rivers, lakes, bays, and oceans. Land elevation, or altitude, may be shown in a map key. National boundaries and major cities may also be included.

The physical map below shows the natural features of Canada. Use the steps to the right to identify the information shown on the map.

Physical Map of Canada

0 400 800 miles
0 400 800 kilometers

Elevation

13,100 ft. (4,000 m)
6,600 ft. (2,000 m)
1,600 ft. (500 m)
650 ft. (200 m)
0 ft. (0 m)
Below sea level

Glacier

ARCTIC OCEAN

Beaufort Sea

Baffin Bay

Davis Strait

60°N
30°W

Mackenzie Mts.
Mackenzie R.
ROCKY MOUNTAINS
COAST RANGES

Interior Plains

Labrador Sea

40°W
50°N

Hudson Bay

PACIFIC OCEAN

CANADIAN SHIELD

Saskatchewan R.

L. Winnipeg

Laurentian Highlands

St. Lawrence R.

Gulf of St. Lawrence

50°W

L. Huron

40°N

L. Superior

L. Michigan

L. Ontario
L. Erie

ATLANTIC OCEAN

Learn the Skill

Step 1: Read the title. It tells you which region's physical features are being represented.

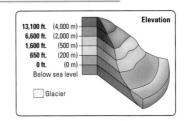

Physical Map of Canada

Step 2: Read the key. It tells you the elevation of land each color represents. A map key may also show boundaries between nations, national capitals, and other cities.

Step 3: Read the scale. It tells you how many miles or kilometers each inch on the map represents.

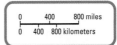

Practice the Skill

A chart can help you organize information given on maps. The chart below organizes information from the map to the left.

Canada	
Bodies of Water	Atlantic Ocean, Pacific Ocean, Arctic Ocean, Hudson Bay, Davis Strait, Baffin Bay, Labrador Sea, Beaufort Sea, Mackenzie River, Lake Winnipeg, Saskatchewan River, Lake Superior, Lake Huron, Lake Erie, Lake Ontario, St. Lawrence River, Gulf of St. Lawrence
Landforms	Rocky Mountains, Coast Ranges, Mackenzie Mountains, Canadian Shield, Interior Plains, Laurentian Highlands

Apply the Skill

Turn to page 52 in the Unit 2 Almanac. Study the physical map of North America. Make a chart listing major physical landforms of North America that you see on the map. You may also include a section in your chart labeled "Countries."

Visual Summary

1–2. ✏️ Write a description for each concept shown below.

From Coast to Coast

_____
_____

Climate and Resources

_____
_____

Facts and Main Ideas

Answer each question below.

3. **Geography** Describe the location of North America.

4. **Geography** What natural processes have changed the geography of North America?

5. **Geography** Which vegetation zones permit farming and ranching?

6. **Economics** How do natural resources affect the economies of the United States and Canada?

7. **History** How have waterways helped people in the past?

Vocabulary

Choose the correct word from the list below to complete each sentence.

river system, p. 67
erosion, p. 67
precipitation, p. 74
vegetation, p. 74

8. Weather measures the temperature, wind speed, and _____ that falls in an area.

9. The _____ that grows in an area is determined by the climate and physical geography of the area.

10. The Mississippi River and its tributaries form one of the major _____(s) on the North American continent.

11. The _____ of soil and rock by the Colorado River helped form the Grand Canyon.

TEST PREP **Read a Physical Map**

Study the map below. Then use the map skills you have learned to answer each question.

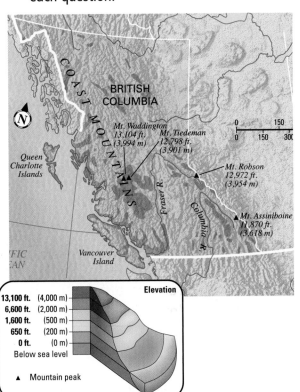

COAST MOUNTAINS

BRITISH COLUMBIA

Mt. Waddington
13,104 ft.
(3,994 m)

Mt. Tiedeman
12,798 ft.
(3,901 m)

Queen Charlotte Islands

Fraser R.

Columbia R.

Mt. Robson
12,972 ft.
(3,954 m)

Mt. Assiniboine
11,870 ft.
(3,618 m)

PACIFIC OCEAN

Vancouver Island

Elevation

13,100 ft. (4,000 m)
6,600 ft. (2,000 m)
1,600 ft. (500 m)
650 ft. (200 m)
0 ft. (0 m)
Below sea level

▲ Mountain peak

12. What is the highest mountain in British Columbia?
- **A.** Mt. Waddington
- **B.** Mt. Tiedeman
- **C.** Mt. Robson
- **D.** Mt. Assiniboine

13. Near what landform does the Fraser River empty into the Pacific Ocean?
- **A.** Queen Charlotte Islands
- **B.** Columbia River
- **C.** Vancouver Island
- **D.** Mt. Robson

TEST PREP Write a short paragraph to answer each question below.

14. Synthesize List the geographic features that contribute to productive farmland and agricultural exports.

15. Draw Conclusions Choose one of the regions of the United States and Canada. Think about what you know about the region's natural resources and economics. What do you think are the economic advantages and disadvantages of the region?

16. Infer What industries that depend on natural resources might flourish in the United States and Canada? Why?

Activities

SPEAKING ACTIVITY Prepare and present a television news report on the Lewis and Clark Expedition. Use the Internet or other library resources to help you prepare your report.

 WRITING ACTIVITY Write a journal entry from the point of view of an early fur trader who traveled across the United States and Canada.

Technology

Writing Process Tips
Get help with your journal entry at www.eduplace.com/kids/hmss05/

Technology

e • **glossary**
e • **word games**
www.eduplace.com/kids/hmss05/

Vocabulary Preview

patriotism

Patriotism is love for one's country. One way citizens can show that they care about their country is to become involved in the political process by voting.
page 88

Constitution

The United States **Constitution** was written by the country's first leaders. This document is the foundation for all laws and the framework for the U.S. government.
page 89

Chapter Timeline

1783
U.S. independence from Britain

1789
Constitution ratified

1775   1800   1850

Reading Strategy

Question As you read the lessons in this chapter, ask yourself questions.

Quick Tip List your questions, and then go back to find the answers.

federal government

The United States has a national government called the **federal government.** It is led by the President. To limit the power of the federal government, there are also state governments.

page 91

technology

The tools and equipment made through scientific discoveries are called **technology.** Technology, such as this satellite, can help locate undiscovered sources of energy.

page 106

| 1865 | 1920 |
| Thirteenth Amendment ends slavery | Women gain right to vote |

1875   1900   1925

We the People

1400   1500   1600   1700   1800   1900   2000

1400–2000

immigrant
equal opportunity
citizenship
democracy
political process
patriotism

Vocabulary Strategy

immigrant

Immigrant begins with **im–**, which sounds like **in.** Immigrants travel to move **in**to a new country.

🎯 **READING SKILL**

Sequence As you read, fill in the chart to show the order of immigration from different countries to the United States.

1	
2	
3	
4	

Build on What You Know Have you ever watched someone make a salad? The lettuce, tomatoes, vegetables, and dressing are mixed together to make one food. The United States is also a mixture. It is a mixture of cultures and people from all over the world that have come together to make one country.

One Country, Many Cultures

Main Idea Thousands of years after Native Americans settled in America, people arrived in the United States from all over the world.

Immigrants have brought unique contributions to the United States from their homelands all over the world. An **immigrant** is someone who chooses to move to a new country. The United States is sometimes called a "melting pot," a "salad bowl," or a "patchwork quilt" to illustrate how U.S. society combines aspects of many cultures. Some features may blend into the culture of the United States, while others retain their original characteristics.

For example, settlers from Great Britain brought English, the most widely spoken language in the United States. Spanish is often spoken in the Southeast and the Southwest, where people from Spain and Mexico settled. French is heard in Louisiana, which was once held by France. People in the United States enjoy the influence of different groups on their foods, music, sports, and other areas of their lives.

Great Seal The motto *E Pluribus Unum* is Latin for "out of many, one." It is on the Great Seal of the United States and many U.S. coins.

Immigrants come to the United States for different reasons. Some are escaping from discrimination, persecution, or war. Others leave their homelands because of famine, earthquake, or other natural disasters. Often, people come to the United States hoping to improve their economic or educational opportunities.

The First Americans

Over the past 500 years, millions of immigrants have come to the land that is now the United States and Canada. However, this land was inhabited long before they arrived. In fact, people have lived in North America for thousands of years.

Native Americans were the first people to inhabit the Western Hemisphere. They came to North America from Eastern Asia 12,000 to 35,000 years ago. Some groups, such as the Mississippians and Anasazi (Navajo for "Ancient Ones"), developed complex civilizations.

The Anasazi civilization developed around A.D. 100 and reached its height in the 11th to 13th centuries. The Anasazi were experts at irrigation. They built homes called cliff dwellings that had from 20 to 1,000 rooms. Remains of these structures survive in the Mesa Verde National Park in Colorado and in other places in the Southwestern United States.

Europeans Arrive

European exploration of the Americas began in the late 1400s. Colonists soon followed the explorers. The British settled along the Atlantic coast, in what is now southeastern Canada and the northeastern United States. Spaniards settled in Florida and came north from Mexico to build towns in the Southwest. Often, the settlers' ways of life and needs for resources conflicted with those of the Native Americans. As the European population grew, competition for land intensified. Europeans often took land from Native Americans. Cultural differences and land disputes led to distrust and war.

European settlers began to plant and harvest crops and started businesses and towns. This created a demand for cheap labor, so Europeans forced some people to migrate to America.

REVIEW Why have people come to the United States?

North American Settlement, 1750

British settlement to 1750
British frontier lands in 1750
Spanish settlement to 1750
Spanish frontier lands in 1750
French settlement to 1750
French frontier lands in 1750
Huron Native American people

Settlement This map shows where Europeans of different nationalities settled when they came to North America. **SKILL** **Interpret a Map** Which three European countries had settlers in North America by 1750?

Slavery in the Colonies

Europeans had been buying people from slave traders in Africa since the 1500s. Beginning in 1619, enslaved Africans were shipped to the American colonies under such harsh conditions that many died during the journey. Those who survived were bought and sold as property and forced to work for free all their lives. Their children were born into slavery. Although these Africans did not arrive by choice, their labor helped build the country, and their influence is seen in our culture today.

In the second half of the 1800s, many Chinese immigrants entered the United States. Some worked in mines, while others helped build the transcontinental railroad. In the 1880s and the 1920s, new laws limited the number of U.S. immigrants from various countries. In 1952, legislation again allowed immigrants of all nationalities to become citizens.

Rights and Responsibilities

Main Idea As citizens of the United States, people have both rights and duties.

Although the United States is among the world's leaders in protecting individual freedom, many U.S. citizens have struggled for their rights. Even after African Americans were freed from slavery in 1865 by the 13th Amendment to the Constitution, they were denied their rights. Women could not vote in the United States until 1920. Native Americans, as well as Hispanics, Asians, the Irish, and other immigrants, have fought against discrimination.

The guarantee of **equal opportunity** in education, employment, and other areas of life has expanded over the years. Today, it is illegal for the government or private institutions to discriminate because of race, gender, religion, age, or disability.

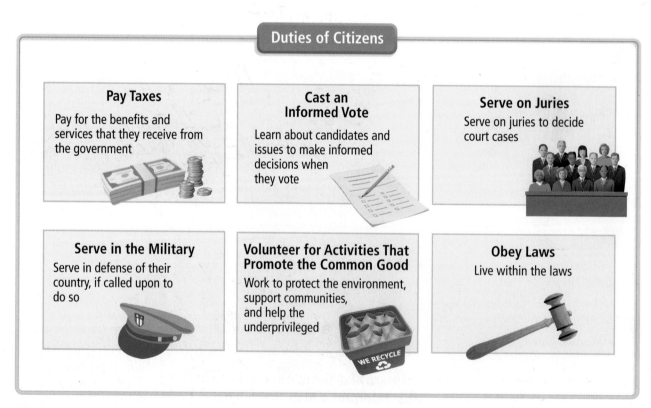

Duties of Citizens

Pay Taxes
Pay for the benefits and services that they receive from the government

Cast an Informed Vote
Learn about candidates and issues to make informed decisions when they vote

Serve on Juries
Serve on juries to decide court cases

Serve in the Military
Serve in defense of their country, if called upon to do so

Volunteer for Activities That Promote the Common Good
Work to protect the environment, support communities, and help the underprivileged

Obey Laws
Live within the laws

Duty U.S. citizens have responsibilities to their country, as well as rights.

Responsibilities of Citizens

U.S. citizens' rights come with important responsibilities. Citizens should help decide who will run their government and what actions it will take. **Citizenship** is a combination of the duties and rights of a citizen. Good citizenship means doing more than the minimum required by law to secure the good of the people. It means participating in one's community to make it a better place to live. Doing volunteer work to help the environment or people in need is one way to participate.

In a democracy, government receives its power from the people. **Democracy** is a Greek word that means "rule of the people." The United States is a democracy, but the people rule through elected representatives. The citizens of a democracy have the responsibility to take part in the political process.

REVIEW Do you think U.S. citizens have greater responsibilities because they have more rights? Explain.

Citizenship IN ACTION

Americans Join Together On September 11, 2001, terrorists hijacked four U.S. planes. They flew two into the twin towers of the World Trade Center in New York City and one into the Pentagon in Arlington, Virginia. Both towers collapsed, and one wing of the Pentagon was damaged. Thousands of people were killed, and hundreds more were injured or trapped under debris. The fourth plane crashed in Pennsylvania after passengers struggled with the hijackers.

During the crisis, Americans like these rescue workers showed their patriotism and heroism. Hundreds of firefighters, police officers, and medical personnel worked tirelessly, risking their own lives to save others. Citizens and companies across the country donated time, blood, supplies, and millions of dollars to the victims and their families through organizations such as the Red Cross and the United Way. Americans came together in response to the attack on their nation.

The Political Process

The **political process** refers to those legal activities through which citizens can change public policy. By becoming involved, citizens demonstrate their **patriotism,** or love for their country.

The Citizenship Pledge New citizens pledge their support of the United States.

Lesson Summary

> **Why Immigrants Came**
> escaping discrimination, persecution, war; economic or educational opportunities; forced as slaves

> **Where Immigrants Came From**
> Eastern Asia, Europe, China, Africa

> **Duties of U.S. Citizens**
> pay taxes, vote, serve on juries, serve in military, volunteer, obey laws

Why It Matters . . .

The ideas and values of U.S. immigrants have helped shape the success of the country in the world today.

Lesson Review

1619	1865	1920
First enslaved Africans arrive	Thirteenth Amendment ends slavery	Women gain right to vote

1600 — 1700 — 1800 — 1900 — 2000

① **VOCABULARY** Write a letter to someone who wants to move to America. Use the words **citizenship, equal opportunity,** and **patriotism.**

② **READING SKILL** Review your chart. When did large numbers of Chinese immigrants enter America?

③ **MAIN IDEA: History** Why do people immigrate to the United States?

④ **MAIN IDEA: Citizenship** What are some of the rights guaranteed to U.S. citizens by the Constitution?

⑤ **MAIN IDEA: Citizenship** What are some responsibilities of U.S. citizens?

⑥ **PEOPLE TO KNOW** Where did the people of the **Anasazi** civilization build their cliff dwellings?

⑦ **TIMELINE SKILL** How many years after enslaved Africans began entering the United States was slavery abolished?

⑧ **CRITICAL THINKING: Draw Conclusions** What would happen to a democracy if citizens only claimed their rights but did not fulfill their duties?

HANDS ON

ART ACTIVITY Think about one of the immigrant populations described. Write and illustrate a magazine article about the contributions this group has made to the culture of the United States.

A Constitutional Democracy

1750   1800   1850   1900   1950   2000

1783–2000

Build on What You Know What kind of plan do you make when you are going to write a report or do a school project? The early leaders of America made a plan when they were forming the new government. They wrote the Constitution, the plan for the government of the United States.

The Law of the Land

Main Idea The United States Constitution explains that the government's power is received from its citizens.

The basis for all U.S. law is the United States **Constitution,** written by the country's first leaders. Amazingly, this document remains the foundation for all laws and the framework for the U.S. government more than 200 years after its creation. The Supreme Court decides whether the actions of states, businesses, and individuals are in accordance with the ideas in the Constitution.

American colonists living under British rule did not have the rights and the protections they wanted. After gaining independence from Great Britain in 1783, they established a nation called the United States of America. The writers of the Constitution designed a government that received its power from the people.

VOCABULARY

Constitution
limited
   government
constitutional
   amendment
Bill of Rights
federal
   government

Vocabulary Strategy

constitutional amendment

Find **mend** in the compound term **constitutional amendment**. An amendment is a way to mend, or fix, a problem with the Constitution.

READING SKILL
Problem and Solution As you read, note the problems the colonists had living under British rule and the solutions they found.

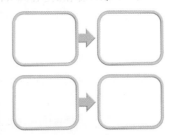

Constitution More than 200 years old, this document is still the basis of U.S. laws and government.

U.S. Constitution

The founders, or early American leaders, believed in **limited government.** They wanted the power of government to be restricted by laws and rules, and wanted to protect people's individual rights and freedoms from government interference. They also knew that a society needs strong laws and a stable government to ensure the common good. They wrote a constitution that achieved both goals. The U.S. Constitution describes and limits the power of the government and its leaders. It also defines the rights of citizens and their role in governing their country. In 1902, President Theodore Roosevelt explained the relationship between U.S. citizens and their government:

66 The government is us; we are the government, you and I. 99

The Constitution Changes

The Constitution went into effect in 1789. A condition of ratifying, or approving, it in many states was the promise of a bill of rights. In 1791, the states adopted ten constitutional amendments proposed by Congress. A **constitutional amendment** is a change or addition to the Constitution. This **Bill of Rights** lists specific freedoms guaranteed to every U.S. citizen. Among them are freedom of speech and religion, the right to a fair trial, and the right to gather peaceably. In all, 27 amendments have adapted the Constitution to the country's changing needs. Some amendments passed after the Bill of Rights include ones that ended slavery, gave women the right to vote, and limited a President's terms to two.

Constitutional Convention The founders of the United States met in Philadelphia to write the Constitution.

Women's Rights Women began the fight for suffrage, or the right to vote, in the early 1800s. In 1920, they succeeded when the Nineteenth Amendment was passed.

Limiting Powers of Government

Main Idea The Constitution limits the powers of the government by separating it into three branches: executive, legislative, and judicial.

Leaders of the new country wanted to limit government power and to preserve each state's right to govern itself. To accomplish these goals, they created a federal system in which power is divided between the **federal government,** or national government, and the state governments. The federal government is a republic headed by the President.

The Constitution gives the federal government specific powers, including establishing an army, waging war, raising money through taxes, and making laws to carry out its duties. All other powers are held by the states. The Constitution does not refer to local government, so each state determines the form of town or county rule.

The Constitution separates powers of government into the executive, legislative, and judicial branches. Each branch has its own job. All are located in the U.S. capital, Washington, D.C.

REVIEW What were two goals that the writers of the Constitution wanted to achieve?

Federal System Under this system of government, national and state governments both share and have their own responsibilities.

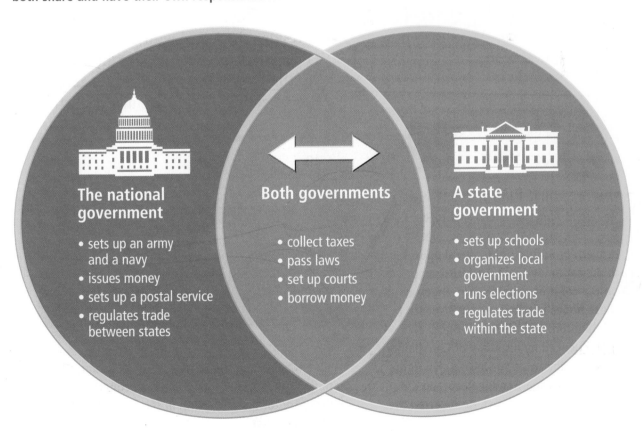

The national government
- sets up an army and a navy
- issues money
- sets up a postal service
- regulates trade between states

Both governments
- collect taxes
- pass laws
- set up courts
- borrow money

A state government
- sets up schools
- organizes local government
- runs elections
- regulates trade within the state

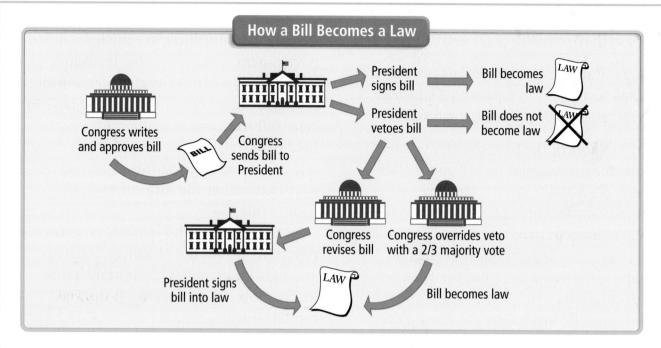

How a Bill Becomes a Law

Congress writes and approves bill → Congress sends bill to President → President signs bill → Bill becomes law

President vetoes bill → Bill does not become law

Congress revises bill ← President vetoes bill

Congress overrides veto with a 2/3 majority vote

President signs bill into law ← LAW ← Bill becomes law

Balance of Power A bill must go through the legislative and the executive branches of government before it can become a law.

Three Branches of Government

Three branches share the powers of the U.S. government. Each branch checks the power of the other branches. The process by which a bill, or a proposal for a new law, becomes a law shows how this balance of power works.

The Executive Branch The President is elected to head the executive branch. The President enforces the laws, serves as commander in chief of the armed forces, and conducts foreign affairs. The Vice-President is elected with the President. The President's cabinet includes the secretaries of the 14 executive departments and other key members of the executive branch.

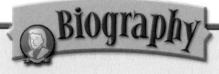

Biography

Martin Luther King Jr. (1929–1968)
Reverend King was a civil rights leader in the 1950s and 1960s. A gifted speaker, he argued for voting rights, equal opportunities in education and jobs, and justice not based on the color of people's skin. He expressed these hopes in a famous 1963 speech in Washington, D.C., shown at right.

Influenced by his study of Christianity and his admiration for India's civil rights leader Mahatma Gandhi, Reverend King used nonviolent protest. He received the Nobel Peace Prize in 1964.

On April 4, 1968, he was assassinated. Since 1986, a U.S. holiday has been observed in January to honor him, and he is remembered around the country for his leadership in the civil rights movement.

The Legislative Branch Congress is made up of two houses—the Senate and the House of Representatives—and makes national laws. Two senators are elected from each of the 50 states. The House of Representatives has 435 members, elected from each state according to its population. The two houses have some shared responsibilities and some separate ones.

The Judicial Branch The judicial branch is the system of federal courts that makes sure all laws and treaties are constitutional, or agree with the U.S. Constitution. The highest federal court, the Supreme Court, has nine justices, or judges, nominated by the President and approved by the Senate.

REVIEW What are the basic powers of each of the three branches of government?

Lesson Summary

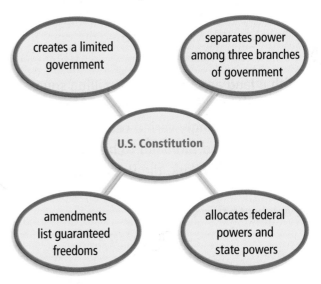

Why It Matters . . .

After more than 200 years, the Constitution continues to protect the freedoms of U.S. citizens.

Lesson Review

1783
U.S. Independence from Britain

1789
Constitution ratified

1791
Bill of Rights adopted

1780   1785   1790

1 **VOCABULARY** Write a paragraph describing how the **Bill of Rights** and **constitutional amendments** affect the **Constitution.**

2 **READING SKILL** What **solutions** to the **problem** of British rule do we still use today?

3 **MAIN IDEA: History** What two goals did the writers of the U.S. Constitution try to achieve?

4 **MAIN IDEA: Citizenship** Why did people think it was important to add the Bill of Rights to the Constitution?

5 **MAIN IDEA: Government** Why does the Constitution create a balance of powers among the three branches of government?

6 **TIMELINE SKILL** How many years after the Constitution was ratified was the Bill of Rights added?

7 **CRITICAL THINKING: Infer** Why do you think Congress is made up of two parts, the Senate and the House of Representatives?

WRITING ACTIVITY If you were going to add an amendment to the Constitution, what would it be? Write a proposal for it. Tell what the law would do, whom it would affect, and why people should support it.

With a land area of over 3.7 million square miles and a population of about 300 million, the United States is an amazingly varied country. From small towns, forests, and farmland to big cities like San Francisco and New York, the United States has a wealth of both human-made and natural features. The poems here celebrate this variety.

CONEY [1]

By Virginia Schonborg

There's hot corn
And franks.
There's the boardwalk [2]
With lots of games,
With chances
To win or lose.
There's the sun.
Underneath the boardwalk
It's cool,
And the sand is salty.
The beach is
Like a fruitstand of people,
Big and little,
Red and white,
Brown and yellow.
There's the sea
With high green waves.
And after,
There's hot corn
And franks.

KNOXVILLE, TENNESSEE

By Nikki Giovanni

I always like summer
best
you can eat fresh corn
from daddy's garden
and okra
and greens
and cabbage
and lots of
barbecue
and buttermilk
and homemade ice-cream
at the church picnic
and listen to
gospel music
outside
at the church
homecoming
and go to the mountains with
your grandmother
and go barefooted
and be warm
all the time
not only when you go to bed
and sleep

SCENIC

By John Updike

O when in San Francisco do
As natives do: they sit and stare
And smile and stare again. The view
Is visible from anywhere.

Here hills are white with houses whence,
Across a multitude of sills,
The owners, lucky residents,
See other houses, other hills.

The meanest[3] San Franciscan knows,
No matter what his past has been,
There are a thousand patios
Whose view he is included in.

The Golden Gate, the cable cars,
Twin Peaks, the Spreckles habitat,[4]
The local ocean, sun, and stars—
When fog falls, one admires *that*.

Here homes are stacked in such a way
That every picture window has
An unmarred prospect of the Bay
And, in its center, Alcatraz.[5]

1. Amusement area in New York City.
2. A wooden walkway over sand.
3. Poorest.
4. In the late 1950s, Twin Peaks was a well-to-do residential neighborhood where a very wealthy family, the Spreckles, lived.
5. An island in San Francisco Bay, site of a former federal prison.

Activities

1. **THINK ABOUT IT** Imagine that you live in one of these places. What kinds of jobs might people have there? What might they do for fun? How does the place where you live influence your daily activities?

2. **WRITE ABOUT IT** Which of the poems creates the strongest image in your mind? Using examples from that poem, write a short paragraph explaining why.

The United States Economy

VOCABULARY

factors of production
GDP
free enterprise/
  market economy
consumer
profit
competition

Vocabulary Strategy

consumer

Consumer includes the word **consume**. A consumer is someone who buys, or consumes, goods and services.

READING SKILL

Cause and Effect As you read, take notes to show the effects on the government when the economy is expanding or declining.

Build on What You Know Have you ever bought something from a store? When you buy something, sell something, earn money, or put money into a bank, you affect the U.S. economy.

The Study of Economics

Main Idea The United States economy is based on freedom of choice about what to buy and sell.

Business start-ups and shutdowns, the rise and fall of investor and consumer confidence, the increase and decrease in the number of people without jobs—all of these changes are part of the economy of the United States. Investors, service providers, manufacturers, and consumers make choices each day, and these choices affect the state of the economy.

Suppose you want a CD recording just released by your favorite music group. To earn the money to pay for it, you might rake your neighbor's leaves or care for his or her child for a few hours. The CD is a good. A good is any object you can buy to satisfy a want. Raking leaves or baby-sitting is a service you provide. A service is an action that meets a want. Your neighbor buys your service to meet his or her want.

People constantly decide which goods and services to buy. They usually satisfy basic needs such as food, clothing, housing, transportation, child care, and medical treatment first. If there is money left over, they might choose to spend it on music CDs, in-line skates, a computer game, or a vacation.

A government must also make decisions. Tax dollars must be set aside to pay for police and fire protection, schools, roads, and military forces. Once these expenses have been determined, other choices can be made.

A Growing Economy

Main Idea Four factors are needed to produce a good.

A nation must produce goods and provide services to support a growing economy. In an expanding economy, citizens have better-paying jobs, so the government collects more tax money. With a strong economy, both people and the government can satisfy more wants and needs.

To sustain a growing economy, business owners must keep production at a high level. Production is the making of goods and services. The four **factors of production** are the ingredients, or elements, needed for production to occur.

Natural Resources Raw materials are used to make goods. Examples include land, water, forests, minerals, soil, and climate.

Labor Resources Workers are needed with the appropriate knowledge, skills, and experience to make goods or provide services.

Capital Resources Machines, factories, and supplies are needed.

Entrepreneurs These are the people who bring natural resources, labor resources, and capital resources together to produce goods and services.

REVIEW After a government has set aside money for basic wants, what additional goods or services might it pay for?

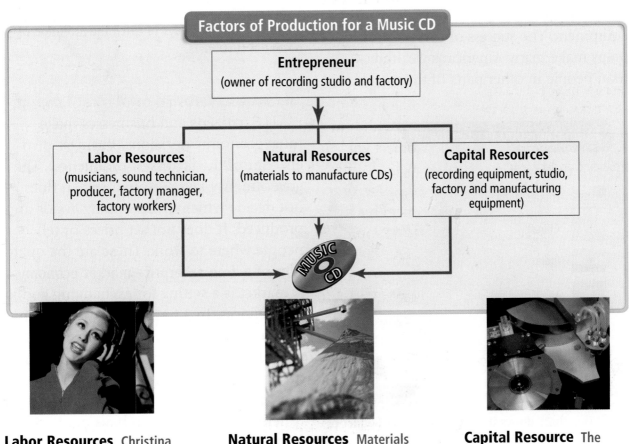

Factors of Production for a Music CD

Entrepreneur
(owner of recording studio and factory)

Labor Resources
(musicians, sound technician, producer, factory manager, factory workers)

Natural Resources
(materials to manufacture CDs)

Capital Resources
(recording equipment, studio, factory and manufacturing equipment)

MUSIC CD

Labor Resources Christina Aguilera's contribution as a singer is one of the labor resources.

Natural Resources Materials such as silicon, a mineral found in sand, are used to produce the compact disc.

Capital Resource The machines that make CDs are a capital resource, one of the four factors of production.

The United States Economy

Main Idea In the United States, consumers and businesses make most economic decisions, while the government's role is limited.

The U.S. economy is one of the wealthiest in the world. One way to measure a country's economy is to look at its **GDP,** or gross domestic product. This tells the total value of the goods and services that a country produces each year. The GDP is also a way to compare the economies of different countries.

U.S. industries include services, such as health care and legal services; communications, such as publishing, television and radio, telephone, and mail delivery; finance, such as banks and stock markets; manufacturing, such as food products, automobiles, and clothing; and electronics, such as televisions, computers, and sound equipment. The success of these industries helps make many Americans wealthier than people in other parts of the world.

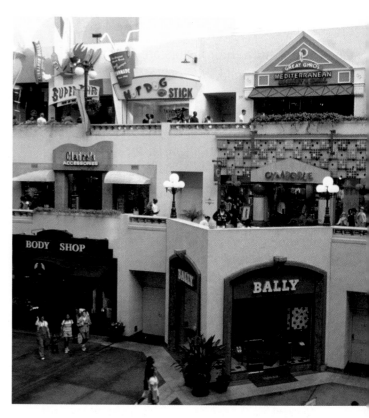

Competition Stores compete in malls and online to attract consumers. They use advertising and appealing store displays to catch the attention of potential customers.

The Free Enterprise or Market Economy

U.S. citizens and businesses make most economic decisions. Business owners control the factors of production. The government plays a limited role. It does not decide which or how many goods are produced. It does not set prices or tell people where to work. These are the qualities of a **free enterprise/market economy.** A market is a setting for exchanging goods and services. In a free enterprise economy, business owners compete in the market with little government interference. Other nations, such as Canada, many countries in Western Europe, Japan, and some Latin American countries, also have market economies.

Estimated 2000 Per Capita* GDP

Country	U.S. Dollars
United States	36,200
China	3,600
India	2,200
Saudi Arabia	10,500
France	24,400
Zimbabwe	2,500

*Per capita means for each person.
Source: CIA World Factbook

GDP This chart shows the gross domestic product of these countries divided by the number of people who live in the country. Developed, industrial countries such as the U.S. and France have high GDPs.

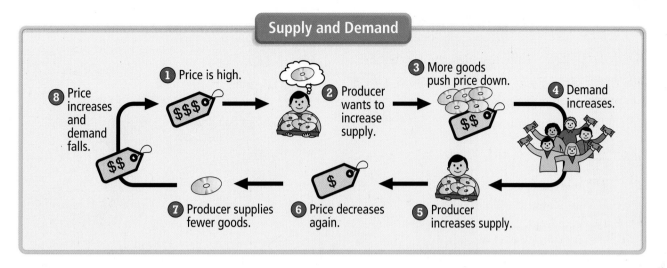

Supply and Demand

Supply and Demand diagram:

1 Price is high.
2 Producer wants to increase supply.
3 More goods push price down.
4 Demand increases.
5 Producer increases supply.
6 Price decreases again.
7 Producer supplies fewer goods.
8 Price increases and demand falls.

Free Market Prices are affected by how much of a good there is and by how many people want the good.

Supply and Demand

In a free enterprise or market economy, the **consumer**—a person who uses goods and services—helps decide what will be produced. Prices affect how products are distributed to consumers.

For example, suppose a music company produces 1,000 CDs priced at $16.95 each, but 1,100 people want to buy them. There are not enough CDs to satisfy the wants of these consumers. Because demand for the good is greater than the supply, the seller can increase the price to $17.95. He or she sells all the CDs and makes an extra $1.00 profit on each.

The seller, like all entrepreneurs, wants to increase profit. **Profit** is the money that remains after all the costs of producing a product have been paid.

Now suppose the seller offers 1,000 more CDs at the original $16.95 price. One hundred sell right away, leaving 900 CDs that no one wants at this price. The seller then reduces the price to $15.95.

Consumers who didn't want the CD at $16.95 may want it at this lower price. Because the supply of the good is greater than the demand, the seller must reduce the price.

Supply and demand explain how price and availability are affected by how much consumers are willing to pay for an item and how much the seller decides to charge for it. The number of CDs offered at each price is the supply. The number of CDs that people will buy at each price is the demand.

In a free enterprise or market economy, many businesses produce similar goods or services. There is competition to attract consumers. **Competition** is the rivalry among businesses to sell goods to consumers and make the greatest profit. To achieve these goals, a company may offer an improved product, manufacture it more cheaply, or sell it at a better price.

REVIEW How does competition help consumers?

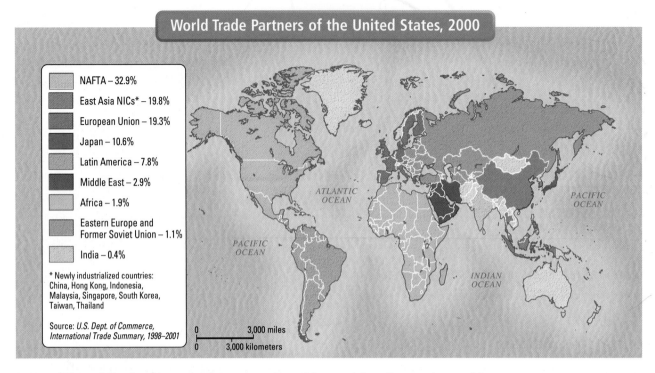

World Trade Partners of the United States, 2000

	NAFTA – 32.9%
	East Asia NICs* – 19.8%
	European Union – 19.3%
	Japan – 10.6%
	Latin America – 7.8%
	Middle East – 2.9%
	Africa – 1.9%
	Eastern Europe and Former Soviet Union – 1.1%
	India – 0.4%

* Newly industrialized countries: China, Hong Kong, Indonesia, Malaysia, Singapore, South Korea, Taiwan, Thailand

Source: *U.S. Dept. of Commerce, International Trade Summary, 1998–2001*

ATLANTIC OCEAN

PACIFIC OCEAN

PACIFIC OCEAN

INDIAN OCEAN

0   3,000 miles
0   3,000 kilometers

International Trade The United States trades with countries all over the world.
SKILL **Interpret a Map** Who are the largest U.S. trade partners? With which countries or regions does the United States trade least?

Other Economic Systems

Main Idea Although more countries than ever have market economies, some countries have command and traditional economies.

Most countries combine features from three types of economic systems: market, command, and traditional economies.

In a command economy, the government decides how many of which goods are produced and sets the prices. Countries such as North Korea and Cuba, with Communist governments, have command economies. China has elements of market and command economies.

In a traditional economy, social roles and culture determine how goods and services are produced, what prices and individual incomes are, and which consumers are allowed to buy certain goods.

The Global Economy

A family's status may determine whether they can own a tractor. Farmers may give much of their produce to community leaders. India has features of both market and traditional economies.

Today, more countries than ever before have market economies. Communication and transportation are fast and dependable, making trade easier among countries. The movement of people, goods, and ideas around the world has helped build a global, or worldwide, economy in which the United States is a leader. Expanding trade can open new markets and keep prices low and quality high for consumers. U.S. citizens buy many cars and clothes from other countries that take part in the global economy.

Trade Barriers

Sometimes countries establish barriers to restrict trade because they prefer to produce their own goods or services. Tariffs, or taxes on imported goods, raise the price to the consumer and make it more difficult for other countries to compete.

Other countries may support free trade. They work to reduce trade barriers, often through free trade agreements. NAFTA, which reduced trade barriers among the United States, Canada, and Mexico, is an example of a free trade agreement. Many economists believe free trade benefits all three countries.

REVIEW Why might countries combine features of different economic systems?

Lesson Summary

- In a free enterprise economy, government is limited. Citizens and businesses make decisions while business owners control production.

- In a command economy, the government makes all decisions about production and pricing of goods.

- In a traditional economy, social roles and culture control production and prices and determine which consumers can buy certain goods.

Why It Matters . . .

The free enterprise economic system has made it possible for the United States to become a leader in the worldwide economy.

Free Trade Cars and car parts are important to North American trade. Car parts from the United States are put together in this Mexican factory.

Lesson Review

❶ **VOCABULARY** Write a paragraph explaining how the **factors of production** affect **consumers** and **profits.**

❷ 🕐 **READING SKILL** What is the **effect** on the government when the economy is in decline?

❸ **MAIN IDEA: Economics** How is the price of goods decided in the U.S. economic system?

❹ **MAIN IDEA: Economics** What are the four factors of production?

❺ **MAIN IDEA: Government** What role does government have in the U.S. market economy?

❻ **EVENTS TO KNOW** How has **NAFTA** changed trade in North America?

❼ **CRITICAL THINKING: Infer** What effect will reducing trade barriers between countries have on the price of goods? Explain.

ART ACTIVITY Write and illustrate an advertisement for a new business showing the goods or services it will produce. Make a chart showing the type of materials, labor, and capital you will need to produce the product.

Skillbuilder

Sequence Events

Sequence is the order in which events follow one another. If you learn to follow the sequence of events through history, you can better understand how events relate to each other.

This passage describes the sequence of events that improved the transportation of natural resources and goods in the United States. Use the steps listed to the right to understand how transportation has improved.

Resources, Goods, and People

The United States could not have developed without new ways of transporting natural resources and goods. In the early 19th century, water provided the fastest way to transport goods. Canals linked some lakes and rivers, so places became more accessible. A little later, steamboats allowed river traffic to go upstream and downstream easily.

By the middle of the century, steam-powered railroads had replaced steamboats because they could reach more places and carry larger loads. At the beginning of the 20th century, people and goods in many cities and towns were linked by railroad.

In the early 1900s, automobiles and trucks began to move raw materials and goods. Airplanes began to transport goods in the 1930s. By the 1950s, paved roads connected much of the country. Today, fast jets also bring goods and people to many parts of the United States.

Learn the Skill

Step 1: Look for time periods of events or discoveries. Some dates may be exact, and others may be indicated only by decades or centuries. Words such as *day, month, year,* or *century* may help you to sequence the events or discoveries.

Step 2: Look for clues about time that allow you to order events according to sequence. Words such as *first, next, later,* and *finally* may help you order events that are not dated.

Practice the Skill

Making a timeline can help you sequence events. This timeline shows the sequence of events in the passage you just read.

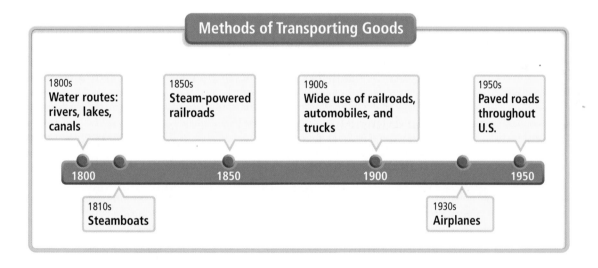

Methods of Transporting Goods

1800s	1850s	1900s	1950s
Water routes: rivers, lakes, canals	Steam-powered railroads	Wide use of railroads, automobiles, and trucks	Paved roads throughout U.S.

1800 — 1850 — 1900 — 1950

1810s Steamboats

1930s Airplanes

Apply the Skill

Turn to Chapter 4, Lesson 1, "We the People." Read about the different groups of people who settled the land that became the United States. Make a list showing the sequence of the arrival of different immigrant groups.

Culture of the United States

READING SKILL

Main Idea and Details As you read, use the graphic organizer to note details that show the influence of world cultures on American culture.

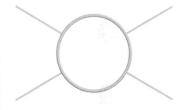

Build on What You Know What do you like to do in your spare time? Many of the things you might enjoy actually came from different cultures. Soccer originated in England. Popular music has influences from all over the world. United States society combines aspects of many cultures.

American Way of Life

Main Idea American life reflects a variety of cultures in religion, customs, traditions, and leisure activities.

People in the United States have brought diverse customs, traditions, and foods from their homelands, but they share many of the same values. **Values** are the principles and ideals by which people live. U.S. citizens care about individual freedoms; equal opportunities for jobs and education; fair treatment of people regardless of race, religion, or gender; and private ownership of property. Many of these values are part of the U.S. Constitution and help define American culture.

U.S. citizens believe they can improve their lives through education. In 1647, Massachusetts established the first colonial public school system. Today, state laws require that all children attend school or be taught at home until they are at least 16. More than 99 percent of U.S. children finish elementary school, and more than 85 percent complete high school.

Early Schoolhouse Some of the oldest schools in the country are in Massachusetts, like this one in Boston.

U.S. Religion

About 70 percent of all U.S. citizens are members of religious groups. Many colonists, such as British Protestants and Catholics, settled in America so that they could worship as they wished. Since then, people with many different religious beliefs have come to the United States. Most Spanish, French, and Italian immigrants were Catholic. In the 1900s, many European Jews settled in the United States. Asian immigrants practice Buddhism and Hinduism. North Africans and Southwest Asians brought Islam. Many Native Americans continue to practice their ancestors' religions.

The Arts and Entertainment

Leisure activities in the United States reflect the influence of other cultures. For example, sports such as tennis, golf, soccer, and even baseball originated in other countries. Tennis came from France, golf from Scotland, and soccer from England. Baseball is probably based on rounders, a game played in Great Britain in the late 1700s. Basketball was invented in the United States by a Canadian and later spread to other countries. Football is played chiefly in the United States and Canada.

REVIEW Why do you think values such as freedom of religion were written into the U.S. Constitution?

Spotlight on CULTURE

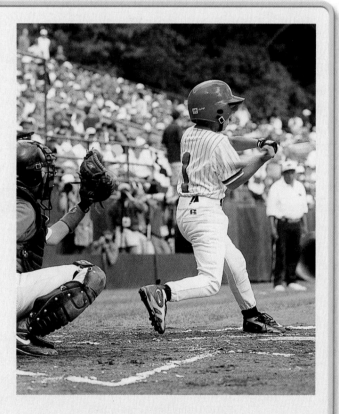

Baseball The American game of baseball, known as the national pastime, probably originated from the old English stick-and-ball game called rounders. In 1845, Alexander Cartwright, a New Yorker, wrote the first official rules, known as the "Knickerbocker Rules," for the American version of the game. The next year, the Knickerbocker team played the first game of baseball under the new rules at Elysian Fields in Hoboken, NJ.

The movement of people caused by the 1849 California Gold Rush and the Civil War helped to spread the game throughout the country. In the 20th century, American travelers and soldiers introduced baseball to many countries. Today, baseball is known around the world and is especially popular in Japan and the Caribbean.

CRITICAL THINKING: Infer How do you think the stick-and-ball game of rounders came to America?

Predict Today, what might help spread American sports to other countries of the world?

World Culture

The movie and television industries and certain musical forms, such as rock 'n' roll, developed in the United States, although they were affected by other cultures. Jazz was greatly influenced by the blues, which is rooted in spirituals once sung by enslaved Africans. Today, artists and audiences around the world enjoy these American musical styles.

The international popularity of U.S. music is an example of the globalization of culture. **Globalization** means spreading around the world. Today, cultural influences often cross national boundaries. People around the world enjoy blue jeans, sodas, and fast food from the United States. McDonald's serves about 45 million people a day in 121 countries.

U.S. citizens eat Japanese sushi, listen to Italian operas, and drive South Korean cars. Literature from many nations is translated into different languages. Print and electronic communication, television, movies, and the Internet provide speedy ways to share the products and creations of different cultures.

U.S. Science and Technology

Main Idea Scientists and inventors use and develop technology to help people around the world.

U.S. scientists are mapping DNA and discovering treatments and cures for diseases. They are also finding new energy sources for industry and homes. Once discoveries are made, inventors create **technology,** such as tools or equipment, to apply the new knowledge in practical ways. Modern technology enables U.S. scientists to work with other scientists from around the world.

Discoveries by U.S. scientists help people throughout the world. Polio, a disease that usually affects children, was widespread in the 1940s and 1950s. Then, U.S. doctors Jonas Salk and Albert Sabin each developed a different vaccine. As a result, great progress has been made toward making the world free of polio.

Polio These maps show the decrease in polio cases worldwide over the last two decades.

SKILL Interpret a Map Which continent had widespread polio in 1988 but was polio-free in 2000?

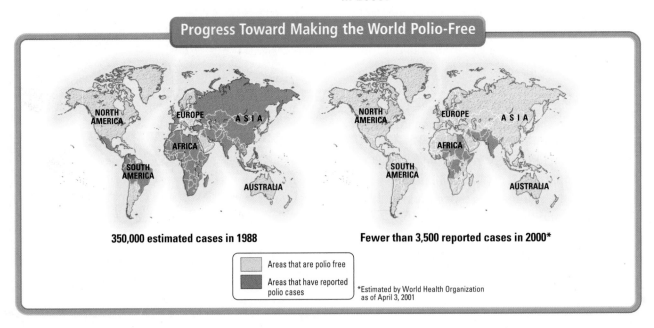

Progress Toward Making the World Polio-Free

350,000 estimated cases in 1988

Fewer than 3,500 reported cases in 2000*

Areas that are polio free

Areas that have reported polio cases

*Estimated by World Health Organization as of April 3, 2001

Negative effects of technology include increased pollution of the environment and the loss of unique cultural features as technology makes it easier for countries to share languages, foods, and customs. Poorer nations may lack the money and skilled labor needed to benefit from new applications of science.

REVIEW Why has technology not had as great an effect on poorer nations?

Jonas Salk This doctor developed a cure for polio, a deadly disease that had spread throughout the world. Today, the world is becoming polio-free.

Lesson Summary

The American way of life reflects the cultures of people from many countries around the world. There is an increasing globalization of culture, science, and technology.

Why It Matters . . .

People around the world are more closely connected than ever before.

Lesson Review

❶ **VOCABULARY** Write a paragraph describing the **globalization** of **technology.** Use both words in your explanation.

❷ **READING SKILL** Which **details** show the influence of world cultures on American art and entertainment?

❸ **MAIN IDEA: Culture** What are some values shared by people in the United States?

❹ **MAIN IDEA: Culture** What are some examples of contributions from other cultures to the American way of life?

❺ **MAIN IDEA: Culture** In what ways does American culture influence people in other countries?

❻ **PEOPLE TO KNOW** How has the globalization of **Jonas Salk's** and **Albert Sabin's** vaccines changed the world?

❼ **CRITICAL THINKING: Evaluate** Do you think globalization has a positive or a negative effect on the world? Support your opinion.

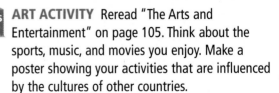

ART ACTIVITY Reread "The Arts and Entertainment" on page 105. Think about the sports, music, and movies you enjoy. Make a poster showing your activities that are influenced by the cultures of other countries.

Review and Test Prep

Visual Summary

1–4.  Write a description for each concept shown below.

We the People	A Constitutional Democracy	The United States Economy	United States Culture

_____	_____	_____	_____
_____	_____	_____	_____

Facts and Main Ideas

Answer each question below.

5. **History** What are some reasons that people have immigrated to the United States?

6. **Government** What were the goals of the early leaders when they wrote the U.S. Constitution?

7. **Government** What were the leaders attempting to do when they set up a system of checks and balances within the federal government?

8. **Economics** What are examples of wants that a government must fund?

9. **Culture** If globalization continues, how will it affect the cultures of the world?

Vocabulary

Choose the correct word from the list below to complete each sentence.

immigrant, p. 84
limited government, p. 90
competition, p. 99
values, p. 104

10. _____ takes place when businesses try to sell similar goods to consumers, and each are trying to make the greatest profit.

11. Many _____s come to the United States hoping to improve their economic condition.

12. Some _____ that Americans share are protection of individual freedom, equal opportunity, and private ownership of property.

13. When a nation's leaders are restricted by laws and rules, this is called _____.

Apply Skills

 TEST PREP Sequence of Events Study the chart below. Then use the chart to answer each question.

> **Civil Rights Movement in the U.S.**

> 1865: Abolition of slavery

> 1870: Right to vote for African American men

> 1920: Right to vote for American women

> 1954: End of school segregation

> 1964: Civil Rights Act

14. When did segregation in schools end?
   A. 1964
   B. 1954
   C. 1865
   D. between 1954 and 1964

15. What relationship did school segregation have to women's right to vote?
   A. School segregation ended before women got the right to vote.
   B. School segregation ended at the same time that women got the right to vote.
   C. Women got the right to vote 34 years after the end of school segregation.
   D. Women got the right to vote 34 years before the end of school segregation.

Critical Thinking

 TEST PREP Write a short paragraph to answer each question below.

16. Synthesize Explain why the economy, form of government, and cultural values of the United States continue to attract so many immigrants each year.

17. Make Inferences What were the major concerns of the leaders who wrote the U.S. Constitution and how did they address them?

Timeline

Use the Chapter Summary Timeline above to answer the question.

18. How many years after the Constitution was adopted was the Thirteenth Amendment added to it?

Activities

 DRAMA ACTIVITY Create and act out a skit depicting an immigrant's first day in the United States. Include examples of American values and culture for the immigrant to experience.

 WRITING ACTIVITY Write a persuasive essay explaining why a country with limited government should have a market economy.

 Technology

Writing Process Tips
Get help with your essay at
www.eduplace.com/kids/hmss05/

Canada Today

Technology

e • **glossary**
e • **word games**
www.eduplace.com/kids/hmss05/

Vocabulary Preview

Parliament

The seat of Canada's government is in the **Parliament.** This legislature sets Canadian laws and policies.
page 118

prime minister

The **prime minister** of Canada is the head of the government. John A. MacDonald was the first prime minister of Canada.
page 118

Chapter Timeline

1867
Canada becomes self-governing

1850   1875   1900

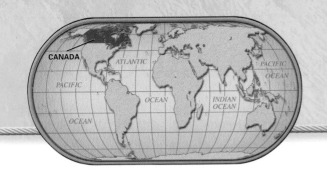

CANADA

Reading Strategy

Summarize Use this strategy to help you understand important information in this chapter.

Quick Tip A summary includes only the most important information. Use the main ideas to help you.

export

An **export** is a good sold to or traded with another country. Canadian exports, such as wheat and wood, are sent to countries around the world. **page 122**

transportation corridor

A path that makes transportation easier is a **transportation corridor.** The St. Lawrence Seaway is a transportation corridor between the Atlantic Ocean and the Great Lakes. **page 123**

1931
Canada joins Commonwealth

1988
Canadian Multicultural Act passed

1950   **1975**   **2000**

Immigrant Roots

| 1500 | 1600 | 1700 | 1800 | 1900 | 2000 |

1600–2000

VOCABULARY

First Nations
multiculturalism
refugee

Vocabulary Strategy

multiculturalism

The prefix **multi–** in **multiculturalism** means "many." Multiculturalism is the acceptance of many cultures.

READING SKILL

Classify As you read, use this chart to list each group of people who settled in Canada and the language they spoke.

Build on What You Know Do you know anyone at school who moved to your neighborhood from another place? The country of Canada was settled by people who came from many countries. As a result, Canada is a country of many different cultures.

Who Are the Canadians?

Main Idea Because it was settled by immigrants from all over the world, Canada has an official policy of acceptance of many cultures.

More than 50 ethnic groups make up the population of Canada. More than two-thirds of Canadians have European ancestry. About 40 percent have British roots and 27 percent share a French heritage. Other Canadians trace their families back to Germany, Italy, and Ukraine, as well as to nations in Africa and Asia.

Samuel de Champlain
This French explorer helped establish the first European settlement in Quebec. He explored and mapped most of New France and its seacoasts and rivers.

The First Nations

People have lived in North America for at least 12,000 years. At times in the past, the levels of the oceans were as much as 300 feet lower than they are today. Then the narrow water passage between Asia and North America—the Bering Strait—became dry land. Small bands of people crossed this land bridge into North America and settled throughout North America and South America.

The Canadians of the **First Nations** are descendants of those first settlers from Asia. In the Arctic north, Inuit and other native people make up more than half the population. Large numbers of First Nations people, including Cree, Micmac, Abenaki, and Ojibwa, live in southern Canada near the United States border.

European Immigrants

The first major wave of European settlement began in the 1600s. Both Britain and France established colonies in what is now Canada. These two countries had a long history of conflict, and they continued their rivalry on the North American continent. Between 1754 and 1763, they fought the French and Indian War for control of North America.

France lost the war and surrendered most of its Canadian territory to Great Britain. However, many French settlers remained, and disputes continued between them and the fast-growing population of British settlers.

REVIEW Who were some of the people of the First Nations?

Spotlight on CULTURE

Totem Poles—Carving History The Haida people in Canada's Queen Charlotte Islands and the Kwakiutl in central British Columbia have been skilled totem carvers for centuries. Early craftspeople believed that red cedar was a gift from the Great Spirit. They used simple tools to carve beautiful, detailed totem poles from these trees.

Totem poles, such as these in Stanley Park, Vancouver, display brightly painted animal figures, or totems. These include eagles, whales, grizzly bears, wolves, ravens, frogs, and halibut. Totems are symbols that tell stories, celebrate important events, and preserve the history of native clans. Totem poles have also been used as grave markers and monuments.

CRITICAL THINKING Make Inferences What do the totem poles tell you about the First Nations people's relationship with nature?
Draw Conclusions What roles do totem poles play in native culture?

Canada and the United Kingdom

In 1791, the British government established itself in two areas in Canada. Upper Canada, now Ontario, had mostly British settlers. Lower Canada, now Quebec, remained largely French. Although hostilities continued between the two populations, in 1867 they were united as the Dominion of Canada, along with Nova Scotia and New Brunswick. Canada became a self-governing nation, although the British monarch remained its head of state.

In 1869, the Hudson's Bay Company sold land to Canada that later became the provinces of Manitoba, Alberta, and Saskatchewan. In 1871, British Columbia joined the Dominion, and Canada now reached to the Pacific Ocean. In 1931, with the enactment of the Statute of Westminster, Canada gained equal status with the United Kingdom and joined the Commonwealth of Nations. In 1982, the last legal connection between Canada and the British Parliament ended, although Canada remains a member of the Commonwealth.

Most of Canada's early immigrants were English, Scottish, Irish, and French. After World War I, other Europeans arrived from countries such as Italy, Poland, and Ukraine. Most Italian immigrants settled in Toronto and Montreal. Most Ukrainians moved to the prairies of central Canada. After World War II, Germans and Dutch entered the country, settling primarily in Ontario and British Columbia. In the 1960s, new immigration laws allowed people to migrate from Africa, Latin America, Asia, and the Pacific Islands.

Canadian Citizens and Citizenship

As Canadian citizens, those of English or French descent have retained their separate languages and identities. Other groups have also kept the traditions of their homelands after settling in Canada. To support these citizen groups, Canada has adopted an official policy of **multiculturalism**—an acceptance of many cultures instead of just one.

Canadian citizens have many of the same rights and responsibilities as U.S. citizens. They must obey Canada's laws. They have the option of voting and participating in the political system. They are guaranteed freedom of religion, speech, and assembly, as well as equal protection and treatment for all under Canadian law.

French Defeat British General James Wolfe's troops defeated the French and captured Quebec in 1759 during the French and Indian War. This painting shows Wolfe's death at the end of the battle his troops won.

Where Canadians Live

Main Idea Most Canadians live where the geography is favorable and there are economic opportunities.

While Canada's land area is second only to Russia's, its population is a relatively small 31 million people. Canadians often live where they find a favorable combination of geographic features and economic opportunities. Three-fourths of the population live in the cities and towns of southern Canada. In this region, the Great Lakes, the St. Lawrence Seaway, numerous rivers, and an excellent railway system provide convenient transportation for people and goods. Some Canadians live on farms in the central prairies and in port cities along the coasts. The northern regions of Canada are rugged and very cold. Few people live in those remote areas.

Vancouver, British Columbia, is called Canada's "Gateway to the Pacific." As Canada's largest port, it trades heavily with Asian countries.

Vancouver This city has many Chinese immigrants from Hong Kong, whose culture has influenced its architecture.

Thousands of Chinese from Hong Kong and many Japanese arrived in Canada at the end of the 20th century. Recent refugees have come from Vietnam, Laos, and Cambodia. **Refugees** are people who flee a country because of war, disaster, or persecution.

REVIEW What geographic and economic features attract people to settle in southern Canada?

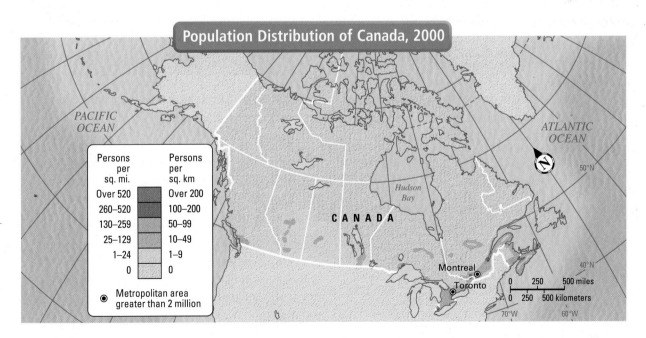

Population Distribution of Canada, 2000

Persons per sq. mi.	Persons per sq. km
Over 520	Over 200
260–520	100–200
130–259	50–99
25–129	10–49
1–24	1–9
0	0

⊙ Metropolitan area greater than 2 million

Population This map shows where people live in Canada.

SKILL **Interpret a Map** In what part of Canada do most Canadians live?

Toronto, City of Immigrants

Toronto, Ontario's capital, is home to one-twelfth of Canada's population but contains one-fourth of its immigrants. More than 70,000 immigrants arrive each year from more than 100 countries in Asia, Europe, the West Indies, and North America. More than 40 percent of Toronto's population is foreign-born, and 10 percent arrived after 1991. Toronto's location, with access to the Atlantic Ocean and the United States, has helped it become a center of industry and international trade.

Lesson Summary

- Originally from Asia, the First Nations people still live in Canada.
- British and French settlers established the first European colonies in the 1600s.
- Canada is part of the British Commonwealth.
- Canada is a nation of many cultures with an official policy of multiculturalism.
- Most Canadians live in southern Canada where transportation and economic opportunities are available.

Why It Matters . . .

Knowing the history of the people of Canada helps in understanding Canada's policy of multiculturalism.

Toronto This city of over two million people is on the shore of Lake Ontario, the easternmost Great Lake. Toronto's skyline is highlighted by the CN Tower.

Lesson Review

	1763	1867	1931
	French and Indian War ends	Canada becomes self-governing	Canada joins Commonwealth

1750 — 1800 — 1850 — 1900 — 1950

1 **VOCABULARY** Use each of the following words in a sentence about immigration to Canada: **First Nations, multiculturalism, refugee.**

2 **READING SKILL** Use your chart to list the languages spoken in Canada.

3 **MAIN IDEA: History** How did the first people reach North America? Who are their descendants?

4 **MAIN IDEA: History** Describe the relationship between the British and Canada in the 1700s and the 1800s.

5 **MAIN IDEA: Citizenship** What are some of the rights and responsibilities of Canadian citizens?

6 **TIMELINE SKILL** How many years after the French and Indian War did Canada become self-governing?

7 **CRITICAL THINKING: Infer** Has the policy of multiculturalism benefited recent immigrants to Canada? Support your conclusion with details from the text.

WRITING ACTIVITY Choose one place in Canada where you might like to live. Look at the information in the Unit Almanac and in this section. Write and illustrate a magazine article about this location.

A Constitutional Monarchy

1970　　　1980　　　1990　　　2000

1980–1995

Build on What You Know You live in a country, the United States. You also live in a state. The governments of the country and of the state work together. In Canada, there are several levels of government too.

Canada's Government

Main Idea Canada is a democracy in which power comes from the constitution and is enacted by Parliament.

Canada is a nation of ten provinces and three territories. The responsibilities of the central government include national defense, trade and banking, immigration, criminal law, and postal service. The provincial governments administer education, property rights, local government, hospitals, and provincial taxes. Territorial governments have fewer responsibilities but still enjoy limited self-government.

Canada is a **constitutional monarchy.** It has a constitution to explain the powers of the government and owes allegiance to a monarch, a king or a queen. The Canadian government consists of the legislative and the judicial branches. Executive duties are within the legislature.

The Parliament Buildings These buildings in Ottawa, Canada's capital, house the legislature of the central government.

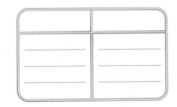

VOCABULARY

constitutional monarchy
Parliament
prime minister
separatist

Vocabulary Strategy

separatist

Separatist comes from the word **separate**. A separatist is someone who wants to separate from the rest of a country.

READING SKILL

Compare and Contrast As you read, take notes to compare and contrast Canada's central government and its provincial governments.

117

Legislature

The British monarch is Canada's head of state. Since the queen or king does not live in Canada, she or he selects a governor-general as a representative. The monarch and the governor-general have little genuine power in Canadian government. They represent the historical traditions of Canada.

Canada's legislature, called **Parliament,** has two bodies, the House of Commons and the Senate. Together they determine Canadian laws and policies. Citizens elect members of the House of Commons. The leader of the party with the most members becomes the head of government, or **prime minister,** who runs the executive branch within the legislature. Senators are chosen by the prime minister from each of the ten provinces and three territories.

Canada has both federal and provincial courts. The highest court is the federal Supreme Court. It is made up of the chief justice of Canada and eight other judges.

Canada is a democracy. Its government is responsible for protecting people's rights.

House of Commons This part of Canada's legislature is elected by its citizens.

Prime Minister Pierre Trudeau led an effort to add a Charter of Rights and Freedoms to the Canadian Constitution in 1982. The Charter is similar to the U.S. Constitution's Bill of Rights. Among other rights, the Charter guarantees freedom of speech and freedom of religion. It protects every citizen's right to vote and to be assisted by a lawyer if arrested. It says that Canadians are free to live and work anywhere in Canada. The Charter also says that people have equal rights regardless of their race, religion, gender, age, or national origin.

Comparing the Canadian and U.S. Governments

Aspects of Government	Canada	United States
Type	Constitutional Monarchy (limited power)	Constitutional Republic (limited power)
Head of State	Monarch	President
Head of Government	Prime Minister	President
Legislature	Parliament	Congress
System	Federal (central and provinces)	Federal (central and states)

Government The United States and Canadian governments are similar but different.

SKILL Interpret a Map Name three ways in which the government of Canada differs from that of the United States. How are the governments of Canada and the United States alike?

Many Cultures, Many Needs

Main Idea Canada's multiculturalism has led to conflicts but continues to be a strength as well.

Canada's people come from different cultures, and many wish to safeguard their special language and customs. Some French-speaking Canadians are **separatists,** or people who want the province of Quebec to become an independent country.

In 1980 and in 1995, separatists asked for a vote on whether Quebec should become independent. Both times the issue was defeated, but the separatists promised to try again.

The federal government wants Quebec to remain part of Canada. Quebec is a major contributor to Canada's economy. Quebec is responsible for half of Canada's aerospace production, half of its information technology, and 38 percent of its high-tech industry. French culture is important in Canada's history and modern-day identity.

REVIEW Why do Canadian separatists want an independent Quebec?

 **Biography**

Pierre Elliott Trudeau (1919–2000)
From 1968 to 1979 and from 1980 to 1984, Pierre Trudeau was Canada's prime minister. Born in Montreal, Quebec, of French and Scottish ancestry, he grew up speaking both French and English. Despite his French-Canadian background, Trudeau successfully opposed Quebec's attempts to separate from Canada. He considered keeping Quebec a part of Canada one of his great achievements.

In 1982, Trudeau also helped enact a new Canadian constitution. At right, British Queen Elizabeth II signs a proclamation in 1982, making the new Canadian Constitution law, while Trudeau, seated, looks on. He worked to establish diplomatic relations with China and achieved Canada's complete independence from the British Parliament.

The Quebec provincial government has passed laws to preserve its citizens' French heritage. In an attempt to satisfy the separatists, Canada's federal government passed the Canadian Multicultural Act in 1988. This act guarantees the right of all Canadians to preserve their cultural heritage. Finding ways to maintain a unified country remains a critical issue in Canada today.

Quebec City
Overlooking the St. Lawrence River, this city is the capital of the province of Quebec and the center of French-Canadian culture.

Lesson Summary

Canada's Government	
Head of State	British Monarch
Head of Government	Prime Minister
Legislature	Parliament made up of House of Commons and Senate
Judiciary	federal Supreme Court, federal and provincial courts

Why It Matters . . .

Canada's form of government has enabled the country to remain united despite conflicts among different groups of citizens.

Lesson Review

1982
Charter of Rights and Freedoms adopted

1988
Canadian Multicultural Act passed

1980 1982 1984 1986 1988 1990

❶ **VOCABULARY** Use the vocabulary words to complete the sentence.

prime minister   Parliament

Canada's legislature is called _____, and it is led by the _____.

❷ **READING SKILL** How are Canada's central government and provincial governments alike?

❸ **MAIN IDEA: Government** What are some similarities and differences between the Canadian and U.S. governments?

❹ **MAIN IDEA: Citizenship** Describe some of the rights guaranteed in the Charter of Rights and Freedoms.

❺ **MAIN IDEA: Culture** What is the purpose of the Multicultural Act?

❻ **TIMELINE SKILL** In what year were Canadians given the legal right to preserve their cultural heritage?

❼ **CRITICAL THINKING: Predict** What might happen if Quebec became a separate country?

HANDS ON

SPEAKING ACTIVITY Imagine that you are giving a speech to the Canadian Parliament in support of the Multicultural Act. Explain why it is important to preserve different cultures.

Canada's Economy

Build on What You Know Think of some jobs that people do in your community. Are any of these jobs related to natural resources in your area? Many people in Canada have jobs that depend on the country's many natural resources.

Contributors to the Economy

Main Idea Canada's rich natural resources and participation in trade have led to a strong economy.

Canada is rich in natural resources. Europeans were first drawn to Canada by the abundant fishing and fur trading. In the 1800s, gold and other minerals were discovered. Today, most Canadians work in the service and manufacturing industries. Canada's skilled labor force, natural resources, and international trade all contribute to the country's economy.

A nation's resources are a source of wealth. The prairie provinces of central Canada have extensive grasslands and good soil, making this area an ideal place to raise beef cattle and grow wheat. On the rich farmlands along the St. Lawrence River, farmers harvest grains, vegetables, and fruit. People plant potatoes and raise dairy cattle on the east coast. The Grand Banks, located off the coast of Newfoundland, is one of the world's most abundant fisheries. The salmon caught off Canada's Pacific coast enrich that area's economy.

VOCABULARY

industry
export
import
**transportation
corridor**
**transportation
barrier**

Vocabulary Strategy

import and export

To remember the difference between **import** and **export,** think of "**in**to" and "**ex**it." Imports come into a country. Exports exit, or leave, a country.

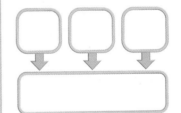

READING SKILL

Cause and Effect As you read, take notes to list some causes of Canada's strong economy.

Yukon Gold Rush When gold was discovered in the Yukon Territory, thousands of people came from all over the world to "strike it rich." This picture shows prospectors using gold dust to pay for merchandise.

121

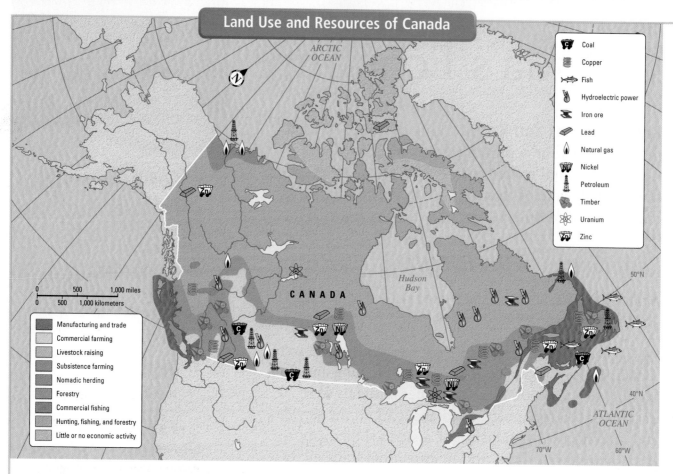

Land Use and Resources of Canada

ARCTIC OCEAN

Legend:
- Coal
- Copper
- Fish
- Hydroelectric power
- Iron ore
- Lead
- Natural gas
- Nickel
- Petroleum
- Timber
- Uranium
- Zinc

CANADA

Hudson Bay

0   500   1,000 miles
0   500   1,000 kilometers

- Manufacturing and trade
- Commercial farming
- Livestock raising
- Subsistence farming
- Nomadic herding
- Forestry
- Commercial fishing
- Hunting, fishing, and forestry
- Little or no economic activity

ATLANTIC OCEAN

50°N
40°N
70°W   60°W

Natural Resources Canada's rich resources support its strong economy.

SKILL **Interpret a Map** For what is most of Canada's land used? Where is most of Canada's commercial farming located?

Industry and Trade

Much of Canada is covered in forests, making the timber industry important, especially in British Columbia. **Industry** refers to any area of economic activity. Mining in the northern territories yields iron ore, gold, silver, copper, and other metals.

Canada's openness to trade has contributed to the growth of its economy. Today almost 80 percent of Canada's raw materials are shipped as exports. **Exports** are goods traded to other countries. Canada's main exports are wood and paper products, fuel, minerals, aluminum, wheat, and oil. These and manufactured goods are sold around the world.

Canada and the United States share a valuable trade partnership. Most of Canada's exports go to the United States. Most of its **imports,** or goods brought into the country, are from the United States. In 1992, Canada, the United States, and Mexico signed the North American Free Trade Agreement, or NAFTA, which lowered trade barriers among the three countries.

Lumber Canada's forests are the largest in North America. Wood and wood products from those forests are important exports.

Industry and the Economy

Main Idea Canada's economy depends on well-educated workers and its transportation industry.

Canada's well-educated workforce is important to its economy. Canadians work in all four types of industry seen in the chart shown below. Since World War II, Canada has shifted from a mostly rural economy to a major industrial and urban economy.

Tertiary, or service, industries, such as health care, recreation, education, transportation, banking, and the government, occupy about two-thirds of Canada's workforce. About 30 percent of Canadians work in secondary, or manufacturing, industries. One of Canada's main products is transportation equipment, including automobiles, trucks, subway cars, and airplanes. Food processing, especially meat and poultry processing, is an important industry in Canada as well. Canada also makes chemicals, medicines, machinery, metal products, steel, and paper.

Transportation

Transportation is a major Canadian industry. The ability to import and export goods and move them from place to place across Canada's vast land area affects many consumers and businesses.

Canada's geography both helps and hinders transportation. Canada has natural **transportation corridors,** or paths that make transportation easier. Rivers and coastal waters, sometimes combined with human-made canals and locks, provide convenient travel routes. The St. Lawrence Seaway, for example, allows oceangoing ships to travel between the Atlantic Ocean and the Great Lakes. Another important route is Canada's transcontinental railway system, which crosses the continent from coast to coast.

REVIEW Why are transportation corridors important to the development of industry?

Industry Canadians work in a wide variety of industries, creating a large economy.

Types of Industry		
Primary Industries	Prepare and process raw materials, such as timber, wheat, and iron ore, so other companies or consumers can use them Examples: **farms; mining companies; logging companies**	
Secondary Industries	Manufacturing—turn raw materials into products that consumers or other businesses can use Examples: **bakeries; car manufacturers; furniture makers**	
Tertiary Industries	Service industries—do not make goods or consume goods; distributors— move goods from the manufacturer to another business or to consumers Examples: **wholesalers; transportation companies (truck, train, airplane, or ship); retailers of food, clothing, and other goods; health care; education; recreation; banking**	
Quaternary Industries	Pass on information Examples: **communication companies, such as Internet service providers and cable companies; financial, research, and other companies that gather and pass on information**	

Canada also has **transportation barriers,** or geographic features that prevent or slow down transportation. In much of the north, snow and ice block travel by land or water. The Rocky Mountains in the west are another major obstacle. Industry develops slowly in regions where transportation is difficult.

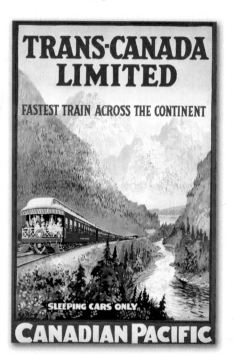

Coast to Coast The Canadian Pacific Railway Company completed a transcontinental line from Montreal to Vancouver in 1885.

Lesson Summary

- Canada's rich natural resources contribute to its economy.
- Canada exports raw materials and manufactured goods around the world, but chiefly to the United States.
- Canada has a well-educated workforce that works mainly in tertiary, or service, industries.
- Canada's geography both helps and hinders transportation.

Why It Matters . . .

Canada is a leader in the global economy.

Lesson Review

1 VOCABULARY Write a paragraph explaining how **transportation corridors** and **transportation barriers** affect Canadian **industry.**

2 READING SKILL What factor do you think has had the greatest **effect** on the Canadian economy? Explain your answer.

3 MAIN IDEA: Economics What important factors have helped build Canada's economy?

4 MAIN IDEA: Economics Give an example of a primary, a secondary, a tertiary, and a quaternary industry.

5 MAIN IDEA: Geography What are some transportation corridors and barriers in Canada?

6 PLACES TO KNOW What natural resource is found in the **Grand Banks** off the coast of Newfoundland?

7 CRITICAL THINKING: Draw Conclusions Why have Canada and the United States become such good trade partners? Support your conclusion with details from the text.

RESEARCH ACTIVITY In the late 1800s, gold was discovered in the Yukon Territory of Canada. Use library or Internet resources to find out about the Yukon Gold Rush and how it affected the history of Canada. Write a report about what you learn.

A Multicultural Society

Build on What You Know What language do you speak? Do you speak more than one? Canada is a country of two languages. In parts of Canada, road signs, newspapers, and television shows are in both English and French.

Canadian Identity

Main Idea Because Canada is a nation of so many cultures, people struggle to define what unites them as a nation.

From 1994 to 2000, the United Nations rated Canada the best of 175 countries in a survey that examines the health, education, and wealth of each country's citizens. Yet, Canadians still seek a **national identity,** or sense of belonging to a nation, to unite its many immigrant cultures.

Many Canadians are **bilingual,** which means they speak two languages. Look at the map on the next page to see where bilingual Canadians live. Canada has two official languages, English and French. Literature, official documents, road signs, newspapers, and television broadcasts are in both languages.

French Culture Business signs on a street in Quebec City reflect the strong influence of French culture.

VOCABULARY

national identity
bilingual
Francophone

Vocabulary Strategy

Francophone

To remember the meaning of **Francophone,** think of **Franco** as meaning "French." Think of **phone** as a way to talk. A Francophone means someone who talks in French.

READING SKILL

Main Idea and Details As you read, note details that support the idea that Canada is a multicultural society.

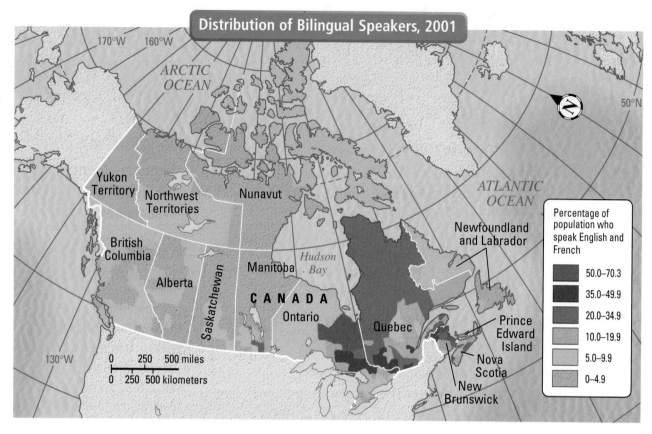

Distribution of Bilingual Speakers, 2001

ARCTIC OCEAN

Yukon Territory

Northwest Territories

Nunavut

British Columbia

Alberta

Saskatchewan

Manitoba

Hudson Bay

CANADA

Ontario

Quebec

ATLANTIC OCEAN

Newfoundland and Labrador

Prince Edward Island

Nova Scotia

New Brunswick

170°W 160°W 130°W 50°N

0 250 500 miles
0 250 500 kilometers

Percentage of population who speak English and French

50.0–70.3
35.0–49.9
20.0–34.9
10.0–19.9
5.0–9.9
0–4.9

Bilingual Nation Many people in Canada speak both French and English.

SKILL **Interpret a Map** What part of Canada has the highest percentage of people who speak both English and French?

Dual Languages

The two languages are not exactly like those spoken in England, the United States, and France. **Francophones** are French-speaking people. Canadian French, based on the French of the first settlers, is pronounced differently from the French spoken in modern France.

Canadian English uses some words, pronunciations, and spellings that differ from those used in the United States. For example, Canadians say *taps* and *serviettes* when people in the United States say *faucets* and *napkins*. Many Canadians write *colour* for *color*, *theatre* for *theater*, and *cheque* for *check*.

The nation's first prime minister, Sir John A. Macdonald, ordered that all official Canadian documents be written using standards set by dictionaries written in England.

Bilingual Many signs in Canada are written in both French and English.

Arts and Entertainment

Canada has rich traditions in the arts, actively supported by government funding. For example, the Canada Council for the Arts gives money to more than 8,400 artists and art organizations each year. Provincial governments also support regional arts programs.

Canadians read many of the same newspapers and magazines, and watch many of the same television shows and movies as do people in the United States. Canadian musicians, such as Neil Young, Joni Mitchell, Sarah McLachlan, Céline Dion, and Shania Twain, are popular in both countries. Comedian-actors Dan Aykroyd and Jim Carrey are also from Canada.

Religion

Christianity is widely practiced in Canada, but many other religions are followed as well, including Buddhism, Hinduism, Islam, and Judaism. Some religions are grounded in a spirituality based on respect for Earth and all forms of life. People of every cultural group are free to worship as they choose.

REVIEW Why does Canada have two official languages?

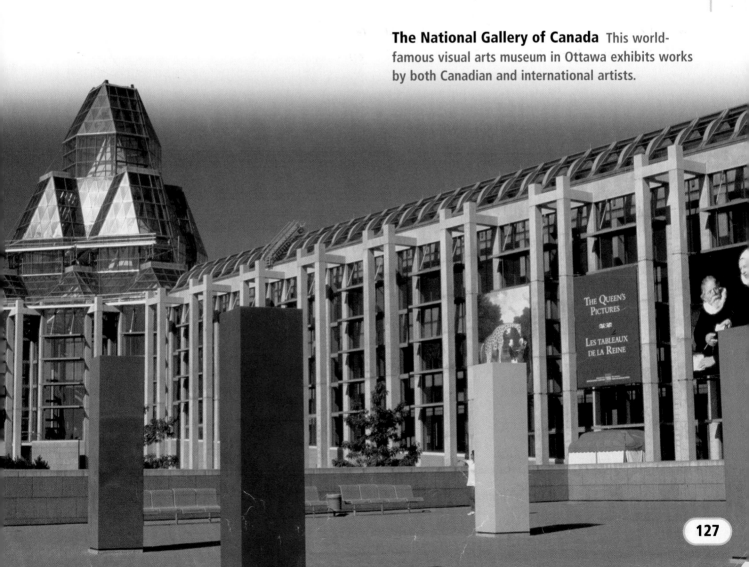

The National Gallery of Canada This world-famous visual arts museum in Ottawa exhibits works by both Canadian and international artists.

Culture Regions

Main Idea Canadians living in different regions often find it hard to agree on national issues.

Most Canadian immigrants during the 1600s, 1700s, and 1800s were European. Recently, more people have arrived from Asia and South America. People who share the same language and background often settle in the same area. As a result, Canada has various culture regions, or areas where many people belonging to one cultural group live together.

Culture regions exist in different parts of Canada. Quebec is home to many French-speaking Canadians. In Nunavut more than 50 percent of the people are Inuit. Almost 16 percent of the population of Vancouver are Chinese, mostly from Hong Kong.

Getting different culture regions to agree on national issues is sometimes difficult. The adoption of the Maple Leaf as Canada's flag in 1965 was one successful effort to unite all Canadians. Speaker of the Senate Maurice Bourget spoke about the importance of the flag:

66 The flag is the symbol of the nation's unity, for it, beyond any doubt, represents all the citizens of Canada without distinction of race, language, belief or opinion. 99

Nunavut This Inuit hunter crouches by his dogsled team.

Flags

Union Jack After 1763, when the United Kingdom won the French and Indian War, the British Royal Union Flag, or Union Jack, became Canada's flag.

Red Ensign Efforts to design a new flag for Canada began in 1925. The Red Ensign, which had the Union Jack in its upper left corner and the Canadian coat of arms on its right side, was raised 20 years later.

Maple Leaf In 1965, the Houses of Parliament adopted the Maple Leaf, which remains the flag of Canada today. The red background is a connection to the Red Ensign, and the maple leaf is Canada's national symbol.

Raising the Maple Leaf A country's flag is an important national symbol.

Conflict and Cooperation

Languages, customs, and lifestyles differ among the cultural groups of Canada. Sometimes these differences lead to conflict. For example, in the second half of the 20th century, some Canadians thought that the thousands of Chinese immigrants settling in the Vancouver area would change Canadian culture through their language and customs.

In 1975, the government began reviewing immigration policy. Chinese groups in Vancouver organized a Chinese-Canadian conference. They asked for continued support of multiculturalism and that immigration laws remain open for all people. The concerned groups solved the problem through human rights laws.

REVIEW How do cultural differences cause conflicts between people?

Notre-Dame This church was built in Montreal between 1824 and 1829. The architecture of the church—as well as the paintings, sculptures, and stained-glass windows inside—attracts many thousands of visitors each year.

Lesson Summary

Many immigrant groups have contributed to Canadian culture. The country is bilingual, displaying the influence of the English and French cultures. These cultures are divided into cultural regions. The multiculturalism of Canada is a strength, but it makes it hard for Canadians to define a national identity.

Why It Matters...

Canada's desire to safeguard its cultural diversity is one of its most serious challenges.

Lesson Review

1 VOCABULARY Choose the correct word to complete each sentence.

bilingual   national identity

Multiculturalism is an important part of Canada's _____.

Someone who speaks both English and French is _____.

2 READING SKILL What **details** illustrate that Canada is a multicultural country?

3 MAIN IDEA: Culture What are the two main languages spoken in Canada?

4 MAIN IDEA: Culture How does Canada support its own arts and entertainment?

5 MAIN IDEA: Culture What do people living in culture regions have in common?

6 EVENTS TO KNOW What happened in 1965 that helped unite all Canadians?

7 CRITICAL THINKING: Generalize Do culture regions create benefits or disadvantages for Canada? Explain your answer.

ART ACTIVITY With a partner, choose a culture region of Canada. Create a mural or collage to show characteristics of the culture.

What Canada Means to Us

Six students from all across Canada are working together on a project. Each won an essay contest, "What Canada Means to Me." Now they are together in Ottawa, Canada's capital, to create a public-service message that will appear on Canadian television. Listen to what they decide to do.

Nallie:
student from
Iqaluit, Nunavut

Characters

Mai-lin:
student from
Vancouver,
British Columbia

Jay:
student from
Regina, Saskatchewan

Stefanie:
student from
Winnipeg, Manitoba

Director: Welcome to the studio. I'd like to congratulate each of you for writing such wonderful essays. Before we get to work, why don't we go around the room and introduce ourselves? Tell us your name, where you are from, and what you wrote about in your essay. Jacques, let's start with you.

Jacques: Hello. My name is Jacques and I'm from Montreal.

Group: Hi, Jacques.

Jacques: Nice to meet you.

Director: What was your essay about?

Jacques: I wrote about how much I like living in a country where there are two official languages. I'm from Quebec, where most people speak French. It's great to be able to talk to people from other parts of Canada who might speak English more often than French.

Diane: Like me. I speak mostly English at home but I understand French, too.

Director: Diane, why don't you introduce yourself to the group?

Diane: Hello. I'm Diane. I live in Fredericton, New Brunswick. My essay was about the debate over our national flag, and how it now stands for all Canadians.

Group: Hello, Diane!

Director: Thank you, Diane. Nallie, how about you?

Nallie: Hi, there. My name is Nallie, and I live in Iqaluit, Nunavut. In my essay, I told the story of how my people, the Inuit, tried since 1972 to gain a homeland. The people of the old Northwest Territories voted to divide the territories. Nunavut became its own territory on April 1, 1999.

Jacques:
student from
Montreal, Quebec

Diane:
student from
Fredericton, New Brunswick

Group: Hi Nallie!

Director: Welcome, Nallie. Go ahead and introduce yourself, Jay.

Jay: Hello. I'm Jay and my essay is also about land. I'm Plains Cree, from Regina, Saskatchewan on the Great Plains. I wrote about how Canada is the land we live in, but it is also the people who live here and our respect for the land.

Group: Hi, Jay.

Director: Thank you. Stefanie?

Stefanie: Hello. Like Jay, I live on the Great Plains, but in Winnipeg, Manitoba. I wrote about how Canada has welcomed people like my grandfather. He came to Canada from the Ukraine when it was still part of the Soviet Union. He told me that he settled in Manitoba because the land and sky reminded him of home.

Director: That's interesting, Stefanie, thank you. Okay, who's next? Mai-lin, how about you?

Mai-lin: Hi, everyone. I'm Mai-lin.

Group: Hi, Mai-lin.

Mai-lin: My family moved from Hong Kong to Vancouver when I was very little. I don't remember much about Hong Kong, so for me, Canada is my home. I wrote about that and also about the 1988 Multicultural Act, which protects Canadians of all cultural backgrounds. Canada is a place where people might have different traditions and cultures, but we are all Canadians.

Nallie: Different cultures, all Canadian. I like that! Maybe that could be our message.

Director:

from Canadian television

Director: I like that, too. Did you all notice that many of you have written about Canada as your home? Let's keep that in mind for our message. How about the rest of you? What do you think?

Jacques: Maybe we could do something that uses the word home, like, "Canada is our home."

Jay: Or how about, "Canada means home"? The word Canada comes from *kanata*, a Huron word meaning a village or settlement.

Stefanie

Director: "Canada means home." Wonderful. Anyone else?

Diane: We could also include the Canadian flag somehow. Maybe we could be by the flag as we say what Canada means to us.

Director: That's a great idea. Each of you could come up with your own message. What do you think?

Mai-lin: Sounds good. It would be like saying that Canada has many meanings…

Stefanie: …and many cultures…

Nallie: …but we are all Canadian.

Director: That's it! I think we've got it, don't you?

Students: Yes!

Director: Excellent work, gang. This will be great. Now let's get going. We have a lot more work to do.

Activities

1. **THINK ABOUT IT** In what ways do the many different people of Canada make it a multicultural society?

2. **WRITE ABOUT IT** With partners, think of a TV message that celebrates the many cultures in the United States. Brainstorm the different cultures that should be represented. Then prepare a script to present to the rest of the class.

Skillbuilder

Identify Cause and Effect

A cause is an event, a person, or an idea that brings about a result, or an effect. An effect is something that results from a cause. Understanding the relationship between cause and effect is key to understanding the world and its cultures.

The following paragraph describes where most Canadians live. Use the steps listed to the right to help you identify why Canadians live there.

Where Canadians Live

Most of Canada's people live within 100 miles of the United States border. This heavily populated area covers only about 10 percent of the country. The mild climate in that part of the country makes living there more pleasant than living in the colder northern regions. People can find jobs more easily in the large cities located near the border. Many Americans who live in Canada can cross the border easily to visit family and friends.

Step 1: Look for the cause of, or reason for, the cause-and-effect relationship. It might be suggested in the title and topic sentence. Ask yourself what happened and why it happened. Writers may indicate a cause-and-effect relationship by using words such as *thus, therefore, so,* and *as a result.* Use those words as clues.

Step 2: Look for the results of the event or action. Ask yourself what happened as a result of the action. You have found the effect.

Step 3: Remember that several causes can combine to create one event. Also remember that one cause can have several effects. Ask yourself if there are other causes or effects.

Practice the Skill

Using a diagram can help you understand causes and effects. The diagram below shows what causes people in Canada to live close to the U.S. border and what effect is created.

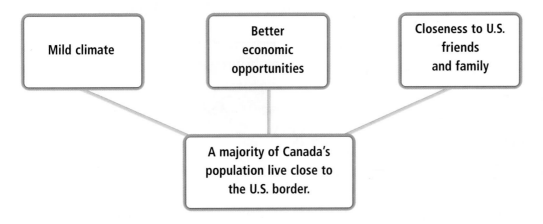

Apply the Skill

Turn to Chapter 5, "Canada Today," Lesson 3, "Canada's Economy," and make a diagram of the causes that have resulted in Canada's strong economy.

Review and Test Prep

Visual Summary

1–4. Write a description for each concept shown below.

Immigrant Roots	Constitutional Monarchy	Canada's Economy	Multicultural Society

Facts and Main Ideas

Answer each question below.

5. **Government** What effects does the policy of multiculturalism have on Canada?

6. **Culture** How has Canada tried to satisfy the needs of its many culture groups?

7. **Economics** How does Canada's wealth of natural resources contribute to its economy?

8. **Geography** What are Canada's chief transportation corridors and barriers?

9. **Culture** How have the native languages of England and France changed in Canada?

Vocabulary

Choose the correct word from the list below to complete each sentence.

First Nations, p. 113
multiculturalism, p. 114
exports, p. 122
transportation barrier, p. 124

10. Because Canada is a nation of many cultures, it adopted an official policy of _____.

11. The descendants of the first Asian settlers are referred to as the _____ people.

12. Almost 80 percent of Canada's raw materials are shipped to other countries as _____.

13. The snow and ice in Northern Canada is a _____ to industry.

CHAPTER SUMMARY TIMELINE

1867
Canada becomes self-governing

1931
Canada joins Commonwealth

1988
Canadian Multicultural Act passed

1850   1900   1950   2000

Apply Skills

 TEST PREP Identify Cause and Effect

Study the chart below. Then use the chart to answer each question.

First Migration to North America

> Climate became colder and more of Earth's water froze.
> **Cause**

> **Effect**
> Ocean water level was as much as 125 feet below its current level.
> **Cause**

> **Effect**
> Land between Asia and North America became dry.
> **Cause**

> **Effect**
> People could walk from Asia to North America.

14. What information does this cause-and-effect chart show?

A. The effects of global warming.

B. What caused North America to become dry.

C. How climate change factored in the first migration to North America.

D. How the first migration caused the climate to become colder.

15. What happened because the ocean level dropped as much as 125 feet?

A. The land was exposed, allowing people to walk between Asia and North America.

B. The Earth's water froze.

C. The climate became colder and colder.

D. The Bering Sea formed, separating Asia and North America.

Critical Thinking

 TEST PREP Write a short paragraph to answer each question below.

16. **Draw Conclusions** Many people in Quebec wanted the province to separate from the rest of Canada. What in Prime Minister Pierre Trudeau's background made him effective in keeping Quebec part of Canada?

17. **Infer** How do you think the policy of multiculturalism affects the way Canadians of different cultures respond to one another?

Timeline

Use the Chapter Summary Timeline above to answer the question.

18. Did Canada join the Commonwealth before or after it became self-governing?

 Activities

HANDS ON SPEAKING ACTIVITY Prepare an interview on the topic of self-government for culture groups. Brainstorm a list of cultural groups and prepare a set of interview questions.

WRITING ACTIVITY Imagine that you have been asked to speak to persuade an audience that Quebec should remain a part of Canada. Write the speech you will give.

 Technology

Writing Process Tips
Get help with your speech at
www.eduplace.com/kids/hmss05/

Review and Test Prep

Vocabulary and Main Ideas

Answer each question below.

1. What effect does **erosion** have on **landforms?**

2. What are some duties of United States **citizenship?**

3. What is a business owner's role in a **free enterprise/market economy?**

4. What is one example of the **globalization** of American culture?

5. How can a Canadian **prime minister** affect **Parliament?**

6. Why are **transportation corridors** important to business?

Critical Thinking

 TEST PREP Write a short paragraph to answer each question below.

7. **Predict** If Quebec had become an independent nation, how might that have affected other culture regions in Canada?

8. **Synthesize** What North American geographic features support productive farmland and agricultural exports?

Apply Skills

 TEST PREP Use the map below and what you have learned about reading a physical map to answer each question.

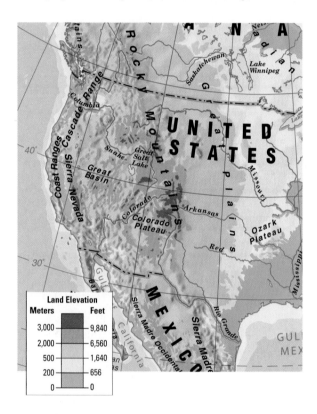

9. What landform does the Colorado River flow through?

   A. Great Salt Lake
   B. Great Basin
   C. Sierra Nevada
   D. Grand Canyon

10. What type of landform is the Great Basin?

    A. Lake
    B. Mountain
    C. Desert
    D. Coastal plain

Unit Activity

The Big Idea

Write a Poem About Being an American Citizen

- Brainstorm a list of duties and responsibilities of being an American citizen.

- Use your ideas in a poem.

- Think about what form you'd like for your poem. You may wish to write a rhyming poem or one without rhymes. Keep rhythm and meter in mind.

- Illustrate your poem and read it aloud.

As a Citizen

As a citizen

I can make my voice heard

By casting a vote

On November the third.

At the Library

Go to your school or public library to find the following books.

We Are Americans: Voices of the Immigrant Experience, by Dorothy and Thomas Hoobler
Immigrants from America's beginnings to the present tell their stories in their own words.

Democracy, by David Downing
Readers learn how democracy works in the United States and around the world.

CURRENT EVENTS

WEEKLY READER

Citizenship Project

Create a volunteer project that your class can do together.

- Find articles on the Weekly Reader Website about volunteer projects kids are doing in your region of the country.

- Find out about needs in your school or community. Who or what needs your help?

- Design a volunteer project to help solve the problem. List the materials needed and prepare a schedule. Prepare a class presentation to persuade your class to get involved in the project.

Technology

Get your information for the project from the Weekly Reader at
www.eduplace.com/kids/hmss05/

Read About It

Look for these Social Studies books in your classroom.

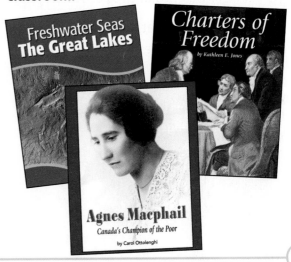

Freshwater Seas
The Great Lakes

Charters of Freedom
by Kathleen E. Jones

Agnes Macphail
Canada's Champion of the Poor
by Carol Ottolenghi

Machu Picchu This complex of ruins is perched high in the Andes Mountains of Peru. The remains of the impressive granite structures were designated a UNESCO World Heritage Site in 1983.

UNIT 3

Latin America

The Big Idea

How can different cultures come together?

❝ *Peace . . . cannot ignore our differences or overlook our common interests. It requires us to work and live together.* ❞

Óscar Arias Sánchez,
Noble Peace Prize winner and former
President of Costa Rica

Almanac

Latin America

Map Labels

Baja California
Gulf of California
Sierra Madre Occidental
Rio Grande
MEXICO
Sierra Madre Oriental

Orizaba
18,854 ft
(5,747 m)

Gulf of Mexico

Yucatán Peninsula

Popocatépet
17,930 ft
(5,465 m)

CENTRAL AMERICA

Tajumulco
13,844 ft
(4,220 m)

BELIZE
HONDURAS
JAMAICA
GUATEMALA
EL SALVADOR
NICARAGUA
COSTA RICA

Isthmus
of Panama

Panama
Canal

PANAMA

Barú
11,400 ft
(3,475 m)

BAHAMAS
CUBA
DOMINICAN REPUBLIC
HAITI

Greater Antilles

W E S T   I N D I E S

Caribbean Sea

Netherlands
Antilles

Lesser Antilles

ATLANTIC OCEAN

VENEZUELA
GUYANA
SURINAME

French
Guiana (Fr.)

Llanos

Orinoco R.

Guiana Highlands

COLOMBIA

Negro R.

ECUADOR

AMAZON BASIN

Amazon R.

PERU

SOUTH AMERICA

Madeira R.

BRAZIL

Xingu R.

Araguaia R.

São Francisco R.

PACIFIC OCEAN

Lake
Titicaca

Mato Grosso
Plateau

BOLIVIA

PARAGUAY

BRAZILIAN HIGHLANDS

Atacama
Desert

A N D E S

Gran Chaco

Paraguay R.

Paraná R.

Mt. Aconcagua
22,831 ft
(6,959 m)

ARGENTINA

Uruguay R.

URUGUAY

Pampas

Plata R.

CHILE

Patagonia

ATLANTIC OCEAN

Tierra
del Fuego

Falkland
Is.

South Georgia I.

Cape Horn

N

Elevation

13,100 ft.	(4,000 m)
6,600 ft.	(2,000 m)
3,275 ft.	(1,000 m)
650 ft.	(200 m)
0 ft.	(0 m)
Below sea level	

▲ Mountain peak

0   500   1,000 miles
0   500   1,000 kilometers

Tropic of Cancer
20°N
Equator
0°
20°S
Tropic of Capricorn
40°S
60°S

100°W   80°W   60°W   40°W

Latin America–United States Landmass and Population

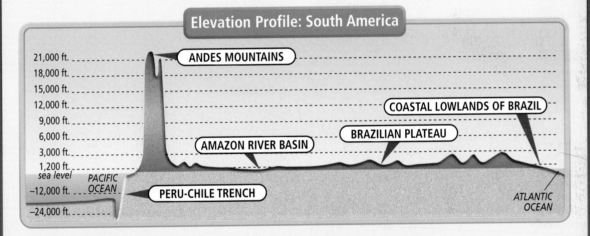

Latin America

United States

LANDMASS

Latin America

7,981,950 square miles

Continental United States

3,165,630 square miles

POPULATION

Latin America
514,662,785

United States
281,421,906

👤 = 50,000,000

Elevation Profile: South America

21,000 ft.
18,000 ft.
15,000 ft.
12,000 ft.
9,000 ft.
6,000 ft.
3,000 ft.
1,200 ft.
sea level
−12,000 ft.
−24,000 ft.

ANDES MOUNTAINS

COASTAL LOWLANDS OF BRAZIL

BRAZILIAN PLATEAU

AMAZON RIVER BASIN

PACIFIC OCEAN

PERU-CHILE TRENCH

ATLANTIC OCEAN

FAST FACTS

✓ **HIGHEST MOUNTAIN:**
Mt. Aconcagua, 22,831 ft.

✓ **HIGHEST RECORDED TEMPERATURE:**
120°F, Rivadavia, Argentina,
December 11, 1905

✓ **HIGHEST AVERAGE ANNUAL PRECIPITATION IN THE WORLD:**
Lloro, Colombia, 523.6 in.

✓ **LONGEST RIVER:**
Amazon River, 3,900 mi. long

✓ **LOWEST RECORDED TEMPERATURE:**
-27°F, Sarmiento, Argentina,
June 1, 1907

✓ **LOWEST AVERAGE ANNUAL PRECIPITATION IN THE WORLD:**
Arica, Chile, 0.03 in.

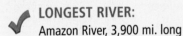

CURRENT EVENTS
WEEKLY (WR) READER

Find out about current events that connect with the content of this unit. See Unit activities at: www.eduplace.com/kids/hmss05/

Country Flag	Country/Capital	Currency	Population (2001 estimate)	Life Expectancy (years)	Birthrate (per 1,000 pop.) (2000)
	Antigua and Barbuda St. John's	East Caribbean Dollar	67,000	70	20
	Argentina Buenos Aires	Peso	37,385,000	75	19
	Bahamas Nassau	Bahamian Dollar	298,000	71	20
	Barbados Bridgetown	Barbadian Dollar	275,000	73	14
	Belize Belmopan	Belizean Dollar	256,000	71	32
	Bolivia La Paz, Sucre	Boliviano	8,300,000	64	28
	Brazil Brasília	Real	174,469,000	63	19
	Chile Santiago	Chilean Peso	15,328,000	76	17
	Colombia Bogotá	Colombian Peso	40,349,000	70	23
	Costa Rica San José	Costa Rican Colon	3,773,000	76	21
	Cuba Havana	Peso	11,184,000	76	13
	Dominica Roseau	East Caribbean Dollar	71,000	73	18
	Dominican Republic Santo Domingo	Dominican Peso	8,581,000	73	25
	Ecuador Quito	U.S. Dollar and Sucre	13,184,000	71	27
	El Salvador San Salvador	Salvadoran Colon	6,238,000	70	29
	Grenada St. George's	East Caribbean Dollar	89,000	65	23
	Guatemala Guatemala City	Quetzal	12,974,000	66	35
	Guyana Georgetown	Guyanese Dollar	697,000	64	18

DATA FILE

Infant Mortality (per 1,000 live births) (2000)	Doctors (per 100,000 pop.) (1997–1998)	Literacy Rate (percentage) (1996–1998)	Passenger Cars (per 1,000 pop.) (1991–1998)	Total Area (square miles)	Map (not to scale)
20.0	114	90	207	171	
17.8	268	96	136	1,073,399	
17.8	152	98	245	5,386	
16.2	125	97	167	166	
30.8	55	93	10	8,867	
60.2	130	83	26	424,164	
33.8	127	85	84	3,300,171	
9.6	110	95	62	292,135	
23.2	116	91	31	440,831	
12.7	141	95	14	19,730	
7.7	530	96	2	42,804	
8.5	49	90	104	290	
40.8	216	82	14	18,704	
29.3	170	90	22	103,930	
27.2	107	71	6	8,124	
10.9	50	96	94	120	
45.0	93	56	9	42,042	
48.6	18	98	34	83,000	

Country Flag	Country/Capital	Currency	Population (2000 estimate)	Life Expectancy (years)	Birthrate (per 1,000 pop.) (2000)
	Haiti Port-au-Prince	Gourde	6,965,000	49	32
	Honduras Tegucigalpa	Lempira	6,406,000	70	33
	Jamaica Kingston	Jamaican Dollar	2,666,000	75	19
	Mexico Mexico City	New Peso	101,879,000	71	23
	Nicaragua Managua	Gold Cordoba	4,918,000	69	28
	Panama Panama City	Balboa	2,846,000	75	20
	Paraguay Asunción	Guarani	5,734,000	74	31
	Peru Lima	New Sol	27,484,000	70	24
	St. Kitts and Nevis Basseterre	East Caribbean Dollar	39,000	71	19
	St. Lucia Castries	East Caribbean Dollar	158,000	72	22
	St. Vincent and the Grenadines Kingstown	East Caribbean Dollar	116,000	72	18
	Suriname Paramaribo	Surinamese Guilder	434,000	71	21
	Trinidad and Tobago Port of Spain	Trinidad and Tobago Dollar	1,170,000	68	14
	Uruguay Montevideo	Uruguayan Peso	3,360,000	75	17
	Venezuela Caracas	Bolivar	23,917,000	73	21
	United States Washington, D.C.	Dollar	281,422,000	77	15

DATA FILE

Infant Mortality (per 1,000 live births) (2000)	Doctors (per 100,000 pop.) (1997–1998)	Literacy Rate (percentage) (1996–1998)	Passenger Cars (per 1,000 pop.) (1991–1998)	Total Area (square miles)	Map (not to scale)
96.3	8	45	5	10,714	
39.8	83	73	14	43,277	
13.4	140	85	17	4,244	
23.4	186	90	87	756,066	
38.7	86	66	16	50,464	
22.7	167	91	54	29,157	
35.3	110	92	14	157,048	
37.1	93	89	20	496,225	
16.9	117	90	130	104	
16.2	47	80	68	238	
14.6	88	82	44	150	
25.6	25	93	111	63,251	
18.3	79	98	107	1,978	
12.9	370	97	147	68,498	
25.5	236	91	68	352,144	
7.0	251	97	489	3,787,319	

Latin America:
Land and History

Technology

e • glossary
e • word games
www.eduplace.com/kids/hmss05/

Vocabulary Preview

tributary

A **tributary** is a river or stream that flows into a larger body of water. There are more than 1,000 tributaries that flow into the Amazon River in South America. **page 153**

deforestation

The process of cutting and clearing away trees from a forest is called **deforestation.** The deforestation of the Amazon rain forest has had both positive and negative effects. **page 153**

Chapter Timeline

About 900
Maya civilization ends

About 1200
Aztec civilization begins

900   1000   1100   1200

Reading Strategy

Monitor and Clarify As you read, check your understanding of the text.

Ask yourself if what you are reading makes sense. Reread if you need to.

hieroglyph

The basic unit of the Mayan writing system is a symbol called a **hieroglyph,** or glyph. These hieroglyphs were the best-developed written language in ancient Latin America. **page 157**

chinampas

Chinampas were floating gardens built by the Aztecs. The Aztecs grew maize, beans, squash, avocados, tomatoes, peppers, and flowers in their *chinampas*. **page 158**

About 1400
Inca civilization begins

1521
Cortés defeats the Aztec

1300   1400   1500   1600

Physical Geography

Build on What You Know The United States is geographically diverse, with mountains and plains, forests and deserts. Latin America is physically diverse as well, but common language and culture tie this large region together.

Defining Latin America

Main Idea Latin America is a vast land of varied geography united by a common language.

Latin America includes Mexico, Central America, the Caribbean, and South America. Because the languages of most of its colonizers—Spanish and Portuguese—are derived from Latin, Europeans later referred to the region's colonies as *Latin America*. Because the region is defined by a cultural connection, in this case language, it is called a culture region.

Mexico is the farthest north of the Latin American countries. You can see that Mexico's major physical features include mountains, plateaus, and plains.

Mexico's two major mountain ranges share the name Sierra Madre (see EHR uh MAH dray). Between the two ranges sits Mexico's large central plateau. The vast northern stretches of the central plateau are desert.

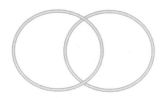

Volcanoes Latin America has many active volcanoes. This volcano, named Mount Popocatépetl (poh puh KAT uh peht uhl) is located near Mexico City.

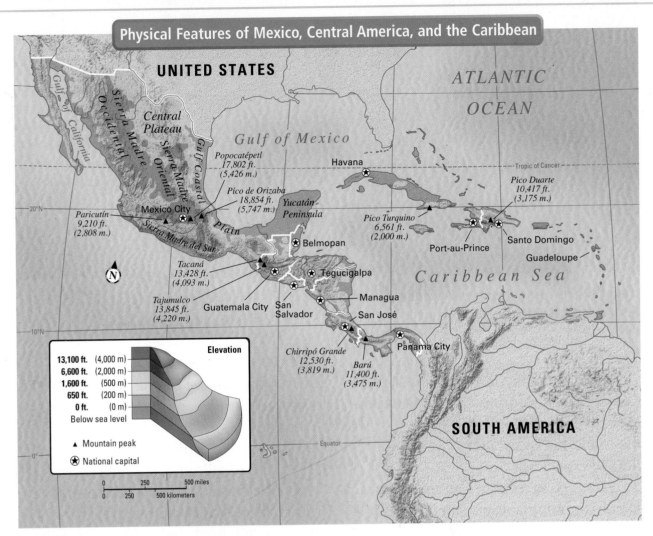

Physical Features of Mexico, Central America, and the Caribbean

UNITED STATES

ATLANTIC OCEAN

Gulf of California

Sierra Madre Occidental

Central Plateau

Gulf of Mexico

Sierra Madre Oriental

Gulf Coastal Plain

Popocatépetl 17,802 ft. (5,426 m.)

Havana

Tropic of Cancer

Pico Duarte 10,417 ft. (3,175 m.)

Pico de Orizaba 18,854 ft. (5,747 m.)

Yucatán Peninsula

20°N

Paricutín 9,210 ft. (2,808 m.)

Mexico City

Sierra Madre del Sur

Pico Turquino 6,561 ft. (2,000 m.)

Belmopan

Port-au-Prince

Santo Domingo

Guadeloupe

Tacaná 13,428 ft. (4,093 m.)

Tegucigalpa

Caribbean Sea

N

Tajumulco 13,845 ft. (4,220 m.)

Guatemala City

San Salvador

Managua

San José

10°N

Chirripó Grande 12,530 ft. (3,819 m.)

Barú 11,400 ft. (3,475 m.)

Panama City

Elevation

13,100 ft. (4,000 m)
6,600 ft. (2,000 m)
1,600 ft. (500 m)
650 ft. (200 m)
0 ft. (0 m)
Below sea level

▲ Mountain peak

⊛ National capital

SOUTH AMERICA

Equator

0   250   500 miles
0   250   500 kilometers

Latin America This map shows the physical features, such as mountains and plains, of Mexico, Central America, and the Caribbean. **SKILL** Interpret a Map What is the tallest mountain in Central America?

Mexico

Now look just south of the central plateau. There you will see Mexico's two highest mountain peaks. Both of these mountains are volcanoes. Volcanic activity and earthquakes frequently plague Mexico and many other parts of Latin America too. They are caused by the movement of five tectonic plates.

At the southern end of the central plateau sits Mexico City, the world's second most populated city. Air pollution there is some of the worst in the world and often reaches dangerous levels.

The city's location has contributed to this problem. The mountains surrounding the city to the east, south, and west trap automobile exhaust and other pollutants that the city's huge population generates.

Another problem of location for Mexico City is the ground on which it was built—a drained lakebed. The vibrations that earthquakes send through Earth grow much stronger and more damaging when they pass through the soft, loose soils of a lakebed, thus making Mexico City highly vulnerable to the effects of earthquakes.

REVIEW How do Mexico's mountains affect life there?

Island Chain Seven islands make up the Caribbean island group that is called Guadeloupe (GWAHD uhl oop). This group is also called the Lesser Antilles.

Central America

Look at the physical map on page 151. Central America forms a bridge between Mexico and South America. To the east are the island nations scattered throughout the Caribbean Sea.

About 80 percent of Central America is hilly or mountainous, and most of it is covered with forests. Rain forests cover much of the lowlands. In the higher regions, deciduous trees cloak many of the slopes.

A string of more than 40 volcanoes lines 900 miles of Central America's Pacific coast, where two tectonic plates crash against each other. This is the most active group of volcanoes in North or South America. Earthquakes also occur frequently. They can completely destroy buildings, towns, and cities. They can also set landslides and mudslides in motion, sending land, houses, and people hurtling down the slopes.

Coral Reefs Some Caribbean Islands have brightly colored coral reefs in the water around them. These reefs are home to many species of fish and colorful coral.

The Caribbean Islands

As you can see on the map (page 151), the Caribbean Islands lie to the east of Central America. Some of these islands, such as St. Kitts and Grenada, are actually the peaks of volcanic mountains rising from the ocean floor. Over thousands of years, the volcanoes erupted, spewing lava that cooled, hardened, and added to the mountains' height.

Other islands, such as the Bahamas, began as coral reefs. Coral is made of organisms that shed hard skeletons when they die. The skeletons pile up, and a reef, or ridge, develops. A coral reef that becomes an island usually encircles a volcanic island and then grows over it.

South America

Look at the map on page 142 of the Unit Almanac. You can see that the equator runs through Ecuador, Colombia, and Brazil. You can also see that only the Isthmus of Panama links South America to North America.

On the map, you can see the Andes mountain range, which stretches over 5,000 miles along South America's west coast. It is the longest continuous mountain range on Earth's surface. Mount Aconcagua (ak uhn KAH gwuh) in Argentina is the highest peak in the Western Hemisphere.

Notice the central plains east of the Andes. The plains in southern South America are called the *Pampas*. South America's largest rivers begin in the Andes, drain the central plains, and then flow into the Atlantic Ocean. They include the Orinoco (awr uh NOH koh), the Paraná-Paraguay-Plata (par uh NAH-PAR uh gwy-PLAH tuh), and the Amazon.

Llamas The llama is a member of the camel family. People raise llamas for their meat and wool.

The Amazon at Risk

In 2000, 22 people explored the Andes's rivers to confirm the source of the Amazon River, which had been discovered in 1971. The mighty river begins in the Peruvian Andes as a trickle of water. It then flows for nearly 4,000 miles to the Atlantic Ocean. No other river carries as much water to the sea. Along with more than 1,000 **tributaries,** which are rivers or streams that flow into a larger body of water, the Amazon drains water from Peru, Ecuador, Colombia, Bolivia, Venezuela, and Brazil.

Deforestation, or the process of cutting and clearing away trees from a forest, has greatly affected the Amazon rain forest. In recent years, Amazon deforestation has provided timber and cleared land for cattle ranches.

Most plants release oxygen into the air and absorb carbon dioxide. By reducing the number of trees and plants, deforestation increases the amount of carbon dioxide in the air.

Others worry that animals who live in the rain forest may need to move—or may die out—when large areas of forest are cut down. The Native Americans that inhabit the rain forest are also at risk of losing the land they live on.

REVIEW What causes so many volcanoes and earthquakes in this region?

153

Climate

Main Idea The climate of most of Latin America is usually warm and humid, or tropical.

A large portion of Latin America lies in the **Tropical Zone,** which, as you can see on the map below, is between the latitudes 23°27' north and 23°27' south. The Tropical Zone may be rainy or dry, but it is typically hot. Also, temperature is always lower at higher elevations, but in the Tropical Zone, all elevations are warmer than they are elsewhere.

The waters in the Caribbean Sea stay warm most of the year and heat the air over them. A warm wind then blows across the islands, keeping the climate warm even in the winter.

El Niño

At times, unusually high air pressure in the south Pacific causes certain winds over the ocean, called trade winds, to die out. Without the trade winds, the ocean's sun-warmed surface water flows eastward, toward North and South America.

The appearance of this warm water off the coast of South America is called **El Niño** (ehl NEE nyaw). It is called *El Niño,* "the Christ child," because it appears yearly at Christmastime.

The warmer water of *El Niño* warms the air. Warmer air holds more water and so releases more rain when it cools. This added precipitation often causes heavy rains and flooding in Latin America and other parts of the eastern Pacific.

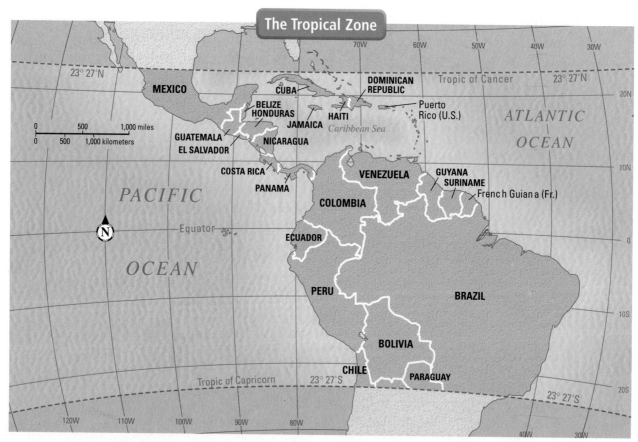

Tropical Zone Much of Latin America falls between the Tropic of Cancer and the Tropic of Capricorn, an area known as the Tropical Zone. **SKILL** **Interpret a Map** Which South American countries are in the Tropical Zone? Where does the equator fall within the Tropical Zone?

Maya Achievements

The ancient Maya studied math and astronomy extensively. The Maya were among the first civilizations in the world known to understand the advanced mathematical concept of zero. They also had an intricate calendar system that included a 260-day calendar of sacred days, a 365-day calendar based on the sun's movement, and a calendar that measured the number of days that had passed since a fixed starting point.

The Maya established the best-developed written language in ancient Latin America. The basic units of the writing system were symbols called **hieroglyphs,** or glyphs. Each glyph represented a word or a syllable. The U.S. lawyer John Lloyd Stephens, while traveling through the Maya area in the 1800s, described his awe at seeing the glyphs and not being able to read them because no one had yet deciphered them.

> 66 **These structures . . . these stones . . . standing as they do in the depths of a tropical forest, silent and solemn, strange in design, excellent in sculpture, rich in ornament . . . their whole history so entirely unknown, with hieroglyphics explaining all, but perfectly unintelligible.** 99

Farming was essential to Maya life. Using a method called slash-and-burn agriculture, the Maya cut down and burned trees, planting crops in their place. After a few years, they let the forest grow back, so the soil could regain its nutrients. Later the area could again be cut, burned, and farmed. The Maya also built up ridges of farming land on floodplains. The floodplains were rich with nutrients, and the ridges kept the crops from getting too wet.

Hi...
Ma...
hi...
m...
th...
n...

Around A.D. 900, the M... began to change. For unkn... the construction of massiv... stone monuments stoppe... abandoned. However, the... did not disappear—they j... More than 6 million Maya... in Guatemala, Belize, and... Mexico and speak dialects... languages of their Maya a...

REVIEW What advances in... astronomy did the Mayans ma...

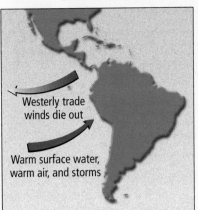

Effects of *El Niño*

Normal Year

El Niño Changes in Pacific winds affect weather in Latin America.

SKILL **Interpret a Diagram** What effect does the increased air pressure of *El Niño* have on the warm surface water of the Pacific?

El Niño Year

Westerly trade winds

Warm surface water

Westerly trade winds die out

Warm surface water, warm air, and storms

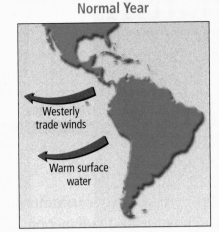

At the same time, areas in the western Pacific, such as Indonesia, may have less rain than usual. These extreme fluctuations in weather affect not only the land and its vegetation, but also marine life and the birds that feed off it. Scientists are still trying to understand the *El Niño* cycles and their effects on the world's weather.

REVIEW What effect does *El Niño* have on weather in Latin America?

Lesson Summary

The physical terrain of Mexico and Central America includes mountain ranges, deserts, forests, and volcanoes. South America has the world's longest mountain range. Most of Latin America lies in a region called the Tropical Zone.

Why It Matters . . .

Physical geography influences Latin America's cultures, offering them both resources and obstacles.

Lesson Review

1 **VOCABULARY** Write a paragraph explaining how the location of Latin America in the **Tropical Zone** affects its climate. Include *El Niño* in your discussion.

2 **READING SKILL Contrast** the landforms of Mexico with the landforms of South America.

3 **MAIN IDEA: Geography** Name two types of natural disasters that occur frequently in Latin America.

4 **MAIN IDEA: Geography** Describe two ways in which the Caribbean Islands formed.

5 **MAIN IDEA: Geography** What happens when increased air pressure causes trade winds to lessen?

6 **CRITICAL THINKING: Infer** Why would nations outside of Latin America care about deforestation of the Amazon? Support your conclusion with details from the text.

WRITING ACTIVITY Look at the map on page 154, which shows the Tropical Zone. Make a list of all the Latin American countries that are wholly or partly in the Tropical Zone.

Ancient Latin America

VOCABULARY

hieroglyph
chinampa
Columbian Exchange

Vocabulary Strategy

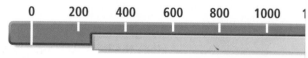
Columbian Exchange

Exchange means "trade." After Columbus's voyages to the Americas, trade between Europe and the Americas was called the **Columbian Exchange,** after Columbus.

READING SKILL

Cause and Effect As you read, use your chart to show the effect of geography on the farming practices of the Incan culture.

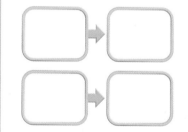

0   200   400   600   800   1000

250–1500

Build on What You Know Where is you located? Have you ever wondered what ma build in the area where you live? In Latin / built cities in jungles, high in the mountai a swampy island.

The Maya

Main Idea The ancient Maya used written langu calendar, and even developed farming methods s

Many ancient civilizations, such as the developed in river valleys and thrived there provided water for both irrigation and trar Latin America, however, some ancient civil ished far from rivers. For example, the May and Central America built cities in dense ju Aztec of Mexico constructed their capital o island. The Inca of South America built cit in the Andes.

In the areas that are today southern an Mexico, western Honduras, Guatemala, El Belize, the ancient Maya built a widesprea Small Maya communities existed as early a From A.D. 250 to A.D. 900, the Maya establ Latin America's most important civilizatio

Olmec Head This colossal statue was carved by the Olmec, Mexico's oldest known civilization.

The Aztec

Main Idea The Aztec built a powerful empire in Mexico.

Where modern Mexico City now stands, the waters of Lake Texcoco once lapped the shores of an island city called Tenochtitlán (teh nohch tee TLAHN). With as many as 200,000 inhabitants, Tenochtitlán served as the capital of the Aztec Empire.

The Aztec were composed of a number of tribes of wandering warriors. Of these, the Mexica (MEH hee kah) were dominant. Mexico took its name from the Mexica.

During the 1200s, the Aztec gradually grew in numbers and military strength until they controlled the region. They dominated until the early 1500s, when the Spanish conquered them.

The Aztec Empire was a warrior society that centered on warfare. All able men, including priests, were expected to join the Aztec army.

Military service was important for two reasons. The first was to maintain a powerful empire, but the second was religious. The Aztec believed that anyone who died in battle had the great honor of dying for Huitzilopochtli (WEE tsuh loh POHCH tlee), the Aztec god of war.

The Aztec held great power over their empire. One reason for their success was that the island location of their capital protected them from attack. However, much of the island was marsh, posing a major challenge to farming. The resourceful Aztec built floating gardens, called *chinampas* (chee NAHM pahs), on which they grew crops. First, they piled up plants from the water. Then they anchored these rafts between trunks of willow trees. Finally, they heaped the lake's fertile mud on the piles to create plots for farming.

The Aztec grew many crops, such as maize, beans, squash, avocados, tomatoes, peppers, and flowers. They also raised turkeys, ducks, geese, and dogs for food.

Aztec *Chinampas* This infographic shows how the Aztec built and farmed the *chinampas*.

willows

crops

plants

mud

The Inca

Main Idea The Inca built an important empire in the Andes.

Around 1400, high in the Andes of Peru, a group of people called the Inca rose up to conquer the people of the surrounding areas. From their capital, Cuzco, the Inca soon ruled a huge empire that included parts of what are now Colombia, Ecuador, Bolivia, northern Chile, and northwestern Argentina.

The Inca built stone terraces to farm on the steep mountainsides. The terraces also helped prevent erosion of the soil. In the desert lands to the west, the Inca built irrigation canals to water their crops. Because of terracing and irrigation, Inca farmers were able to grow crops such as potatoes, maize, and a grain called *quinoa*.

Quipu The Inca kept accounting records by tying knots in a series of strings called *quipu* (KEE poo). The significance of knots and colors remain a mystery.

Stone roads were a major technological feat of the Inca. These roads are still in use today. Having no written language or knowledge of the wheel, Inca rulers ordered roads built on which runners carried verbal messages to distant places. The runners worked in relay teams stationed along the roads. One runner told the message to the next. Messages could travel 150 miles a day along the stone roads. This system of communication was important to the Inca because their empire spread out over thousands of miles.

REVIEW How did the Aztecs use Lake Texcoco to their advantage?

Spotlight on CULTURE

Inca Weaving The Inca had no formal written language, but they used weaving as a means of representing ideas. Using wool sheared from llamas and alpacas, as well as many colorful plant dyes, the Inca wove images into the fabrics they wore and traded. Concepts related to the passing of seasons, agricultural practices, and history were all represented in the weavings. In Peru today, Edwin Sulca Lagos is famous for his Inca-inspired weavings. This one is covered in designs from the Inca calendar.

CRITICALLY THINKING Hypothesize What sorts of images might the Inca have used to convey concepts such as time or seasons?

Identify Problems What risks did the Inca face by recording ideas only on fabric?

Inca Stonework

The Inca are known for their stonework. They erected many massive buildings, some with stones weighing as much as 200 tons. Wooden rollers were used to move these heavy stone blocks. The most remarkable of Inca stonework is the city of Machu Picchu (MAH choo PEEK choo), which still stands almost 8,000 feet above sea level. The walls of Machu Picchu were constructed so that they appear to emerge from the mountainsides. Around them, terraces connected by stairways run down the steep slopes. (See photograph on pages 140–141.)

Montezuma II He was a great warrior who was feared throughout the Aztec Empire.

The Spanish in Latin America

Until about 500 years ago, Latin America was populated solely by Native Americans. In the 1500s, the Spanish arrived in the region. One famous Spanish soldier, Hernán Cortés (ehr NAHN kawr TEHS), captured the Aztec ruler, Montezuma II (mahn tih ZOO muh), in 1519. He claimed the Aztec empire for Spain in 1521 and renamed it New Spain. A decade later, another Spanish soldier, Francisco Pizarro, defeated the Inca ruler, Atahualpa (ah tuh WAHL puh), and claimed Atahualpa's empire for Spain.

Once in control of Latin America, the Spanish enslaved many Native Americans and forced them to do labor, such as mining silver. The Spanish also worked hard to convert the Native Americans to Christianity.

Europeans also exposed the Native Americans to diseases. Smallpox and other diseases from Europe killed millions of Native Americans between 1500 and 1900. Smallpox had long been widespread in Europe, and most Europeans were at least partly immune. Native Americans, however, had no immunity to it because it had never before existed in the Americas.

Within months of the Spanish soldiers' arrival in Mexico, many thousands of Native Americans got sick with smallpox and died from it— including Montezuma II's successor. Smallpox proved far more deadly to Native Americans than Spanish swords and cannons.

Latin America and Spain also exchanged culture. Ships carrying Latin American goods sailed to Spain. The Spanish soon began growing corn, peppers, and tomatoes—crops they had never seen before. Manufactured products from Spain, especially textiles, were also shipped to Latin America. So were foods and animals.

Aztec Sun Stone The Aztec civilization had its own calendar. This stone carving also honors the Aztec sun god, whose face is shown in the center. It is 13 feet across.

This trade was part of the **Columbian Exchange,** or the exchange of goods and ideas between European countries and their colonies in North and South America.

REVIEW How did building stone roads improve the ability of the Inca rulers to control a large region?

Lesson Summary

Three ancient empires flourished in Latin America. The Maya lived in dense jungles and developed calendars, hieroglyphs, and slash-and-burn agriculture. The Aztec Empire centered on warfare and was based in a capital city built on a lake. The Inca lived high in the mountains and built stone roads and used terrace farming.

Why It Matters . . .

These ancient Latin American cultures serve as models for how successful civilizations develop.

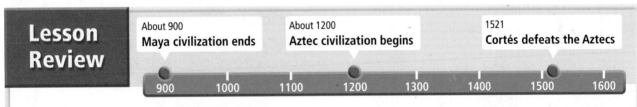

Lesson Review

| About 900 Maya civilization ends | About 1200 Aztec civilization begins | 1521 Cortés defeats the Aztecs |

900   1000   1100   1200   1300   1400   1500   1600

❶ **VOCABULARY** Use **Columbian Exchange** in a paragraph that lists some of the plants and animals that were new to the Americas and new to Europe.

❷ **READING SKILL** What was the **effect** of the mountainous terrain on Incan agriculture?

❸ **MAIN IDEA: Culture** Describe the writing system that the Maya developed.

❹ **MAIN IDEA: Government** How did the Inca pass important messages across great distances?

❺ **MAIN IDEA: Economics** What was the Columbian Exchange?

❻ **PEOPLE TO KNOW** Who was **Hernán Cortés** and what did he do in Latin America?

❼ **TIMELINE SKILL** In what year did the Aztec Empire end?

❽ **CRITICAL THINKING: Compare and Contrast** Compare and contrast the Maya civilization with the Aztec civilization.

 WRITING ACTIVITY Imagine you live in the Aztec capital, Tenochtitlán, and have spent the day constructing *chinampas*. Write a letter to a friend describing the process.

Andean Agriculture

Long before the rise of the Inca Empire, people living in the Andes had learned to farm the steep valley walls by building terraces into the sides of the mountains. They had also learned to build canals, many of them lined with stone, to carry water to their crops. The Inca improved and expanded the existing terraces and canals until they could feed 15 million people, with enough food left over to put away stores for three to seven years.

Mountain Extremes In the Andes, valley walls rise as high as 10,000 feet, and temperatures can span a 55-degree range.

Canals Inca canals stretched for miles. They were often lined and covered with stones. Some were cut through solid rock.

Architect Workers directed by royal architects built stone retaining walls. Inside the walls, they placed layers of stone, clay, gravel, and topsoil. This combination allowed water to slowly work its way to lower terraces.

Tools The Inca had few farm tools. The most widely used was the *taclla,* or digging stick. It consisted of a pointed hardwood pole with a footrest for pushing the tool into the ground. Some *tacllas* had metal tips. The other main tools were hoes and clubs.

Crops The Inca grew maize, hundreds of kinds of potatoes, and many other crops. Farmers had to plant crops adapted to many different climates because of the great variations in altitude and temperature.

Activities

1. **THINK ABOUT IT** Why did people living in the Andes need to build terraces and canals?

2. **WRITE ABOUT IT** What role did agriculture play in the building and maintenance of the Inca Empire?

Skillbuilder

Find and Summarize the Main Idea

When you find and summarize the main idea, you restate the subject of a written passage in fewer words. You include only the main idea and the most important details. It is important to use your own words when summarizing.

The passage below tells about the climate in Latin America. Use the steps listed to the right to help you find the main idea and summarize a passage.

The Tropical Zone

A large portion of Latin America lies within the Tropical Zone, which is the region between the latitudes 23°27' north and 23°27' south. The Tropical Zone may be rainy or dry, but it is typically hot. Although temperature is always lower at higher elevations, in the Tropical Zone, all elevations are warmer than in non-Tropical areas.

Learn the Skill

Step 1: Look for a topic sentence stating the main idea. This is often at the beginning of a section or paragraph. Briefly restate the main idea in your own words

Step 2: Include key facts, numbers, dates, amounts, or percentages from the text.

Step 3: After writing your summary, review it to see that you have included the main idea and the most important details.

Practice the Skill

You can write your summary in a paragraph. The paragraph below summarizes the passage you just read.

Much of Latin America is in the Tropical Zone. This zone is between latitudes 23°27' north and 23°27' south. Usually, the Tropical Zone is hot. Also, the elevations in the Tropical Zone are warmer than the same elevations in other places.

Apply the Skill

Turn to page 160 in Chapter 6, Lesson 2, "Ancient Latin America." Read "The Spanish in Latin America," find the main idea, and write a paragraph summarizing the passage.

Visual Summary

1–2.  Write a description for each concept shown below.

Physical Geography

Ancient Latin America

Facts and Main Ideas

Answer each question below.

3. **Geography** Describe two problems that Mexico City faces because of its location.

4. **Geography** How have tectonic plates affected Latin America's physical geography? Give two examples.

5. **History** Why was warfare so important to the Aztec?

6. **Culture** Describe two means of communication used by the Inca.

7. **History** What changes took place in Latin America once the Spanish took control?

Vocabulary

Choose the correct word from the list below to complete each sentence.

tributaries, p. 153
El Niño, p. 154
hieroglyphs, p. 157
chinampas, p. 159

8. The Maya often carved _____ on stone monuments.

9. There are more than 1,000 _____ that flow into the Amazon River.

10. _____ solved the problem of how to farm in marshland.

11. There are heavy rains and flooding in Latin America during an _____ period of weather.

About 900	About 1200	About 1400	1521
Maya civilization ends	Aztec civilization begins	Inca civilization begins	Cortés defeats the Aztec

900   1000   1200   1300   1400   1500   1600

Apply Skills

 TEST PREP Find and Summarize the Main Idea Read the text below. Then use the text to answer each question.

Inca Stone Roads

Stone roads were a major technological feat of the Inca and are still in use today. Having no written language or knowledge of the wheel, the Incan rulers ordered roads built for runners to carry verbal messages to distant places. The runners worked in relay teams stationed along the roads. Messages could travel 150 miles. This system of communication was important to the Inca because their empire spread out over thousands of miles.

12. What is the main idea of the paragraph?
   A. The Inca communicated using stones.
   B. Messages could travel 150 miles a day along the stone roads.
   C. The Inca relied on verbal messages relayed by wheels.
   D. The Inca relied on roads and runners for their communication system.

13. What details support the main idea?
   A. The Inca had no written language, the Inca never heard of the wheel, and Inca rulers ordered that roads be built.
   B. Inca messengers could run fast and the Inca roads are still in use today.
   C. The empire was spread out over thousands of miles. The Inca had no written language or knowledge of the wheel.
   D. The Inca invented the wheel to use on their stone roads.

Critical Thinking

 TEST PREP Write a short paragraph to answer each question below.

14. **Synthesize** How are the farming methods of the Maya, the Aztec, and the Inca examples of people adapting to their environment?

15. **Draw Conclusions** Around A.D. 900, the Maya civilization—though not the people—began to disappear. What might have contributed to this decline?

Timeline

Use the Chapter Summary Timeline above to answer the question.

16. What civilizations were flourishing in 1492?

 Activities

 SPEAKING ACTIVITY Imagine that you are a meteorologist on a local television station in a city located in the Tropical Zone. Prepare and present a weather report for your local area.

 WRITING ACTIVITY Write a letter to the editor of a newspaper taking a stand either for or against deforestation of the Amazon rain forest. Support your opinion with facts.

Technology
Writing Process Tips
Get help with your letter at
www.eduplace.com/kids/hmss05/

Technology

e • **glossary**
e • **word games**
www.eduplace.com/kids/hmss05/

Vocabulary Preview

hacienda

A *hacienda* is a big farm or ranch. Between 1920 and 1940, the Mexican government broke up the giant haciendas and divided the land among small farmers or community farms.
page 180

distribution

The **distribution** of goods is important for businesses to succeed. The Mexican government promoted the building of highways, railroads, and airports to aid in the distribution of products to their markets. **page 188**

Chapter Timeline

1821
Mexican independence from Spain

1845
Texas joins U.S.

| 1800 | 1825 | 1850 | 1875 |

Reading Strategy

Predict and Infer Use this strategy as you read the lessons in this chapter.

Quick Tip Look at the pictures in a lesson to predict what it will be about. What will you read about?

tourism

Tourism is the business of helping people travel on vacations. So many people come to enjoy Mexico's warm weather and beautiful beaches that tourism is now Mexico's second-largest business.
page 189

fiesta

A **fiesta** is a holiday in a village or town, with parades, games, and feasts. Fiestas are usually of religious origin, but they can also be just big neighborhood parties.
page 195

1920
Mexican Revolution ends

1992
NAFTA approved

1925   1950   1975   2000

The Roots of Modern Mexico

1500   1600   1700   1800   1900   2000

1500–1850

Build on What You Know Have you ever read a story or seen a movie where someone pretended to be friendly in order to get something he or she wanted? When the Spanish came to Mexico, they pretended to be friendly, but actually wanted to conquer Mexico.

The Founding of New Spain

Main Idea After conquering the Aztec, the Spanish established the colony of New Spain.

The leader of the Spanish army that first landed on the shores of Mexico was Hernán Cortés. He hoped to win new lands for Spain, as well as gold and glory for himself.

Cortés reached the east coast of Mexico in 1519 with about 500 soldiers. He claimed the land for the king and queen of Spain. Quickly, however, he learned that the land was ruled by the powerful Aztec emperor Montezuma II.

Montezuma II ruled an empire of between 5 and 6 million people. However, many of his Native American subjects wanted to be free. They helped the Spanish conquer the Aztec king. They did not expect that the Spanish would become their new rulers.

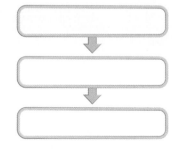

Armor Aztec shields, made of animal hide or woven plant materials were often decorated with feathers. They offered less protection than Spanish metal helmets and armor.

A Clash of Cultures

Montezuma II heard about the arrival of the Spanish, and soon he welcomed Cortés with gifts. He even allowed Cortés to stay in a royal palace in the Aztec capital, Tenochtitlán. Within a week, Cortés took Montezuma II prisoner—and took control of the Aztec Empire.

Other Aztec leaders drove the Spanish from Tenochtitlán. However, during the fighting that followed, Montezuma II was killed. The Spanish then retook the city, greatly aided by their Native American allies.

The Spanish also had an essential advantage over the Aztec: their weapons. The Aztec had only war clubs, spears, and arrows. The Spanish soldiers had steel swords, armor, guns, and cannons, as well as horses. The invading army destroyed Tenochtitlán street by street.

Festivals Mexicans today celebrate Catholic holy days that the Spanish established. This festival honors Our Lady of Guadalupe.

New Spain

The fall of Tenochtitlán in 1521 marked the end of the Aztec Empire and the beginning of Spanish rule in Mexico. The Spanish called their empire "New Spain," just as the English called their territory in North America "New England." Where Tenochtitlán had stood, the Spanish established Mexico City as their capital. Spain ruled Mexico for the next 300 years.

The Spanish victory caused more than a change of rulers in Mexico. The Spanish introduced a different way of life to the region. They brought new animals, such as horses, cattle, sheep, and pigs. They also brought new trades, such as ironsmithing and shipbuilding. They brought a new religion as well—Christianity.

Because the Roman Catholic Church was powerful in Spain, it soon became powerful in New Spain. Catholic priests set up churches, schools, and hospitals. Sometimes Native Americans accepted Christianity willingly. Sometimes, though, they were forced to become Christian against their will.

REVIEW Why did some Native Americans help the Spanish fight the Aztec?

Changes in Mexico

Main Idea After rebels gained independence from Spain, Mexico fought with the United States over Texas land in the Southwest.

The Native Americans had to accept many new ways of life, but the old ways were not lost entirely. For instance, an essential element of Native American cooking was the tortilla, a flat, round bread made from corn. Tortillas are still made daily all over Mexico. As with food, many other aspects of the two cultures blended in the new Mexican culture.

A new multilayered society developed in Mexico. The ruling class were Spanish officials who were born in Spain. They were called *peninsulares* (peh neen soo LAH rehs) because they were from the Iberian Peninsula in Europe.

A second class were *criollos* (kree AW yaws), people who were born in Mexico but whose parents were born in Spain. *Criollos* were often wealthy and powerful, but they were not in as high a social class as the *peninsulares*.

A *mestizo* (mehs TEE saw) is a person who is of Spanish and Native American ancestry. *Mestizos* formed the third layer of New Spain's society.

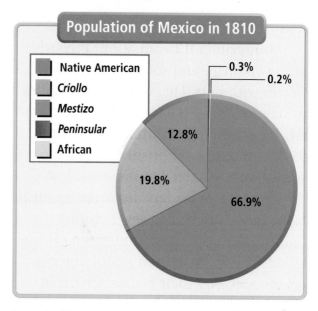

Population of Mexico in 1810

- Native American
- *Criollo*
- *Mestizo*
- *Peninsular*
- African

0.3%
0.2%
12.8%
19.8%
66.9%

Population Mexico was made up of many different cultures.

SKILL **Read a Graph** What percentage of the Mexican population in 1810 was Native American?

A fourth group of people arrived in Mexico unwillingly—the enslaved Africans brought by European slave ships. African farming techniques, musical traditions, and crafts soon blended into the Mexican culture.

New Spain's largest group was the Native Americans. They made up the bottom layer of society. The rulers of Spain set up in Mexico a system called *encomienda* (ehn kaw MYEHN dah). Under this system, Spanish men were each given a Native American village to oversee. The villagers had to pay tribute—in goods, money, or labor—to this Spaniard. They were essentially enslaved. The results of their labor helped to make Spain rich. However, the villagers lived in poverty and hardship.

Traditional Fabrics Skilled craftsworkers weave a variety of fabrics, creating blankets and clothing. Many of the designs are influenced by the art of Native American cultures.

The War of Independence

Based on earlier European and American political writers, many Mexican religious and political leaders in the early 1800s were saying that Mexicans should be free to choose their own government. They argued that Mexico should be independent from Spain. The demand for Mexican independence grew stronger after 1808, when France conquered Spain.

Then, before dawn on September 16, 1810, the farmers in the mountain village of Dolores heard their church bells ringing. At the church, their priest, Father Miguel Hidalgo, gave a fiery speech urging them to throw off Spanish rule. No one knows the exact text of the speech, but it is known as the *Grito de Dolores* (Cry of Dolores). Urged on by his words, a small army of Native Americans and *mestizos* marched with Father Hidalgo toward Mexico City. Along the way, thousands more joined them.

Father Hidalgo's army had few weapons. Mostly, his men carried clubs and farm tools, such as sickles and axes. When they faced the government soldiers, the farmers were soon defeated. Father Hidalgo was captured and executed, but the revolution he had sparked did not die.

New leaders took Father Hidalgo's place. A few wealthy Spanish nobles and many *criollos* joined the fight for independence. The struggle lasted for 11 years.

In 1821, the rebels finally overthrew the Spanish government, and Mexico became independent. However, the *peninsulares* and *criollos* still ruled the country. Native Americans and *mestizos* benefited little from independence from Spain.

REVIEW What effect did the *Grito de Dolores* have on the Mexican struggle for independence?

Biography

Father Hidalgo Father Miguel Hidalgo y Costilla, shown in the center of this illustration, was born in 1753. He was a *criollo* who felt great sympathy for the Native Americans and *mestizos*. As a priest in the small village of Dolores, Father Hidalgo joined a secret group that fought for Mexico's independence.

Father Hidalgo is known as the Father of Mexican Independence. Every September 16, Mexicans shout slogans from the *Grito de Dolores* in celebration of their independence and Father Hidalgo.

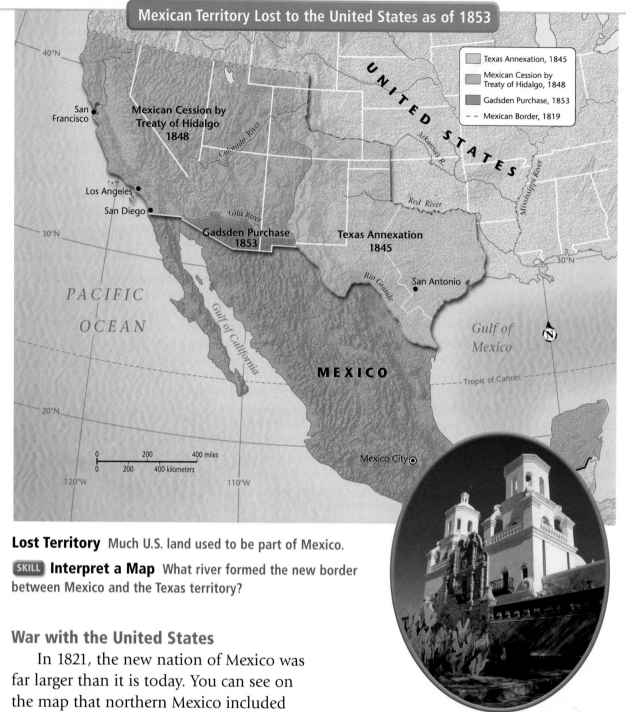

Mexican Territory Lost to the United States as of 1853

Texas Annexation, 1845
Mexican Cession by Treaty of Hidalgo, 1848
Gadsden Purchase, 1853
- - - Mexican Border, 1819

UNITED STATES

San Francisco
Mexican Cession by Treaty of Hidalgo 1848
Colorado River
Arkansas R.
Mississippi River
Los Angeles
San Diego
Gila River
Red River
Gadsden Purchase 1853
Texas Annexation 1845
30°N
PACIFIC OCEAN
Rio Grande
San Antonio
Gulf of California
Gulf of Mexico
MEXICO
Tropic of Cancer
20°N
0   200   400 miles
0   200   400 kilometers
Mexico City
120°W   110°W

Lost Territory Much U.S. land used to be part of Mexico.

SKILL **Interpret a Map** What river formed the new border between Mexico and the Texas territory?

War with the United States

In 1821, the new nation of Mexico was far larger than it is today. You can see on the map that northern Mexico included much of what is now the Southwestern United States. Spanish explorers claimed this entire region in the 1500s and 1600s. Spanish and Mexican priests built missions there in the 1600s.

Much of this land was desert. Travel was slow and communication difficult. Mexico was at war with Native Americans in this region, such as the Apache and the Comanche tribes. For all these reasons, few Mexicans settled there.

Mission You can still see this Spanish mission, built in 1700, in Arizona today.

To encourage settlement, the Mexican government invited foreigners to move into these northern lands. Most of the newcomers were from the United States and still felt some loyalty to that country. By the 1830s, settlers in Texas from the United States greatly outnumbered those from Mexico.

Texas Independence

In 1835, many settlers in Texas decided to break away from Mexico and rose in revolt. After several fierce battles, the Texans won their independence. They set up the Republic of Texas in 1836.

Most Texans wanted to become part of the United States. In 1845, the United States agreed, but Mexico and the United States could not agree where the boundary between Texas and Mexico should be. Each side claimed land that the other wanted.

In 1846, the dispute grew into a war. During the next two years, U.S. forces won control of northern Mexico; it was made official when Mexico was forced to sign the Treaty of Guadalupe Hidalgo.

A few years later, in 1853, the Gadsden Purchase gave the United States more of Mexico's northern land. The two countries have since made slight adjustments to the border, but they have not fought a war again.

REVIEW What ideas from other parts of the world did Mexicans agree with?

Lesson Summary

- After Hernán Cortés defeated the Aztecs, Spain began ruling in Mexico. They set up a multilayered society that was based on class. Within this society, the Roman Catholic Church was very powerful. The *encomienda* system gave Spaniards control over Native American villages.

- After an 11-year struggle, Mexican rebels finally won independence from Spain. Fifteen years later, Texas gained independence from Mexico. Texas soon joined the United States.

- The United States and Mexico went to war over the border between Texas and Mexico. The Treaty of Guadalupe Hidalgo and the Gadsden Purchase gave the United States part of Mexico's northern land.

Why It Matters . . .

The culture of Mexico today reflects the influences of and interactions among these groups.

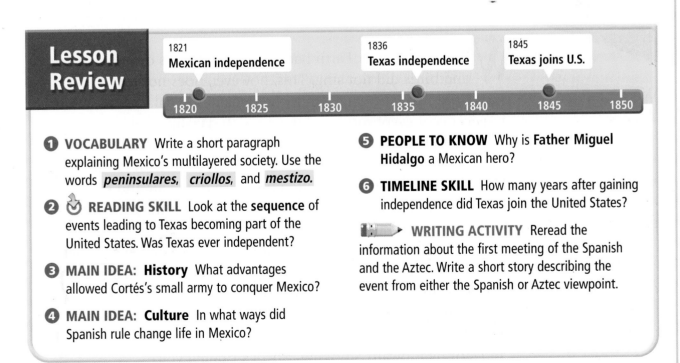

Lesson Review

| 1821 Mexican independence | 1836 Texas independence | 1845 Texas joins U.S. |

1820 — 1825 — 1830 — 1835 — 1840 — 1845 — 1850

❶ **VOCABULARY** Write a short paragraph explaining Mexico's multilayered society. Use the words *peninsulares*, *criollos*, and *mestizo.*

❷ **READING SKILL** Look at the **sequence** of events leading to Texas becoming part of the United States. Was Texas ever independent?

❸ **MAIN IDEA: History** What advantages allowed Cortés's small army to conquer Mexico?

❹ **MAIN IDEA: Culture** In what ways did Spanish rule change life in Mexico?

❺ **PEOPLE TO KNOW** Why is **Father Miguel Hidalgo** a Mexican hero?

❻ **TIMELINE SKILL** How many years after gaining independence did Texas join the United States?

WRITING ACTIVITY Reread the information about the first meeting of the Spanish and the Aztec. Write a short story describing the event from either the Spanish or Aztec viewpoint.

Latin American Folk Lore

How Quetzalcoatl Brought Music to the World

This Mexican folktale was first written down as a poem in Nahuatl (NAH waht uhl), the language of the Aztec, in the 1500s. The myth on which it is based may be a thousand years older. It was passed by word of mouth from one storyteller to another for centuries. This tale is about the serpent Quetzalcoatl (ket sahl koh AHT I), the Lord of the Winds, who helped the god Smoking Mirror bring music to Earth.

When time began, Earth had no music. Brooks did not babble, and birds did not sing. This, however, does not mean that music did not exist. High in the heavens in the Palace of the Sun, musicians of every sort filled the air with dazzling notes.

The god Smoking Mirror envied this music, and he knew that the Sun would never share his prized possession with Earth. Therefore, Smoking Mirror lifted his voice to the air and shouted in every valley and cave for his friend Quetzalcoatl, the feathered serpent who was also Lord of the Winds.

At a distance just beyond the horizon, Quetzalcoatl slumbered in silence. At the sound of Smoking Mirror's call, Quetzalcoatl slowly opened one eye and muttered with a sigh, "What does Smoking Mirror want now? Just as I find a dream, he finds a problem." With that being said, he whirled his serpent body 'round and stormed toward Smoking Mirror's ringing voice.

When Quetzalcoatl reached Smoking Mirror, he asked, "What is the matter now?" Smoking Mirror replied, "This morning, as I walked upon the bright and brilliant Earth that the two of us created, I realized that it is incomplete."

Quetzalcoatl responded doubtfully, "That is not so! There are beautiful creeks and colorful birds in the world! Don't you smell the fragrance of the rose or feel the soft grass beneath your feet?"

"I do," responded Smoking Mirror, "but there is no music! Earth cannot sing its joy when there is no music. That is why I must ask you to go to the Palace of the Sun and return with musicians who are able to spread music across Earth."

"The musicians are faithful servants of the Sun," replied Quetzalcoatl. "They will never leave him." Smoking Mirror remained silent. After a while, the silence began to bother Quetzalcoatl, and he realized the importance of music. So up he went, through the blue smoke of the sky, to the Palace of the Sun.

The Sun saw the Lord of the Winds coming and told his musicians that they must be very quiet, or the feathered serpent would carry them away to the dark and silent Earth. As Quetzalcoatl reached the palace, the glorious music stopped, and the musicians turned their instruments away from the feathered serpent.

But with his command over the wind, Quetzalcoatl brought forth fierce storm clouds that blocked the radiance of the Sun. He then produced his own light as a guide for the frightened musicians. Mistaking the serpent's light for the light of the Sun, the musicians stepped into Quetzalcoatl's embrace. The feathered serpent gently floated the musicians to Earth.

When the musicians saw Smoking Mirror, they knew instantly that they had been tricked. What they saw, however, was not the horrible place described by the Sun. Instead, Earth was full of wondrous colors and activity. It was still within reach of the Sun's warming rays. The musicians then embarked on journeys throughout the world. On their way, they taught the birds to sing, the brooks to babble, the leaves to rustle, and the people to make music of their very own.

Activities

1. **THINK ABOUT IT** What does this folktale suggest about the role of music in Aztec society? Why might this folktale be popular in Mexico today?

2. **WRITE ABOUT IT** Write a dialogue involving the musicians, Quetzalcoatl, and the Sun, in which Quetzalcoatl tries to persuade the musicians to come with him to Earth and the Sun urges them to stay. As a class, compare and contrast the arguments each side makes.

Government in Mexico

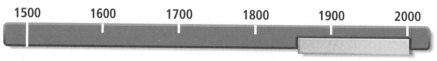

1500   1600   1700   1800   1900   2000

1855–2000

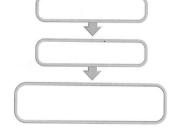

Build on What You Know Which president of the United States do you consider a hero? You might answer Abraham Lincoln or George Washington. In Mexico, many people might answer Benito Juárez. When he was president, he supported many reforms.

A Struggle for Power

Main Idea Benito Juárez's reform movement led to a new constitution.

The constitution of 1917 was written as a response to the struggles of the previous century. During that time, Mexico spent many years fighting wars. In 1821, Mexico won its war for independence from Spain. Two decades later, Mexicans entered into and then lost a war with the United States over Texas, California, and other lands. During all these years, still another struggle was going on—a struggle for power within Mexico.

In the years after independence, army leaders often took over Mexico's government. In some parts of the country, bandits attacked travelers. Elsewhere, Mexicans fought with Spanish landowners. Everywhere, a few people enjoyed great wealth, while many suffered in poverty.

Venustiano Carranza This Mexican president organized the meetings that resulted in the 1917 constitution.

Benito Juárez Brings Reform

By the 1850s, many Mexicans were eager for reform. They found a leader in Benito Juárez, a man who rose from poverty to become president of Mexico and a hero to his people. He became minister of justice in 1855, and he later became chief justice of the Supreme Court. In 1858, he gained the presidency, giving control of the Mexican government to the reformers.

The reformers wrote a new constitution for Mexico in 1857. For the first time, Mexicans had a bill of rights, promising them freedom of speech and equality under the law. The constitution of 1857 also ended slavery and forced labor. However, the new constitution did not promise freedom of religion. Nor did it make Catholicism Mexico's official religion, as many church leaders had hoped it would. The reformers also cut back the army's power in the government.

Battle Mexican forces fight their way to victory in an early battle against the French in 1862.

Response to Reform

These reforms stirred up a storm of controversy. Church leaders, army leaders, and wealthy landowners were outraged. From 1858 to 1860, the War of Reform raged between the reformers and their opponents.

The War of Reform left Mexico so weak—because of death, debt, and unemployment—that the country was an easy target for foreign takeover. Spain, Britain, and France sent troops into Mexico. In 1863, after more than a year of fighting, the French marched into Mexico City and established themselves in control of the country. They made a European nobleman named Maximilian emperor. Maximilian did not reign long. The Mexicans overthrew Maximilian and executed him in 1867.

That same year, Benito Juárez and the reformers returned to power. Juárez remained president until his death in 1872. Unfortunately, his successors cared about reform less than he had. Poverty and lack of education remained problems. A few families held most of the political and economic power. Not until the 20th century did a new wave of reform begin.

REVIEW What sorts of concerns led Mexicans to fight in the Mexican Revolution?

Benito Juárez He was a Zapotec, one of the many Native American groups in Mexico. He grew up in a mountain village, studied law, and then went into politics.

The Mexican Revolution

Main Idea The divisions between the rich and the poor led to the Mexican Revolution and a new constitution.

By 1910, the divisions between rich and poor in Mexico were huge. Just 800 families owned more than 90 percent of the farmland. Of Mexico's 15 million people, 10 million owned no land at all.

Once again, many Mexicans decided to fight for reforms. And once again, the struggle turned bloody. From 1910 to 1920, Mexico endured the Mexican Revolution.

The Revolution was a fight among many armies. Almost every part of Mexico had an army of rebels and reformers with particular goals. One of the first revolutionary leaders was a wealthy rancher named Francisco Madero, who became president in 1911. For Madero and his supporters, the key issue was free, honest elections. For others, however, the most important problem was landownership.

Mexican Freedom Fighters These men fought for freedom during the Mexican Revolution. Villa was a leader in the north of Mexico. Madero wanted honest elections. Zapata fought for farmers' rights.

The Problem of Land

Poor farmers wanted land of their own. They believed the government should give each farm family a few acres by breaking up the giant **haciendas.** A *hacienda* is a big farm or ranch, often as large as 40,000 or 50,000 acres. Much of the *hacienda* land had once belonged to village farmers. But a law passed in 1883 allowed some of the wealthiest ranch owners to easily take away land from the village farmers. During the 1880s and 1890s, the ranch owners took over millions of acres of land owned by village farmers, and that land became part of their *haciendas.*

Emiliano Zapata was a legendary fighter for farmers' rights. With his famous motto—"Land and Liberty!"— Zapata gathered an army in the south of Mexico and urged farmers to join him.

> 66 Join me. . . . We want a much better president. Rise up with us because we don't like what the rich men pay us. It is not enough for us to eat and dress ourselves. I also want for everyone to have his piece of land so that he can plant and harvest corn, beans, and other crops. What do you say? Are you going to join us? 99

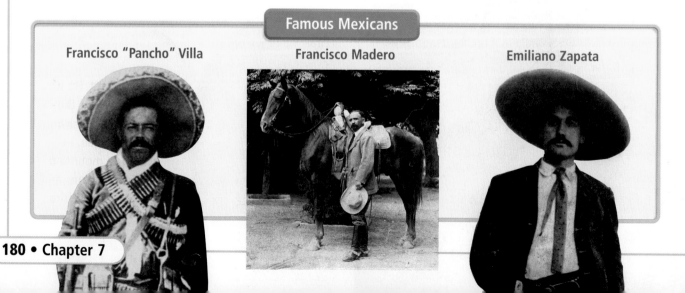

Famous Mexicans

Francisco "Pancho" Villa   Francisco Madero   Emiliano Zapata

Hacienda Like this one, many of Mexico's *haciendas* were situated on huge pieces of land.

Mexican Flag This flag combines symbols from the Aztec and from the period of independence.

A Continuing Revolution

Over the course of a decade, dozens of large and small armies fought with one another. In 1913, Madero was murdered. The same fate befell Zapata in 1919. Between 1910 and 1920, more than 1 million Mexicans died in the battles of the Revolution. In 1920, a new government managed to make peace among the many armies. The fighting was over, but the Revolution—the effort to reform Mexico's government and economy—went on.

In 1917, a new constitution was written, and one of its promises was to distribute land more equally among the people. Between 1920 and 1940, the government broke up many of the giant *haciendas*. Millions of acres were divided among small farmers or given to **ejidos.** An *ejido* (eh HEE daw) is a community farm owned by all the villagers together. Farmers were proud and happy to have their own land once again.

The idea of the Revolution was so important and popular among new Mexicans that the most powerful political party called itself the party of the Revolution. Its name changed several times, but the word *revolution* was always part of it. Today, it is called the Institutional Revolutionary Party (Partido Revolucionario Institucional, or PRI). This party won every presidential election in Mexico from 1929 until 2000, with power passing peacefully from one president to the next.

REVIEW How did the 1917 constitution respond to concerns about landownership?

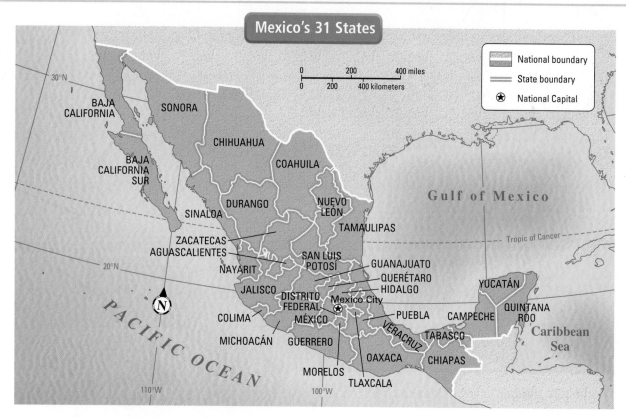

Mexico's 31 States

National boundary
State boundary
★ National Capital

Mexican States Like the United States, Mexico is made up of many states.

SKILL **Interpret a Map** Which Mexican states border the United States? Which two states form a peninsula on the Pacific coast?

Mexico's Government Today

Main Idea Like the United States, Mexico is a democracy and a republic with three branches of government.

December 1, 2000, was a historic occasion in Mexico. On that day, Vicente Fox became Mexico's new president. Fox was the first president in more than 70 years who did not belong to the PRI. Instead, he belonged to the National Action Party (Partido Acción Nacional, or PAN). The election of a president from a party other than the PRI confirmed that Mexico was entering a time of new political possibilities.

Mexico's official name is *Estados Unidos Mexicanos,* or the United Mexican States. Thirty-one states make up the nation of Mexico.

Mexico is a democracy and a republic. All Mexicans who are 18 or older have the right to vote. The Mexican government has three branches. As in the United States, these branches are the executive, legislative, and judicial.

Like the United States, Mexico has a federal system of government. Power is shared between the national government and state governments.

Voters in each state elect a governor. Each state also has its own legislature that makes laws. However, the national government has some control over the state governments. For example, the president and the national Senate together can remove a state governor from office.

Most towns and villages depend on money from the national government. Therefore, a local government has less say in its town's affairs than the national government does. However, local governments do provide essential public services, such as maintaining sewer systems and public safety.

REVIEW What is the official name of Mexico?

Lesson Summary

> The War of Reform raged between reformers and church leaders, army leaders, and wealthy landowners.

> The effort to reform Mexico's government and economy led to the Mexican Revolution in 1910.

> Mexico entered a new political era with the election of a president from the National Action Party and not the PRI.

Why It Matters...

Other countries, such as the United States, are more willing to work as partners with Mexico because its government is democratic.

Stamps The Mexican government issues stamps that celebrate its people and achievements.

Lesson Review

1858
Benito Juárez becomes president

1920
Mexican Revolution ends

1850   1860   1870   1880   1890   1900   1910   1920   1930

1 VOCABULARY Write a short paragraph explaining how life on an *ejido* would be similar to farm life before *haciendas.*

2 READING SKILL What was one constitutional reform that helped the poor people of Mexico?

3 MAIN IDEA: Citizenship What changes did reformers such as Benito Juárez help bring about in Mexico?

4 MAIN IDEA: History Why was the Mexican Revolution fought among many armies?

5 MAIN IDEA: Economics How did the Mexican government help farmers gain land of their own?

6 TIMELINE SKILL Did Benito Juárez become president before or after the end of the Mexican Revolution?

7 CRITICAL THINKING: Compare and Contrast How did different groups view the need for reform and change in Mexico during the years from 1850 to 1940?

HANDS ON

SPEAKING ACTIVITY Think about a constitution's bill of rights. Write a speech explaining why a bill of rights is important to citizens.

Skillbuilder

Read a Graph

Graphs use pictures and symbols, along with words, to show information. There are many different kinds of graphs. Bar graphs, line graphs, and pie graphs are the most common. Bar graphs compare numbers or sets of numbers. The length or height of each bar shows a quantity. It is easy to compare different categories using a bar graph.

The bar graph shows the number of Mexican state governors who belong to each political party. Use the steps listed to help you interpret the graph.

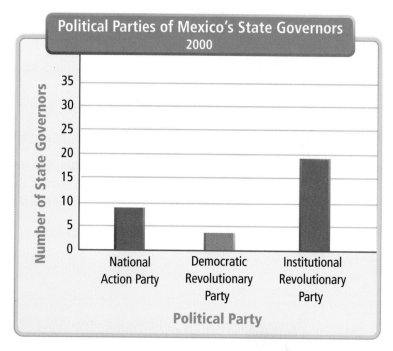

Political Parties of Mexico's State Governors 2000

Number of State Governors

Political Party

National Action Party

Democratic Revolutionary Party

Institutional Revolutionary Party

Learn the Skill

Step 1: Read the title to identify the main idea of the graph.

Step 2: Read the vertical axis (the one that goes up and down) on the left side of the graph. This one shows the number of state governors. Each bar represents the number of Mexican state governors who were members of a particular political party.

Step 3: Read the horizontal axis (the one that runs across the bottom of the graph). This one shows the three political parties of Mexico's governors in 2000.

Step 4: Summarize the information given in each part of the graph. Use the title to help you focus on what information the graph is presenting.

Practice the Skill

Writing a summary will help you understand the information in the graph. The paragraph below summarizes the information from the bar graph.

In the year 2000, the state governors in Mexico belonged to three different political parties. The majority belonged to the Institutional Revolutionary Party. The next largest group was the National Action Party, and the smallest number of governors belonged to the Democratic Revolutionary Party. This shows that the Institutional Revolutionary Party was probably the most powerful party in Mexico.

Apply the Skill

Turn to page 172 in Chapter 7, Lesson 1, "The Roots of Modern Mexico." Look at the graph entitled "Population of Mexico in 1810," and write a paragraph summarizing what you learned from it.

Mexico's Changing Economy

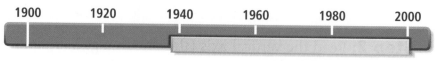

1900	1920	1940	1960	1980	2000

1938–2000

Build on What You Know What kind of work would you like to do when you grow up? You have many choices of different kinds of work. For much of Mexico's history, most Mexicans had little choice but to be farmers. It was not until the 1950s that large numbers of Mexicans started working in other kinds of jobs.

Farming in a Time of Change

Main Idea The Mexican government has moved to private ownership of farms and business.

The 1938 decision that the government would own Mexico's oil industry was made in an effort to expand Mexico's economy. The expansion was necessary because, from ancient times until the mid-1900s, most Mexicans worked in just one industry—farming. Since the 1950s, great numbers of Mexicans have left farming for other kinds of work. However, farming is still important to Mexico's economy.

About one-fourth of Mexican workers are farmers. Many small farmers still work on the *ejidos*, or community farms, that were set up after the Revolution. Although the *ejido* system gave land to many poor villagers, it did not lift them out of poverty.

Farmers could not use the land as security for a bank loan because they did not really own their land—the *ejido* did. Without much money, they could not buy the necessary tools and equipment that they needed, such as tractors, plows, or fertilizer. Because they had to continue to farm in the old ways, with hand tools on worn-out soil, *ejido* farmers had little chance of success.

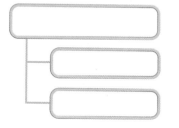

Increased Productivity Some private farms turn out hundreds of crates of produce at once.

Reform

In 1991, Mexican president Carlos Salinas de Gortari decided it was time to change the *ejido* system. Under Salinas's new laws, farmers could vote to divide their *ejido* into individual farms. Each farm family would have its own piece of land. The family could sell, rent, or trade its land. This process of replacing community ownership with individual, or private, ownership is called **privatization.**

The supporters of privatization hope that private farms will be able to grow more crops. Many of these farms are run like big businesses. Banks lend them money so they can afford to buy and use modern machinery. They can then grow the crops that Mexico sells to other countries, such as cotton, coffee, sugar cane, and strawberries.

Ejidos still make up about half the farmland in Mexico. This is partly because some farmers do not want to divide their *ejidos* into private farms. They worry that privatization might once again put most of the country's land into the hands of a few wealthy people.

The Growth of Business and Industry

During the mid-1900s, industry became a larger part of Mexico's economy because the Mexican government took steps to encourage its growth. For example, the government built new power plants to supply energy for factories. It also constructed homes for factory workers.

The Mexican government also helped new companies get started by lending them money from the national bank. Sometimes the government lowered taxes on businesses or helped companies pay back money they had borrowed.

The new policies encouraged production. As a result, new factories sprang up that made products such as steel, chemicals, paper, soft drinks, and textiles. The Mexican government also promoted the building of highways, railroads, and airports to aid manufacturers in the distribution of goods. **Distribution** is the process of moving products to their markets.

REVIEW How does using land on an *ejido* differ from owning one's own land?

The Growth of Factories and Trade

In the same way that it was privatizing farms, the Mexican government during the 1990s began to privatize businesses. It raised millions of dollars by selling businesses, such as banks, mines, and steel mills, to private companies. By 2000, only a few key industries—such as the oil industry—were still in government hands.

During the 1990s, many of Mexico's fastest-growing factories were situated along its border with the United States. These factories are called *maquiladoras*. In Mexico, a **maquiladora** (mah kee lah DAW rah) is a factory that imports duty-free parts from the United States to make products that it then exports back across the border. The lack of a tax on the parts helps keep operating costs low. Also, most of Mexico's *maquiladoras* are owned by foreigners, who save money because wages are lower in Mexico than in countries such as the United States. Although the wages are not great, *maquiladoras* have provided hundreds of thousands of jobs in Mexico.

New Industries In this Mexican factory, workers make car parts.

Giving tax breaks on trade items is also a goal of the North American Free Trade Agreement (NAFTA). NAFTA has reduced taxes on items traded among Mexico, the United States, and Canada. However, some Mexicans are not sure NAFTA is a good idea—they worry that having such close ties to the United States and Canada gives those countries too much influence over Mexico. Despite these concerns, Mexico has nearly doubled its trade with the United States and with Canada since NAFTA was approved in 1992.

Citizenship IN ACTION

Na Bolom Since 1951, an organization called Na Bolom (headquarters shown) has tried to help maintain Mexico's national heritage. Na Bolom works with the Maya living in the southeastern part of Mexico to uphold their traditional ways of life while also developing their economic opportunities. The group also tries to protect the often-threatened resources of the surrounding environment, such as the rain forest.

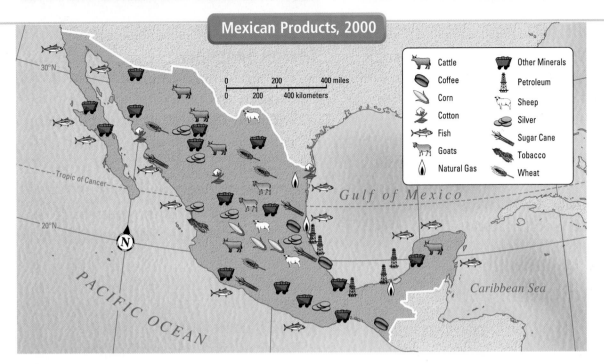

Mexican Products, 2000

Cattle · Coffee · Corn · Cotton · Fish · Goats · Natural Gas · Other Minerals · Petroleum · Sheep · Silver · Sugar Cane · Tobacco · Wheat

Natural Resources Mexico produces natural goods such as livestock, crops, and minerals. **SKILL** **Interpret a Map** In what region of Mexico is oil produced? What resource is found all over Mexico?

Mexico's Rich Resources

Main Idea Mexico's most important industries are based on petroleum and tourism.

Just as gold and silver drew the Spanish to Mexico in the 1500s, other minerals that are found there attract worldwide interest today. While Mexico produces more silver than any other country in the world, it also mines lead, zinc, graphite, sulfur, and copper.

By far the most important of Mexico's natural resources is petroleum, or oil. In 1938, the Mexican government decided to **nationalize,** or establish government control of, the oil industry. Today, when many other businesses have been privatized, the oil industry is still government owned. An agency called PEMEX (which stands for Petróleos Mexicanos, or Mexican Petroleum) runs the industry. PEMEX is Mexico's largest and most important company. Oil is Mexico's biggest export, and the United States is its largest buyer.

Tourism Is Big Business

Mexico's second-largest business is tourism. **Tourism** is the business of helping people travel on vacations. Tourists come to Mexico to enjoy its warm weather and its sunny beaches. Many people also visit the ancient Native American ruins and Mexico City's spectacular museums.

A popular tourist place in Mexico is Cancún, on the country's southeastern coast. The story of Cancún shows the effect tourism has had on Mexico's economy.

Until 1970, Cancún was a small Maya village of about 100 people. Its shoreline had white sand beaches and palm trees. The weather was sunny almost every day.

In 1970, the Mexican government decided Cancún was an ideal place for a holiday resort. Working together, the government and private businesses built an airport, new roads, and skyscraper hotels.

REVIEW How has nationalization affected Mexico's oil industry?

Today, more than 2.5 million people from all over the world visit Cancún's resorts each year. Because of the tourism boom, the once tiny village has become a city with about 500,000 people.

Other popular resort towns also attract tourists. Cozumel is on the east coast, near Cancún. Acapulco and Puerto Vallarta are popular resorts on the west coast of Mexico.

Rattlesnake Tourists who travel to Santa Catalina Island, off western Mexico, can see rattleless rattlesnakes. These snakes live nowhere else on Earth.

Lesson Summary

- The Mexican government is trying to make the economy stronger by supporting many different kinds of industries.
- The *ejido* system is being replaced with privatization of farms, which makes farming more profitable for individuals.
- In the 1990s, the government built new factories and supported privatization of businesses.
- NAFTA and *maquiladoras* support international trade.
- The greatest contributors to the Mexican economy now are the oil industry and tourism.

Why It Matters . . .

Mexico's successful expansion of its economy has helped the nation to prosper.

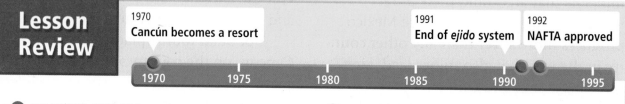

Lesson Review

1970 — Cancún becomes a resort
1991 — End of *ejido* system
1992 — NAFTA approved

1970 1975 1980 1985 1990 1995

1 **VOCABULARY** Write a short paragraph discussing the effect of **privatization** or **nationalization** on Mexico's economy. Use these words in your explanation.

2 **READING SKILL** Give a **detail** that supports the **main idea** that Mexico is rich in natural resources.

3 **MAIN IDEA: Economics** How has privatization changed the *ejido* system?

4 **MAIN IDEA: Government** What part has Mexico's government played in the growth of industry?

5 **TIMELINE SKILL** In what year was tourism encouraged as a growing industry?

6 **CRITICAL THINKING: Form and Support Opinions** Do you think the privatization of farmland in Mexico has been a positive step for Mexico's farmers? Why or why not?

CHART ACTIVITY Draw a flow chart that shows the process by which goods are produced and distributed by a *maquiladora*.

Mexico's Culture Today

Build on What You Know Do you live in a city or in the country? The United States has both rural and urban areas where people live and work. Mexico also has urban and rural areas, and the lifestyles of people in these two areas are very different from each other.

Mexico's Blend of Cultures

Main Idea Mexico today is a blend of Native American and Spanish traditions mixed with modern culture.

Mexican culture today reflects a mix of traditions. This mix includes three main cultures. The first two, Native American and Spanish, have long histories. The third culture, modern Mexican, results from the natural changes Mexicans have gone through over time.

A plaza near the center of Mexico City symbolizes the traditions that have come together in Mexico. At the center of this Plaza of Three Cultures stand the stone ruins of the Aztec marketplace. Nearby, a Spanish Catholic church borders the plaza. Beyond the plaza, skyscrapers rise against the sky and stand as landmarks of modern Mexico.

Mexico City This city's plaza, the Zócalo, is the center of one of the world's largest cities.

VOCABULARY

rural
urban
fiesta

Vocabulary Strategy

fiesta

Fiesta sounds similar to **feast**. A fiesta is a big party where people often eat a feast.

READING SKILL

Compare and Contrast As you read, complete the chart to show the differences between rural and urban Mexico.

Mexican Architecture and Art

Just as Mexico's architecture reveals the multiple layers of its culture, so do other art forms. A series of historical murals decorates the walkways of the National Palace in Mexico City. Painted by Diego Rivera, one of Mexico's most celebrated 20th-century artists, these murals depict scenes from the Aztec Empire, New Spain, and the Mexican Revolution. Rivera's wife, Frida Kahlo (FREE duh KAH loh), is another favorite Mexican painter. After being injured badly in a bus accident, Kahlo painted many famous self-portraits from her bed.

Mexican literature also echoes the country's three cultural traditions. Octavio Paz, who won the Nobel Prize in literature in 1990, often writes about the connections between elements of Mexico's past.

Frida Kahlo (1907-1954) She taught herself how to paint and created brightly colored self-portraits.

Mexican Muralist After the Mexican Revolution, artist Diego Rivera (1886–1957) painted a series of famous murals on the walls of the National Palace in Mexico City. Rivera wanted to use his art to remind Mexicans of the important events in their country's past. This mural shows a typical day in the Aztec capital, Tenochtitlán—now Mexico City.

CRITICAL THINKING Synthesize What aspects of Aztec society was Rivera celebrating in this mural?

Recognize Details Identify three activities depicted in the mural.

Life in the City

About one of every five Mexicans lives in Mexico City. Thousands of people move there each year, hoping to work in factories or attend one of the city's universities or colleges. While Mexico City is by far the largest city in the country, many other cities and towns are growing quickly. Like Mexico City, they offer a blend of opportunities and problems.

With more than 18 million inhabitants, Mexico City is the second-largest city in the world, after Tokyo, Japan. It is also the cultural center of Mexico. The great marble Palace of Fine Arts houses the national opera, theater, and symphony. It is also home to the famous Ballet Folklórico, a group that performs spectacular dances based on Mexican traditions.

Growth has, however, created problems. Streets are jammed with traffic. Car exhaust creates a blanket of smog over the city. The government has responded to the pollution problem in a number of ways. One solution was to free taxi drivers from paying taxes on their vehicles if they drive cars that pollute less.

As is true in most large cities, a noticeable gap exists between the lives of Mexico City's rich and poor citizens. While luxurious homes and fine shopping centers line some streets, many people also live in poverty.

REVIEW How are Mexico's three cultures expressed in Mexico City?

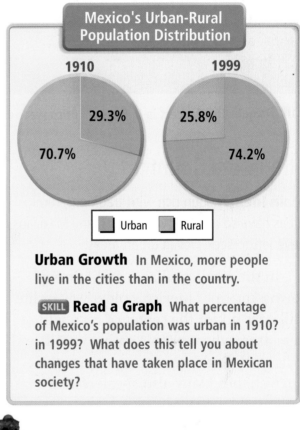

Mexico's Urban-Rural Population Distribution

1910
29.3%
70.7%

1999
25.8%
74.2%

■ Urban ■ Rural

Urban Growth In Mexico, more people live in the cities than in the country.

SKILL Read a Graph What percentage of Mexico's population was urban in 1910? in 1999? What does this tell you about changes that have taken place in Mexican society?

Mexico City Aztec ruins, Spanish colonial architecture, and modern high-rises share space in Mexico's capital.

modern high-rises

Spanish colonial architecture

Aztec ruins

193

Folk Dance The dancers in Ballet Folklórico wear detailed, bright costumes.

Life in the Countryside

Main Idea Though rich with traditions, rural areas have so much poverty that many Mexicans have left to seek jobs in urban areas.

In the smaller villages and farming towns, much of Mexico's older way of life still goes on. At the center of each village is a plaza, where people gather to talk and visit with neighbors. Most people speak Spanish, but many also speak Native American languages.

Each village sets aside one day a week as market day. People gather in the plaza to buy, sell, or trade food, clothing, and other goods. Farmers come in from surrounding areas, bringing vegetables and handicrafts. The scent of freshly baked tortillas and frijoles, or beans, fills the air.

Mexico's **rural** areas—those in the countryside—face the serious problem of poverty. Some homes have only one room and a dirt floor. Farmhouses may lack electricity and running water. These hardships have driven many rural Mexicans to seek jobs in **urban,** or city, settings.

Education is also more limited in the rural areas than in the urban ones. Without education, it is especially hard for people to escape poverty.

Holidays

On September 16, Mexico celebrates their Independence Day. To celebrate, Mexicans reenact Father Hidalgo's call in 1810 to rise up against Spanish rule. Then people watch fireworks, dance, and play music in the streets late into the night.

Another major holiday has a somber name—the Day of the Dead. Nevertheless, Mexicans see it as a joyful time. They set aside November 1 and 2 to remember and honor their loved ones who have died.

Mexicans decorate the graves with candles and flowers. Bakeries sell loaves of bread shaped like bones, and many stores sell small candy skulls. Relatives gather for meals at the cemeteries and decorate the gravesites with brightly colored flowers. While eating picnics of spicy meat dishes and sugary desserts, family members share favorite stories about departed loved ones.

At least once a year, each village or town celebrates a **fiesta.** A fiesta is a holiday with parades, games, and feasts. It usually takes place on a saint's day—a day set aside by the Catholic Church to honor the memory of a holy person. While these days have religious origins, they are also celebrated as big neighborhood parties.

REVIEW Compare and contrast Mexican Independence Day with the U.S. Independence Day, celebrated on July 4.

Day of the Dead This gravesite is decorated for the Mexican holiday.

Lesson Summary

- Mexican culture is a mixture of Native American, Spanish, and modern Mexican cultures.

- Mexican cities offer jobs and educational opportunities, but have problems with traffic and pollution.

- Mexico's older way of life is preserved in the countryside, but people there face problems of limited education and poverty.

- In addition to local fiestas, Mexicans celebrate Independence Day and the Day of the Dead.

Why It Matters . . .

Cultures change over time, but understanding their histories can help you better understand their characteristics today.

Lesson Review

1. **VOCABULARY** Choose the correct word to complete each sentence.

   urban   rural

   Poverty is a problem in Mexico's _____ areas. Most people in Mexico live in Mexico City or other _____ areas.

2. **READING SKILL** Which offers more economic advantages, urban or rural life?

3. **MAIN IDEA: Culture** What three traditions mix in Mexico's culture today?

4. **MAIN IDEA: Geography** Why is Mexico City growing so rapidly?

5. **EVENTS TO KNOW** Describe a typical family celebration on the **Day of the Dead.**

6. **CRITICAL THINKING: Compare** Do you see any similarities between the mix of cultural traditions in Mexico and the mix in the United States? What are they?

WRITING ACTIVITY Imagine that you are traveling through Mexico. Write a journal entry describing what you saw and did in its cities and towns.

Visual Summary

1–4. ✏️ Write a description for each concept shown below.

| The Roots of Modern Mexico | Government in Mexico | Mexico's Changing Economy | Mexico's Culture Today |

_____

_____

Facts and Main Ideas

Answer each question below.

5. **History** How was Mexico's War of Independence connected to events elsewhere in the world at that time?

6. **Economics** What concerns did Mexicans in the 1800s and 1900s have about land ownership?

7. **Government** What was unique about Mexico's presidential election in 2000?

8. **Economics** What is the role of oil in Mexico's economy?

9. **History** What are some of the problems caused by Mexico City's rapid growth?

Vocabulary

Choose the correct word from the list below to complete each sentence.

peninsulares, p. 172
ejido, p. 181
privatization, p. 187
urban, p. 194

10. When _____ replaced community ownership, farmers made their community farms into individual farms.

11. Mexico City is an example of an _____ setting.

12. An _____ was owned by all the villagers who worked the land together.

13. The _____ came from the Iberian Peninsula and moved to Mexico as the ruling class.

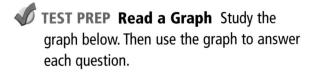

1821 Mexican independence

1845 Texas joins U.S.

1920 Mexican Revolution ends

1992 NAFTA approved

1800   1825   1850   1875   1900   1925   1950   1975   2000

Apply Skills

 TEST PREP **Read a Graph** Study the graph below. Then use the graph to answer each question.

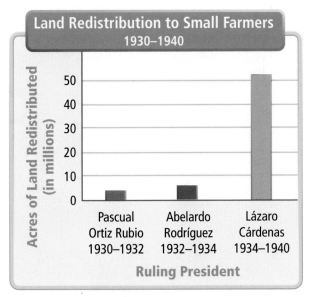

Land Redistribution to Small Farmers
1930–1940

Acres of Land Redistributed (in millions)

50
40
30
20
10
0

Pascual Ortiz Rubio 1930–1932

Abelardo Rodríguez 1932–1934

Lázaro Cárdenas 1934–1940

Ruling President

14. About how much land did President Cárdenas give to small farmers?

 A. less than 10 million acres

 B. almost 50 million acres

 C. almost 50 thousand acres

 D. 40 million acres

15. How much more land did Cárdenas give than Rodríguez?

 A. almost 35 million acres

 B. almost 40 million acres

 C. almost 45 million acres

 D. about 5 million acres

Critical Thinking

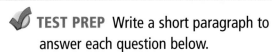 TEST PREP Write a short paragraph to answer each question below.

16. **Infer** Do you think the Mexican government's decision in the 1990s to privatize farming and business was a good one? Explain.

17. **Analyze** Why do modern artists use images from both Mexico's past and its present in their works?

Timeline

Use the Chapter Summary Timeline above to answer the question.

18. How many years of independence will Mexicans celebrate on this year's Independence Day?

Activities

SPEAKING ACTIVITY Work with a group of classmates to create a news show about the experience of Mexicans during the Mexican Revolution.

WRITING ACTIVITY Write and illustrate a colorful travel brochure to persuade tourists to visit Cancún. Use information from the chapter to help you.

Technology
Writing Process Tips
Get help with your brochure at www.eduplace.com/kids/hmss05/

Chapter 8

Central America and the Caribbean Islands

Technology

e • **glossary**
e • **word games**
www.eduplace.com/kids/hmss05/

Vocabulary Preview

dictator

A **dictator** is a person who has complete control over a country's government. Fidel Castro has been the dictator of Cuba since 1959.

page 203

sugar cane

Sugar cane is a plant from which sugar is made. From the 1600s to the 1800s, growing sugar cane was the main industry of the Caribbean Islands.

page 206

Chapter Timeline

1821
Guatemala independence

| 1820 | 1835 | 1850 | 1865 | 1880 |

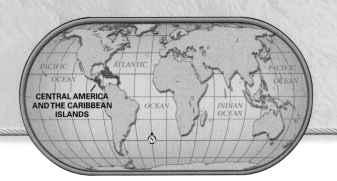

Reading Strategy

Question As you read the lessons in this chapter, ask yourself questions to check your understanding.

Quick Tip

Ask yourself what you want to know more about. Write your question and go back to it once you finish reading.

diversify

When economies **diversify,** they conduct business activities in a variety of industries. The West Indian economy used to rely on the sugar business, but it diversified into pineapples, bananas, and some manufacturing. **page 207**

departamento

Guatemala is divided into 22 states. Each state is called a ***departamento.*** Like a state in the United States, each *departamento* has a governor. **page 218**

1902 Cuba independence	1903 Panama independence		1961 Cuba becomes communist	

1895	1910	1925	1940	1965

Establishing Independence

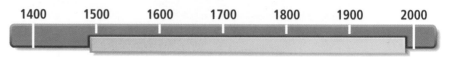

1400   1500   1600   1700   1800   1900   2000

1492–1990

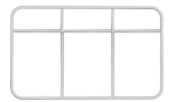
Build on What You Know Think how much the freedoms we have in the United States mean to us. The people of Central America and the Caribbean had to work long and hard to enjoy the freedoms that we may take for granted in a democracy.

Central America and the Caribbean

Main Idea West Indians are a mix of Spanish, Native American, and African descent.

Central America includes seven nations—Belize, Guatemala, Honduras, El Salvador, Nicaragua, Costa Rica, and Panama. Its neighbors—St. Domingue, now called Haiti, and the other islands of the Caribbean—are known as the West Indies. They include 13 nations and 11 dependencies. A **dependency** is a place that is governed by or closely connected with another country. For example, Puerto Rico is a dependency of the United States.

Cultures People of many different cultures live in the Caribbean.

Political Map of Central America and the Caribbean in 2001

Central America and the Caribbean There are many different important countries in this part of the world. **SKILL** **Read a Political Map** Which two nations are located on the same island?

Peoples of the Caribbean

When Christopher Columbus reached the West Indies in 1492, about 750,000 Native Americans lived there. The Europeans forced Native Americans to work on plantations and in mines. The harsh labor, plus European diseases unknown in the Americas, killed many Native Americans. Others died in battles with the Europeans. Soon, nearly all the Native Americans on the islands had died.

Without Native Americans to use for labor, European rulers looked for a new source of workers. By the 1520s, the Spanish began bringing shiploads of enslaved Africans to the West Indies. Other European nations joined in the slave trade. From the 1500s to the mid-1800s, about 10 million enslaved Africans arrived in the West Indies. As a result, many people in the Caribbean today are **mulattos** (mu LAT ohz), or people who have African and European ancestry.

Central American People

In Central America, the situation for the Native Americans was different. When the Spanish arrived in 1501, many Native Americans withdrew to the inland mountains and thus survived what proved to be a deadly encounter with the Spanish elsewhere. Today, one-fifth of Central Americans are Native Americans.

The slave ships also arrived in Central America, bringing Africans to the region. Africans from the Caribbean also migrated to the area. As the years passed, the Spanish, Native Americans, and Africans intermarried. Those people with mixed European and Native American ancestry are called **ladinos** (luh DEE naws), and they make up about two-thirds of Central America's population today.

REVIEW How did geography help the Native Americans in Central America survive the arrival of Europeans?

From Colonies to Independence

Main Idea Over time, Central American and West Indian colonies gained their independence.

From the 1500s to the 1800s, European nations ruled Central America and the West Indies as colonies. These differed from the dependencies of today. Usually, a dependency is free to break off its connection to the other country, but a colony must either win its independence or be granted it.

Spain was the first European country to colonize this region. Soon, however, the French, Dutch, and English set up their own colonies in the islands. While they found the gold they were looking for, they also found another source of wealth—sugar. Soon many of the islands were home to sugar plantations. Most of the workers who grew and cut the sugar cane were enslaved.

By the 1800s, the people of Central America and the Caribbean Islands began to demand their independence. In 1804, the French colony of St. Domingue became the first nation in the region to win independence.

Other nations soon followed St. Domingue's example. In 1821, Guatemala, Honduras, Costa Rica, and Nicaragua declared independence from Spain. At first they united, but since 1839, they have existed as separate nations.

Relations with the United States

The United States of America is the largest neighbor of Central America and the West Indies. U.S. policies have long played a part in shaping the region's history.

Until the early 1900s, people who wanted to travel from one side of North or South America to the other had two choices. They could make the long, dangerous trip by land or sail all the way around South America. The Isthmus of Panama is only about 40 miles wide, and by 1900, first France, then the United States were eager to build a canal across it to connect the two oceans.

At that time, Panama was part of the South American nation of Colombia. The United States tried to buy from Colombia a strip of land on the isthmus. Colombia refused, and so the United States urged the people of Panama to break away. Soon, Panama did revolt. After establishing its own country in 1903, Panama agreed to lease the United States land to build a canal. The canal opened in 1914 and soon became one of the most important transportation routes in the world. Now ships only had to sail the 50 miles from one end of the canal to the other.

Central Americans
The people of Central America today reflect the region's rich mix of cultures and people.

lookout

ship entering lock

train

lock

Panama Canal The United States controlled the Panama Canal and the land around it until December 31, 1999, when control passed to Panama. By using the Panama Canal, ships can save thousands of miles by not sailing around South America.

NICARAGUA

Caribbean Sea

Panama Canal

COSTA RICA

Panama City

N

PANAMA

COLOMBIA

PACIFIC OCEAN

The Spanish-American War

Long after Central America broke free of Spanish rule, Spain continued to control Cuba and Puerto Rico. During the late 1800s, the islanders there rebelled many times without success.

In 1898, the United States declared war on Spain. It wanted to help the people of Cuba and Puerto Rico gain freedom from Spain. It also wanted to protect the U.S.-owned sugar cane plantations on the islands. By the end of the short war, Spain had lost its last colonies in the Americas. Puerto Rico became a U.S. dependency, a territory under the control of another nation. Cuba became an independent country, but the U.S. military set up bases there and kept control over the country.

Dictatorships and Democracy

Independence did not necessarily bring freedom to the people of Central America and the West Indies. Only Costa Rica has been a democracy since the beginning of the 20th century.

Nearly all the other countries have spent many years under the rule of dictators. A **dictator** is a person who has complete control over a country's government. At times, dictators ruled Guatemala, Honduras, Panama, El Salvador, Haiti, and the Dominican Republic. Dictators often used violence to grab and keep power.

REVIEW How did the Spanish-American War affect Cuba and Puerto Rico?

Most countries in Central America and the West Indies now have democratically elected governments. The people of these countries removed most of their dictators, one by one. For example, in 1990, Nicaraguans replaced dictatorial rule by electing Violetta Barrios de Chamorro (vee oh LE tuh BA ree ohs day chah MOH roh) as president. However, elected leaders sometimes refuse to give up power, thus becoming dictators. Sometimes, elections are not run fairly. Nevertheless, freedom is more widespread than it was 50 years ago.

Violetta Barrios de Chamorro
Nicaragua's first female president governed from 1990 to 1996.

Lesson Summary

Europeans brought in African slave labor when many Native Americans died.

The United States influenced Panama to break away from Colombia so the Panama Canal could be built.

The Spanish-American War brought independence for Cuba and made Puerto Rico a U.S. dependency.

Dictatorships ruled Central America and the West Indies for much of their history.

Why It Matters . . .

The quest for democracy continues in Central America and the Caribbean, as it does elsewhere in the world today.

Lesson Review

1898 **Spanish-American War** 1903 **Panama independence** 1914 **Panama Canal completed**

1895   1900   1905   1910   1915

① **VOCABULARY** Choose the correct word to complete each sentence.

   dependency   dictator

   Panama used to be ruled by a _____ who made all the decisions for the government.
   Puerto Rico was a _____ of the United States after independence from Spain.

② **READING SKILL** What was a **solution** to the United States' need to build a canal to connect the Atlantic and Pacific Oceans?

③ **MAIN IDEA: History** Why are there more Native Americans in Central America today than in the Caribbean?

④ **MAIN IDEA: Government** Describe the difference between dependencies and colonies.

⑤ **MAIN IDEA: History** List two reasons why the United States declared war on Spain.

⑥ **EVENTS TO KNOW** How did the opening of the Panama Canal in 1914 change transportation?

⑦ **TIMELINE SKILL** How many years after Panama's independence was the canal built?

⑧ **CRITICAL THINKING: Evaluate** Why have some countries in Central America and the Caribbean had trouble establishing democracies?

HANDS ON

DRAMA ACTIVITY Use library or Internet resources to learn about François Dominique Toussaint L'Ouverture, the man who led Haiti to independence. Pick one event from his life to dramatize.

Economies and Cultures

Build on What You Know Have you ever seen an advertisement for vacations or cruise ships to the Caribbean? Many people like to visit there to enjoy the sunny weather and beautiful beaches. Many Caribbean Islands depend on tourism for their economies.

The Economies

Main Idea Because an economy that depends on a single product can be unstable, the Caribbean Islands had to find new businesses to support their economy.

In the Caribbean, the economies of most islands have depended on growing one or two crops to sell to other countries. However, the islanders have also worked hard to create new businesses as well as new industries.

Grenada This island is a favorite destination in the Caribbean, with its crater lakes, waterfalls, fragrant spice trees, and rain forests.

VOCABULARY

sugar cane
single-product economy
diversify

Vocabulary Strategy

single-product economy

Single means "one." A **single-product economy** is dependent on just one product for jobs and income.

READING SKILL

Compare and Contrast As you read, complete the Venn diagram to compare and contrast the cultures of Central America and the Caribbean.

Coffee This important cash crop grows well in the cool highlands of Central America.

Sugar Cane Many Caribbean islanders worked on plantations growing sugar cane.

Caribbean Sugar Cane

For most of the colonial period, the Caribbean Islands focused mainly on one industry—growing sugar cane. From the 1600s to the 1800s, most islanders worked on sugar cane plantations. In the early years, the majority of these workers were enslaved. Even after slavery ended by the late 1800s, most workers owned no land of their own. Instead, they planted, tended, and cut sugar cane on plantations owned by the wealthy.

During the colonial period, most of the islands traded only with their ruling countries. Cuba, for example, sold its sugar to Spain and bought goods from Spain in return. But after the colonial period ended, many of the islands traded mostly with the United States.

Sugar was so valuable that plantation owners raised few other crops. Most did not even grow food. Many of the islands had to buy almost all their food from other countries. A country that depends on just one product for almost all its jobs and income has a single-product economy.

A single-product economy can be unstable—if something happens to that single product, the country's economy will be ruined. By the late 1800s, the sugar business in the West Indies was in trouble. People raising sugar cane in other parts of the world offered the West Indies fierce competition. Steam-powered machines allowed these foreigners to process sugar cane at lower prices. The people of the West Indies had to find new ways to make a living.

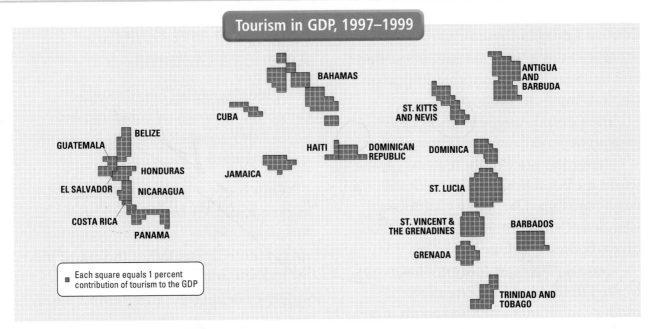

Tourism in GDP, 1997–1999

BAHAMAS

ANTIGUA AND BARBUDA

CUBA

ST. KITTS AND NEVIS

BELIZE

GUATEMALA

HAITI

DOMINICAN REPUBLIC

DOMINICA

HONDURAS

JAMAICA

EL SALVADOR

NICARAGUA

ST. LUCIA

COSTA RICA

ST. VINCENT & THE GRENADINES

BARBADOS

PANAMA

GRENADA

TRINIDAD AND TOBAGO

Each square equals 1 percent contribution of tourism to the GDP

Tourism This map shows the economic value of tourism in these countries. GDP, or gross domestic product, is the yearly value of goods and services produced in a country. **SKILL Interpret a Map** In this cartogram, countries with a greater percentage of GDP coming from tourism are larger than countries with a smaller percentage. In which country does tourism make up the greatest percentage of GDP?

New Crops and Industries

The islanders found they needed to diversify their economies. To **diversify** an economy means to invest in a variety of industries. People began to raise other crops, such as pineapples and bananas. Industries, such as textiles, medical supplies, and electronic equipment, also developed in the Caribbean.

One of the most important industries in the Caribbean Islands is tourism. With warm weather and beautiful beaches, the islands attract tourists from around the world.

The landscapes of the Caribbean Islands contain sandy beaches, coral lagoons, grassy plains, mountains, and volcanoes. The year-round warm climate creates lush, green landscapes. More than 8 million tourists flock to the area each year. On some of the smaller islands, such as Antigua and Barbuda, tourism is now the major industry.

Central America

After the Spanish Central American countries became independent in the 1820s, they wanted to increase their trade with other nations. To do so, they needed to develop exports. During the 1800s, several Central American countries began to produce coffee. Soon it became an important export crop for Costa Rica, Guatemala, Honduras, El Salvador, and Nicaragua. In exchange for their exports, Central American countries purchased imports from other parts of the world.

In the late 1800s, a major new export business got started in Central America. U.S.-based United Fruit Company (UFCO) set up huge banana plantations in the hot, wet lowlands of Central America.

REVIEW How have the people of the West Indies tried to overcome the problems of a single-product economy?

Central America Diversifies

UFCO did a huge amount of business, and bananas became another important Central American product.

The Central American economies grew to depend on bananas and coffee. Whenever the price of these items on the world market fell, Central Americans faced hardship. Like many Caribbean islanders, Central Americans wanted to diversify their economies.

Central American countries have worked to build more factories and produce more manufactured goods. Costa Rica, for example, has built factories that make machinery, furniture, cloth, and medicine. The countries of the region have also developed tourism as an industry.

Visitors arrive by the thousands in Guatemala to see the spectacular ruins of Maya temples. As different businesses grow, Central Americans will not be as dependent on agriculture as they were in the past.

Caribbean and Central American Cultures

Main Idea Europeans brought Roman Catholicism to the region, but African and Native American beliefs have also influenced religious practices.

Each country in the Caribbean has its own particular way of life. Native American, African, and European influences blend differently from place to place.

In the Caribbean, people speak a variety of languages. These reflect the area's history.

Music, too, shows a blending of cultures. From Cuban salsa to Jamaican reggae, much Caribbean music combines African and European styles to make something completely new. The rap music that is popular in the United States also has Caribbean roots. Some of the first rappers to perform in the United States introduced to this country the Jamaican technique of mixing together tracks from different songs.

María Elena Cuadra Movement In Central America, poverty and unemployment are widespread. In Nicaragua, many women take jobs in factories, like the one shown here, under poor conditions and for low wages.

Since 1994, the María Elena Cuadra Movement of Working and Unemployed Women (MEC) has been working to improve the position of women at work and in the home. MEC protects workers' rights, trains women in new skills, and lends money to women to start their own small businesses.

A Blend of Cultures

The countries of Central America share a common history. In their cultures, the Native American and Spanish heritages blend. In most of Central America, people speak Spanish. Central Americans also speak about 80 Native American languages, nearly half of which are Maya languages.

Roman Catholicism is the most widespread religion in the West Indies. However, many islanders practice religions that have African influences. In Haiti, elements of Catholic and African religious practices combine in the religion known as voodoo.

In Cuba, Yoruba beliefs from Africa combine with Catholic beliefs in the religion called Santeria. In Trinidad, the Shango religion blends Catholic, Baptist, and West African beliefs.

In recent years, millions of Central Americans have become Protestants and Mormons. Also, some ancient Maya religious beliefs still thrive. An example is the companion spirit.

Many Maya people today believe that when a person is born, so is an animal. That animal, the companion spirit, lives through the same experiences as the person does. A person usually learns about his or her companion spirit in dreams.

REVIEW What cultures are reflected in the music of the region?

Spotlight on CULTURE

Merengue Dancing is a popular pastime in Latin America. One of the favorite dances (and the national dance of the Dominican Republic) is the merengue (at right). This dance form originated in the neighboring nations of Haiti and the Dominican Republic. It is known for its unique dance step, called a sliding step, in which the dancer always rests his or her weight on the same foot. People commonly explain this step with one of two legends. One legend says that enslaved people developed the step while chained to one another at the leg. Another legend has it that a Dominican war hero, wounded in the leg during a revolt, designed the step. Whatever the true story behind the dance, the merengue did arise as a folk dance in rural areas. Later it became a favorite of ballroom dancers.

CRITICAL THINKING Draw Conclusions
What do the two legends about the origins of the merengue's sliding step tell you about the significance of dancing in Latin American culture?

Synthesize What different roles do you think dancing can play in a culture?

Many Central American towns are known for their crafts, such as weaving, embroidery, pottery, silversmithing, and basketmaking. Many of the styles and methods used originated with ancient Native Americans. For example, many weavers use a backstrap loom—a 2,000-year-old device consisting of threads that are attached to a fixed post or tree on one end and a belt on the other end.

Master Weaver By placing the belt around her waist, the weaver stretches the threads tight to weave on them.

Lesson Summary
- The colonial period encouraged single-product economies. As countries gained independence, they diversified by raising various tropical crops and encouraging the growth of industries such as tourism.
- Each country in the Caribbean has its own culture, but they all blend Native American, African, and European influences.
- The Central American countries share a common history so their cultures blend Native American and Spanish influences.

Why It Matters...
Though small in size, the region exports its culture and products to the United States and beyond.

Lesson Review

❶ **VOCABULARY** Explain why sugar cane's influence led to a single-product economy.

❷ 📖 **READING SKILL** Compare and contrast the influence of Europe on Caribbean and Central American culture.

❸ **MAIN IDEA: Economics** List some ways in which sugar production affected the lives of Caribbean people.

❹ **MAIN IDEA: Economics** How have Central American countries diversified their economics?

❺ **MAIN IDEA: Culture** How do the religions in Central America and the Caribbean reflect the regions' histories?

❻ **FACTS TO KNOW** What is the most widespread religion in Central America?

❼ **CRITICAL THINKING: Infer** How do you think the success of a foreign-owned company affects a country?

HANDS ON

CHART ACTIVITY A country with a single-product economy risks losing a great deal if that product fails. Make a chart of the factors that put the country in this risky position but that it cannot control.

Cuba Today

1800 1825 1850 1875 1900 1925 1950 1975 2000 2025

1895–2000

Build on What You Know In your neighborhood, neighbors have some things in common and some differences. Cuba is a close neighbor of the United States. We have some things in common with Cuba and some big differences.

Independence and Revolution

Main Idea Many years after Cuba became an independent country, Fidel Castro set up a Communist government, causing tensions with the United States.

Cuba, the largest island in the Caribbean, still suffered Spanish rule long after many other Latin American countries gained independence. In 1895, Cubans led by José Martí continued fighting for the nation's independence. Three years later, the Spanish-American War reached the island. By the end of the war, Cuba had gained its independence from Spain. However, the United States maintained great influence over the nation.

VOCABULARY

Communism
malnutrition

Vocabulary Strategy

malnutrition

The prefix **mal** means "bad" or "poor." **Malnutrition** means having poor nutrition.

READING SKILL

Cause and Effect As you read, use the chart to take notes about the effects of Cuba forming a Communist government.

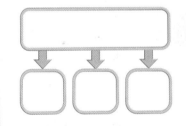

Fidel Castro While hiding deep in the Sierra Maestra mountains, Castro organized his followers for revolution.

211

Cuban Independence

Before the Spanish-American War, the United States wanted to add Cuba to the nation. After the Spanish-American War ended, the United States appointed a military governor for Cuba. From 1899 to 1902, the U.S. Army stayed in Cuba to keep peace and help set up a new government. Most Cubans resented the U.S. presence. However, during these years, Cubans and U.S. soldiers did build many needed roads, bridges, and public schools.

In 1902, the U.S. Army withdrew from Cuba, which then became independent. However, the United States insisted that it still had the right to send soldiers to Cuba at any time. The U.S. Navy also kept a large base for its ships at Guantánamo Bay.

After independence, Cuba had a series of leaders. Some were elected, and some took power by force. Most governed as dictators. Cuba's dictators were careful to stay friendly with the United States. They welcomed U.S. businesses and tourists. Havana, Cuba's capital, offered tourists luxury hotels and casinos. Most Cubans, however, remained poor.

Revolution Takes Hold

Time and again, Cubans protested against the dictators. In the 1950s, Cubans who were angry at the government found a leader for their cause. He was a young lawyer named Fidel Castro. Born in 1927 to a wealthy family, Castro was known for being a dynamic speaker. In college, he developed a deep interest in politics. By late 1956, Castro and a few followers had established headquarters for their revolution in the mountains of southeastern Cuba.

A few at a time, Cubans began to join Castro's small army. The rebel army won several battles against government troops. As the revolution grew stronger, Cuba's dictator, Fulgencio Batista (fool HEHN see oh buh TEES tuh), fled the country on January 1, 1959. On January 8, 1959, Castro and his followers marched triumphantly into Havana. More than half a million Cubans greeted them joyfully. In a speech to the crowds, Castro promised that Cuba would have no more dictators.

Economic Extremes The two extremes of life in Cuba are apparent in this contrast of one of Havana's fancy hotels with one simple dwelling.

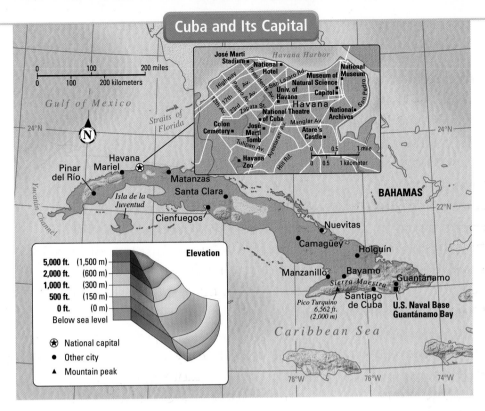

Cuba and Its Capital

Havana Harbor

José Martí Stadium
National Hotel
Museum of Natural Science
National Museum
Univ. of Havana
Capitol
Havana
National Theatre of Cuba
National Archives
Colon Cemetery
José Martí Tomb
Atare's Castle
Havana Zoo

Gulf of Mexico

Straits of Florida

Pinar del Río
Mariel
Havana
Matanzas
Santa Clara
Isla de la Juventud
Cienfuegos
Yucatán Channel

BAHAMAS

Nuevitas
Camagüey
Holguín
Manzanillo
Bayamo
Guantánamo
Sierra Maestra
Santiago de Cuba
Pico Turquino 6,562 ft. (2,000 m)
U.S. Naval Base Guantánamo Bay

Caribbean Sea

Elevation
5,000 ft. (1,500 m)
2,000 ft. (600 m)
1,000 ft. (300 m)
500 ft. (150 m)
0 ft. (0 m)
Below sea level

★ National capital
● Other city
▲ Mountain peak

Havana The capital of Cuba has many interesting historical and cultural sites.

SKILL Interpret a Map
Havana is located between what two latitudes?

Castro Takes Power

The revolution had succeeded. Castro became the new commander-in-chief of Cuba's army. By July 1959, he had taken full control of Cuba's government.

> ❝ We cannot ever become dictators. Those who do not have the people with them must resort to being dictators. We have the love of the people, and because of that love, we will never turn away from our principles. ❞

Castro took power in Cuba during the Cold War—a period of conflict between the United States and the Soviet Union. Castro needed the friendship of a powerful country. The Soviet Union was eager to have Cuba as an ally. It proved its interest in the smaller country by engaging in large-scale trade with Cuba as well as by providing Cuba with weapons. This attention helped Castro choose to side with the Soviet Union in the Cold War.

The Soviet Union practiced an economic and political system known as **Communism.** Under this system, the government plans and controls a country's economy—in effect, the government owns the country's farms, factories, and businesses. Soon, Castro began to adopt Communist policies for Cuba's economy. His government took over the big sugar cane plantations, many of which had been owned by U.S. companies. His government then took over U.S. banks, oil refineries, and other businesses on the island.

In return, the United States cut off all trade with Cuba. Cubans could no longer sell their huge sugar crop to the United States. Instead, the Soviet Union bought Cuba's sugar. The Soviet government also sent weapons, farm machinery, food, and money to Cuba. In 1961, Castro declared that he and Cuba were Communist.

REVIEW What actions did Castro take that went against his 1959 promise?

Castro as Dictator

While the poor usually supported Castro's policies, many wealthier Cubans did not. They were particularly upset when he redistributed land so that no family or farm owned more than a certain amount.

Castro also imprisoned people who spoke out against him. As a result, Cubans who opposed Castro began to flee to the United States and other countries. Over the years, hundreds of thousands of people left Cuba.

Government control over the economy is stronger in Cuba than almost anywhere else in the world. The government owns factories, hotels, and restaurants. There is very little free enterprise.

Castro has kept a tight hold on power for more than 40 years. Without ever being elected, he has remained head of state. His government has controlled all newspapers and radio and television stations. No one has been allowed to criticize his actions or the government. Despite his 1959 promise, Castro became a dictator.

Living in Cuba

Main Idea Since the collapse of the Soviet Union, Cubans have suffered from food shortages and other hardships.

Since the Cuban revolution, the Cuban economy has changed in many ways. Since the collapse of the Soviet Union in 1991, Cuba has struggled to maintain its Communist way of life without Soviet aid.

Sugar is Cuba's most important product in the world economy. The yearly sugar cane harvest is a key event for Cuba's economy. Once, workers with machetes cut the tough canes by hand. Then, with Soviet help, Castro's government bought huge machines to cut most of the cane. The cane harvest grew to record size.

While the Soviet Union was powerful, it traded oil, grain, and machinery with Cuba for sugar. Most of these products were worth more than sugar, so the Soviet Union was, in large part, supporting Cuba's economy.

Government Farms One of Castro's Communist policies was to take government control of farms, such as this one.

Protests In recent years, Cubans like these have continued to protest Castro's policies. Many protesters have been jailed or killed.

Education and Health Care

As with the economy, ways of life in Cuba have been greatly affected by Communism. Both education and health care reflect these changes.

After the revolution, Cuba's government set up many new schools. In the 1960s, teachers and even schoolchildren went into small villages to teach those who could not read or write. Many older people who had never had the chance to go to school learned to read for the first time.

Today, Cuban children must go to public school from ages 6 to 12. They can choose whether to continue their education after that. All schools are free, including college. Besides their academic subjects, students must take classes that teach Communist beliefs.

Like education, all health care in Cuba is paid for by the government. Cuba's health care system is probably the largest in Latin America. Every small village has a clinic.

However, Cuba had economic problems in the 1990s that affected both education and health care. Lack of fuel for buses and cars prevented some children from getting to school. Food shortages caused malnutrition. **Malnutrition** is poor health due to a lack of eating the right kinds of food. It often causes sickness. From the 1960s to the 1980s, Cuba had almost wiped out malnutrition. Since 1990, malnutrition has again become a problem in Cuba.

REVIEW In what ways did Cubans benefit under the Communist system?

Schools These Cuban school children sing their national anthem.

Health Care Workers The Cuban government pays for clinics and hospitals.

Arts, Sports, and Holidays

Both Castro's government and earlier dictators have placed strict limits on what artists, writers, and filmmakers may say in their work. As a result, some Cubans have fled to other countries in search of greater freedom of expression.

However, some art forms thrive in Cuba. Music is part of everyday life there. The unique sound of Cuban music combines African drums and Spanish guitars. Each different style and rhythm has its own name—son, mambo, cha-cha, rumba, salsa.

A Cuban holiday, Carnival, takes place at the end of July. Cities and villages celebrate the end of the sugar harvest with festivals filled with music and dancing.

Sports are also popular in Cuba. The nation's favorite sport is baseball. Cuba's baseball team won a gold medal at the Olympics in 1996.

Lesson Summary

After gaining independence, Cuba had a series of leaders until the 1950s, when Fidel Castro led an overthrow of the government. Castro aligned Cuba with the Soviet Union and, in 1961, made Cuba a Communist country. Castro has continued to lead Cuba even after the collapse of the Soviet Union. Boycotts by the United States and the loss of Soviet support however led to economic hardship for the Cuban people.

Why It Matters . . .

At the end of the 20th century, Cuba was the only Communist country in the Western Hemisphere.

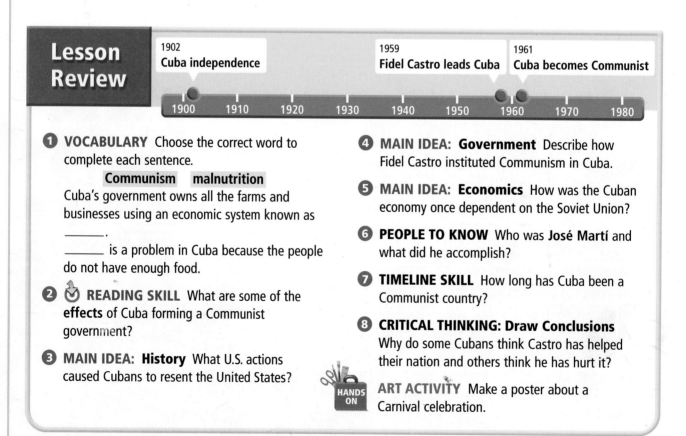

Lesson Review

1902 **Cuba independence**

1959 **Fidel Castro leads Cuba**

1961 **Cuba becomes Communist**

1900 1910 1920 1930 1940 1950 1960 1970 1980

1 **VOCABULARY** Choose the correct word to complete each sentence.

  Communism **malnutrition**

Cuba's government owns all the farms and businesses using an economic system known as _____.

_____ is a problem in Cuba because the people do not have enough food.

2 **READING SKILL** What are some of the **effects** of Cuba forming a Communist government?

3 **MAIN IDEA: History** What U.S. actions caused Cubans to resent the United States?

4 **MAIN IDEA: Government** Describe how Fidel Castro instituted Communism in Cuba.

5 **MAIN IDEA: Economics** How was the Cuban economy once dependent on the Soviet Union?

6 **PEOPLE TO KNOW** Who was **José Martí** and what did he accomplish?

7 **TIMELINE SKILL** How long has Cuba been a Communist country?

8 **CRITICAL THINKING: Draw Conclusions** Why do some Cubans think Castro has helped their nation and others think he has hurt it?

HANDS ON

ART ACTIVITY Make a poster about a Carnival celebration.

Guatemala Today

1800 1825 1850 1875 1900 1925 1950 1975 2000 2025

1821–2000

Build on What You Know What is the most important crop grown in our part of the country? If you lived in Guatemala, your answer would probably be "coffee." The export of coffee, sugar, and bananas has made the Guatemalan economy thrive.

Guatemala's Government

Main Idea After a series of dictators and military leaders and a long civil war, Guatemala became a democratic republic.

In 1821, along with three other Central American states, Guatemala gained independence from Spain. It broke from the other states in 1839 to become the nation we know today. Between 1821 and 1839, peasants in the mountains had staged revolts against the government. In 1837, an uneducated farmer, Rafael Carrera (rah fy EHL kuh REHR uh), led a revolt and emerged as a new leader for Guatemala. In 1854, he took over the presidency, which he held until his death in 1865.

After Carrera died, a steady flow of dictators filled Guatemala's presidency. In 1944, a set of military officers revolted and won control of the nation. One of these officers, Jacobo Arbenz Guzmán (YAH koh boh AHR bayns gooz MAHN), saw the need for social reforms in Guatemala. When he became president in 1951, Arbenz decided to develop a market economy and raise Guatemala's standard of living. Arbenz also redistributed 1.5 million acres of land to 100,000 families. As in Mexico, the goal of redistributing land was to give many more people access to land that they could farm.

VOCABULARY

departamento

Vocabulary Strategy

*de***part***amento*

The word **part** is in *departamento*. A state is a part of a country. A *departamento* is a Guatemalan state.

READING SKILL

Sequence As you read, use the chart to list the sequence of events that led to Guatemala's current form of government.

Jacobo Arbenz Guzmán Born in 1913, he was president of Guatemala from 1951 to 1954.

The United States Steps In

Serious opposition to Arbenz's redistribution program arose in the United States. Both United Fruit Company and the U.S. government owned much land in Guatemala. Arbenz established a policy of giving farmers any land that was not already being used. Eighty-five percent of UFCO's land in Guatemala was unused. Thus, UFCO was at great risk of losing that land.

The United States took action in 1954. Accusing Arbenz of supporting Communism—a political system that the United States believed threatened national safety—the U.S. Central Intelligence Agency (CIA) supported an invasion of Guatemala's capital, Guatemala City. A Guatemalan colonel, Carlos Castillo Armas (CAR lohs kah STEE yoh AR mahs), led the attack. A frightened Arbenz quickly gave in. A new government, backed by the United States, took control of Guatemala.

After 1954, Guatemala's government was ruled mainly by military officers. During much of this era, a civil war raged between government forces and rebels who opposed the government. Many people who expressed disagreement with government policy were murdered. More than 100,000 Guatemalans were killed or kidnapped before a peace agreement was reached in 1996.

Government's Three Branches

Guatemala's current constitution was written in 1985. It established the nation's government as a democratic republic with three branches. They are executive, legislative, and judicial.

A president heads Guatemala's executive branch. He or she is elected by the people every four years and may not be reelected. The president appoints a cabinet, or a group of advisers, to carry out the government's work.

Guatemala's legislative branch is called Congress. It has 113 members who are elected to four-year terms. Guatemala's Congress is unicameral, or has one chamber. Members of Congress may be reelected.

Guatemala's judicial branch has different levels of courts, somewhat like the United States. Unlike U.S. Supreme Court justices, whom the President appoints to serve for as long as they choose, Guatemala's Supreme Court judges are elected to five-year terms.

Guatemala is a federal republic, so the national government shares power with state and local governments. Governors head Guatemala's 22 states, called **departamentos** (deh pahr tah MEHN taws). The president appoints each of the governors. Mayors elected by popular vote oversee the city governments.

Economy and Culture

Main Idea Guatemala's economy is based on agriculture, some manufacturing, and tourism.

At the turn of the century, Guatemala had the largest gross domestic product (GDP) in Central America. It also had the fastest growing GDP in the region.

Guatemala's dominant industry is agriculture, which employs more than half of its work force. The nation's economy largely relies on the export of agricultural products. Since 1870, coffee has been Guatemala's leading export. Other agricultural exports include sugar, a spice called cardamom, and bananas.

Banana production began in the early 1900s, when U.S. companies built banana plantations in Guatemala. These fruit companies also developed railroads, ports, and communication systems in order to transport the bananas to foreign markets.

REVIEW Given the opposition to the new government after Guzmán's overthrow, do you think it continued social reforms?

Important Crop Millions of pounds of bananas are produced on Guatemala's many banana plantations.

National Palace Since the 1930s, Guatemala City's National Palace has housed the government's offices.

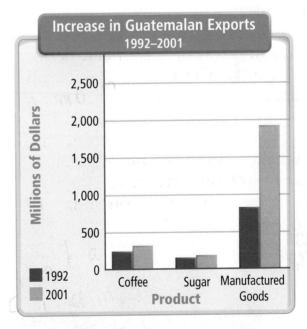

Increase in Guatemalan Exports
1992–2001

Millions of Dollars

- 1992
- 2001

Product: Coffee, Sugar, Manufactured Goods

Growing Economy Guatemala's growing textile and clothing industry is an important part of Guatemala's manufactured exports.
SKILL Read a Graph How much did the export of manufactured goods increase between 1992 and 2001?

Industry

Guatemala also relies on manufacturing to bring in money. Food, beverages, and clothing are among its manufactured goods. These goods are sold both within Guatemala and as exports to other countries.

While other Central American nations purchase many of Guatemala's manufactured goods, the United States purchases more of Guatemala's exports than any other country does.

In past years, Guatemala's economy has boomed with the sale of both textiles and clothing. Also, new nontraditional agricultural products, such as cut flowers and winter fruits, are selling quite well on the international market.

Tourism is also a strong industry in Guatemala. People are attracted to Guatemala's warm climate, lush vegetation, and beautiful culture. Tourists are also interested in the many ancient Maya ruins that they can visit in Guatemala.

Living in Guatemala

More than half of Guatemala's people are Maya. The rest are *ladinos*. In Guatemala, *ladinos* are either of mixed Maya and Spanish ancestry, or they are of Maya ancestry but no longer practice Maya ways or speak Maya languages. Like the ancient Maya, most of Guatemala's Maya today work in agriculture and live in small rural villages. They speak Maya languages, though many of them also speak Spanish. They wear traditional clothing, much of which they weave by hand.

Guatemalan children are required to attend school from the age of 7 through 13. However, about one-third do not. Most of these children live in rural areas that have no schools. Only 15 percent of Guatemalans attend high school.

Mayan Crafts This Guatemalan woman sells many traditional Maya handwoven cloths and rugs.

Modern Housing Many Guatemalans live in apartment complexes like these.

Daily life in Guatemala is a matter of extremes. On the one hand, rural Guatemalans have few of the comforts that North Americans take for granted, such as indoor bathrooms, running water, and electricity. Outside the cities, most homes are very small, and many have dirt floors.

On the other hand, urban Guatemalans live in modern homes, attend schools and universities, and go to theaters, museums, and restaurants. Many of the cultural influences in the cities, such as movies, restaurant chains, clothing styles, magazines, cars, and television programs, come from foreign countries. The cultural influences in the rural areas are much more local in origin.

REVIEW Does Guatemala have a single-product economy? Why or why not?

Lesson Summary

- In 1996, a peace agreement was reached after decades of dictators and civil war.

- Guatemala currently is a democratic republic with three branches of government.

- Guatemala's strong economy relies mostly on agriculture.

- Rural life is very different than urban. While rural Guatemalans live in poor conditions, urban dwellers enjoy modern conveniences and have higher levels of education.

Why It Matters . . .

Guatemala's increased stability has improved its relationship with its neighbors, such as the United States.

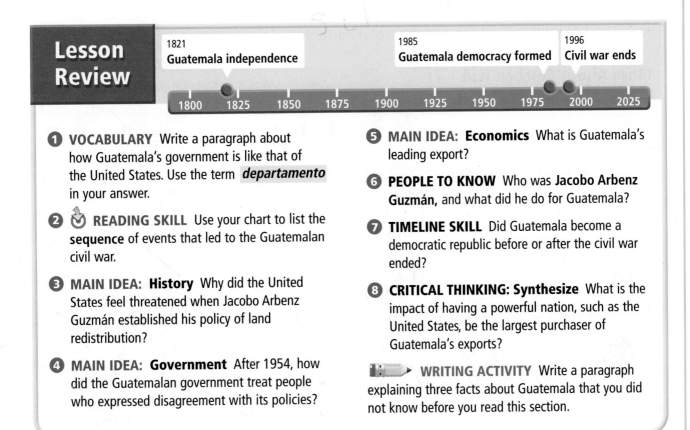

Lesson Review

1821 **Guatemala independence**

1985 **Guatemala democracy formed**

1996 **Civil war ends**

1800 1825 1850 1875 1900 1925 1950 1975 2000 2025

1. **VOCABULARY** Write a paragraph about how Guatemala's government is like that of the United States. Use the term *departamento* in your answer.

2. **READING SKILL** Use your chart to list the **sequence** of events that led to the Guatemalan civil war.

3. **MAIN IDEA: History** Why did the United States feel threatened when Jacobo Arbenz Guzmán established his policy of land redistribution?

4. **MAIN IDEA: Government** After 1954, how did the Guatemalan government treat people who expressed disagreement with its policies?

5. **MAIN IDEA: Economics** What is Guatemala's leading export?

6. **PEOPLE TO KNOW** Who was **Jacobo Arbenz Guzmán,** and what did he do for Guatemala?

7. **TIMELINE SKILL** Did Guatemala become a democratic republic before or after the civil war ended?

8. **CRITICAL THINKING: Synthesize** What is the impact of having a powerful nation, such as the United States, be the largest purchaser of Guatemala's exports?

WRITING ACTIVITY Write a paragraph explaining three facts about Guatemala that you did not know before you read this section.

EXPLORE THE MYSTERIES OF CHICHÉN ITZÁ

You are a movie director making a documentary film called *Mysteries of the Maya.* You are shooting your film at the ruins of Chichén Itzá (chee CHEHN ee TSAH), a city of stone deep in the jungle of Mexico's Yucatán Peninsula. Many things about the Maya culture are still a mystery. You want to inform your audience about Chichén Itzá, but you also want to make them feel the mood of the place—awesome and mysterious.

On these pages you will find challenges that you and your crew will face in making the documentary. Working with your crew, decide which one of these problems you will solve. Divide the work among crew members. Look for helpful information below. Keep in mind that you will present your solution to the class.

More About Chichén Itzá

- **City was founded by Maya** about sixth century A.D.

- The name, which means **"mouth of the wells of Itzá,"** refers to the site's two deep natural wells, or cenotes. The Itzá were a Maya group.

- One **cenote** supplied water. The other, about 200 feet across, was sacred to the rain god. Human sacrifices, mostly young people, were thrown into it, along with gold and jade ornaments.

- The Maya had many gods. **Chac** was the rain god. Kukulcan was pictured as a feathered serpent.

- Major buildings—**Pyramid of Kukulcan** (El Castillo), **Temple of the Warriors, Great Ball Court**—were built about A.D. 900–1200.

- City was abandoned about A.D. 1450.

Temple of Kukulcan/
El Castillo ("The Castle")

Four-sided pyramid represents the **Maya calendar** in several ways.

At the **spring and fall equinoxes**, sunlight falls on one staircase in a pattern that looks like a serpent creeping down the pyramid.

Four steep stairways, with 91 steps each, climb each side of the pyramid. Including the top platform, **the steps total 365.** There are 18 flat platforms—the number of months in the Maya calendar.

Activities

1. **THINK ABOUT IT** Draw a diagram of El Castillo and label its important parts.

2. **WRITE ABOUT IT** Imagine that you are at the Temple of Kukulcan during the spring or fall equinox. Write a diary entry about what you see.

223

Skillbuilder

Read a Political Map

Political maps show the boundaries of nations and other political areas, such as dependencies. Lines show these boundaries. Often political maps also show capitals and other cities.

The political map below shows the nations of Central America. Use the steps listed at right to identify the information shown on the map.

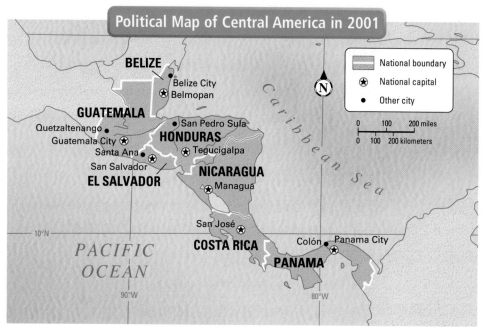

Political Map of Central America in 2001

BELIZE
• Belize City
⊛ Belmopan

GUATEMALA
Quetzaltenango •
Guatemala City ⊛
Santa Ana •
San Salvador •
EL SALVADOR

• San Pedro Sula
HONDURAS
⊛ Tegucigalpa

NICARAGUA
⊛ Managua

San José ⊛
COSTA RICA

Colón •
PANAMA
⊛ Panama City

Caribbean Sea

PACIFIC OCEAN

N

	National boundary
⊛	National capital
•	Other city

0   100   200 miles
0   100   200 kilometers

10°N

90°W   80°W

Learn the Skill

Step 1: Read the title. It tells you which region's political areas are being represented.

Step 2: Read the key. It tells you what each symbol stands for. This key shows boundaries between nations, national capitals, and other cities.

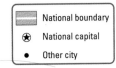

Step 3: Read the scale. It tells you how many miles or kilometers each inch represents.

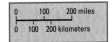

Practice the Skill

A chart can help you organize information given on maps. The chart below organizes information about the map you just studied.

Central America

Countries	Capitals	Other Cities
Guatemala	Guatemala City	Quetzaltenango
Belize	Belmopan	Belize City
Honduras	Tegucigalpa	San Pedro Sula
El Salvador	San Salvador	Santa Ana
Nicaragua	Managua	
Costa Rica	San José	
Panama	Panama City	Colón

Apply the Skill

Turn to Chapter 8, Lesson 1, "Establishing Independence." Study the political map of Central America and the Caribbean on page 201. Make a chart listing the nations of the Caribbean and the capitals that are shown on the map.

Visual Summary

1–4.  Write a description for each concept shown below.

| Establishing Independence | Economies and Cultures | Cuba Today | Guatemala Today |

Facts and Main Ideas

Answer each question below.

5. **History** Why did the United States want to build the Panama Canal?

6. **Economics** What risk did Caribbean islanders face by having single-product economies?

7. **Economics** What two crops did Central American economies depend on before the countries diversified their economies?

8. **Government** How did Cuba's relationship with the Soviet Union affect Cuba?

9. **Economics** Why did Jacobo Arbenz Guzmán's program of land redistribution upset leaders in the United States?

Vocabulary

Choose the correct word from the list below to complete each sentence.

dependency, p. 200
ladinos, p. 201
diversify, p. 207
Communism, p. 213

10. When people of the West Indies began to _____ they started raising pineapples and bananas.

11. Two-thirds of Central America's population today is made up of _____, people who have mixed Native American and European ancestry.

12. Puerto Rico is governed by the United States as a _____.

13. In 1961, Fidel Castro imposed _____ in Cuba.

CHAPTER SUMMARY TIMELINE

1821
Guatemala independence

1902
Cuba independence

1903
Panama independence

1961
Cuba becomes Communist

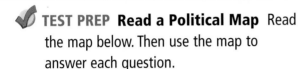

1800   1825   1850   1875   1900   1925   1950   1975

Apply Skills

 TEST PREP **Read a Political Map** Read the map below. Then use the map to answer each question.

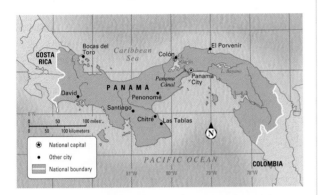

14. What political region is represented on the map?

   A. Panama

   B. Costa Rica

   C. Caribbean Sea

   D. Las Tablas

15. What city is the capital of this country?

   A. David

   B. Chitré

   C. Panama City

   D. Panama Canal

16. What two other countries are shown on this map?

   A. Panama and Colombia

   B. Panama and Costa Rica

   C. Costa Rica and the Caribbean

   D. Costa Rica and Colombia

Critical Thinking

 TEST PREP Write a short paragraph to answer each question below.

17. **Draw Conclusions** How do you think Fidel Castro's control of newspapers and television and radio stations has helped keep him in power?

18. **Contrast** Contrast the fates on Native Americans in the Caribbean Islands and in Central America after Europeans took over.

Timeline

Use the Chapter Summary Timeline above to answer the question.

19. How long after Cuba won independence from Spain did Panama gain independence?

Activities

 SCIENCE ACTIVITY The Caribbean Islands are prone to hurricanes. Working in pairs, hypothesize why hurricanes develop and travel through this region. Then use library and Internet resources to find the answer. Write your hypothesis and explanation.

 WRITING ACTIVITY Imagine you have traveled to one of the Caribbean Islands. Write a letter to a friend describing what you saw.

 Technology

Writing Process Tips
Get help with your letter at
www.eduplace.com/kids/hmss05/

Technology

e • **glossary**
e • **word games**
www.eduplace.com/kids/hmss05/

Vocabulary Preview

Pan-American

The area relating to all of the Americas—North, South, and Central—is **Pan-American.** The Organization of American States (OAS) was formed to discuss Pan-American issues.

page 233

urbanization

When people move from the countryside to cities, it is called **urbanization.** Urbanization in South America is caused by the promise of jobs, schools, and health services offered in cities.

page 238

Chapter Timeline

1822
Brazil independence

1824
Bolívar frees Peru from Spanish

1800   1820   1840   1860   1880

SOUTH AMERICA

Reading Strategy

Monitor and Clarify Use this strategy as you read to check your understanding of the text.

Stop to check that you understand what you are reading. Reread if you need to.

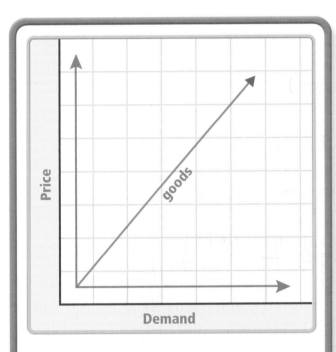

inflation

When goods and services are in great demand, producers can charge much higher prices for them, causing **inflation.** In Brazil and other parts of the world, many people can no longer afford basic goods and services, because of inflation. **page 243**

oasis

A fertile region in a desert, watered by a spring, stream, or well, is an **oasis.** Most of the cities in Peru are located in or near an oasis. **page 247**

1948
OAS formed

1985
Brazil democracy restored

| 1900 | 1920 | 1940 | 1960 | 1980 |

Establishing Independence

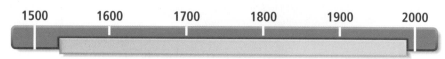

VOCABULARY

Pan-American

Vocabulary Strategy

Pan-American

Pan means "all." **Pan-American** means "all of the Americas."

READING SKILL

Cause and Effect Note the effects that colonization had on the native people of South America.

Build on What You Know Your class is made up of many individual students, but you share similarities. Classmates may be born in the same year, live in the same neighborhood, or have the same sixth-grade teacher. South America is a big continent of many countries, but they share similar histories.

Colonialism and Independence

Main Idea In the 1820s, after nearly 300 years of European rule and exploitation, most of South America gained independence.

In 1531, Spanish explorer Francisco Pizarro landed on the coast of what is now the South American country of Peru. He had with him horses, guns, cannons, and about 200 soldiers. His forces began the long climb up into the Andes Mountains, following the Inca road that led to the city of Cajamarca (kah hah MAHR kah).

When Pizarro first encountered the Inca, he found a kingdom weakened by a bitter civil war. Pizarro quickly captured and executed the Inca ruler, and the Inca Empire soon fell under Spanish control.

Meanwhile, Portugal had claimed what is now Brazil, and so the Portuguese began to settle the region. However, dense rain forests prevented much exploration of the region's interior. The Portuguese therefore built most of their settlements along the Atlantic Coast.

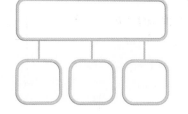

Francisco Pizarro He conquered the Inca Empire, using his superior military forces.

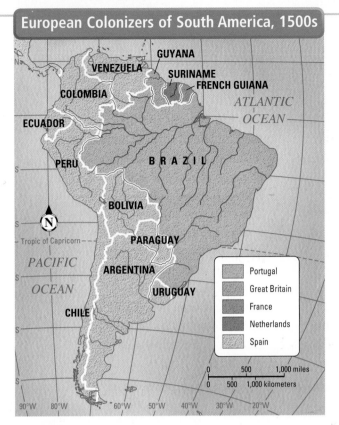

European Colonizers of South America, 1500s

GUYANA
VENEZUELA
SURINAME
FRENCH GUIANA
COLOMBIA
ECUADOR
ATLANTIC OCEAN
PERU
B R A Z I L
BOLIVIA
PARAGUAY
Tropic of Capricorn
PACIFIC OCEAN
ARGENTINA
URUGUAY
CHILE

	Portugal
	Great Britain
	France
	Netherlands
	Spain

0   500   1,000 miles
0   500   1,000 kilometers

90°W 80°W 60°W 50°W 40°W 30°W 20°W

Colonies Many different European nations established colonies in South America.

SKILL **Interpret a Map** What countries, other than Spain and Portugal, established colonies in South America?

Colonial South America

Many Spanish and Portuguese settlers soon made their way to South America. As happened throughout the New World, the arrival of the Europeans led to the deaths of many Native Americans. Millions died from disease or overwork. As the Native American population shrank, the Europeans imported enslaved Africans to work mainly on the large sugar cane plantations in Brazil.

For nearly 300 years, the Europeans ruled much of South America. Spain and Portugal between them claimed most of the land. Ships loaded with South American silver, gold, and sugar regularly sailed to these two countries. Both, especially Spain, grew enormously wealthy from their South American colonies.

Independence

In the early 1800s, Spain and Portugal were still taking most of the wealth out of the South American colonies. People of Spanish or Portuguese descent born in South America wanted to share in the political and economic power. They were encouraged by the results of the American Revolution in 1776 and the French Revolution in 1789.

At the same time, the *mestizos* and mulattos wanted to bring about change because they were often treated no better than slaves. South Americans soon decided to fight for independence.

Beginning in 1810, two generals led a series of wars for independence. One was Simón Bolívar (see MOHN boh LEE var), whose leadership freed the northern parts of South America. The other was José de San Martín (san mahr TEEN). He was responsible for defeating Spanish forces in the south. By 1825, nearly all of Spanish South America was independent.

Meanwhile, Brazil gained its independence without a major war. When the French general Napoleon Bonaparte invaded Portugal in 1807, the Portuguese royal family fled to Brazil.

After Napoleon's later defeat, the Portuguese king returned to Portugal in 1821. He left his son Pedro to be regent of Brazil. When the Brazilians demanded their freedom in 1822, Pedro agreed. Brazil then named Pedro its emperor.

REVIEW How did Brazil gain its independence differently from other South American countries?

Biography

Simón Bolívar Simón Bolívar (shown at left) was born in Caracas, Venezuela, in 1783. As a teenager, Bolívar lived in Spain. He was influenced by the European Enlightenment and the philosophers Voltaire and Rousseau. A dream of freedom and independence for Hispanic America stirred Bolívar's soul, and he returned to South America.

Bolívar became a leader of the revolution in Venezuela in 1810. His clever military tactics led to victory over the Spanish and the creation of the republic of Gran Colombia, which included what are now Colombia, Panama, Venezuela, and Ecuador. Bolívar became president of Gran Colombia and continued fighting farther south. Victorious there, he soon became the president of Peru and Bolivia, which was named for him. Because of his role in gaining South American independence from Spain, Bolívar is often called "the Liberator." He died in Colombia in 1830.

South America Today

Main Idea Following independence, many South American governments went through upheavals but now most countries are democratic.

South America's new independence did not lead to a stable, fair society, as revolutionary leaders had hoped. These leaders had little experience in government. Many of them wanted to establish constitutions that set limits on the powers of government. Doing this would allow citizens to participate in government.

However, wealthy citizens and former Spanish officials in South America wanted to keep their property and power. They did not want all citizens to have a say in government. To maintain order and to protect their interests, the powerful often gave control of the government to the military. This frequently resulted in unlimited governments, in which one person or one group held total power. In other cases, military leaders used their armies to take over limited governments in South America. By the 1990s, however, the majority of governments in South America were democratic.

Independence South American countries gained independence from European nations.
SKILL **Read a Timeline** For each country on the timeline, what event occurred on the date given?

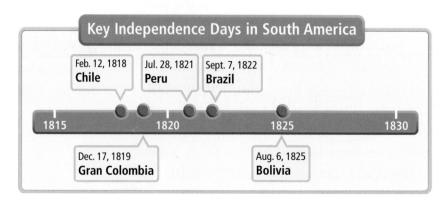

Key Independence Days in South America

| Feb. 12, 1818 **Chile** | Jul. 28, 1821 **Peru** | Sept. 7, 1822 **Brazil** |

| Dec. 17, 1819 **Gran Colombia** | Aug. 6, 1825 **Bolivia** |

1815 — 1820 — 1825 — 1830

Organization of American States An OAS official and a U.S. government official are shown here using a map of South America to discuss Pan-American issues.

South American Cooperation

Simón Bolívar tried to create a united South America—a nation of states like the United States. Although he was not successful, in the late 1800s the U.S. government began encouraging Pan-American unity. *Pan* means "all," so **Pan-American** means "all of the Americas."

In 1948, Latin American nations joined with the United States to form the Organization of American States (OAS). The OAS promotes economic cooperation, social justice, and the equality of all people. It encourages democracy within its member nations. For example, OAS officials observe elections to make sure they are run fairly. The organization also helps settle conflicts among its members. In 1979, the OAS established a special court to protect human rights in its member countries.

The countries of South America will probably never join together in the way that Simón Bolívar envisioned. They are, however, working together to achieve justice and a better life for all their people.

The People of South America

Until the 1800s, immigrants to South America came mostly from Spain and Portugal. During the 1880s, South America attracted many more European immigrants.

The new immigrants helped build South America's economy by establishing a variety of industries. Also, as all immigrants do, they brought their own customs to their new home. For example, the British introduced the game of football (which people in the United States call soccer), and it quickly became a popular sport across South America.

There are many ethnic groups within South America's population—Native Americans, descendants of Europeans or of enslaved Africans, and people of mixed ancestry. Some of these groups live in particular regions, while others are more widespread.

REVIEW Why do you think the United States wanted to establish Pan-American ties?

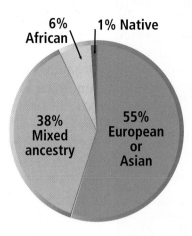

A Mix of Peoples Brazil is made up of people from many different ethnic backgrounds.

Today, many Africans live in the tropical lowlands where their enslaved ancestors worked. Native Americans make up a large part of the population in the Andean nations of Peru, Bolivia, and Ecuador. The majority of South Americans, however, are of mixed ancestry.

Lesson Summary

- Beginning in 1531 and continuing for nearly 300 years, Europeans ruled much of South America.

- A series of civil wars gained South America's freedom from Spain. Brazil peacefully obtained freedom from Portugal.

- In 1948, Latin American nations joined with the United States to form the Organization of American States.

- The majority of South Americans are either *mestizos* or mulattos, though immigrants have also had an influence on culture.

Why It Matters . . .

Because the United States has close economic and political ties with South America, it is important to understand the history of the region.

Lesson Review

1822 — **Brazil gains independence**

1948 — **OAS formed**

1820 · 1840 · 1860 · 1880 · 1900 · 1920 · 1940 · 1950

1. **VOCABULARY** Write a paragraph explaining how **Pan-American** nations are working together.

2. **READING SKILL** List some **effects** of colonization on the lives of the native people of South America.

3. **MAIN IDEA: Economics** From what South American products did European nations profit?

4. **MAIN IDEA: Geography** How has South America's population changed since the 1500s?

5. **MAIN IDEA: Government** What challenges have many South American governments faced in recent years?

6. **PEOPLE TO KNOW** Who was **Simón Bolívar** and what was his dream for South America?

7. **TIMELINE SKILL** How many years after Brazil gained independence was the OAS formed?

8. **CRITICAL THINKING: Synthesize** What challenges do you think South Americans faced in their fights for independence?

HANDS ON

ART ACTIVITY Imagine you work for the Organization of American States. Make a poster that highlights the benefits the organization offers its members.

Economies and Cultures

Build on What You Know Imagine that you could only trade sports cards with one other person. You would be limited in the number and kinds of cards you could trade. The countries of North and South America used to be limited in trade too. Now, they have formed a trade agreement.

Geography and Trade in South America

Main Idea Many South American nations face similar challenges while also facing similar possibilities.

Many South American nations have found that working together results in greater economic opportunity. Partly this is because they face similar challenges and possibilities. A common factor influencing many of the region's economies is geography. South America's physical geography presents the region with both transportation barriers and transportation corridors.

Amazon River The longest river in South America, the Amazon is an important transportation corridor for the South American economy.

235

Barriers and Corridors

South America's transportation barriers have interfered with trade and contacts with other cultures. For example, Portuguese explorers had trouble penetrating the dense Amazon rain forest. Because of this, they built their settlements along the coastline. Today, rain forests and rugged regions such as the Andes still prevent easy travel across the continent.

South America also has transportation corridors, such as the Amazon River system. Before the Europeans arrived, Native Americans canoed along the Amazon and its tributaries. Today, ocean-going vessels enter the Amazon system on Brazil's north coast. They carry goods such as food, clothing, and tools. They bring back lumber, rubber, animal skins, Brazil nuts, and other raw materials for shipment overseas.

Natural Resources

The rich natural resources of South America include abundant minerals and fertile land. However, few South American countries have fully developed their natural resources.

Under the surface of South America's land lie many precious minerals—including gold, iron ore, lead, petroleum, tin, and copper. Many South American countries mine these minerals for export. For example, Chile mostly mines copper, Bolivia has a great amount of tin, and Colombia supplies the world with emeralds.

Copper Mines, such as this one in Chile, provide minerals for export.

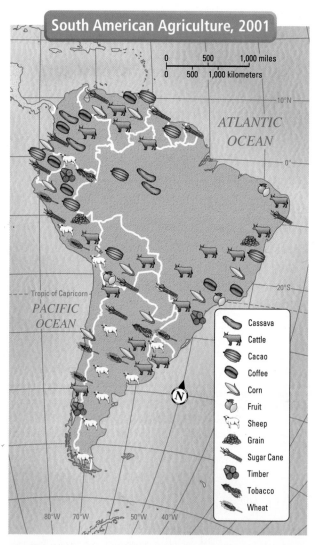

South American Agriculture, 2001

0 500 1,000 miles	
0 500 1,000 kilometers	

ATLANTIC OCEAN

Tropic of Capricorn
PACIFIC OCEAN

10°N
0°
20°S

Cassava
Cattle
Cacao
Coffee
Corn
Fruit
Sheep
Grain
Sugar Cane
Timber
Tobacco
Wheat

80°W   70°W   50°W   40°W

Agriculture South America produces many crops and livestock. **SKILL** **Interpret a Map** Name an agricultural product from southern South America.

Farming and Industry

South America is not only rich in mineral resources, but it also boasts some of the largest farms in the world. These farms produce goods for export, such as beef, grain, sugar, wool, bananas, and coffee.

Most of South America's farms, however, are small. On these farms, individual farmers struggle to grow even enough food to feed their families. Many poor farmers have given up and moved to cities, hoping to find jobs there.

The most important South American industrial countries are Venezuela, Chile, Argentina, and Brazil. In fact, Brazil is one of the most important industrial nations in the world. It manufactures enough cars and trucks to supply the entire continent. Brazil also manufactures computers, televisions, and airplanes. In other South American countries, manufactured goods include shoes, furniture, beverages, and textiles.

Lack of funding prevents many South American countries from developing manufacturing. To improve their economies, countries may cooperate economically. For example, in 1994, the heads of 34 North and South American countries met in Miami, Florida, at the first Summit of the Americas.

There, they agreed to create the huge Free-Trade Zone of the Americas, which would include almost every country in North and South America by the year 2005. In a **free-trade zone,** people and goods move across borders without being taxed. Many South Americans are confident that the Free-Trade Zone of the Americas will lead to greater prosperity in the region.

Country	Literacy Rate	Life Expectancy
Argentina	96%	75 years
Bolivia	83%	64 years
Brazil	85%	63 years
Chile	95%	76 years
Colombia	91%	70 years
Ecuador	90%	71 years
Guyana	98%	64 years
Paraguay	92%	74 years
Peru	89%	70 years
Suriname	93%	71 years
Uruguay	97%	75 years
Venezuela	91%	73 years

Economic Indicators These statistics indicate how well a country's economy is doing.

SKILL **Interpret a Chart** Which nation has the highest literacy rate? Which has the lowest? What is the life expectancy in Brazil?

Economic cooperation among nations can be challenging if some economies are strong and others are weak. Differences can be measured by **economic indicators,** statistics that show how a country's economy is doing. The literacy rate shows the percentage of a country's people who can read and write. Life expectancy, or the average age to which people in a country live, gives clues about a country's health care and nutrition.

REVIEW How do South America's small farms and large farms differ?

Daily Life in South America

Main Idea South America is a region of contrasts, with wealthy and middle-class people in urban areas and extreme poverty in slums and rural areas.

South America is home to both urban and rural areas. Many of the urban areas are enormous. City populations include some very wealthy people and many middle-class people who work in government or business. Millions more, however, live in extreme poverty.

For the past 50 years or so, South America has experienced major **urbanization,** meaning that many people have moved from the countryside to cities. Multiple factors caused this movement to occur.

One factor is the growth of manufacturing jobs in cities. Because many rural people lived in poverty, without enough land to support their families, the promise of jobs, schools, and health services drew them to cities.

Today, several South American cities rank among the largest in the world. In 2000, São Paulo (sown POW loh) in Brazil was home to nearly 18 million people, and Buenos Aires (BWAY nos AIR ays) in Argentina had nearly 13 million people. Houses cannot be built quickly enough to keep up with the growing number of people. Large slums surround South America's biggest cities. In these areas, people live in shacks of cardboard, wood scraps, or tin. They often have no electricity or running water.

Spotlight on CULTURE

Gabriela Mistral Chilean poet Gabriela Mistral (1889–1957; shown at left) used poetry to express her deep feelings for the people and land of South America, as in this poem, "Chilean Earth." She particularly loved children, and their rhymes and lullabies influenced her writing.

South Americans and people around the world greatly admire Mistral's work. As the first South American to win the Nobel Prize in Literature, she became a symbol of the hopes and dreams of a whole continent.

CRITICAL THINKING Draw Conclusions What about Chile does Mistral celebrate in this poem?

Infer Why do you think Mistral's poetry inspired many South Americans?

Chilean Earth

We dance on Chilean earth
more beautiful than Lia and Raquel:
the earth that kneads men,
their lips and hearts without bitterness.

The land most green with orchards,
the land most blond with grain,
the land most red with grapevines,
how sweetly it brushes our feet!

Its dust molded our cheeks,
Its rivers, our laughter,
and it kisses our feet with a melody
that makes my mother sigh.
For the sake of its beauty,
we want to light up the fields with song.
It is free,
and for freedom we want
to bathe its face in music.

Tomorrow we will open its rocks;
we will create vineyards and orchards;
tomorrow we will exalt its people.
Today we need only to dance!

Despite the terrible poverty of millions, the arts in South America have thrived. The region's literature is admired throughout the world. The Nobel Prize in Literature has been given to three South Americans—Chilean poets Gabriela Mistral (mih STRAHL) and Pablo Neruda (neh ROO duh), and Colombian novelist Gabriel García Márquez (gar SEE uh MAR kez). Many South American poets and writers express their unique cultural heritage in their work. South American novelists also founded a literary style, magical realism, in which everyday reality mixes with fantasy.

Music, too, is an important part of the culture of South America. The traditional music of the Andean regions, called *huayno*, is played on flutes and drums. Some forms of music, such as salsa, have African roots. As South Americans move to urban areas, musicians there are combining traditional musical styles with rock and other popular types of music from Europe and North America.

REVIEW How has urbanization affected South American music?

Lesson Summary

Why It Matters . . .

Cultural elements from South America are popular around the world.

Lesson Review

❶ **VOCABULARY** Use **free-trade zone** and **economic indicator** in a paragraph about economic cooperation.

❷ **READING SKILL** What positive **conclusions** can you draw about South America's economy? What negative **conclusions**?

❸ **MAIN IDEA: Geography** Name one geographic feature that is a transportation barrier and one that is a transportation corridor.

❹ **MAIN IDEA: Economics** List five of South America's important natural resources.

❺ **MAIN IDEA: Culture** Name the three South Americans who have won the Nobel Prize in Literature.

❻ **PLACES TO KNOW** What city in Brazil grew by millions of people because of job opportunities there?

❼ **CRITICAL THINKING: Analyze** What challenges do South American countries face in building strong economies?

HANDS ON **MAP ACTIVITY** Look at the physical map of South America on page 144. Locate major mountains and rivers. Write a short description of a way to overcome one of South America's transportation barriers.

Trading Partners

Have you ever wondered where the food you eat comes from? Those grapes you are about to eat might be from Chile. The coffee your parents drink might be from Colombia. More and more goods are traded between the United States and South America. In addition, South American nations are forming trade groups to increase trade among themselves. Members of a trade group create a free-trade zone. They do not tax goods imported from other member nations, making those goods cheaper. The main exports of one MERCOSUR nation can fill the import needs of another member of the trade group. Such economic cooperation is helping South American nations develop their economies and improve the lives of their people.

MERCOSUR is a South American trade group formed by Brazil, Argentina, Chile, Uruguay, and Paraguay.

The Southern Common Market

BRAZIL
Brasilia
PARAGUAY
Asunción
CHILE
Santiago   Buenos   URUGUAY
            Aires   Montevideo
ARGENTINA

km 0   500   1000
mi 0   500   1000

⊛   National capital
—   National border

Balance of Trade

Country	Value of Exports	Value of Imports
Argentina	$25.3 billion	$9 billion
Brazil	$59.4 billion	$46.2 billion
Chile	$17.8 billion	$15.6 billion
Paraguay	$2 billion	$2.4 billion
Uruguay	$2.1 billion	$1.9 billion

MERCOSUR These nations generally have a favorable balance of trade. That means they export more than they import.

Cattle Ranching The ranches of this region produce beef products that are in demand worldwide.

Shipping Goods The rain forests and mountains of South America can be a barrier to overland trade between its nations. Because of this, ships carry most of South America's traded goods.

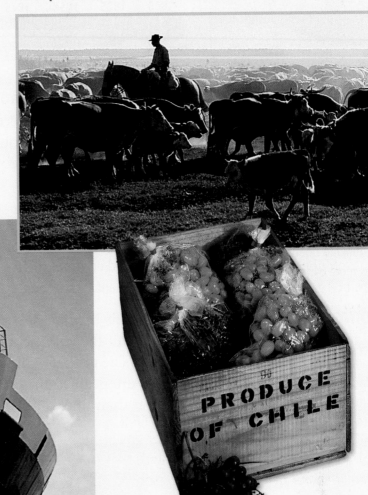

Chilean Fruit Fruit exports are one of the ways Chile has diversified its economy. The fruit is shipped by sea to North America.

Activities

1. **SHOW IT** Trace with your finger on the map the flow of traded goods between Chile, Brazil, and Argentina. Tell what kind of goods are traded to and from these nations.

2. **SPEAK ABOUT IT** Write a short speech explaining why joining a trade group and free-trade zone can help a South American nation.

241

Brazil Today

| 1800 | 1825 | 1850 | 1875 | 1900 | 1925 | 1950 | 1975 | 2000 |

1822–2000

VOCABULARY

inflation

Vocabulary Strategy

inflation

When you **inflate** a balloon, you make it bigger. **Inflation** means that prices grow bigger, making goods and services more expensive.

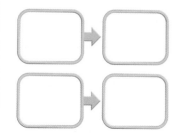 **READING SKILL**

Problem and Solution As you read, list problems that Brazil faced. Look for the government's solution to each problem.

Build on What You Know You know that the United States has the strongest economy in North America. In South America, Brazil not only has the strongest economy, but it is also the largest country, with the most people.

Brazil: Regional Leader

Main Idea As the largest country in South America, Brazil has achieved economic success while facing challenges such as unemployment.

Brazil is the largest country in South America, covering almost half the continent. Its population of 172 million is close in size to the combined population of all the other South American countries. Brazil's gross domestic product is larger than that of any other South American country.

São Paulo This coastal city is one of Brazil's most populated and important areas.

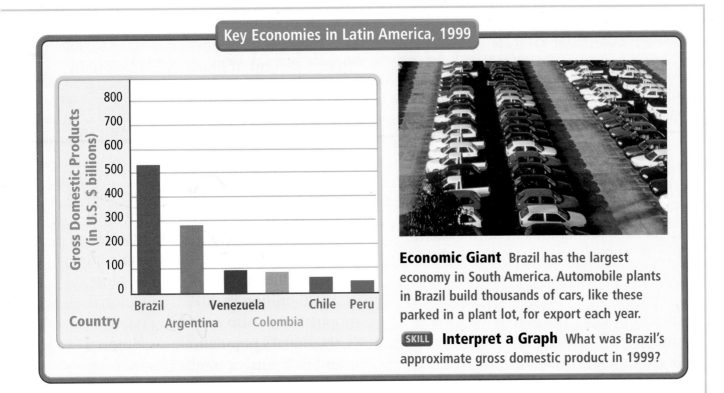

Gross Domestic Products (in U.S. $ billions)

800
700
600
500
400
300
200
100
0

Country: Brazil, Argentina, Venezuela, Colombia, Chile, Peru

Economic Giant Brazil has the largest economy in South America. Automobile plants in Brazil build thousands of cars, like these parked in a plant lot, for export each year.

SKILL Interpret a Graph What was Brazil's approximate gross domestic product in 1999?

Government and Economy

After gaining independence from Portugal in 1822, Brazil was ruled by a series of emperors. In 1889, Brazil became a constitutional republic. Beginning in 1930, a series of dictators and military leaders ruled Brazil. Democratic government was restored in 1985. Power today is shared by a president, an elected congress, and a court system.

Brazil has the largest economy in South America. The country's gross domestic product is nearly twice that of Argentina, which is the next largest economy in South America.

In Brazil, the government controls or influences certain industries to help the economy grow. For example, in the 1950s, the government promoted the building of automobile factories to cut down on the number of cars imported into Brazil. By the late 1980s, Brazil was building more than 1 million vehicles a year, enough to export some to other countries.

In the world, Brazil is second only to the United States in exporting crops. When it comes to coffee, Brazil produces more than any other country in the world. Brazil is also a leading producer of oranges, bananas, and corn.

Even though Brazil's economy is the strongest in Latin America, many Brazilians are unemployed. Unemployment results when not enough businesses hire workers, or when workers do not have the education or training they need for the jobs available. Even those who have jobs may face hard times, especially due to inflation. **Inflation** is a general increase in the price of goods or services. It occurs when goods or services are in great demand, allowing producers to charge higher prices for them. The combination of unemployment and inflation has led to much poverty in Brazil.

REVIEW What are the two biggest challenges to Brazil's economy?

The People of Brazil

Main Idea Brazil is a blend of European and African cultures that are reflected in Brazil's music, food, and religions.

When explorers from Portugal arrived in Brazil in 1500, as many as 5 million Native Americans lived there. During the 1500s, the Portuguese established large sugar cane plantations in northeastern Brazil. At first, they enslaved Native Americans to work on the plantations. Soon, however, many Native Americans died of disease. The plantation owners then turned to Africa for labor. Eventually, Brazil brought over more enslaved Africans than any other North or South American country.

Today, Native Americans make up less than 1 percent of Brazil's population. In northeastern Brazil, most people have African ancestors, while many people in Brazil have both European and African ancestors.

Today, four out of five Brazilians live in cities. Brazil's two largest cities, São Paulo and Rio de Janeiro, are growing quickly. In 2000, São Paulo's population was close to 18 million. At the rate it is growing, the population will be more than 20 million in 2015. The national population is also increasing rapidly. In 1999, Brazil's population was almost 172 million. If current trends continue, by 2025 it could reach 210 million.

Because of much crowding along Brazil's Atlantic coast, the government wanted people to move into Brazil's vast interior. In 1956, it decided to create a new capital, Brasília, 600 miles inland. Now, like every other city in Brazil, Brasília has problems with overcrowding.

Brazil's lively culture is a blend of influences from the many cultural groups that have come to Brazil over the centuries. Brazil's music, foods, and religious practices reflect that blend.

Brazilian languages, religions, and musical traditions all reflect the multiple roots of Brazil's culture. For example, Brazil's official language is Portuguese. Included in Brazilian Portuguese, however, are many words from Tupi-Guarani (TOO pee-gwah ruh NEE), the language of Native Americans from the interior of northern Brazil.

Overcrowding The rapid growth of Brazil's cities, such as São Paulo, has put many stresses on the nation.

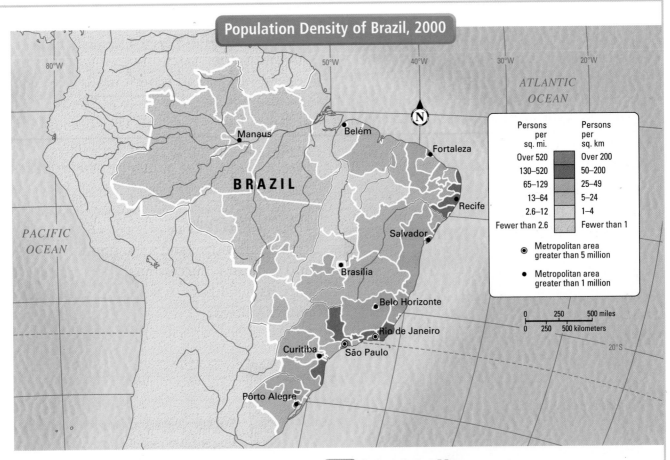

Population Density of Brazil, 2000

Persons per sq. mi.	Persons per sq. km
Over 520	Over 200
130–520	50–200
65–129	25–49
13–64	5–24
2.6–12	1–4
Fewer than 2.6	Fewer than 1

◉ Metropolitan area greater than 5 million

● Metropolitan area greater than 1 million

Population Most people in Brazil live on the coast. **SKILL Interpret a Map**
How many cities in Brazil have populations greater than 5 million? Which parts
of Brazil are nearly unpopulated?

Religion and Holidays

Most Brazilians are Catholic, the religion brought to Brazil by the Portuguese. However, the number of non-Catholics is increasing. In 1940, only 5 percent of Brazilians were not Catholic. In 2000, non-Catholics had risen to 20 percent of the population because immigrants and missionaries had brought other religions to Brazil. Even so, more Catholics live in Brazil than in any other country in the world.

African religions thrive in Brazil. For example, many people worship the African sea goddess Iemanjá. African influences can also be heard in Brazilian music.

Carnival Mask Dancers often wear masks like the one shown here.

A Brazilian holiday called Carnival highlights the country's cultural diversity. This famous festival occurs during the four days before Lent. Carnival includes huge parades and street parties. In Rio de Janeiro, groups of African Brazilians perform samba dances. The dancers wear elaborate costumes of feathers and brightly colored, sparkling cloth.

REVIEW What problems can rapid population growth cause?

245

Brazilian football, called soccer in the United States, is a sport that most of the country gets excited about. Brazil is often a finalist in the World Cup, the sport's world championship competition. Brazilians enjoy watching professional football; millions of them also enjoy playing the game.

Lesson Summary

Brazil dominates South America, both geographically and economically. Though it is the strongest economy in South America, it has problems with unemployment, inflation, and overcrowding. Brazilian culture is a mixture of European and African cultures.

Why It Matters . . .

Brazil's huge land area, population, and economic success enable it to influence its neighbors in South America and North America.

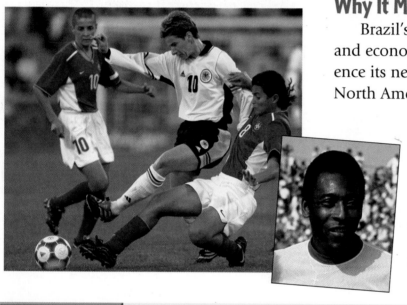

Soccer Players on Brazil's women's soccer team move in for the win. Brazilian soccer hero Pelé (PAY lay) smiles for the crowd.

Lesson Review

1822 Brazil independence	1930 dictators gain power	1985 democracy restored

1800 1825 1850 1875 1900 1925 1950 1975 2000

1 **VOCABULARY** Use inflation in a short paragraph that explains the economic hardships it causes.

2 **READING SKILL** Look at the Brazilian government's **solution** to the problem of overcrowding. Did this solution solve the problem?

3 **MAIN IDEA: Economics** Why can Brazil be described as an "economic giant"?

4 **MAIN IDEA: Geography** Where do most people in Brazil live today?

5 **MAIN IDEA: Government** Why did the Brazilian government move the capital inland to Brasília?

6 **MAIN IDEA: Culture** What is the largest religious group in Brazil?

7 **TIMELINE SKILL** How many years after Brazil gained independence from Portugal did it form a democratic government?

8 **CRITICAL THINKING: Draw Conclusions** Why do you think Brazil's economy is the most successful in South America?

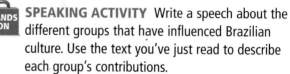

SPEAKING ACTIVITY Write a speech about the different groups that have influenced Brazilian culture. Use the text you've just read to describe each group's contributions.

Peru Today

1821–2000

Build on What You Know You know that living in a desert, a rain forest, or very high mountains makes it hard for people to earn a living. In Peru, all three of these landforms make life difficult.

The Land of Peru

Main Idea Peru's physical features make agriculture and mining difficult.

Though Peru is rich in resources, its physical geography also presents problems. Three types of landforms exist in Peru: mountains, rain forest, and desert. Each type has its own special characteristics, but all three are transportation barriers rather than transportation corridors. Traveling from one part of Peru to another is not easy.

Look at the map on the next page. You can see that the Andes Mountains run the entire length of Peru, dividing the country in two. In places, the mountains are so steep that they are practically impassable. Notice that rain forests are located off the eastern slopes of the Andes. Now look to the west of the Andes, along the Pacific coast. Here the northern stretches of Chile's Atacama Desert reach into Peru. Most of Peru's cities, large farms, and factories are located in the desert, in or near oases. An **oasis** is a fertile region in a desert that formed around a river or spring.

▶ **VOCABULARY**

oasis
guerrilla warfare

Vocabulary Strategy

| oasis

A synonym for **oasis** is **refuge**. An oasis is a refuge in the desert where there are water and plants.

◎ **READING SKILL**
Compare and Contrast As you read, complete the chart to compare and contrast life in a Peruvian city with life in rural Peru.

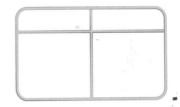

Cool Desert Because of cold currents in the Pacific Ocean, Peru's desert has an average summer temperature of only 73°F.

The Economy of Peru

Peru has many resources, but it also has many problems. The country's harsh geography hinders its economy. For example, the cold, rocky highlands and the cool, dry desert cover so much area that there is not enough farm land to feed the growing population.

Like many other countries, Peru must import certain foods. These include grains, vegetable oils, and some meats, many of which come from the United States. However, Peruvians do grow sugar cane, cotton, and coffee for export. Southern Peru has a large dairy industry. Meats from cattle, sheep, alpaca, and goats are also processed and distributed within the country.

The cold waters along the Pacific Coast are fine fishing grounds. Sardines and anchovies are the most important fish in the Peruvian catch. They are dried and made into fishmeal, which is sold as feed for livestock throughout the world.

Peru is an important supplier of metals such as silver, copper, and bismuth. It also contains oil and gold deposits. However, the richest deposits of minerals in the country exist in dense rain forests and at elevations of over 12,000 feet. Because it is difficult to mine in these locations, Peru's mineral resources have not brought the country the great wealth that they could.

Physical Features of Peru

Gulf of Guayaquil

Amazon R.

rainforest

ANDES MOUNTAINS

Elevation

13,100 ft.	(4,000 m)
6,600 ft.	(2,000 m)
1,600 ft.	(500 m)
650 ft.	(200 m)
0 ft.	(0 m)

Below sea level

N

Lake Titicaca

0   250   500 miles
0 250   500 kilometers

84°W   80°W   76°W   72°W

Peru The majestic Andes Mountains form the backbone of South America.

SKILL **Interpret a Map** Through which of Peru's landforms does the Amazon River run? What is the highest elevation shown on this map?

Farming Cotton is an important export. These cotton plants grow in Ica, Peru.

Fishing Tons of anchovies are caught off the coast of Peru each year.

Peru's Government and People

Main Idea Peru has had problems with unstable governments and overcrowding in cities.

Peru declared itself independent of Spain in 1821. The nation was not completely free, however, until December of 1824, when Simón Bolívar finally drove out the Spanish. Following independence, Peru's military leaders began fighting one another. Struggles between military and civilian leaders continued until late in the 20th century.

Perhaps the greatest struggle in Peru's modern history arose in the early 1980s. At that time, Communist groups rose up to fight against the democracy that they felt was failing Peru. The most powerful of these groups was Sendero Luminoso (sen DAIR oh loo mih NOH soh), or Shining Path.

Sendero Luminoso fought for changes using **guerrilla warfare,** or nontraditional military tactics characterized by small groups using surprise attacks. The military responded, and many citizens died in the crossfire. Until Sendero Luminoso's leader, Abimael Guzmán Reynoso (ah bee mah EHL gooz MAHN ray NAW saw), was imprisoned in 1992, the civil war continued.

The 1990s did not bring better times to Peru. From 1990 to 2000, Alberto Fujimori, the son of Japanese immigrants, was president. At first, many of Peru's poor rural people supported him. By May 2000, however, he and his officials were accused of corruption. Many resignations followed.

In November, Fujimori abandoned the presidency and fled to Japan. The new president, Alejandro Toledo (al eh HAHN droh toh LAY doh), faced the challenge of trying to win back the trust of Peruvians after the government scandals.

REVIEW What are Peru's three most important industries?

Mining A freight train transports copper ingots through Peru.

Alpaca Related to the llama, the alpaca is prized for its fine, long wool used to make clothing.

Quechua Like this mother and daughter, many Quechua live in the Andes of Ecuador, Peru, and Bolivia.

Native Americans of Peru

Today, more Native Americans live in Peru than in any other South American country. Forty-five percent of Peru's people are Native Americans—the descendants of the Inca. Many of these people are Quechua (KEHCH wuh), people who live in the Andes highlands and speak the Inca language, Quechua. Along with Spanish, Quechua is one of Peru's official languages. Many people in the highlands speak the language of another Native American group, the Aymara (eye mah RAH). The Inca conquered the Aymara in the 15th century, but the language lived on.

After Native Americans, *mestizos* are Peru's next largest group. Peru's population also includes people with European, African, and Asian ancestors.

Most of Peru's people live in cities or towns. Lima is Peru's capital and its biggest city, with about 7 million people. Lima has grown very quickly, which poses some severe problems. At the dawn of the 21st century, many neighborhoods lacked basic city services, such as electricity, running water, and public transportation.

Many of Peru's rural farmers are very poor. They farm such small plots of land that often they cannot grow enough to feed their families. These rural people, who are mainly Native Americans, often move to the cities in search of a better life. However, many have little education and cannot speak Spanish, making it hard to find work.

Citizenship IN ACTION

Committee to Protect Journalists In a democracy, freedom of the press helps to prevent wrongdoing by the government. In Peru, for example, many administrators resigned in disgrace after journalists exposed widespread corruption in Alberto Fujimori's administration. Elsewhere, however, many governments have jailed journalists like the one shown here for their reports.

The Committee to Protect Journalists (CPJ) was formed in 1981 to promote freedom of the press. CPJ tracks abuses against the press all over the world, makes the abuses public, and organizes protests.

Peruvian Culture

Peru's religions reflect its multiple cultural traditions. Catholicism is the national religion of Peru, and more than 90 percent of Peruvians are Catholic. However, because Peru was once the heart of the Inca Empire, many Inca religious practices also still exist. At times, the Inca and Catholic customs mix. For example, some villages honor Catholic saints with festivals that often include the traditions of the Incas.

The literature of Peru reveals modern themes as well as traditional ones. Peru's most famous novelist, Mario Vargas Llosa (MAHR yoh VAHR guhs YOH suh), is known for his belief that a novel should represent life to the fullest.

One of the most famous Peruvian composers is Andre Sas. Many of his compositions highlight the influence of native music.

César Vallejo (SAY sar vuh YAY hoh) is Peru's most famous poet and is considered one of the world's best Spanish-language poets. His poetry describes what life is like for Peru's Native Americans.

REVIEW How has fighting between military and civilian leaders affected people's daily lives in Peru?

Lesson Summary

Peru's challenging physical features make transportation within the country difficult. Although Peru has many natural resources, including farming, fish, and mining, its harsh geography contributes to its poor economy. With an unstable government, overcrowded cities, and difficult landscapes, Peru has many economic problems.

Why It Matters...

Peru's economic problems also affect its trading partners, including the United States.

Lesson Review

1821
Peru declares its independence from Spain

1824
Bolívar frees Peru from Spanish

1800   1821   1822   1823   1824   1825

❶ **VOCABULARY** Use **oasis** in a paragraph about Peru's cities and their location.

❷ 🔖 **READING SKILL** How does Peruvian life in cities **compare** to that in rural areas?

❸ **MAIN IDEA: Geography** Describe the three types of landforms in Peru.

❹ **MAIN IDEA: Economics** Describe the challenges facing Peru's economy.

❺ **MAIN IDEA: Culture** Which group makes up the largest part of Peru's population?

❻ **PEOPLE TO KNOW** Who were the **Sendero Luminoso,** or Shining Path?

❼ **TIMELINE SKILL** How may years after Peru declared independence did Simón Bolívar defeat the Spanish?

❽ **CRITICAL THINKING: Analyze** Why did Peru's guerrillas believe they had to use violence to bring about change? Were they right to do so? Explain.

HANDS ON

ART ACTIVITY Make a poster to advertise Peru's natural resources to possible trade partners around the world.

Skillbuilder

Read a Timeline

A timeline is a visual list of dates and events shown in the order in which they occurred. Timelines can be horizontal or vertical. On horizontal timelines, the earliest date is on the left. On vertical timelines, the earliest date is usually at the top.

The timeline below shows the dates of expeditions to explore the Amazon River. Use the steps listed to the right to help you read the timeline.

Exploration of the Amazon River

1500
Vicente Yáñez Pinzón, Spanish, explores lower river.

1637
Pedro Teixeria, Portuguese, begins trip upstream.

1848
H.W. Bates, English, begins collecting animal species.

1910
Harvard's Institute of Geographical Exploration starts exploring.

1500   1600   1700   1800   1900   2000

1560
Pedro de Ursua, Spanish, explores from Huallaga River downstream.

1799
Alexander von Humboldt, German, leads mapmaking trip.

1851
U.S. government sends expedition.

Step 1: Read the title. It will tell you the main idea of the timeline.

Step 2: Read the dates at the beginning and the end of the timeline. These will show the period of time that the timeline covers.

Step 3: Read the dates and events in order, beginning with the earliest one. Think about how each event may have influenced later events. Take note of which nations were involved in each expedition.

Step 4: Summarize the main idea of the timeline. Remember that the title will help you focus on the main idea.

Practice the Skill

Writing a summary can help you understand the information shown on a timeline. The summary states the time period covered and the main idea of the timeline.

> The timeline covers the period between 1500 and 1925. During that period of time, people from Europe and the United States explored the Amazon River. The timeline shows that on their expeditions, people explored the river, made maps, and collected animal species.

Apply the Skill

Turn to page 232 in Chapter 9, Lesson 1. Look at the timeline entitled "Key Independence Days in South America" and write a paragraph summarizing what you learned from it.

Visual Summary

1–4. Write a description for each concept shown below.

Establishing Independence

_____
_____

Economies and Cultures

_____
_____

Brazil Today

_____
_____

Peru Today

_____
_____

Facts and Main Ideas

Answer each question below.

5. **History** What caused the death of so many Native Americans after the arrival of the Europeans in South America?

6. **Geography** List three of South America's major natural resources?

7. **Government** Why did the government of Brazil build the city of Brasília?

8. **Geography** Describe the three types of landforms that make up Peru.

9. **Culture** How does the Native American population in Peru compare in size with the Native American populations elsewhere in South America?

Vocabulary

Choose the correct word from the list below to complete each sentence.

Pan-American, p. 233
economic indicators, p. 237
inflation, p. 243
oasis, p. 247

10. A farm in Peru is usually located in or near an _____ because there would be water there.

11. The formation of the Organization of American States was an attempt at _____ unity.

12. To compare the economies of Brazil and Peru, look at their _____.

13. When the price of goods and services goes higher, it is a time of _____.

CHAPTER SUMMARY TIMELINE

1822 Brazil independence	1824 Bolívar frees Peru from Spanish		1948 OAS formed	1985 Brazil democracy restored

1800 ● ● 1825 | 1850 | 1875 | 1900 | 1925 | 1950 ● | 1975 ● | 2000

Apply Skills

 TEST PREP Read a Timeline Read the timeline below. Then use the timeline to answer each question.

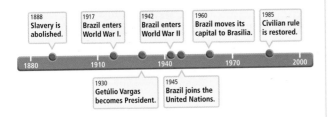

1888 Slavery is abolished.	1917 Brazil enters World War I.	1942 Brazil enters World War II	1960 Brazil moves its capital to Brasilia.	1985 Civilian rule is restored.

1880 ● | 1910 ● | ● 1940 | 1970 ● | 2000

1930 Getúlio Vargas becomes President.	1945 Brazil joins the United Nations.

14. What period is covered in the timeline?

   A. 1800 to 1900

   B. a period of 250 years

   C. 1880 to 2000

   D. 1880 to 1985

15. What events has Brazil participated in with other countries of the world?

   A. ending of slavery, formation of UN

   B. World Wars I and II, formation of UN

   C. World Wars I and II, moving the capital

   D. declaring independence, moving the capital, formation of UN

16. How long after Getúlio Vargas became president did Brazil enter the United Nations?

   A. 10 years

   B. 15 years

   C. 200 years

   D. cannot tell from timeline

Critical Thinking

 TEST PREP Write a short paragraph to answer each question below.

17. Compare and Contrast Brazil and Venezuela both gained independence from European countries. How did the road to freedom for Brazil contrast with that of Venezuela?

18. Synthesize When South American nations form trade blocs, how is that different from uniting politically?

Timeline

Use the Chapter Summary Timeline above to answer the question.

19. Which country gained indepence first, Brazil or Peru?

Activities

 SPEAKING ACTIVITY Work with a group of classmates to create a news show about the experience of Mexicans during the Mexican Revolution.

 WRITING ACTIVITY Imagine that you are in a plane, flying over Peru. Write a journal entry about what you see from your flight.

 Technology

Writing Process Tips
Get help with your journal entry at
www.eduplace.com/kids/hmss05/

Review and Test Prep

Vocabulary and Main Ideas

Write a sentence to answer each question below.

1. What is a disadvantage of **deforestation** in the Amazon rain forest?

2. How does *El Niño* affect Latin America?

3. How important is **tourism** to Mexico's economy?

4. What is the disadvantage of a **single-product economy?**

5. How was the sugar industry in Cuba affected by **Communism?**

6. What has caused increased **urbanization** in South America?

7. How would **inflation** affect a country's **economic indicators?**

Critical Thinking

 TEST PREP Write a short paragraph to answer each question below.

8. **Compare and Contrast** Compare and contrast the Aztec *chinampas* and the Inca stone terraces. Explain why each culture used that style of farming.

9. **Cause and Effect** What effect do you believe a free-trade zone will have on South American economies?

Apply Skills

 TEST PREP **Read a Graph** Study the graph below. Then use the graph to answer each question.

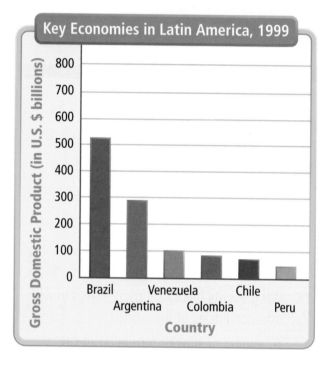

Key Economies in Latin America, 1999

10. Which country has a gross domestic product about twice the size of Argentina's?

   A. Venezuela
   B. Brazil
   C. Colombia
   D. Chile and Peru combined

11. Which country in Latin America has the largest economy?

   A. Peru
   B. Venezuela
   C. Argentina
   D. Brazil

Create a Cultural Celebration Oral Report

- Choose a holiday or event celebrated in Central or South America.

- Use library resources or the Internet to find out about the celebration.

- Create visuals to accompany your oral report. Make sure they give your classmates a feel for the celebration.

- Present your findings to the class in a 5-minute oral report.

At the Library

The following books are found at your school or public library.

Golden Tales: Myths, Legends, and Folktales from Latin America, by Lulu Delacre
Tales from 13 Latin American countries are told here.

Esperanza Rising, by Pam Muñoz Ryan
Tragedy forces Esperanza to leave the good life in Mexico and join other Depression-era migrant workers in California.

CURRENT EVENTS
WEEKLY (WR) READER

Connect to Today

Create a newspaper about Latin America today.

- Find current articles on the Weekly Reader Web site about events in Latin American countries.

- Write a short newspaper article on each event. Be sure to begin with the 5 Ws— who, what, where, when, and why. Draw a picture or map to illustrate each story.

- Assemble the articles into a newspaper and publish it for the class to read.

 Technology

Get your information for the newspaper articles from the Weekly Reader at **www.eduplace.com/kids/hmss05/**

Read About It

Look for these Social Studies books in your classroom.

The Colosseum Completed in A.D. 80,
the Colosseum in Rome, Italy, held 50,000
spectators. There they watched battles
between gladiators, among other contests.
The Colosseum is the largest structure
that survives from the Roman Empire

Europe, Russia, and the Independent Republics

The Big Idea

How do governments protect and limit people's freedom?

"*The basis of a democratic state is liberty.*"

Aristotle,
Greek philosopher

THE COLOSSEUM

PACIFIC OCEAN

PACIFIC OCEAN

ATLANTIC OCEAN

EUROPE, RUSSIA, AND THE INDEPENDENT REPUBLICS

OCEAN

Europe, Russia, and the Independent Republics

20°W   20°E   40°E   60°E   80°E   100°E

Franz Josef Land

ARCTIC OCEAN

Svalbard

Novaya Zemlya

Kara Sea

Barents Sea

N

0   500   1,000 miles
0   500   1,000 kilometers

Norwegian Sea

Arctic Circle

ICELAND

60°N

SWEDEN   FINLAND

Dvina R.

RUSSIA

West Siberian Plain

Central Siberian Plateau

NORWAY

ESTONIA

Jutland   LATVIA
DENMARK   LITHUANIA

North Sea   RUS.

Baltic Sea

IRELAND   NETH.
UNITED KINGDOM   GERMANY   POLAND   BELARUS

Central Russian Upland

Volga R.   *Kama R.*

Ural Mountains

Ob R.   *Yenisey R.*
Ob R.   *Angara R.*

BEL.   *Rhine R.*
LUX.   CZECH R.   UKRAINE   *Dnieper R.*   *Don R.*
ATLANTIC OCEAN   *Carpathian Mts.*
FRANCE   SWITZ.   SLOVAKIA   *Irtysh R.*
AUS. HUNGARY   MOLDOVA   KAZAKHSTAN   *Sayan Mts.*
Mt. Blanc   SLO.   ROMANIA
15,771 ft.   CRO.   *Mt. Elbrus*
(4,807 m)   BOS. & H.   *Danube R.*   *18,510 ft.*
40°N   SERB.   *(5,642 m)*   *Aral Sea*
Douro R.   & MON. BULGARIA   *Black Sea*   *Caucasus*   UZBEKISTAN   KYRGYZSTAN
Pyrenees   ITALY   ALB. MAC.   GEORGIA   *Caspian Sea*
Iberian Peninsula   *Corsica*   *Sardinia*   GREECE   ARMENIA   TURKMENISTAN   TAJIKISTAN
PORTUGAL   SPAIN   *Mt. Etna*   AZERBAIJAN
10,902 ft.
(3,323 m)   *Crete*
Sicily   *Mediterranean Sea*

20°N

180°E

Climates of Europe, Russia, and the Independent Republics

N

ARCTIC OCEAN   ARCTIC OCEAN

Arctic Circle

60°N   60°N

ATLANTIC OCEAN   PACIFIC OCEAN

Black Sea

40°N

Mediterranean Sea

0   1,000   2,000 miles
0   1,000   2,000 kilometers

Desert	Humid continental
Semiarid	Subarctic
Mediterranean	Tundra
Marine west coast	Highland
Humid subtropical	

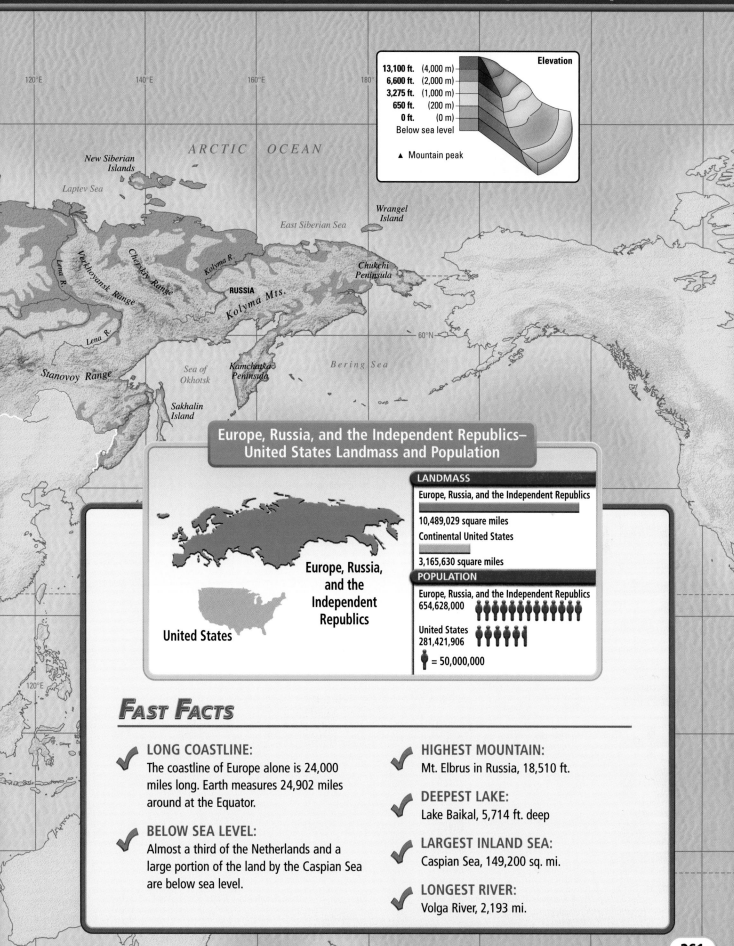

Elevation

13,100 ft.	(4,000 m)
6,600 ft.	(2,000 m)
3,275 ft.	(1,000 m)
650 ft.	(200 m)
0 ft.	(0 m)
Below sea level	

▲ Mountain peak

ARCTIC OCEAN

New Siberian Islands

Laptev Sea

Wrangel Island

East Siberian Sea

Verkhoyansk Range

Chersky Range

Lena R.

Kolyma R.

Chukchi Peninsula

RUSSIA

Kolyma Mts.

60°N

Lena R.

Stanovoy Range

Bering Sea

Sea of Okhotsk

Kamchatka Peninsula

Sakhalin Island

120°E 140°E 160°E 180°

120°E

Europe, Russia, and the Independent Republics– United States Landmass and Population

Europe, Russia, and the Independent Republics

United States

LANDMASS

Europe, Russia, and the Independent Republics

10,489,029 square miles

Continental United States

3,165,630 square miles

POPULATION

Europe, Russia, and the Independent Republics
654,628,000

United States
281,421,906

= 50,000,000

FAST FACTS

✔ **LONG COASTLINE:**
The coastline of Europe alone is 24,000 miles long. Earth measures 24,902 miles around at the Equator.

✔ **BELOW SEA LEVEL:**
Almost a third of the Netherlands and a large portion of the land by the Caspian Sea are below sea level.

✔ **HIGHEST MOUNTAIN:**
Mt. Elbrus in Russia, 18,510 ft.

✔ **DEEPEST LAKE:**
Lake Baikal, 5,714 ft. deep

✔ **LARGEST INLAND SEA:**
Caspian Sea, 149,200 sq. mi.

✔ **LONGEST RIVER:**
Volga River, 2,193 mi.

Almanac

Country Flag	Country/Capital	Currency	Population (2001 estimate)	Life Expectancy (years)	Birthrate (per 1,000 pop.) (2000)
	Albania Tiranë	Lek	3,510,000	71	19
	Andorra Andorra la Vella	French Franc	68,000	83	11
	Armenia Yerevan	Dram	3,336,000	75	10
	Austria Vienna	Euro*	8,151,000	78	10
	Azerbaijan Baku	Manat	7,771,000	70	15
	Belarus Minsk	Ruble	10,350,000	68	9
	Belgium Brussels	Euro*	10,259,000	78	11
	Bosnia-Herzegovina Sarajevo	Conv. Mark	3,922,000	73	13
	Bulgaria Sofia	Lev	7,707,000	71	8
	Croatia Zagreb	Kuna	4,334,000	73	11
	Czech Republic Prague	Koruna	10,264,000	75	9
	Denmark Copenhagen	Danish Krone	5,353,000	77	12
	Estonia Tallinn	Kroon	1,423,000	70	8
	Finland Helsinki	Euro*	5,176,000	78	11
	France Paris	Euro*	59,551,000	79	13
	Georgia Tbilisi	Lavi	4,989,000	73	9
	Germany Berlin	Euro*	83,029,000	77	9

*On January 1, 2002, the euro became the common currency for the member nations of the European Union that choose to adopt it.

DATA FILE

Infant Mortality (per 1,000 live births) (2000)	Doctors (per 100,000 pop.) (1990–1998)	Literacy Rate (percentage) (1991–1998)	Passenger Cars (per 1,000 pop.) (1996–1997)	Total Area (square miles)	Map (not to scale)
41.3	129	83	10 (1990)	11,100	
6.4	253	100	552	174	
41.0	316	98	2	11,506	
4.9	302	100	468	32,378	
83.0	360	99	36	33,436	
15.0	443	100	111	80,154	
5.6	395	99	434	11,787	
25.2	143	86	23	19,741	
14.9	345	98	202	42,822	
8.2	229	98	160	21,830	
4.6	303	99	428	30,448	
4.7	290	100	339	16,637	
13.0	297	99	294	17,413	
4.2	299	100	378	130,560	
4.8	303	99	437	212,934	
53.0	436	99	80	26,911	
4.7	350	100	504	137,830	

Almanac

Country Flag	Country/Capital	Currency	Population (2001 estimate)	Life Expectancy (years)	Birthrate (per 1,000 pop.) (2000)
	Greece Athens	Euro*	10,624,000	78	10
	Hungary Budapest	Forint	10,106,000	71	9
	Iceland Reykjavik	Krona	278,000	80	15
	Ireland Dublin	Euro*	3,841,000	76	15
	Italy Rome	Euro*	57,680,000	78	9
	Kazakhstan Astana	Tenge	16,731,000	65	14
	Kyrgyzstan Bishkek	Som	4,753,000	67	22
	Latvia Riga	Lat	2,385,000	70	8
	Liechtenstein Vaduz	Swiss Franc	33,000	73	14
	Lithuania Vilnius	Litas	3,611,000	72	10
	Luxembourg Luxembourg	Euro*	443,000	77	13
	Macedonia Skopje	Denar	2,046,000	73	15
	Malta Valletta	Lira	395,000	77	12
	Moldova Chisinau	Leu	4,432,000	67	11
	Monaco Monaco	French Franc	32,000	79	20
	Netherlands Amsterdam	Euro*	15,981,000	78	13
	Norway Oslo	Krone	4,503,000	79	13
	Poland Warsaw	Zloty	38,634,000	74	10

DATA FILE

Infant Mortality (per 1,000 live births) (2000)	Doctors (per 100,000 pop.) (1990–1998)	Literacy Rate (percentage) (1991–1998)	Passenger Cars (per 1,000 pop.) (1996–1997)	Total Area (square miles)	Map (not to scale)
6.7	392	97	223	50,950	
8.9	357	99	222	35,919	
4.0	326	100	489	39,768	
6.2	219	100	292	27,135	
5.5	554	98	540	116,320	
59.0	353	99	61	1,048,300	
77.0	301	97	32	76,641	
16.0	282	100	174	24,595	
5.1	100	100	592 (1993)	62	
15.0	395	100	242	25,174	
5.0	272	100	515	999	
16.3	204	89	132	9,927	
5.3	261	91	321	124	
43.0	400 (1995)	99	46	13,012	
5.9	664	100	548	0.6	
5.0	251	100	372	16,033	
4.0	413	100	399	125,050	
8.9	236	99	195	124,807	

Country Flag	Country/Capital	Currency	Population (2001 estimate)	Life Expectancy (years)	Birthrate (per 1,000 pop.) (2000)
	Portugal Lisbon	Euro*	10,066,000	76	11
	Romania Bucharest	Leu	22,364,000	70	11
	Russia Moscow	Ruble	145,470,000	67	8
	San Marino San Marino	Italian Lira	27,000	80	11
	Slovakia Bratislava	Koruna	5,415,000	73	11
	Slovenia Ljubljana	Tolar	1,930,000	75	9
	Spain Madrid	Euro	40,038,000	78	9
	Sweden Stockholm	Krona	8,875,000	80	10
	Switzerland Bern	Franc	7,283,000	80	11
	Tajikistan Dushanbe	Ruble	6,579,000	68	21
	Turkmenistan Ashgabat	Manat	4,603,000	66	21
	Ukraine Kiev	Hryvnya	48,760,000	68	8
	United Kingdom London	Pound	59,648,000	77	12
	Uzbekistan Tashkent	Som	25,155,000	69	23
	Vatican City Vatican City	Vatican Lira/Italian Lira	870 (2000)	N/A	N/A
	Serbia & Montenegro Belgrade	New Dinar	10,677,000	73	11
	United States Washington, D.C.	Dollar	281,422,000	77	15

DATA FILE

Infant Mortality (per 1,000 live births) (2000)	Doctors (per 100,000 pop.) (1990–1998)	Literacy Rate (percentage) (1991–1998)	Passenger Cars (per 1,000 pop.) (1996–1997)	Total Area (square miles)	Map (not to scale)
6.0	312	91	295	35,514	
20.5	184	98	106	92,042	
20.0	421	100	120	6,592,812	
8.8	252	99	955	23	
8.8	353	100	185	18,923	
5.2	228	99	343	7,819	
5.7	424	97	384	195,363	
3.5	311	100	417	173,730	
4.8	323	100	460	15,942	
117.0	201	99	31	55,251	
73.0	300 (1997)	98	N/A	188,455	
22.0	299	100	97	233,089	
5.7	164	100	434	94,548	
72.0	309	88	37	173,591	
N/A	N/A	100	N/A	0.17	
10.4	203	98	173	39,448	
7.0	251	97	489	3,787,319	

Chapter 10

Western Europe:
Land and History

Technology

e • glossary
e • word games
www.eduplace.com/kids/hmss05/

Vocabulary Preview

fjord

A **fjord** is a long, narrow, deep inlet of the sea that is located between steep cliffs. Fjord is a Norwegian word that describes a common land-form in Northern Europe.
page 271

philosopher

If you think about and study why the world is the way it is, you are a **philosopher.** Some of the greatest philosophers of all time, including Socrates, Plato, and Aristotle, lived in ancient Greece. **page 278**

Chapter Timeline

509 B.C.
Roman Republic formed

| 600 | 500 | 400 | 300 | 200 |

EUROPE

Reading Strategy

Summarize Use this strategy to help you understand important information in the chapter.

Quick Tip Take notes as you read. Then highlight the most important information.

empire

Rome grew from a republic into an **empire.** An empire is a vast land that is ruled by just one, very powerful man—the emperor. Augustus was the first emperor of the Roman Empire.
page 288

guild

A **guild** is an association of tradespeople and craftspeople formed to protect workers' rights. In the Middle Ages, guilds set wages and prices, helped settle disputes, and established standards for quality. **page 296**

27 B.C.
Rome becomes an empire

A.D. 313
Christianity official Roman religion

| 0 | 100 | 200 | 300 | 400 |

Geography and Climate

VOCABULARY

peninsula
fjord
plain

Vocabulary Strategy

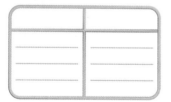

plain

A **plain** is a large, flat area of land, often without many trees. Plain can also mean "not decorated." Think of a plain as a place not "decorated" with trees.

READING SKILL

Categorize As you read, list examples of the landforms in Europe.

Build on What You Know You know that the geography of an area can make travel and transportation difficult. Europeans took advantage of the Atlantic Ocean, surrounding seas, and the continent's many rivers to travel and to trade with one another.

The Geography of Europe

Main Idea Europe is a continent of varied geographic features, with towering mountains, broad plains, and busy rivers.

Today, cars, airplanes, and trains are common forms of high-speed transportation across Europe. Before the 19th century, however, the fastest form of transportation was to travel by water.

Look at the map of Europe on page 260 of the Unit Almanac. Water surrounds the continent to the north, south, and west. The southern coast of Europe borders the warm waters of the Mediterranean Sea. Europe also has many rivers. The highly traveled Rhine and Danube rivers are two of the most important. The Volga, which flows nearly 2,200 miles through western Russia, is the continent's longest. For hundreds of years, these and other waterways have been home to boats and barges carrying people and goods inland across great distances.

The Channel Tunnel This underwater tunnel, also called the Chunnel, connects England and France. Trains make the 31-mile trip under the English Channel in only 20 minutes.

Landforms and Waterways

Several large **peninsulas,** or bodies of land surrounded by water on three sides, form the European continent. In Northern Europe, the Scandinavian Peninsula is home to Norway and Sweden. Along the jagged shoreline of this peninsula are beautiful fjords (fyawrdz). A **fjord** is a long, narrow, deep inlet of the sea located between steep cliffs.

In Western Europe, the Iberian Peninsula includes Portugal and Spain. The Iberian Peninsula is separated from the rest of the continent by a mountain range called the Pyrenees (PEER uh neez). The entire continent of Europe, itself surrounded by water on three sides, is a giant peninsula.

Fjords The Scandinavian Peninsula is the location of many spectacular fjords, such as this one in Norway.

Mountain ranges, including the towering Alps, also stretch across much of the continent. Along Europe's eastern border, the Ural Mountains (YUR uhl) divide the continent from Asia. The many mountain ranges of Europe separated groups of people from one another as they settled the land thousands of years ago. This is one of the reasons why different cultures developed across the continent.

Not all of Europe is mountainous. A vast region called the Great European Plain stretches from the coast of France to the Ural Mountains. A **plain** is a large, flat area of land, usually without many trees. The Great European Plain is the location of some of the world's richest farmland. Ancient trading centers attracted many people to this area, which today includes some of the largest cities in Europe—Paris, Berlin, Warsaw, and Moscow.

REVIEW Why were waterways so important for the movement of European people and goods?

Climate and Natural Resources

Main Idea Europe has abundant natural resources and a climate that supports agriculture.

The Gulf Stream is a strong ocean current that flows from the Gulf of Mexico across the Atlantic Ocean to Europe. It carries warm water and warm, moist air, which contribute to Europe's mild climate. The Gulf Stream warms the water of some Northern European ports, allowing them to remain open in the winter when they might otherwise be frozen.

Although the Gulf Stream brings warm air and water to Europe, the winters are still severe in the mountains and in the far north. In some of these areas, cold winds blow southward from the Arctic Circle and make the average temperature fall below 0°F in January. The Alps and the Pyrenees, however, protect the European countries along the Mediterranean Sea from these chilling winds. In these warmer parts of Southern Europe, the average temperature in January stays above 50°F.

The summers in the south are usually hot and dry, with an average July temperature around 80°F. This makes the Mediterranean coast a popular vacation spot. Elsewhere in Europe, in all but the coldest areas of the mountains and the far north, the average July temperature ranges from 50°F to 70°F.

Europe also has rich soil and plentiful rainfall. The average precipitation for the Great European Plain, for example, is between 20 and 40 inches per year. The map on page 273 shows the agricultural uses of the land, highlighting the major crops. Notice that few parts of the continent are too cold or too hot and dry to support some form of agriculture. These characteristics have made Europe a world leader in crop production.

REVIEW What two factors have made Europe a world leader in crop production?

The Alps These tall mountains remain snowcapped year-round.

Southern Europe Brightly colored buildings dot the hills along the Mediterranean coast.

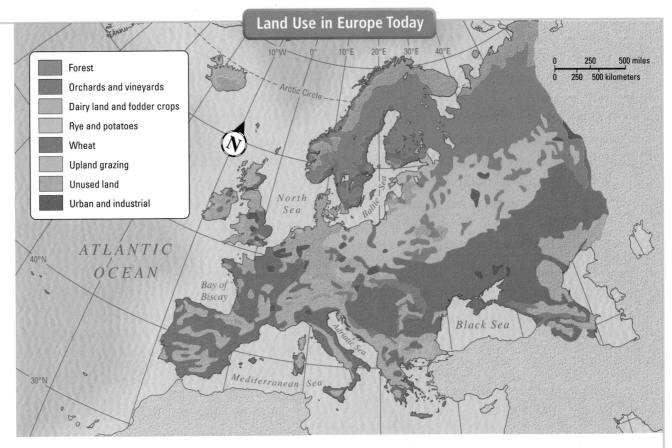

Land Use in Europe Today

Legend:
- Forest
- Orchards and vineyards
- Dairy land and fodder crops
- Rye and potatoes
- Wheat
- Upland grazing
- Unused land
- Urban and industrial

ATLANTIC OCEAN

North Sea

Baltic Sea

Bay of Biscay

Adriatic Sea

Black Sea

Mediterranean Sea

Arctic Circle

Land Use The land in Europe supports a variety of industries and the rich soil supports a great deal of agriculture. **SKILL** **Interpret a Map** What are the three most common uses of land in Europe?

Sheep Shepherds tend their livestock on grassy hills. Many parts of Europe, as the land use map (above) shows, are good for upland grazing such as this.

Europe has a large variety of natural resources, including minerals. The rich coal deposits of Germany's Ruhr (rur) Valley region have helped to make that area one of the world's major industrial centers. Russia and Ukraine have large deposits of iron ore, which is used to make iron for automobiles and countless other products.

Factories European industry uses the abundant natural resources of the region to produce goods that are sold all over the world.

Lesson Summary

Europe benefits from a varied landscape that is rich in natural resources. Europe's great rivers, such as the Rhine, Danube, and Volga, have provided transportation of goods and people for centuries. Mountain ranges, such as the Alps and Pyrenees, used to separate groups of people and continue to form different climates in different parts of the continent. Europe's climate, plentiful rainfall, and rich soil have made it good for agriculture. Mineral wealth, including coal and iron, has helped make Europe one of the world's most important industrial regions.

Why It Matters...

The development of Europe's diverse cultures has been shaped by the continent's diverse geography.

Lesson Review

1 VOCABULARY Explain the significance of **peninsula** and **plain** to the geography of Europe.

2 READING SKILL Would you put the Alps in the **category** of mountains, plains, or peninsulas?

3 MAIN IDEA: Geography What separates Europe from Asia?

4 MAIN IDEA: Economics How do waterways, such as rivers and seas, strengthen trade in Europe?

5 MAIN IDEA: Geography How does the Gulf Stream affect the climate of Europe?

6 PLACES TO KNOW What are two major mountain ranges in Europe?

7 CRITICAL THINKING: Cause and Effect How did Europe's many mountain ranges affect its development?

WRITING ACTIVITY Imagine that you have moved from the Scandinavian Peninsula to a home on the European coast of the Mediterranean Sea. Write a letter home to a friend or family member telling him or her about the differences you notice most between the two parts of Europe.

Ancient Greece

| 800 | 600 | 400 | 200 |

750 B.C.–322 B.C.

Build on What You Know You know how important voting is to a democracy such as the United States. In a democracy, citizens take part in government by voting. The earliest forms of democracy developed in ancient Greece.

The Land and Early History of Greece

Main Idea In ancient Greece, communities grew up around cities that grew into independent states.

The Greek Peninsula is mountainous, which made travel by land difficult for early settlers. Most of the rocky land also contains poor soil and few large trees, but settlers were able to cultivate the soil to grow olives and grapes.

The greatest natural resource of the peninsula is the water that surrounds it. The ancient Greeks depended on these seas for fishing and trade, and they became excellent sailors.

Metropolis The ancient Greeks called the city-state they came from their metropolis, which meant "mother-city." Today, metropolis means any large urban area, such as Athens (shown below).

VOCABULARY

city-state
polis
oligarchy
philosopher

Vocabulary Strategy

city-state

Look at the word **city-state.** It is made of two words you know: **city**—a center of population, and **state**—an area with a single government. A nation centered on a city and its surrounding territory is a city-state.

READING SKILL

Main Idea and Details As you read, take notes about the contributions of ancient Greece to the modern world.

275

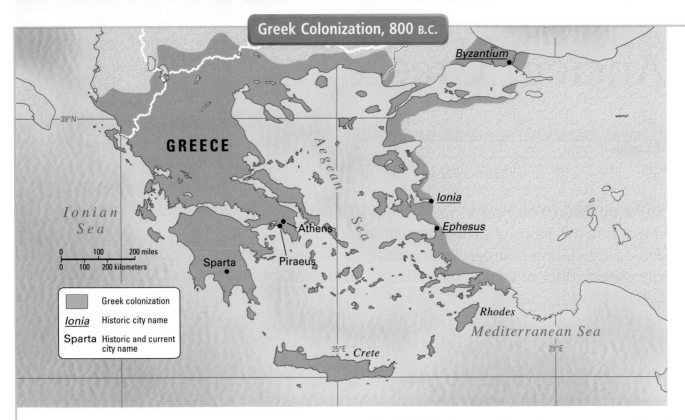

Byzantium

GREECE

Ionia

Ephesus

Ionian Sea

Athens

Sparta   Piraeus

	Greek colonization
Ionia	Historic city name
Sparta	Historic and current city name

Rhodes
Mediterranean Sea

Crete

The Growth of Colonies

As the ancient Greek population grew, people created city-states. A **city-state** included a central city, called a **polis,** and surrounding villages. Each ancient Greek city-state had its own laws and form of government. The city-states were united by a common language, shared religious beliefs, and a similar way of life.

By the mid-700s B.C., the Greeks were leaving the peninsula in search of better land and greater opportunities for trade. During the next 200 years, they built dozens of communities on the islands and coastline of the Aegean Sea (ih JEE uhn). Some Greeks settled as far away as modern-day Spain and North Africa.

Once established, these distant Greek communities traded with each other and with those communities on the Greek Peninsula. This made a great variety of goods available to the ancient Greeks, including wheat for baking bread, timber for building boats, and iron ore for making strong tools and weapons.

Greek Colonies Greek settlements surrounded the Aegean Sea. **SKILL Interpret a Map** What was the southernmost Greek territory at this time?

Individual Forms of Government

Some ancient Greek city-states were oligarchies (AHL ih gahr kees). An **oligarchy** is a system in which a few powerful, wealthy individuals rule. The word *oligarchy* comes from an ancient Greek word meaning "rule by the few." Other city-states were ruled by a tyrant, a single person who took control of the government against the wishes of the community.

Still other ancient Greek city-states developed an early form of democracy. The word *democracy* comes from an ancient Greek word meaning "rule by the people." In a democracy, citizens take part in the government. The various forms of democracy in the world today all have their origins in Greek democracy.

Athens and Sparta

Athens, centrally located on the Greek Peninsula, was one of the largest and most important ancient Greek city-states. By the end of the sixth century B.C., Athens had developed a democratic form of government. Athenian citizens took part in political debates and voted on laws, but not everyone who lived in Athens enjoyed these rights. Participation in government was limited to free, adult males whose fathers had been citizens of Athens. Women, slaves, and foreign residents could not take part in government.

Athens's chief rival among the other Greek city-states was Sparta. Located in the southernmost part of the Greek Peninsula, Sparta was an oligarchy. It was ruled by two kings, who were supported by other officials. Sparta, like Athens, had a powerful army. Each city-state's army helped protect it from slave rebellions, guard it against attack by rival city-states, and defend it from possible foreign invaders.

Literature and the Arts

Main Idea The ancient Greeks made remarkable achievements in literature and philosophy.

In 480 B.C., the Persians, who controlled a large empire to the east, tried to conquer the Greek Peninsula. Several Greek city-states, including Athens and Sparta, joined forces to defeat the Persians. In the years following this victory, the ancient Greeks made remarkable achievements in literature, learning, and architecture.

To honor their gods and goddesses, the ancient Greeks created myths and wrote poems and plays. Some of the greatest Greek plays were written during the fifth century B.C. During that time, the playwrights Aeschylus (EHS kuh luhs), Sophocles (SAHF uh kleez), and Euripides (yu RIHP ih deez) wrote tragedies. Tragedies are serious plays that have unhappy endings. Many of these stories have been the basis for modern films and operas.

In addition to using the gods as characters, ancient Greek playwrights sometimes poked fun at important citizens, including generals and politicians. Aristophanes (ar ih STAHF uh neez) was a popular writer of comedies of this type.

REVIEW What were the three forms of government most common in ancient Greek city-states?

Spartan Soldier Sparta was the only city-state with a permanent army. Spartan boys began military training at the age of seven and stayed in the army until they were thirty years old.

Philosophers

Ancient Greece was the birthplace of some of the finest thinkers of the ancient world. Socrates (SAHK ruh teez) was an important philosopher of the fifth century B.C. A **philosopher** studies and thinks about why the world is the way it is. Socrates studied and taught about friendship, knowledge, and justice. Another great philosopher, Plato (PLAY toh), was a student of Socrates who studied and taught about human behavior, government, mathematics, and astronomy.

The ancient Greek philosopher Heraclitus (hehr uh KLY tuhs) wrote the following lines.

> **66** One cannot step twice into the same river, for the water into which you first stepped has flowed on. **99**

Many people continue to study and write about the same philosophical questions that these, and other, ancient Greek philosophers explored.

The Spread of Greek Culture

The city-states of ancient Greece were constantly at war with one another. By the fourth century B.C., this fighting had weakened their ability to defend themselves against foreign invaders. In 338 B.C., King Philip II of Macedonia conquered the land. After Philip died, his son, Alexander—who had been taught by Aristotle—took control.

Acropolis Ancient Greek builders created some of the world's most impressive architecture. They built several beautiful temples atop the Acropolis (uh KRAHP uh lihs) in Athens, shown below.

Biography

Aristotle At the age of 17, Aristotle (384–322 B.C.) began studying philosophy with Plato. After Plato died, Aristotle received his most important assignment—to teach Alexander, the teenage son of King Philip II of Macedonia.

After teaching Alexander, Aristotle returned to Athens. There he taught and wrote about poetry, government, and astronomy. He started a famous school called the Lyceum (ly SEE uhm). Aristotle also collected and studied plants and animals. The work of this brilliant philosopher continues to greatly influence scientists and philosophers today.

Alexander the Great was an excellent military leader, and his armies conquered vast new territories. As Alexander's empire expanded, Greek culture, language, and ideas were spread throughout the Mediterranean region and as far east as modern-day India. Upon Alexander's death, however, his leading generals fought for control of his territory and divided it among themselves. This marked the end of one of the great empires of the ancient world.

REVIEW Name two famous philosophers of ancient Greece who were teacher and student.

Alexander the Great This mosaic shows Alexander riding into battle on his beloved horse, Bucephalus (byoo SEHF uh luhs).

Lesson Summary

> Achievements of Ancient Greeks

> City-states in different regions developed different forms of government.

> Myths, poems, and plays created by ancient Greeks continue to influence modern arts.

> Ancient Greek philosophical questions are studied and written about today.

> Alexander the Great spread Greek culture, language, and ideas throughout the Mediterranean region.

Why It Matters . . .

The achievements of the ancient Greeks continue to influence culture, science, and politics in the world today.

Lesson Review

480 B.C.
Athens and Sparta defeat Persians

338 B.C.
Philip II of Macedonia conquers Greeks

500 — 450 — 400 — 350 — 300 — 250

❶ **VOCABULARY** Write a paragraph explaining what it means to live in a **city-state** ruled by an **oligarchy.** Use these words in your paragraph.

❷ **READING SKILL** What **detail** supports the **main idea** that ancient Greeks developed political ideas that are important today?

❸ **MAIN IDEA: Geography** Why were the surrounding areas of water an important natural resource of the Greek Peninsula?

❹ **MAIN IDEA: Government** Which people were allowed to participate in the government of ancient Athens?

❺ **MAIN IDEA: History** How did Alexander the Great help to spread Greek culture?

❻ **FACTS TO KNOW** Which of the two main rival city-states in ancient Greece was an oligarchy?

❼ **TIMELINE SKILL** In what year did Philip II of Macedonia conquer the Greek city-states?

❽ **CRITICAL THINKING: Analyze** Why was the fifth century B.C. a remarkable time in ancient Greek history?

HANDS ON

SPEAKING ACTIVITY Reread the information about the three forms of government common in ancient Greece. Present an oral report that compares and contrasts two of the forms.

Extend Lesson 2

Readers' Theater

Flying High

Daedalus and Icarus

Plays in ancient Greece often taught lessons. Sometimes, a play retold one of the ancient Greek myths. Myths are traditional stories dealing with ancestors, heroes, and supernatural beings, like gods. Myths usually try to explain some belief or practice and often have a moral. The myth of Daedalus (DEHD uhl uhs) cautioned against pride. Listen to this ancient Greek myth. Do you see the lesson in the story?

Characters

Chorus Member One
Chorus Member Two
Chorus Member Three
King Minos (MY nuhs): the ruler of Crete
Daedalus: an architect and engineer from Athens
Icarus (IHK uhr uhs): the young son of Daedalus

Chorus Member 1: In ancient Greece, Daedalus was the greatest architect and builder of all time. His skill has never been matched.

Chorus Member 2: He was admired by all, and he admired himself as well. He built a palace on Crete.

Chorus Member 3: Daedalus had a son named Icarus. Daedalus loved Icarus and delighted in showing the small boy how to build things.

Chorus Member 1: Yet King Minos of Crete refused to let Daedalus return to Athens.

King Minos: You will always be treated well here. The people hold you in high honor. You will live well, but you can never leave. I will not share your talent or your secrets with any other king.

Daedalus: But Athens is my home!

Icarus: I can't wait to see Athens!

Chorus Member 2: King Minos stared down at Icarus, then at Daedalus.

King Minos: If you try to escape, I will punish not just you, but your son, Icarus, as well.

Chorus Member 3: With that, King Minos marched out of the room.

Chorus Member 1: Daedalus looked down at Icarus, who was beginning to cry.

Daedalus: I will think of something. I am the greatest builder and engineer in the world! I will find some way for us to escape this island. But in the meantime, you must run and play as always so King Minos does not suspect our plans.

Icarus: I will, Father. I know you can do this! I'm so happy!

King Minos

281

Chorus Member 2: Weeks went by, and Daedalus sat in the window of his workshop, high in a tower, watching birds, clouds, and wind.

Daedalus: I have an idea. I want you to play near the cliffs and along the shore, and every day, I want you to bring every feather you can find back to our workshop.

Icarus: I will, but why?

Daedalus: I am going to make wings! We will fly across the sea to Athens.

Chorus Member 3: And so it happened. Day after day, Icarus carried feathers to the workshop. There, Daedalus used strips of wood and wax to fashion them into wings.

Daedalus: Listen to me carefully, Icarus. Our wings will carry us from Crete to the mainland of Greece. We can glide, and if we flap our wings hard enough, we can climb.

Icarus: I can't wait! We will be like birds!

Daedalus: But we are not birds! If we fly too low, the waves of the sea will make our feathers wet, and we will fall into the water and drown. If we fly too high, the heat of the sun will melt the wax in our wings, and the feathers will fall out.

Chorus Member 1: Daedalus and Icarus strapped their wings to their arms. Then they stood in the window of their tower.

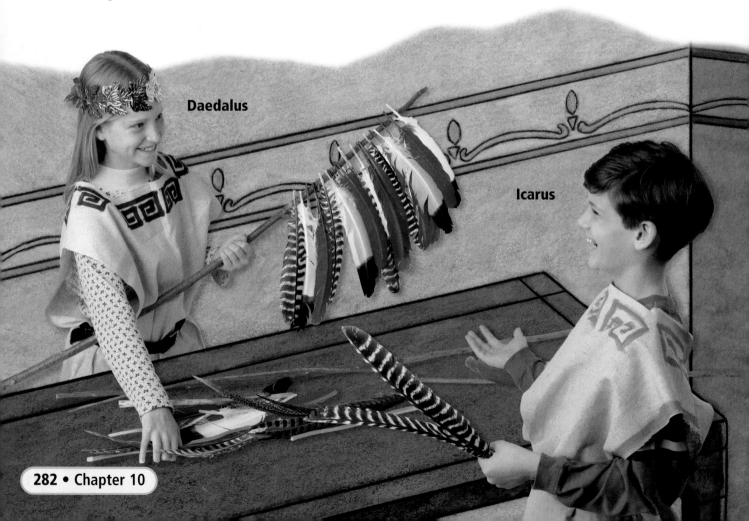

Daedalus

Icarus

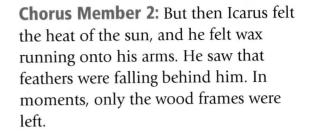

Daedalus: Remember my warning, Icarus. Stay with me in the sky!

Icarus: Don't worry so much!

Chorus Member 2: With that, Icarus plunged from the window. Daedalus followed.

Icarus: This is wonderful!

Chorus Member 3: Icarus soared and glided, swooping up and down around his father.

Daedalus: Icarus! Stay near me! It is dangerous to fly too high or too low!

Icarus: Look at me! I'm flying like a bird!

Chorus Member 1: Icarus flew high above the clouds, laughing and singing. He ignored his father's cries and warning.

Chorus Member 2: But then Icarus felt the heat of the sun, and he felt wax running onto his arms. He saw that feathers were falling behind him. In moments, only the wood frames were left.

Icarus: Father!

Daedalus: Icarus!

Chorus Member 3: Daedalus beat his wings and dove, trying to catch Icarus as he fell.

Chorus Member 1: But Daedalus could only watch as Icarus fell into the sea. Daedalus circled the waves, flying as low as he dared, but he saw only a few feathers on the waves.

Daedalus: I never should have made these wings! Who am I to try to outsmart nature, and turn a boy into a bird? My son has been destroyed by our own pride! No one will ever know how these wings were made!

Chorus (together): Daedalus never revealed the secret of the design of his wings. He had learned the lesson that pride comes before the fall.

Activities

1. **THINK ABOUT IT** How did the ancient Greeks use the myth of Daedalus and Icarus to teach a moral?

2. **WRITE ABOUT IT** Ancient Greeks created myths to explain things in the natural world that they did not understand. With partners, create a myth that explains something from nature as the ancient Greek myths did.

Skillbuilder

Make a Generalization

To make generalizations means to make broad judgments based on information. When you make generalizations, you should gather information from several sources.

The following three passages contain different information on the government of ancient Athens. Use the steps listed below to make a generalization about Athenian government based on the passages.

Athenian citizens took part in political debates and voted on laws, but not everyone who lived in Athens enjoyed these rights. Participation in government was limited to free, adult males whose fathers had been citizens in Athens.

—*World Cultures and Geography*

In return for playing their parts as soldiers or sailors, ordinary Athenians insisted on controlling the government.

—*Encyclopaedia Britannica*

Unlike representative democracies or republics, in which one man is elected to speak for many, Athens was a true democracy: every citizen spoke for himself.

—*Classical Greece*

Learn the Skill

Step 1: Look for all the information that the sources have in common. These three sources all explain about Athenian government.

Step 2: Form a generalization that describes ancient Athenian government in a way that all three sources would support. State your generalization in a sentence.

Using a chart can help you make generalizations. The chart below shows how the information you just read can be used to generalize about the government of ancient Athens.

Athenian citizens took part in political debates and voted on laws.	Ordinary Athenians insisted on controlling the government.	Athens was a true democracy: every citizen spoke for himself.

Generalizations: In ancient Athens, the government was a democracy in which ordinary people regularly took part.

Turn to Chapter 10, Lesson 2, "Ancient Greece." Read the sections on literature and philosophy. Also read about ancient Greek writings in an encyclopedia, a library book, or on the Internet. Then make a chart like the one above to form a generalization about the importance of knowledge and learning to the ancient Greeks.

Ancient Rome

800 600 400 200 0 200 400

750 B.C.–A.D. 313

Build on What You Know You have probably ridden on one of the interstate highways in the United States. Our highways help people and goods move quickly throughout our huge country. Over 2,000 years ago, ancient Romans built roads throughout their empire for the same reason. Some of their roads are still in use today!

The Beginnings of Ancient Rome

Main Idea From a collection of small villages, Rome grew to control most of the Mediterranean region.

Ancient Rome began as a group of villages located along the banks of the Tiber River in what is now Italy. There, early settlers herded sheep and grew wheat, olives, and grapes. Around 750 B.C., these villages united to form the city of Rome.

For more than 200 years, kings ruled Rome. Then, in 509 B.C., Rome became a republic. A **republic** is a nation in which power belongs to the citizens, who govern themselves through elected representatives.

The Roman **Senate** was an assembly of elected representatives. It was the single most powerful ruling body of the Roman Republic. Each year, the Senate selected two leaders, called consuls, to head the government and the military.

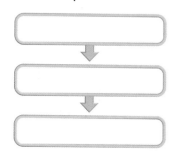

Market This carving depicts a typical Roman marketplace.

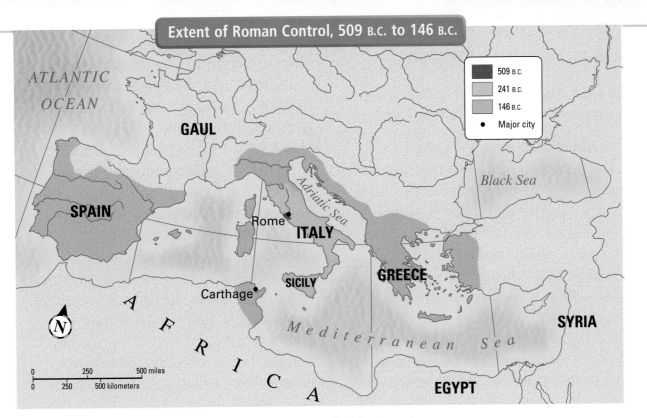

ATLANTIC
OCEAN

GAUL

SPAIN

Adriatic Sea

Rome
ITALY

Black Sea

Mediterranean Sea

SICILY

GREECE

Carthage

A F R I C A

N

SYRIA

EGYPT

509 B.C.
241 B.C.
146 B.C.
• Major city

0   250   500 miles
0   250   500 kilometers

Roman Rule By the second century B.C., Rome controlled land on three continents. **SKILL** **Interpret a Map** Around which body of water was Roman control located in 146 B.C?

The Republic

At first, most of the people elected to the Senate were patricians (puh TRIHSH uhns). In ancient Rome, a **patrician** was a member of a wealthy, landowning family who claimed to be able to trace its roots back to the founding of Rome. The patricians also controlled the law, since they were the only citizens who were allowed to be judges.

An ordinary, working male citizen of ancient Rome—such as a farmer or craftsperson—was called a **plebeian** (plih BEE uhn). Plebeians had the right to vote, but they could not hold public office until 287 B.C., when they gained equality with patricians.

Over hundreds of years, Rome grew into a mighty city. By the third century B.C., Rome ruled most of the Italian Peninsula. This gave Rome control of the central Mediterranean.

The city-state of Carthage, which ruled North Africa and southern Spain, controlled the western Mediterranean. To take control over this area as well, Rome fought Carthage and eventually won.

As Rome's population grew, its army also expanded in size and strength. Under the leadership of ambitious generals, Rome's highly trained soldiers set out to conquer new territories one by one.

As Rome's control over its neighbors expanded, its culture and language continued to spread into Spain and Greece. By the end of the second century B.C., the Romans ruled most of the land surrounding the Mediterranean Sea. The ancient Romans even called the Mediterranean *mare nostrum* (MAH ray NOH struhm), which means "our sea."

REVIEW What was the most powerful body of government in the Roman Republic?

287

From Republic to Empire

Main Idea The Roman Empire grew into one of the greatest empires in the ancient world.

As the Roman Republic grew, its citizens became a more and more diverse group of people. Many Romans practiced different religions and followed different customs, but they were united by a common system of government and law. In the middle of the first century B.C., however, Rome's form of government changed.

Julius Caesar, a successful Roman general and famous speaker, was the governor of the territory called Gaul. By conquering nearby territories to expand the land under his control, he increased both his power and his reputation. The Roman Senate feared that Caesar might become too powerful, and they ordered him to resign. Caesar, however, had other ideas.

Rather than resign, Caesar fought a long, fierce battle for control of the Roman Republic. In 45 B.C., he finally triumphed and returned to Rome. Caesar eventually became dictator of the Roman world. A dictator is a person who holds total control over a government. Caesar's rule marked the end of the Roman Republic.

The Beginning of the Roman Empire

Julius Caesar had great plans to reorganize the way ancient Rome was governed, but his rule was cut short. On March 15, 44 B.C., a group of senators, angered by Caesar's plans and power, stabbed him to death on the floor of the Roman Senate. A civil war then erupted that lasted for several years.

In 27 B.C., Caesar's adopted son, Octavian, was named the first emperor of Rome. This marks the official beginning of the Roman Empire. An **empire** is a nation or group of territories ruled by a single, powerful leader, or emperor. As emperor, Octavian took the name Augustus.

Emperor Sculptures of Augustus were sent all over the Roman Empire to let people know what their ruler looked like.

Julius Caesar When this powerful general became dictator, he had his likeness stamped on coins such as this one.

Roman Achievements

Augustus ruled the Roman Empire for more than 40 years. During this time, called the Augustan Age, the empire continued to expand. To help protect the enormous amount of land under his control, Augustus sent military forces along its borders, which now extended northward to the Rhine and Danube rivers.

While the Roman army kept peace, architects and engineers built many new public buildings. Trade increased, with olive oil, wine, pottery, marble, and grain being shipped all across the Mediterranean. Lighthouses were constructed, too, to help ships find their way into port.

The Augustan Age was also a time of great Roman literature. One of the most famous works of the age is the *Aeneid* (ih NEE ud). This long poem tells the story of Rome's founding. Augustus himself asked the famous poet Virgil to write it.

The period of peace and cultural growth that Augustus created in the Roman Empire was called the "Pax Romana" (pahks roh MAH nah). The Pax Romana, or Roman Peace, lasted for 200 years.

REVIEW What part did Julius Caesar play in the change from republic to empire?

Ancient Road Roman engineers created a vast system of roads uniting the Roman Empire. The roads were so well built that over 2000 years later, some are still in use, such as the one above.

Roman Empire For 200 years, the Romans controlled almost all of the land surrounding the Mediterranean Sea.

SKILL Interpret a Map Name two continents on which the Roman Empire was located.

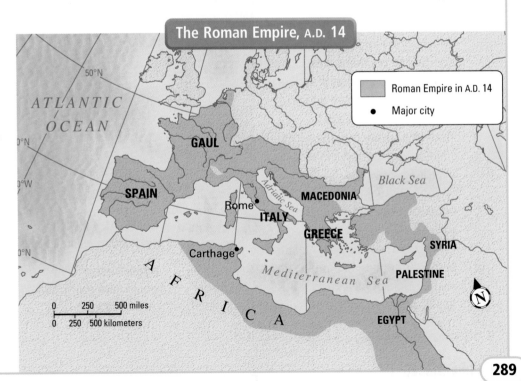

The Roman Empire, A.D. 14

- Roman Empire in A.D. 14
- Major city

50°N

ATLANTIC OCEAN

GAUL

SPAIN

Rome
ITALY

Carthage

MACEDONIA

Black Sea

GREECE

SYRIA

PALESTINE

AFRICA

Mediterranean Sea

EGYPT

Adriatic Sea

0   250   500 miles
0   250   500 kilometers

N

The Rise of Christianity

Main Idea The Roman Empire helped to spread Christianity throughout the world.

In the years following the death of Augustus in A.D. 14, a new religion from the Middle East began to take hold in the rest of the Mediterranean world. The religion was Christianity. At first, Christianity became popular mainly in the eastern half of the Roman Empire. Many followers there preached about its teachings. Christianity spread along the transportation network constructed by the Romans. By the third century A.D., this religion had spread throughout the empire.

Most earlier Roman leaders had tolerated the different religions practiced throughout the empire. Christians, however, were viewed with suspicion and suffered persecution as early as A.D. 64. Roman leaders and people of other religions even blamed the Christians for natural disasters. Many Christians during this time were punished or killed for their beliefs.

Christian Image This early Christian painting shows Moses in a scene from the Bible.

Architecture Various inventions helped the Roman Empire grow and prosper. In addition to buildings and roads, Roman architects and engineers constructed water systems called aqueducts. Ancient aqueducts were raised tunnels that carried fresh water over long distances.

Built throughout the empire, aqueducts poured millions of gallons of water into Rome and other cities every day. They supplied clean water to private homes, fountains, and public baths. Today, some ancient Roman aqueducts still stand in France, Spain, and even on the outskirts of Rome itself.

CRITICAL THINKING Analyze Motives Why did Romans want a way to transport water?

Hypothesize Do you think the Roman Empire would have grown so large and prosperous without the aqueducts?

The First Christian Emperor

Things changed when Constantine became emperor of Rome in A.D. 306. In A.D. 312, before a battle, Constantine claimed to have had a vision of a cross in the sky. The emperor promised that if he won the battle, he would become a Christian. Constantine was victorious, and the next year he fulfilled his promise. Christianity became the official religion of the Roman Empire.

Today, Christianity has nearly two billion followers worldwide.

REVIEW How did the Roman Empire help spread Christianity?

Constantine As the first Christian emperor of Rome, he helped end persecution of Christians.

Lesson Summary

> Around 750 B.C., villages united to become Rome.

> In the sixth century B.C., Rome became a republic.

> Rome defeated Carthage to take control of most of the Mediterranean region.

> The Roman Republic expanded to control all of the Mediterranean and much of Europe by the second century B.C.

> In 27 B.C., Rome became an empire, beginning a 200-year period of peace called the "Pax Romana."

Why It Matters . . .

The cultural achievements of the Romans continue to influence the art, architecture, and literature of today.

Lesson Review

509 B.C.	27 B.C.	313 A.D.
Roman Republic formed	Rome becomes an empire	Christianity official Roman religion

600　　400　　200　　0　　200　　400

1. **VOCABULARY** Use the words **republic** and **empire** in a paragraph comparing the forms of government in the Roman Republic and the Roman Empire.

2. **READING SKILL** What **sequence** of events led to Augustus becoming Rome's first emperor?

3. **MAIN IDEA: Geography** On what river is the city of Rome located?

4. **MAIN IDEA: Citizenship** What helped to unite the many different citizens of the Roman Republic?

5. **MAIN IDEA: History** How did Christianity spread throughout the Roman Empire?

6. **TIMELINE SKILL** How many years did the Roman Republic exist?

7. **PLACES TO KNOW** During the reign of Augustus, what European rivers marked the northern border of the Roman Empire?

8. **CRITICAL THINKING: Draw Conclusions** Why was ancient Rome able to control most of the land surrounding the Mediterranean Sea?

HANDS ON

CHART ACTIVITY Review the information about the beginnings of ancient Rome. Create a chart that compares the two important classes of Roman society: patricians and plebeians.

The Middle Ages

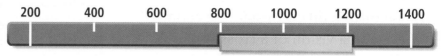

800–1215

Build on What You Know During the summer, has it ever felt like the entire world was just your neighborhood, family, and friends? In the Middle Ages in Europe, most people knew nothing but their own village.

Western Europe in Collapse

Main Idea The long period between the fall of the Roman Empire and the beginning of the modern world is called the Middle Ages.

When Emperor Constantine came to power in A.D. 306, the Roman Empire was already in serious decline. A weakened Roman army was unable to defend the Empire's borders from increasing attacks from Germanic invaders called the Visigoths. In A.D. 476, the Visigoths attacked the city of Rome and overthrew the Emperor Romulus Augustus. This event marked the end of the Roman Empire in the West.

As the Roman Empire collapsed in the fifth century, more and more people fled to the countryside to escape invaders from the north and east. Eventually, there was no central government to maintain roads, public buildings, or water systems. Most towns and cities in Western Europe shrank or were totally abandoned. Long-distance travel became unsafe, and trade less common.

The period of history between the fall of the Roman Empire and the beginning of the modern world is called the Middle Ages, or **medieval** (mee dee EE vuhl) era. During this time, many of the advances and inventions of the ancient world were lost. Without a strong central government, many Europeans turned to military leaders and the Roman Catholic Church for leadership and support.

Charlemagne and the Christian Church

Among the most famous military leaders was the Germanic King Charlemagne (SHAHR luh mayn). In the late 700s, Charlemagne, or Charles the Great, worked to bring political order to the northwestern fringes of what had been the Roman Empire. This great warrior not only fought to increase the size of his kingdom, he also worked to improve life for those who lived there.

Eventually, news of Charlemagne's accomplishments spread to Rome. Although the old empire was gone, Rome was now the center of the Catholic Church. The Pope recognized that joining forces with Charlemagne might bring greater power to the Church.

In 800, the Pope crowned Charlemagne as the new Holy Roman Emperor. During Charlemagne's rule, education improved, the government became stronger, and Catholicism spread. But after Charlemagne's death, Western Europe was once again without a strong political leader.

Religious Communities
Medieval convents and monasteries often were located in hard-to-reach areas.

The Role of the Church

Throughout Western Europe in medieval times, each community was centered around a church. The Church offered religious services, established orphanages, and helped care for the poor, sick, and elderly. It also hosted feasts, festivals, and other celebrations. As communities grew, their members often donated money and labor to build new and larger churches.

Some people chose to dedicate their lives to serving God and the Church. These religious people were called monks and nuns. Monks were men who devoted their time to praying, studying, and copying and decorating holy books by hand. Monks lived in communities called monasteries. Many monasteries became important centers of learning in medieval society.

Women who served the Church were called nuns. In the Middle Ages, it was common for a woman to become a nun after her husband died. Nuns prayed, sewed, taught young girls, cared for the poor, and also copied and decorated books. They lived in secluded communities called convents.

REVIEW Who provided leadership during the Middle Ages?

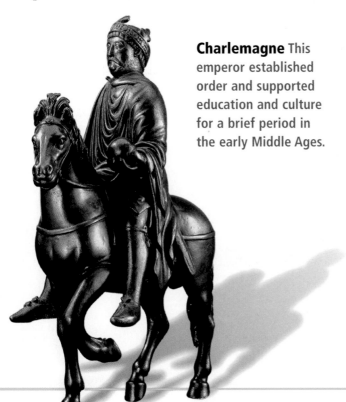

Charlemagne This emperor established order and supported education and culture for a brief period in the early Middle Ages.

Two Medieval Systems

Main Idea Medieval government was largely based on land ownership.

During the Middle Ages, almost all the land was owned by powerful nobles—lords, kings, and high church officials. The central government was not very strong. The nobles sometimes even controlled the king and constantly fought among themselves. To protect their lands and position, nobles developed a system known as feudalism.

Feudalism was a system of political ties in which the nobles, such as kings, gave out land to less powerful nobles, such as knights. In return for the land, the noble, called a vassal, made a vow to provide various services to the lord. The most important was to furnish his lord with knights, foot soldiers, and arms for battle.

The parcel of land granted to a vassal by his lord was called a fief (feef). The center of the lord's fief was the manor, which consisted of a large house or castle, surrounding farmland, villages, and a church. A fief might also include several other manors or castles belonging to the fief-owner's vassals.

On the manor, peasants lived and farmed, but they usually did not own the land they lived on. In exchange for their lord's protection, the peasants contributed their labor and a certain amount of the food they raised. Some peasants, known as serfs, actually belonged to the fief on which they lived. They were not slaves, but they were not free to leave the land without the permission of the lord. This system, in which the lord received food and work in exchange for his protection, is known as **manorialism.**

Medieval Defense Medieval castles were built to defend the surrounding country and towns. They were usually located on high ground with a series of walls and towers.

Medieval Ways of Life

Main Idea The lives of medieval nobles and peasants were slowly changed by the growth of towns and cities.

Medieval nobles had more power than the peasants. However, the difference in the standard of living between the very rich and the very poor was not as great as the difference today.

The manor houses or castles may have been large, but they were built more for defense than for comfort. Thick stone walls and few windows made the rooms cold, damp, and dark. Fires added warmth but made the air smoky. Medieval noble families may have slept on feather mattresses, but lice and other pests were a constant annoyance. Most castles did not have indoor plumbing.

Peasant Life

Peasants lived outside the castle walls in small dwellings, often with dirt floors and straw roofs. They owned little furniture and slept on straw mattresses. It was common for peasant families to keep their farm animals inside their homes.

Peasants often worked two or three days a week for their lord, harvesting crops and repairing roads and bridges. The rest of the week they farmed their own small plots. Many days were religious festivals during which no one worked.

REVIEW What role did manors play in the feudal system?

Middle Class This stained glass window shows a wine merchant. Many people who worked in towns saved money and built businesses. This led to the rise of the middle class.

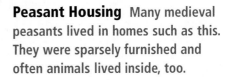

Peasant Housing Many medieval peasants lived in homes such as this. They were sparsely furnished and often animals lived inside, too.

295

The Growth of Medieval Towns

By the middle of the 11th century, life was improving for many people in Western Europe. New farming methods increased the supply of food and shortened the time it took to harvest crops. Fewer farmers were needed, and workers began to leave the countryside in search of other opportunities. People moved back into towns or formed new ones that grew into booming centers of trade. The population increased, and more and more people owned property or started businesses.

Over time, the towns of the late Middle Ages grew in size, power, and wealth. The citizens of these towns began to establish local governments and to elect leaders.

As competition among local business-people grew, tradespeople and craftspeople created their own guilds, or business associations. Similar to modern trade unions, a **guild** protected workers' rights, set wages and prices, and settled disputes. Membership in a guild was also a common requirement for citizens who sought one of the few elective public offices.

Governments Challenge the Church

The Pope insisted that he had supreme authority over all the Christian lands. Kings and other government leaders, however, did not agree that the Pope was more powerful than they were.

Magna Carta This document, which limited the power of the king, influenced the creators of the U.S. Constitution.

Towns Merchants and craftspeople became important members of society during the Middle Ages.

The Magna Carta

The rulers of Western Europe also struggled for power with members of the nobility. In England, nobles rebelled against King John. In 1215, the nobles forced the English king to sign a document called the Magna Carta (MAG nuh KAHR tuh), or Great Charter. This document limited the king's power and gave the nobles a larger role in the government.

REVIEW Why did people create guilds?

King John High taxes and failures on the battlefield made King John one of the most hated kings of England.

Lesson Summary

- The Middle Ages was the era between the collapse of the Roman Empire in the fifth century and the beginning of the modern world.

- As the Roman Empire collapsed, people left towns and cities, and central government disappeared.

- During this period, many Europeans turned to military leaders and the Roman Catholic Church.

- For centuries, people lived under the systems of feudalism and manorialism.

- Slowly, towns and cities grew, and began to elect their governments.

Why It Matters ...

Some developments that occurred during the Middle Ages continue to affect life in Europe today.

Lesson Review

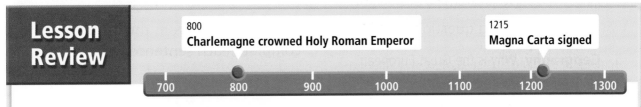

	800 Charlemagne crowned Holy Roman Emperor				1215 Magna Carta signed	
700	800	900	1000	1100	1200	1300

1 **VOCABULARY** Use **medieval** and **feudalism** to complete the sentence.
For centuries during the _____ period, the main organization of society was _____.

2 **READING SKILL** What was a **cause** of the development of feudalism and manorialism?

3 **MAIN IDEA: History** Why is this era of European history called the Middle Ages?

4 **MAIN IDEA: Culture** Describe the role of the Church in medieval society.

5 **MAIN IDEA: Economics** How did manorialism help both nobles and peasants?

6 **PEOPLE TO KNOW** Who was **Charlemagne** and what did he accomplish?

7 **EVENTS TO KNOW** What happened in Western Europe in the middle of the 11th century that improved life for many people?

8 **TIMELINE SKILL** Was Charlemagne emperor before or after the signing of the Magna Carta?

9 **CRITICAL THINKING: Compare and Contrast** How did life differ for nobles and peasants under feudalism?

WRITING ACTIVITY Review the information about peasants, or serfs. Write a series of short journal entries describing what a week in the life of a serf might have been like during the Middle Ages.

Visual Summary

1–4. Write a description for each image below.

Geography and Climate	Ancient Greece	Ancient Rome	Middle Ages

Facts and Main Ideas

Answer the following questions.

5. **Geography** Why is the Great European Plain an important region?

6. **History** What caused the people of Athens to join forces with their rival city-state, Sparta, in 480 B.C.?

7. **Government** Why did the Roman Senate ask Julius Caesar to resign?

8. **Economics** What contributed to the growth of towns during the Middle Ages?

9. **Citizenship** Why did people turn to the Roman Catholic Church for leadership and support during the Middle Ages?

Vocabulary

Choose a word from the list below to complete each sentence.

peninsula, p. 271
oligarchy, p. 276
feudalism, p. 294

10. The Roman Empire was centered in what is now Italy, a large _____ in Europe.

11. Following the collapse of the Roman Empire, the political system in Europe was _____.

12. The control of government by a small group of wealthy, powerful individuals is an _____.

509 B.C.
Roman Republic formed

27 B.C.
Rome becomes an empire

A.D. 313
Christianity official Roman religion

600   400   200   0   200   400

Apply Skills

 TEST PREP **Make a Generalization**
Read the passages and then answer the questions.

> "[The ancient Greeks] believed there were many gods and that those gods controlled the universe."
>
> —*Greek Gods and Heroes*
>
> "Each [Roman] home had a special niche or place for the household gods. Every aspect of nature had its particular spirit too."
>
> —*The New Book of Knowledge*

13. What information do these passages have in common?
    A. They explain a variety of different ancient religions.
    B. They discuss the governments of Greece and Rome.
    C. They describe the trade and commerce of Greece and Rome.
    D. They describe the religious beliefs of ancient Romans and Greeks.

14. What generalization can you make from these passages?
    A. Both ancient Greeks and ancient Romans had household gods.
    B. Both ancient Greeks and ancient Romans believed in many gods.
    C. Both ancient Greeks and ancient Romans traded on the Mediterranean.
    D. Both ancient Greeks and ancient Romans tried to expand their empires.

Critical Thinking

TEST PREP Write a short paragraph to answer each question below.

15. **Draw Conclusions** Many myths and plays of ancient Greece have been the basis for modern films and dramas. What does this indicate about these ancient stories and characters?

16. **Cause and Effect** How did the long, peaceful reign of Augustus help to promote architecture, literature, and art in the Roman Empire?

Timeline

Use the Chapter Summary Timeline above to answer the question.

17. How long was Rome an empire before Christianity became its official religion?

 Activities

 ART ACTIVITY Design and create a poster announcing a sculpture show in ancient Rome. Include a drawing of one of the sculptures, a description of the event, and a short explanation for why the sculpture was carved.

 WRITING ACTIVITY Write a diary entry about the daily life of a noble or knight living on a manor in the 13th century.

Technology

Writing Process Tips
Get help with your diary entry at
www.eduplace.com/kids/hmss05/

The Growth of New Ideas

Technology

e • **glossary**
e • **word games**
www.eduplace.com/kids/hmss05/

Vocabulary Preview

Reformation

Martin Luther was one of the driving forces behind the Protestant **Reformation.** This 16th-century movement sought to reform, or change, the practices of the Roman Catholic Church.
page 306

circumnavigate

The explorer Ferdinand Magellan had a daring idea. He believed that if he kept sailing west from Europe, he would eventually **circumnavigate,** or sail completely around, the world.
page 312

Chapter Timeline

1492
Columbus reaches the Americas

1400   1500   1600

RUSSIA

ATLANTIC

WESTERN
EUROPE

PACIFIC

PACIFIC
OCEAN

OCEAN

INDIAN
OCEAN

OCEAN

Reading Strategy

Question As you read, ask yourself questions to check your understanding.

quick Tip Write down a question you have and answer it when you finish reading.

labor force

As factories were built in cities, they needed workers, or a **labor force,** in order to operate. Factory laborers worked long hours and received low pay.
page 317

czar

Russia was ruled by a **czar,** or emperor, from 1547 until 1917. Czar Peter the Great introduced many ideas from Western Europe to Russia.
page 321

1789
French Revolution begins

1917
Russian Revolution

1800   1900   2000

Renaissance Connections

1200	1300	1400	1500	1600	1700

1300–1600

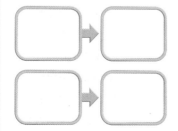

Build on What You Know Have you ever noticed how new ideas can spread quickly through your school? You might have heard a new musical group that you really like. Soon, everyone seems to be listening to the group. New ideas spread through Europe in a similar way as the Middle Ages ended.

Rebirth of Europe

Main Idea The rebirth of art, literature, and ideas during the Renaissance changed European society.

The **Crusades** —a series of expeditions from the 11th to the 13th centuries by Western European Christians to capture the Holy Lands from Muslims—greatly changed life in Western Europe. The Crusades opened up trade routes, linking Western Europe with southwestern Asia and North Africa. They also helped Europeans rediscover the ideas of ancient Greece and Rome.

Crusades King Louis IX of France led his army to the Holy Land during the eighth Crusade.

The Renaissance

Over time, this interest in the ancient world sparked a new era of creativity and learning in Western Europe. This cultural era, which lasted from the 14th to the 16th century, is called the **Renaissance.**

The Renaissance began on the Italian Peninsula in the mid-14th century. During this time, many artists, architects, writers, and scholars created works of great importance. These included beautiful paintings, large sculptures, impressive buildings, and thought-provoking literature. As new ideas and achievements spread across the continent of Europe, they changed the way people viewed themselves and the world.

Florence Once a wealthy city-state, this city remains an important economic and cultural center of Italy. The Duomo, shown here, is a symbol of the city's Renaissance past.

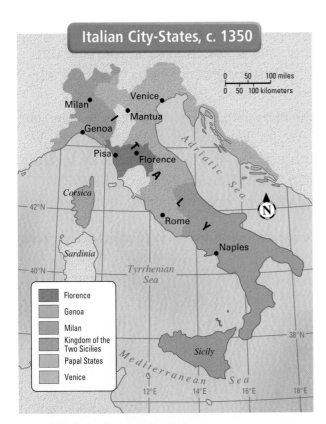

City-States The Italian peninsula was made up of independently governed realms.

SKILL **Interpret a Map** Which city-state does not have access to water?

The Italian City-States

In the 14th century, the Italian Peninsula was divided into many independent city-states. Some of these city-states, such as Florence, were bustling centers of banking, trade, and manufacturing.

The wealthy businesspeople who lived in these city-states were members of a new class of aristocrats. Unlike the nobles of the feudal system, these aristocrats lived in cities. Their wealth came from earning money and producing goods rather than from the lands they owned or inherited wealth.

Religion was important to people's daily life during the Renaissance, but many wealthy Europeans began to turn increased attention to the material comforts of life.

REVIEW How did the new class of aristocrats in the Renaissance differ from the nobles of the feudal system?

Palazzo The wealthy merchants in Italy built large palaces, called palazzos, such as Florence's Palazzo Medici shown here.

Aristocrats

New wealth allowed aristocratic families to build large homes for themselves in the city centers, decorating them with luxurious objects. They ate expensive food and dressed in fine clothes and jewels, often acquired as a result of the expanded trade routes. Aristocrats also placed increased emphasis on education and the arts.

Learning and the Arts Flourish

Main Idea Newly wealthy European merchants strongly supported artists and architects.

Wealthy citizens were proud of their city-states and often became generous patrons. A patron gave artists and scholars money and, sometimes, a place to live and work. They hired architects and designers to improve local churches, to design grand new buildings, and to create public sculptures and fountains. As one Italian city-state made additions and improvements, others competed to outdo it.

As part of the competition to improve the appearance and status of their individual city-states, patrons wanted to attract the brightest and best-known scholars and poets of the time. Patrons believed that the contributions of these individuals would, in turn, add to the greatness of their city-states and attract more wealth.

Most medieval art was based on religious subjects. Painters and sculptors of the early Renaissance created religious art too, but they also began to depict other subjects. Some made portraits for wealthy patrons. Others created works showing historical scenes or mythological stories.

The Medici Family Among the most famous patrons of the Renaissance were the Medici (MEHD uh chee). They were a wealthy family of bankers and merchants. In fact, they were the most powerful leaders of Florence from the early 1400s until the 1700s.

Along with Lorenzo, pictured here, the Medici family included famous princes and dukes, two queens, and four popes. Throughout the 15th and 16th centuries, the Medici supported many artists, including Botticelli, Michelangelo, and Raphael. Today, Florence is still filled with important works of art made possible by the Medici.

One of the most famous artists and scientists of the Renaissance was **Leonardo da Vinci** (lee uh NAHR doh duh VIHN chee) (1452–1519). Among his best-known paintings are the *Mona Lisa*, a portrait of a young woman with a mysterious smile, and *The Last Supper*. Da Vinci was more than just a talented painter, however.

Throughout his life, da Vinci observed the world around him. He studied the flow of water, the flight of birds, and the workings of the human body. Da Vinci, who became a skilled engineer, scientist, and inventor, filled notebooks with thousands of sketches of his discoveries and inventions. He even drew ideas for flying machines, parachutes, and submarines—hundreds of years before they were built.

The Northern Renaissance

As the new Renaissance ideas about religion and art spread to Northern Europe, they inspired artists and writers working there. The Dutch scholar and philosopher Desiderius Erasmus (ih RAS muhs) (1466–1536), for example, criticized the church for its wealth and poked fun at its officials. During the late 16th and early 17th centuries, another writer—the Englishman **William Shakespeare**—wrote a series of popular stage plays. Many of his works, including *Romeo and Juliet* and *Macbeth*, are still read and performed around the world.

REVIEW How did the subject matter of Renaissance art differ from medieval art?

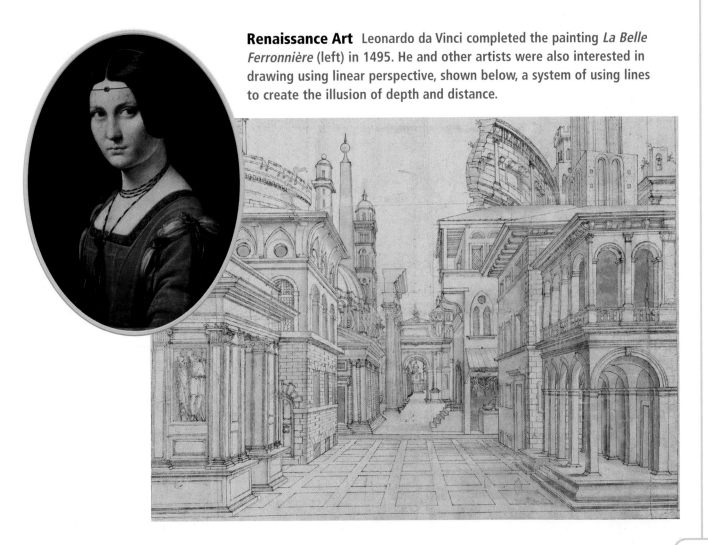

Renaissance Art Leonardo da Vinci completed the painting *La Belle Ferronnière* (left) in 1495. He and other artists were also interested in drawing using linear perspective, shown below, a system of using lines to create the illusion of depth and distance.

The Reformation

Main Idea In the 1500s, the authority of the Roman Catholic Church was challenged, changing the religious organization of Europe.

Roman Catholicism was still the most powerful religion in Western Europe. Some of the views of the northern Renaissance writers and scholars, however, were in conflict with the Roman Catholic Church. These new ideas would eventually lead to the **Reformation,** a 16th-century movement to change church practices.

The German monk Martin Luther (1483–1546) was one of the most important critics of the church. The wealth and corruption of many church officials disturbed him. Luther also spoke out against the church's policy of selling indulgences—the practice of forgiving penance, or punishment for sins, in exchange for money.

A Conflict over Religious Beliefs

In 1517, Luther wrote The 95 Theses, or statements of belief, attacking the sale of indulgences and other church practices. Copies were printed and handed out throughout Western Europe. After this, Luther was excommunicated, or cast out of the Roman Catholic Church. Luther then went into hiding and translated the Bible from Latin into German so that all literate, German-speaking people could read it. Under Luther's leadership, many Europeans began to challenge the practices of the Roman Catholic Church.

Luther's followers were called Protestants because they protested events at an assembly that ended the church's tolerance of their beliefs. Many people in Western Europe still supported the church, however. This conflict led to religious wars that ended in 1555. At that time, the Peace of Augsburg declared that German rulers could decide the official religion of their own state.

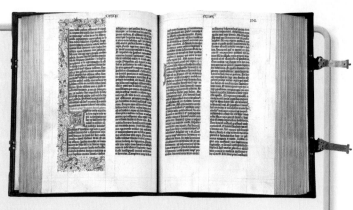

The Printing Press Until the Renaissance, each copy of a book had to be written by hand—usually by monks or nuns. A Renaissance invention, however, changed that forever. Around 1450, a German printer named Johann Gutenberg (YOH hahn GOO tuhn berg) began to use a method of printing with movable type. This meant that multiple copies of books, such as this Bible, could be printed quickly and less expensively.

Although many Renaissance books dealt with religious subjects, printers also published plays, poetry, works of philosophy and science, and tales of travel and adventure. As greater numbers of books were published, more and more Europeans learned to read.

CRITICAL THINKING Recognize Effects What were three effects of the invention of Gutenberg's printing press?

Synthesize Before the printing press, who produced the books?

By 1600, Protestantism had spread to England and the Scandinavian Peninsula. Protestants pushed to expand education for more Europeans. They did this because being able to read meant being able to study the Bible. They also encouraged translation of the Bible into the native language of each country.

The Roman Catholic Church responded to Protestantism by launching its own movement in the mid-16th century. As part of this movement, called the Counter Reformation, the church stopped selling indulgences. New religious orders, such as the Society of Jesus, or the Jesuits, were formed.

REVIEW How did Protestants get their name?

Martin Luther His writings and actions changed Christianity.

Lesson Summary

> **The Rebirth of Europe**

> The Crusades opened trade for Europe and helped Europeans rediscover the ideas of ancient Greece and Rome.

> The Renaissance was a new era of creativity and learning.

> New wealth from trade encouraged developments in the arts, architecture, and learning.

> The views of some northern Renaissance writers and scholars led to the Reformation.

Why It Matters . . .

Many accomplishments of the Renaissance are high points of Western culture and continue to inspire artists, writers, and thinkers of today.

Lesson Review

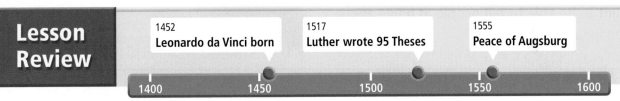

1452
Leonardo da Vinci born

1517
Luther wrote 95 Theses

1555
Peace of Augsburg

1400 1450 1500 1550 1600

❶ **VOCABULARY** Use **Reformation** in a paragraph explaining how conflict over religious ideas changed Western Europe.

❷ **READING SKILL** What **effect** did wealthy city-states have on Renaissance art, literature, and architecture?

❸ **MAIN IDEA: History** Where and when did the Renaissance begin?

❹ **MAIN IDEA: Culture** What was the Counter Reformation?

❺ **PEOPLE TO KNOW** What were two reasons that **Martin Luther** became a critic of the Roman Catholic Church?

❻ **TIMELINE SKILL** In what year did the religious wars end between Roman Catholics and Protestants?

❼ **CRITICAL THINKING: Analyze** Why do you think Protestantism spread so quickly in Northern Europe?

WRITING ACTIVITY Write a letter to an imagined patron for support to create a project—such as a public sculpture, park, fountain, or building—to beautify your community.

Spend a Day in

Renaissance Florence

You are a traveler visiting Florence, Italy, in the year 1505. It is exciting to be here now. All over Europe, people have heard about the Renaissance, or cultural rebirth, that is taking place in this beautiful city. Artists, architects, writers, and scientists are turning out brilliant work. In the day you spend here, you want to learn about this new cultural movement. You want to be able to tell people at home about Renaissance Florence.

Major Figures of the Renaissance

- **Filippo Brunelleschi** (1377–1446), architect of the Duomo and the Pitti Palace.

- **Dante** (1265–1321), poet, author of *Divine Comedy*. Dante pioneered the usage of everyday language, instead of Latin, in literature.

- **Isabella d'Este** (1474–1539), noblewoman and patron of many artists.

- **Leonardo da Vinci** (1452–1519), painter, sculptor, engineer, scientist.

- **Michelangelo** (1475–1564), sculptor, painter, architect; sculptor of *David* (1504).

- **Raphael** (1483–1520), painter and architect.

Duomo This dome stands on the Piazza del Duomo, an open square. In 1418, Filippo Brunelleschi won a contest to build a dome over an unfinished church. He invented new methods and machines to build it. As in earlier domes, vaults or pointed arches support the dome. Brunelleschi added a circular support wall, called a drum, to build it higher.

The City Florence is built on both sides of the Arno. Florence's population during the Renaissance was about 100,000. Besides its artists, Renaissance Florence was known for its craftworkers, especially goldsmiths and leatherworkers.

Ponte Vecchio ("Old Bridge") Built in 1345, this is one of several bridges across the Arno River. Shops, especially those of goldsmiths, line both sides of the bridge.

Pitti Palace This palace is another creation of architect Filippo Brunelleschi. Built for the wealthy merchant Luca Pitti around 1440, the original palace was expanded and improved by later ruling aristocrats in Florence, such as the powerful Medici family.

Isabella d'Este Isabella d'Este was a well-educated noble. As a patron of the arts she supported local writers, poets, and painters. Isabella also exchanged ideas about art with other Italian artists, including Raphael.

Activities

1. **THINK ABOUT IT** Imagine you are an ordinary young Florentine living in 1505. What would have interested or impressed you most about the city? Why?

2. **WRITE ABOUT IT** Choose one major figure who lived in Florence during the Renaissance and research his or her life. Then write a short first-person monologue in which, speaking as that person, you describe your life and work.

309

Traders, Explorers, and Colonists

VOCABULARY

circumnavigate
imperialism

Vocabulary Strategy

circumnavigate

Divide the word **circumnavigate** into two parts, **circum** and **navigate**. Circum contains **circ** for **circle.** Circumnavigate means to completely circle, or navigate around the world.

READING SKILL

Compare and Contrast
Take notes to compare and contrast exploration and colonization by different European countries.

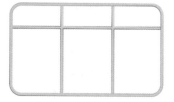

Build on What You Know Have you ever tried to find a new way to get to school? Have you looked for shortcuts? In the 1500s, Europeans started to look for a new way to get to Asia. To their surprise, they found the Americas.

Trade Between Europe and Asia

Main Idea As they competed for trade with Asia, European countries sent ships around Africa and across the Atlantic Ocean.

For centuries before the Renaissance, European traders traveled back and forth across the Mediterranean. Merchants commonly journeyed from southern Europe to North Africa and to the eastern Mediterranean. Spices were one of the most important items traded at this time.

Spices were in great demand by Europeans. Before refrigeration, meat and fish spoiled quickly. To help preserve food and to improve its flavor, people used spices such as pepper, cinnamon, nutmeg, and cloves. These spices came from Asia. For centuries, Italian merchants from Genoa and Venice controlled the Asian spice trade. They sailed to ports in the eastern Mediterranean, where they would purchase spices and other goods from traders who had traveled across Asia. The Italian merchants would then bring these goods back to Europe.

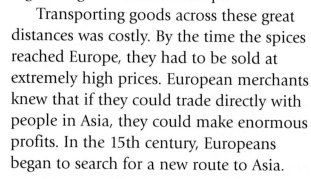

Astrolabe Sailors calculated their ship's position with the astrolabe. It measured the position of the sun and stars in relation to the horizon.

Transporting goods across these great distances was costly. By the time the spices reached Europe, they had to be sold at extremely high prices. European merchants knew that if they could trade directly with people in Asia, they could make enormous profits. In the 15th century, Europeans began to search for a new route to Asia.

Henry the Navigator This Portuguese prince supported sailing expeditions around Africa and helped advance the science of navigation.

Leaders in Exploration

The small country of Portugal is at the westernmost part of the European continent. Portuguese sailors had navigated the waters of the Atlantic Ocean for centuries. As shown on the map on page 312, they traveled down the west coast of Africa and as far west into the Atlantic as Madeira, the Azores, and the Canary Islands.

In the early 1400s, Portugal's Prince Henry the Navigator decided to send explorers farther down the coast of Africa. He believed that if explorers could find a way around Africa, it might be a shortcut to Asia. Portuguese explorers returned home from these expeditions with gold dust, ivory, and more knowledge of navigation. By the time Henry died in 1460, the Portuguese had ventured around the great bulge of western Africa to present-day Sierra Leone.

Bold Portuguese explorers continued to push farther down the African coast. Finally, in 1488, Bartolomeu Dias (bahr too loo MAY oo DEE uhsh) rounded the southern tip of Africa. The Portuguese named the tip the Cape of Good Hope.

Less than ten years later, Vasco da Gama (VAS koh deh GAH muh) led a sea expedition all the way to Asia. Da Gama and his crew traveled for 317 days and 13,500 miles before reaching the coast of India. They were the first Europeans to discover a sea route to Asia. Now, the riches of Asia could be brought directly to Europe. After setting up trading posts along the coast of the Indian Ocean, Portugal ruled these waterways.

Portugal was not the only European country to understand that whoever controlled trade with Asia would have great power and wealth. Spain and England quickly entered the race to find a direct sea route of their own.

Some explorers believed that the shortest way to Asia was to sail west across the Atlantic Ocean. Queen Isabella of Spain agreed to fund an expedition across the Atlantic.

In August 1492, an Italian named Christopher Columbus and 90 crew members left Spain aboard three ships—the *Santa Maria*, the *Pinta*, and the *Niña*. The Atlantic Ocean proved to be wider than maps of the time suggested. On October 12, after weeks at sea, the crew spotted land. Although Columbus thought he had found Asia, they were off the coast of an island in the Caribbean. This was still a great distance from their spice-rich destination.

REVIEW What land did Columbus reach, and where did he think he was?

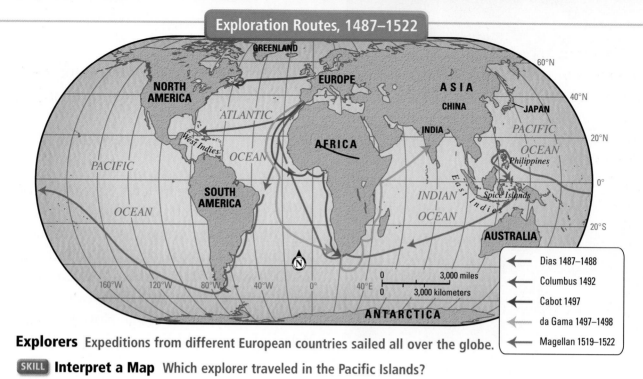

Exploration Routes, 1487–1522

Dias 1487–1488
Columbus 1492
Cabot 1497
da Gama 1497–1498
Magellan 1519–1522

Explorers Expeditions from different European countries sailed all over the globe.

SKILL **Interpret a Map** Which explorer traveled in the Pacific Islands?

After Columbus

Main Idea European exploration changed the lives of people on both sides of the Atlantic.

The kings and queens of Europe sent explorers in search of a direct trade route to Asia. These expeditions, however, turned out to have unexpected results.

In 1519, Spain funded an expedition for the Portuguese explorer Ferdinand Magellan (muh JEHL uhn). Magellan left Spain with five ships and more than 200 sailors. As they traveled west, the crew battled violent storms and rough seas. Food was in short supply, and starving sailors ate rats and sawdust. Some died of disease.

By the time Magellan and his ships reached the Philippines in Asia, the sailors had spent 18 long months at sea. Then, during a battle there, Magellan and several crew members were killed. The expedition returned to Spain after a three-year journey. Only one boat and 18 crew members succeeded. They were the first people to **circumnavigate,** or sail completely around, the world.

King Henry VII of England did not want Portugal and Spain to claim all the riches of Asia. He funded a voyage by Italian-born Giovanni Caboto, called John Cabot by the English, who believed that a northern route across the Atlantic Ocean might be a shortcut to Asia. When they reached land, however, they most likely had landed in present-day Newfoundland in Canada.

European countries founded many new colonies along the coastal areas of Africa and North and South America. This practice of one country controlling the government and economy of another country or territory is called **imperialism.**

These conquered lands were already home to large, self-ruling populations. They had their own cultural traditions.

The European monarchs were Christians. They had strong religious beliefs, and they sent missionaries and other religious officials to help convert conquered peoples to Christianity.

Without knowing it, the European explorers and colonists carried diseases with them, including smallpox, malaria, and measles. These diseases were unknown in the Americas, and killed hundreds of thousands of people there.

European explorations also led to an expanding slave trade. The Portuguese purchased West Coast African people to work as slaves back in Portugal, where the work force had been reduced by plague. In other colonized areas, such as Mexico and parts of South America, Europeans forced conquered peoples to work the land where they lived. For hundreds of years, Africans and conquered peoples of the Americas would be forced to work under horrible conditions.

REVIEW What effect did European exploration have on people in Africa?

Lesson Summary

- European countries competed for the riches from trade with Asia. Portugal found a route around Africa.

- Christopher Columbus was the first European to reach the Americas.

- Ferdinand Magellan's crew was the first to circumnavigate the world.

- Portugal, Spain, and England established colonies in Africa and North and South America.

- European conquerors brought European culture and ideas to the new lands, but also disease and slavery.

Why It Matters . . .

Today, citizens of the Americas and Africa continue to feel the effects of European exploration and colonization.

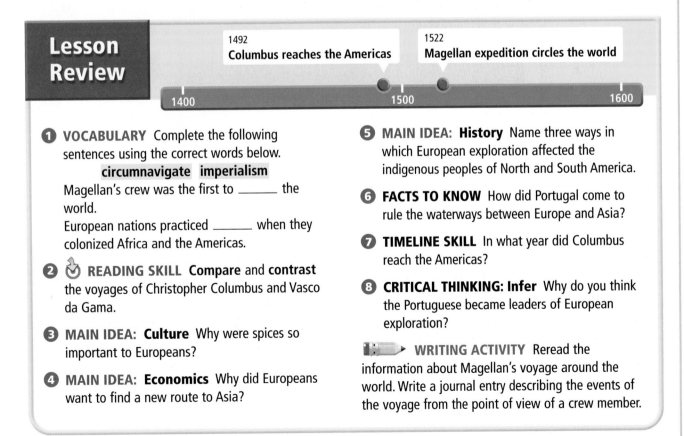

Lesson Review

1492
Columbus reaches the Americas

1522
Magellan expedition circles the world

1400   1500   1600

1. **VOCABULARY** Complete the following sentences using the correct words below.
   circumnavigate   imperialism
   Magellan's crew was the first to _____ the world.
   European nations practiced _____ when they colonized Africa and the Americas.

2. 📖 **READING SKILL** **Compare** and **contrast** the voyages of Christopher Columbus and Vasco da Gama.

3. **MAIN IDEA: Culture** Why were spices so important to Europeans?

4. **MAIN IDEA: Economics** Why did Europeans want to find a new route to Asia?

5. **MAIN IDEA: History** Name three ways in which European exploration affected the indigenous peoples of North and South America.

6. **FACTS TO KNOW** How did Portugal come to rule the waterways between Europe and Asia?

7. **TIMELINE SKILL** In what year did Columbus reach the Americas?

8. **CRITICAL THINKING: Infer** Why do you think the Portuguese became leaders of European exploration?

✏️ **WRITING ACTIVITY** Reread the information about Magellan's voyage around the world. Write a journal entry describing the events of the voyage from the point of view of a crew member.

Research Topics on the Internet

The Internet is a computer network that connects libraries, museums, universities, government agencies, businesses, news organizations, and private individuals all over the world. Each location on the Internet has a home page with its own address, or URL (universal resource locator). With a computer connected to the Internet, you can reach the home pages of many organizations and services. The international collection of home pages, known as the World Wide Web, is an excellent source of up-to-date information about the regions and countries of the world.

The Web page shown below is the European Reading Room at the Library of Congress Web site. Use the steps listed to the right to help you understand how to research topics on the Internet.

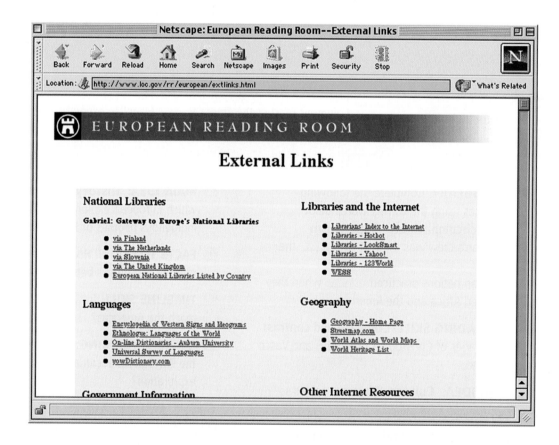

Learn the Skill

Step 1: Once on the Internet, go directly to the Web page. For example, type http://www.loc.gov/rr/european/extlinks.html in the box at the top of the Web browser and press ENTER. The Web page will appear on your screen.

Location: http://www.loc.gov/rr/european/extlinks.html

Step 2: Explore the European Reading Room links. Click any of the links to find more information about a subject. These links take you to other Web sites.

National Libraries

Gabriel: Gateway to Europe's National Libraries

- via Finland
- via The Netherlands
- via Slovenia
- via The United Kingdom
- European National Libraries Listed by Country

Step 3: Always confirm information you have found on the Internet. The Web sites of universities, government agencies, museums, and trustworthy news organizations are more reliable than others. You can often find information about a site's creator by looking for copyright information or reviewing the home page.

Practice the Skill

Use the Web page to the left to answer these questions.
1. Which link will take you to a list of European National Libraries?
2. What is a link that will take you to an on-line dictionary?

Apply the Skill

Turn to Chapter 11, Lesson 1, "Renaissance Connections." Reread the lesson and make a list of topics you would like to research.

The Age of Revolution

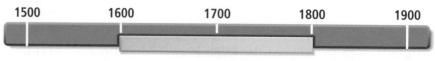

1500   1600   1700   1800   1900

1600–1800

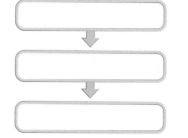
Build on What You Know Have you ever visited a doctor because you felt ill? The doctor may have given you medicine. The discovery of medicines to treat diseases was just one result of the Scientific Revolution in Europe.

Changes in Science and Industry

Main Idea Scientific and Industrial Revolutions in Europe transformed the world.

In the 1600s and 1700s, scientists and inventors made so many discoveries that Europe experienced what became known as the **Scientific Revolution.** This revolutionary period of scientific discovery changed the way Europeans looked at the world and helped create modern societies.

In Italy, Galileo Galilei (gal uh LEE oh gal uh LAY) (1564–1642) studied the stars and planets using a new invention called the telescope. Later in Holland, Antoni van Leeuwenhoek (LAY vuhn huk) (1632–1723) used a microscope to explore an unknown world found in a drop of water. The Swedish botanist Carolus Linnaeus (lih NEE uhs) (1707–1778) even developed a system to name and classify all living things on Earth.

Telescope In 1610, Galileo used his telescope to discover that Jupiter had moons.

Watch This silver watch was made in 1724 by John Canter of Salisbury, England.

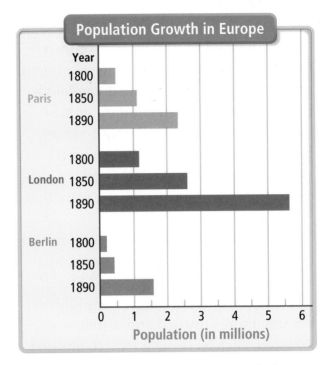

Population Growth in Europe

Population (in millions)

City Growth During the Industrial Revolution, urban population boomed.

SKILL Interpret a Chart Which city had the largest growth in population?

The Workshop of the World

Many inventions of the Scientific Revolution began to change the way people worked all across Europe. Machines performed jobs that once had been done by humans and animals. This brought about such great change that it led to a revolution in the way goods were produced: the **Industrial Revolution.**

Machines were grouped together to make products in large factories. Early factories were built in the countryside near streams and rivers so that they could be powered by water. By the late 1700s, however, new steam engines were used to power the machinery. More and more factories could now be built in cities. People, in turn, moved from the countryside to the cities in search of work.

The Industrial Revolution began in England in the late 1700s. The first English factories made textiles, or cloth. The steam-powered machines of the textile industry produced large amounts of goods quickly and cheaply. So many factories were built in England that the country earned the nickname "The Workshop of the World."

Hard Work for Low Pay

The Industrial Revolution created a need for workers, or a **labor force,** in cities. The workers who ran the textile machines made up part of this labor force. Most workers could earn more income in cities than on farms, but life could be hard. Factory laborers worked long hours and received low pay. In fact, many families often sent their children to work to help create more income.

In 1838, women and children made up more than 75 percent of all textile factory workers. Children as young as seven were forced to work 12 hours a day, six days a week.

REVIEW How did the Scientific Revolution lead to the Industrial Revolution?

The Spread of Industrialization

The textile industry in 18th-century England was one step in the development of an economic system called **capitalism.** In this system, factories and other businesses that make and sell goods are privately owned. Private business owners make decisions about what goods to produce. They sell these goods at a price that will earn a profit.

Industrialization spread from England to other countries, including Germany, France, Belgium, and the United States. Cities in these countries grew rapidly and became more crowded and dirtier. Diseases, such as cholera (KAHL uhr uh) and typhoid (TY foyd) fever, spread. Smoke from factories blackened city skies, and pollution fouled the rivers.

The French Revolution

Main Idea The French Revolution in 1789 transformed the politics of Europe.

Along with changes in science, technology, and the economy came new ideas about government. In the late 18th century, many ordinary citizens began to fight for more political rights.

By the 1780s, the French government was deeply in debt because of bad investments and the costs of waging wars. Life was miserable for the common working people. Poor harvests combined with increased population had led to food shortages and hunger. People were forced to pay heavy taxes. At the same time, the French king, Louis XVI, and his queen, Marie Antoinette, continued to enjoy an expensive life at court, entertaining themselves and the French nobility.

The citizens of France demanded changes in the government, without success. Then, on July 14, 1789, angry mobs stormed a Paris prison called the Bastille (ba STEEL). The attack on this prison, which reflected the royal family's power, became symbolic of the French Revolution.

Revolts spread from Paris to the countryside, and poor and angry workers burned the homes of the nobility. By 1791, France had a new constitution that gave civil rights to French citizens.

Factory Factories, like this one in Sheffield, England, were found throughout Western Europe by the mid-19th century.

The Bastille
This prison used to be a military fortress. Today, the French celebrate Bastille Day, their most important national holiday, on the anniversary of the storming of the Bastille.

Guillotine
During the Reign of Terror, this kind of killing machine was used to end the lives of French royalty and nobility.

The French Republic

In 1792, France became a republic. King Louis XVI was found guilty of treason, or betraying one's country. In 1793, he and Marie Antoinette were sentenced to death. They were beheaded on the guillotine (GIHL uh teen).

Still, France was not at peace. The new revolutionary leaders refused to tolerate any disagreement. Between 1793 and 1794, these new leaders executed 17,000 people. This period of bloodshed became known as the Reign of Terror.

French leaders continued to struggle for power until 1799, when General Napoleon Bonaparte (nuh POH lee uhn BOH nuh pahrt) took control. The French Revolution and the disorder that followed were finally over.

REVIEW Why did French citizens demand a new government?

The new sense of equality brought about by the Revolution stirred feelings of pride and loyalty to their nation among the French. Before this, most people felt a stronger connection to their king or queen or to their religion. Soon, the citizens of other European nations began to fight for more political power. Slowly, they, too, won more rights.

Lesson Summary

Scientific discoveries in the 16th and 17th centuries changed the way Europeans looked at the world. Ideas and inventions created in the Scientific Revolution led to the Industrial Revolution. Factories and steam-powered machines transformed the economy of Europe and the United States. Along with changes in science, technology, and the economy came new ideas about government. Ordinary citizens began to fight for more political rights.

Why It Matters...

European revolutions in science, technology, and politics helped to create modern societies throughout the world.

Napoleon Bonaparte This general crowned himself emperor of France in 1804. He led France to victory in what became known as the Napoleonic Wars.

Lesson Review

1789	1799
French Revolution begins	**Napoleon Bonaparte rules France**

1600   1700   1800   1900   2000

❶ **VOCABULARY** Write a short paragraph explaining the relationship between **capitalism** and the **labor force.**

❷ 🕮 **READING SKILL** Europe's Age of Revolutions followed a logical order. Write a short paragraph to explain the **sequence** of changes that transformed society.

❸ **MAIN IDEA: History** Describe at least three inventions or discoveries of the Scientific Revolution.

❹ **MAIN IDEA: Economics** How did the Industrial Revolution change the way people in Europe worked?

❺ **MAIN IDEA: Government** What changes occurred in France after the French Revolution?

❻ **PEOPLE TO KNOW** Who was **Antoni van Leeuwenhoek?**

❼ **TIMELINE SKILL** How many years after the start of the French Revolution did Napoleon come to power?

❽ **CRITICAL THINKING: Cause and Effect** How did industrialization change the cities to which it spread?

MUSIC ACTIVITY Reread the section about the French Revolution. Write a poem or lyrics for a folk song that describe the events from the point of view of a common citizen or a member of the royal family.

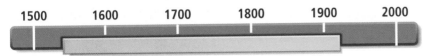

The Russian Empire

| 1500 | 1600 | 1700 | 1800 | 1900 | 2000 |

1547–1918

Build on What You Know Have you ever been with a group of people, such as in a club or on a sports team, where just one person wanted to make all of the decisions, no matter what anyone else thought? That's how life was in the huge country of Russia for hundreds of years.

Russia Rules Itself

Main Idea Strong leaders who held all the power built Russia into a large empire.

Russia, geographically the world's largest nation, is located in both Europe and Asia. It takes up large parts of both continents, and both continents have helped shape its history.

Mongols from eastern Asia conquered Russia in the 13th century and ruled it for about 200 years. During the 15th century, Russia broke free of Mongol rule. At this time, the most important Russian city was Moscow, located in the west.

In 1547, a 16-year-old leader in Moscow was crowned the first **czar** (zahr), or emperor, of modern Russia. His official title was Ivan IV, but the people nicknamed him Ivan the Terrible. Ivan was known for his cruelty, especially toward those he viewed as Russia's enemies. During his rule of 37 years, the country was constantly at war.

VOCABULARY

czar
unlimited government

Vocabulary Strategy

czar

The word **czar** is a Russian form of the word **caesar,** the title of ancient Rome's first emperor. The czar was the emperor of Russia.

READING SKILL

Compare and Contrast As you read, use your chart to list differences between Russian emperors.

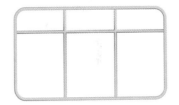

Crown Ivan the Terrible is believed to have worn this fur-trimmed crown at his coronation in 1547.

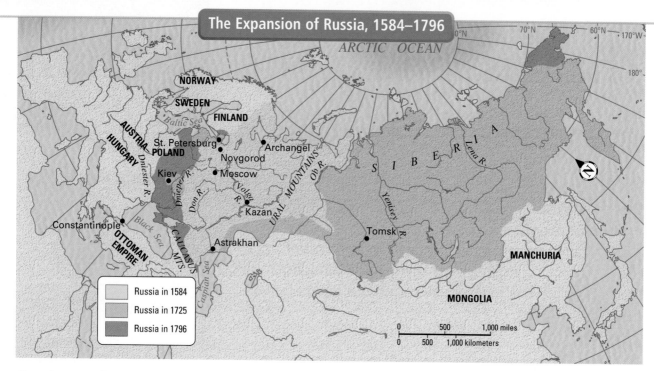

The Expansion of Russia, 1584–1796

Russian Empire This large country stretched from Eastern Europe to the Pacific Ocean.

SKILL **Interpret a Map** What body of water did Russia gain access to in 1796?

The Czars of Russia

During the reigns of Ivan the Terrible and the czars who followed him, Russia had an **unlimited government.** This is a form of government in which a single ruler holds all the power. The people have no say in how the country is run.

The first Russian czars were often in conflict with the Russian nobles, who possessed much land and wealth. The czars viewed the nobles as a threat to their control. Ivan the Terrible ordered his soldiers to murder Russian nobles and church leaders who opposed him.

The poor farmers, or peasants, of Russia also suffered under the first czars. New laws forced the peasants to become serfs, who had to remain on the farms where they worked.

In addition to strengthening their control over the Russian people, the czars wanted to gain new territory. Rulers such as Peter the Great and Catherine the Great conquered neighboring lands.

A Window on the West

An intelligent man with big ideas for his country, Peter the Great ruled Russia from 1682 to 1725. After defeating Sweden in war and winning land along the Baltic Sea, Peter built a port city called St. Petersburg. This city, which Peter saw as Russia's "window on the west," became the new capital.

One of Peter's goals was to have closer ties with Western Europe. He hoped to use the ideas and inventions of the Scientific Revolution to modernize and strengthen Russia. During his rule, Peter reformed the army and the government and built new schools. He even ordered Russians to dress like Europeans and to shave off their beards. Peter's reforms made Russia stronger, but they did not improve life for Russian peasants.

A Great Empress

Catherine the Great took control of Russia in 1762 and ruled until her death in 1796. Catherine added vast new lands to the empire, including the present-day countries of Ukraine (yoo KRAYN) and Belarus (behl uh ROOS). Like Peter the Great, Catherine borrowed many ideas from Western Europe. She started new schools and encouraged art, science, and literature. Catherine also built new towns and expanded trade.

During Catherine's reign, Russia became one of Europe's most powerful nations. The lives of the peasants, however, remained miserable. Catherine thought about freeing them, but she knew the nobles would oppose her. When the peasants rebelled in the 1770s, Catherine crushed their uprising.

REVIEW Why did the Russian people give Czar Ivan IV the nickname Ivan the Terrible?

Catherine the Great She continued Peter the Great's practice of bringing the ideas of Western Europe to Russia.

The Hermitage Museum One of the world's largest art museums is the Hermitage in St. Petersburg. It contains many works of art, including French, Spanish, and British paintings. Part of the collection is in the Winter Palace, a former royal residence.

Both Peter the Great and Catherine the Great collected European art. On a trip to Amsterdam in 1716, Peter bought paintings by the famous Dutch artist Rembrandt. About 50 years later, Catherine bought more than 200 works of art when she visited Germany. These royal collections became part of the Hermitage when it opened as a public museum in 1852.

CRITICAL THINKING Analyze Motives Why did Peter the Great and Catherine the Great collect art from Western Europe?

Make Inferences Why do you think the works of art were displayed in a museum?

A Divided Russia

Main Idea Russia was a large and powerful empire, but the country's citizens had few rights and struggled with poverty.

In the 19th century, Russia remained a divided nation. Most people were poor peasants, and most of the wealth belonged to the nobles. This division would lead to conflict and eventually to a political revolution.

Many Russian nobles sent their children to be educated in Germany and France. In fact, many noble families spoke French at home, speaking Russian only to their servants. The Western Europeans introduced many new ideas to the Russian nobles, among them the idea that a nation's government should reflect the wishes of its citizens.

Many Russian nobles were army officers or government officials. Most supported the czar and were proud of Russia's growing power. In 1825, one group of nobles tried to replace the government. Their attempt to gain more power failed.

In the 19th century, the Russian serfs still had no land or money of their own. They worked on farms owned by others and received little help from the Russian government.

In 1861, Alexander II decided to end serfdom in Russia. He hoped that freeing the serfs would help his country compete with Western Europe. The serfs had to pay a heavy tax, though, and the land they were given was often not good for farming. Most former serfs felt that they had gained very little.

Bloody Sunday

The serfs were not the only unhappy Russians. Many university students, artists, and writers believed that the government's treatment of the serfs was unfair. Some joined groups that tried to overthrow the government. In addition, workers in Russia's cities complained about low pay and poor working conditions.

In 1905, a group of workers marched to the royal palace in St. Petersburg with a list of demands. Government troops shot many of them. News of the events of this "Bloody Sunday" spread across Russia, making people even angrier with the government and czar.

Nicholas and Alexandra The last czar and czarina of Russia were killed in 1918 by revolutionaries.

The End of the Russian Empire

In 1914, World War I began. Nicholas II ruled Russia, but he failed to keep his country out of the battle. Russia, whose allies included the United Kingdom and France, suffered terrible losses fighting Germany and its allies.

During World War I, there were food shortages in the cities and workers went on strike. Russian revolutionaries organized the workers against the czar. Even the Russian army turned against their ruler, and in 1917, Nicholas was forced to give up power. On July 17, 1918, Nicholas II and the royal family (the Romanovs) were executed, ending more than 300 years of rule by the Romanov family and nearly 400 years of czarist rule. This overturning of the Russian monarchy is known as the Russian Revolution.

REVIEW What events led to the Russian Revolution?

Lesson Summary

Ivan the Terrible becomes first czar of Russia in 1547.

Peter the Great and Catherine the Great expand and modernize the Russian Empire.

Alexander II ends serfdom in Russia in 1861.

Nicholas II gives up power, and in 1918, czarist rule ends.

Why It Matters . . .

Russia has had a great influence on world politics and is experiencing a period of great change.

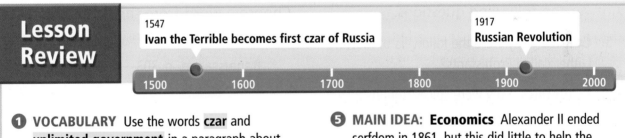

Lesson Review

1547
Ivan the Terrible becomes first czar of Russia

1917
Russian Revolution

1500 1600 1700 1800 1900 2000

① **VOCABULARY** Use the words **czar** and **unlimited government** in a paragraph about Ivan the Terrible.

② **READING SKILL** **Contrast** the rulers Ivan the Terrible and Catherine the Great.

③ **MAIN IDEA: Government** What effects did an unlimited government have on Russian peasants?

④ **MAIN IDEA: History** How did Peter the Great help reform Russia?

⑤ **MAIN IDEA: Economics** Alexander II ended serfdom in 1861, but this did little to help the serfs. Why?

⑥ **PEOPLE TO KNOW** Who was **Peter the Great** and how did he change Russia?

⑦ **TIMELINE SKILL** How many years was Russia ruled by czars?

⑧ **CRITICAL THINKING: Cause and Effect** Why did "Bloody Sunday" anger the people of Russia?

WRITING ACTIVITY Look at the map on page 322 that shows the expansion of Russia. Write a brief summary to describe how the Russian nation grew from the 1500s to 1800.

Visual Summary

1–4. ✏️ Write a description for each image below.

The Renaissance	Traders, Explorers, and Colonists	The Age of Revolution	The Russian Empire

Facts and Main Ideas

Answer the following questions.

5. **Culture** Why were the followers of Martin Luther called Protestants?

6. **Economics** Why were spices from Asia so expensive when sold in Europe?

7. **History** When and where did the Industrial Revolution begin?

8. **Government** What conditions in France during the 1780s led to the French Revolution?

9. **Culture** What ideas did Catherine the Great borrow from Western Europe?

Vocabulary

Choose a word from the list to complete each sentence below.

Renaissance, p. 303
imperialism, p. 312
capitalism, p. 318

10. The _____, a rebirth in Europe of interest in learning, creativity, and the arts, began in what is now Italy.

11. Private ownership of factories and other businesses that sell goods is called _____.

12. _____ is the practice of one country controlling the government and economy of another country or territory.

1492
Columbus reaches the Americas

1789
French Revolution begins

1917
Russian Revolution

1400 1500 1600 1700 1800 1900 2000

Apply Skills

 TEST PREP **Research Topics on the Internet** Look at the Web page shown here. Then apply what you learned about researching topics on the Internet to answer the questions.

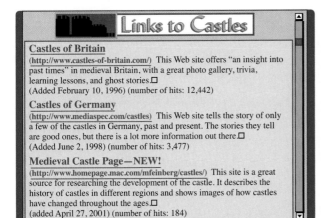

Links to Castles

Castles of Britain
(http://www.castles-of-britain.com/) This Web site offers "an insight into past times" in medieval Britain, with a great photo gallery, trivia, learning lessons, and ghost stories.□
(Added February 10, 1996) (number of hits: 12,442)

Castles of Germany
(http://www.mediaspec.com/castles) This Web site tells the story of only a few of the castles in Germany, past and present. The stories they tell are good ones, but there is a lot more information out there.□
(Added June 2, 1998) (number of hits: 3,477)

Medieval Castle Page—NEW!
(http://www.homepage.mac.com/mfeinberg/castles/) This site is a great source for researching the development of the castle. It describes the history of castles in different regions and shows images of how castles have changed throughout the ages.□
(added April 27, 2001) (number of hits: 184)

13. What is the subject of this Web site?
    A. Germany
    B. Britain
    C. Castles
    D. Medieval farming

14. Which site would you visit to learn about the history of castles throughout Europe?
    A. Castles of Britain
    B. Medieval Castle Page
    C. Castles of Germany
    D. All of these sites

Critical Thinking

 TEST PREP Write a short paragraph to answer each question below.

15. **Cause and Effect** What were the effects of the Renaissance on life in Western Europe?

16. **Draw Conclusions** In 19th-century Russia, the lives of poor citizens were very different from those of wealthy citizens. How do you think this division led to political revolution?

Timeline

Use the Chapter Summary Timeline above to answer the question.

17. Which revolution occurred first, the French Revolution or the Russian Revolution?

Activities

 SPEAKING ACTIVITY Prepare a persuasive speech to try to convince a European monarch to pay for ships to sail west across the Atlantic Ocean in 1490.

 WRITING ACTIVITY Write an editorial from a French newspaper in the 1780s from the point of view of someone who wants political changes.

 Technology

Writing Process Tips
Get help with your editorial at
www.eduplace.com/kids/hmss05/

Technology

e • glossary
e • word games
www.eduplace.com/kids/hmss05/

Vocabulary Preview

colonialism

By 1914, Great Britain had colonies all around the world. The sun literally never set on the British Empire. During this period of **colonialism** in Europe, many European nations had colonies in Africa and Asia.

page 332

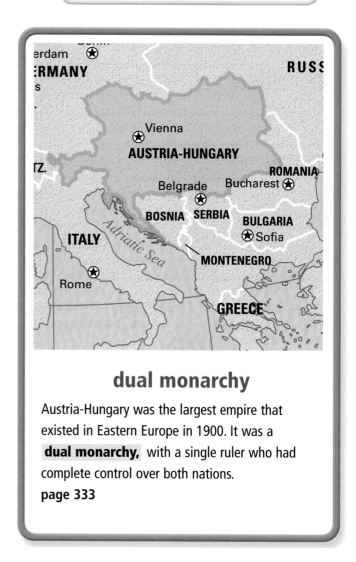

dual monarchy

Austria-Hungary was the largest empire that existed in Eastern Europe in 1900. It was a **dual monarchy,** with a single ruler who had complete control over both nations.

page 333

Chapter Timeline

1914
World War I begins

1900	1910	1920

EUROPE AND THE FORMER SOVIET UNION

Reading Strategy

Predict and Infer Use this strategy as you read the lessons in this chapter.

Quick Tip

Look at the pictures in a lesson to predict what it will be about. What will you read about?

alliance

When Archduke Franz Ferdinand of Austria-Hungary was murdered by a Serb nationalist in 1914, it caused Austria-Hungary to declare war on Serbia. Serbia had an **alliance,** or agreement to unite for a common cause, with Russia, and Russia declared war on Austria-Hungary. **page 337**

Cold War

After World War II, Europe was divided between East and West. The United States supported the West, and the Soviet Union supported the East. Both sides avoided open war because they feared nuclear weapons. Instead, a **Cold War** existed for nearly 40 years. **page 348**

1933 Hitler elected in Germany	1939 World War II begins	1949 NATO formed

1930   **1940**   **1950**

European Empires

Build on What You Know Are you a fan of your school's sports teams? You may cheer for your teams and take great pride in their victories. You may even consider rival teams as the "enemy." In a similar way, people in European countries in the 19th century began to feel pride for their nations. This sometimes led to conflict.

VOCABULARY

nationalism
colonialism
dual monarchy

Vocabulary Strategy

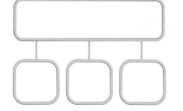

nationalism

Look for the word **nation** in nationalism. **Nationalism** is a strong sense of pride in one's nation or ethnic group.

 READING SKILL

Cause and Effect As you read, take notes to show the effects of nationalism on countries in Europe.

The Spread of Nationalism

Main Idea At the beginning of the 20th century, growing nationalism and colonialism changed Europe.

During the late 19th and early 20th centuries, **nationalism,** or strong pride in one's nation or ethnic group, influenced the feelings of many Europeans. An ethnic group includes people with similar languages and traditions, but who are not necessarily ruled by a common government.

In part, the spread of nationalism was fueled by the fact that more Europeans than ever before could vote. For centuries, many monarchs had unlimited power. In country after country, however, citizens demanded the right to elect lawmakers who would limit their monarch's authority. This kind of government is called a constitutional monarchy. A constitutional monarchy not only has a king or queen, but also a ruling body of elected officials. The United Kingdom is one example of a constitutional monarchy.

House of Commons These elected officials limit the power the British monarch.

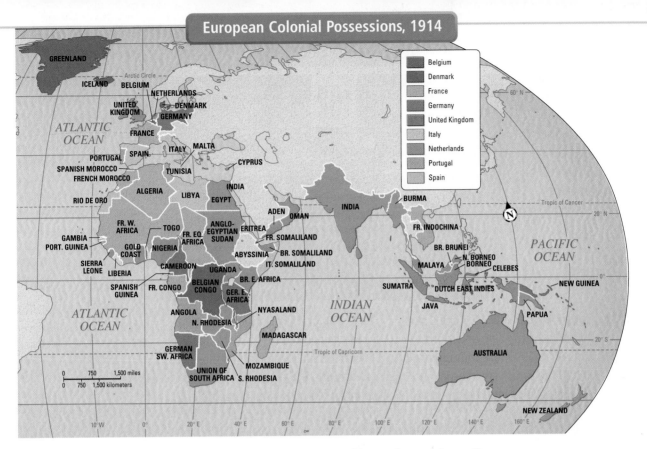

European Colonial Possessions, 1914

Legend:
- Belgium
- Denmark
- France
- Germany
- United Kingdom
- Italy
- Netherlands
- Portugal
- Spain

GREENLAND, ICELAND, BELGIUM, NETHERLANDS, UNITED KINGDOM, DENMARK, GERMANY, FRANCE, ATLANTIC OCEAN, PORTUGAL, SPAIN, ITALY, MALTA, CYPRUS, SPANISH MOROCCO, FRENCH MOROCCO, TUNISIA, RIO DE ORO, ALGERIA, LIBYA, EGYPT, INDIA, ADEN, OMAN, BURMA, FR. W. AFRICA, TOGO, FR. EQ. AFRICA, ANGLO-EGYPTIAN SUDAN, ERITREA, FR. SOMALILAND, INDIA, FR. INDOCHINA, GAMBIA, PORT. GUINEA, GOLD COAST, NIGERIA, ABYSSINIA, BR. SOMALILAND, IT. SOMALILAND, BR. BRUNEI, MALAYA, N. BORNEO, BORNEO, PACIFIC OCEAN, SIERRA LEONE, LIBERIA, CAMEROON, UGANDA, BR. E. AFRICA, CELEBES, SPANISH GUINEA, FR. CONGO, BELGIAN CONGO, GER. E. AFRICA, SUMATRA, DUTCH EAST INDIES, NEW GUINEA, ATLANTIC OCEAN, ANGOLA, NYASALAND, INDIAN OCEAN, JAVA, PAPUA, N. RHODESIA, MADAGASCAR, GERMAN SW. AFRICA, MOZAMBIQUE, UNION OF SOUTH AFRICA, S. RHODESIA, AUSTRALIA, NEW ZEALAND

0   750   1,500 miles
0   750   1,500 kilometers

Colonialism Many European countries had colonies in Africa, Asia, and Australia.

SKILL Interpret a Map Which Western European country possessed the most land?

Constitutional Monarchies

By 1900, many countries in Western Europe had become constitutional monarchies. Citizens of these countries strongly supported the governments that they helped to elect. When one country threatened another, most citizens were willing to go to war to defend their homeland.

The Defense of Colonial Empires

At the beginning of the 20th century, many Western European countries—including France, Italy, the United Kingdom, Germany, and even tiny Belgium—had colonies in Asia and Africa.

Colonies supplied the raw materials that the ruling countries needed to produce goods in their factories back home. Asian and African colonies, sometimes larger than the ruling country, were also important markets for manufactured goods.

REVIEW How does a constitutional monarchy differ from a democracy?

India In the 1600s, the British East India Company established trading posts in India. In 1858, Britain took over complete control of India.

Australia In 1770, the British explorer Captain James Cook claimed the eastern coast of Australia for Britain. Later, Britain claimed the entire continent, and in 1901, the colonies became the Commonwealth of Australia.

South Africa In 1815, Cape Colony in South Africa came under British control. In 1909, the South Africa Act united the British colonies in southern Africa into the Union of South Africa.

New Zealand In 1840, the native Maori signed the Treaty of Waitangi, giving Britain sovereignty in the country. In 1852, New Zealand was granted self-government but still remained part of the empire.

British Empire In 1914, the United Kingdom could truthfully state that the sun never set on the British Empire.

The Fight for Colonies

This was a period of **colonialism,** when European nations worked to control more colonies. Western European nations spent much of their wealth on building strong armies and navies. Their military forces helped to defend borders at home as well as colonies in other parts of the world. Colonies were so important that the ruling countries sometimes fought one another for control of them. They also struggled to extend their territories.

Austria-Hungary

By the end of the 19th century, most nations of Western and Northern Europe had become industrialized. The majority of Eastern Europe, including Russia, remained agricultural. These Eastern European countries imported most of their manufactured goods from Western and Northern Europe.

Dual Monarchy Austria-Hungary was a large empire in Central Europe.

SKILL **Interpret a Map** Name three countries that bordered Austria-Hungary.

Austria-Hungary, 1900

The largest empire in Eastern Europe in 1900 was Austria-Hungary. The empire was a **dual monarchy,** in which one ruler governs two nations. As you can see in the map on page 332, Austria-Hungary also included parts of many other present-day countries, including Romania, the Czech Republic, and portions of Poland.

REVIEW Why do you think governing a dual monarchy was difficult?

Franz Joseph I He was emperor of Austria when it became a dual monarchy with Hungary.

Lesson Summary

By the beginning of the 20th century, more Europeans than ever had the right to vote. In country after country, people changed their government to a constitutional monarchy. As nationalism grew, people were more willing to fight wars in defense of governments they elected. Citizens were also willing to fight in order to defend or expand their governments' colonies in Africa and Asia.

Why It Matters . . .

Feelings of nationalism continue to lead to conflicts that change the map of Europe.

Lesson Review

1 **VOCABULARY** Choose the correct word to complete each sentence.

　　　colonialism　**dual monarchy**

Because the emperor of Austria-Hungary ruled two nations, this empire was a ＿＿＿＿. During the period of ＿＿＿＿, European countries ruled most of Africa and Asia.

2 **READING SKILL** What **effect** did colonialism and nationalism have on the military of European countries?

3 **MAIN IDEA: Government** Identify one reason for the spread of nationalism in Europe.

4 **MAIN IDEA: Geography** On what continents did European countries have most of their colonies?

5 **MAIN IDEA: Economics** How did the nations of Eastern Europe differ from those of Western and Northern Europe at the end of the 19th century?

6 **FACTS TO KNOW** What was the largest empire in Eastern Europe in 1900?

7 **CRITICAL THINKING: Draw Conclusions** Why were colonies so important to European nations?

HANDS ON **MAP ACTIVITY** Choose one of the European colonies on the map on page 331 and use library resources to find out more about its geography. Draw a map showing the colony's major landforms.

Fionn Mac Cumhail and the
Giant's Causeway

Irish Folktales

Fionn Mac Cumhail, more commonly known as Finn MacCool, is a familiar figure in Irish folktales. He first appears in the ancient Celtic tales known as the Fenian cycle. In the following story, retold by Una Leavy, Fionn is portrayed as a clever giant, hard at work with the Fianna, his band of Irish warriors. They begin to build a bridge from Ireland to Scotland, because, as the boastful Fionn says, "There are giants over there that I'm longing to conquer." Plans suddenly change, however, and Fionn must go home.

Fionn Mac Cumhail and the Fianna worked quickly on the bridge, splitting stones into splendid pillars and columns. Further and further they stretched out into the ocean. From time to time, there came a distant rumble. "Is it thunder?" asked the Fianna, but they went on working. Then one of their spies came ashore. "I've just been to Scotland!" he said. "There's a huge giant there called Fathach Mór. He's doing long jumps—you can hear the thumping. He has a magic little finger with the strength of ten men! He's in training for the long jump to Antrim."

Fionn's face paled. "The strength of ten men!" he thought. "I'll never fight him. He'll squash me into a pancake." But he could not admit that he was nervous, so he said to the Fianna, "I've just had a message from Bláithín, my wife. I must go home at once—you can all take a holiday."

He set off by himself and never did a man travel faster. Bláithín was surprised to see him. "And is the great causeway finished already?" she asked.

"No indeed," replied Fionn.

"What's the matter?" Bláithín asked. So Fionn told her.

"What will I do, Bláithín?" he asked. "There's the strength of ten men in his magic little finger. He'll squish me into a jelly!"

Bláithín laughed. "Just leave him to me. Stoke up the fire and fetch me the sack of flour. Then go outside and find nine flat stones." Fionn did as he was told. Bláithín worked all night making ten oatcakes. In each she put a large flat stone, all except the last. This one she marked with her thumbprint. "Go and cut down some wood," she said. "You must make an enormous cradle." Fionn worked all morning. The cradle was just finished when there was a mighty rumble and the dishes shook.

"It's him," squealed Fionn.

"Don't worry!" said Bláithín. "Put on this bonnet. Now into the cradle and leave me to do the talking."

"Does Fionn Mac Cumhail live here?" boomed a great voice above her.

"He does," said Bláithín, "though he's away at the moment. He's gone to capture the giant, Fathach Mór."

"I'm Fathach Mór!" bellowed the giant. "I've been searching for Fionn everywhere."

"Did you ever see Fionn?" she asked. "Sure you're only a baby compared with him. He'll be home shortly and you can see for yourself. But now that you're here, would you do me a favor? The well has run dry and Fionn was supposed to lift up the mountain this morning. There's spring water underneath it. Do you think you could get me some?"

"Of course," shouted the giant as he scooped out a hole in the mountain the size of a crater.

Fionn shook with fear in the cradle and even Bláithín turned pale. But she thanked the giant and invited him in. "Though you and Fionn are enemies, you are still a guest," she said. "Have some fresh bread." And she put the

oatcakes before him. Fathach Mór began to eat. Almost at once he gave a piercing yell and spat out two teeth.

"What kind of bread is this?" he screeched. "I've broken my teeth on it."

"How can you say such a thing?" asked Bláithín. "Even the child in the cradle eats them!" And she gave Fionn the cake with the thumbprint. Fathach looked at the cradle. "Whose child is that?" he asked in wonder.

"That's Fionn's son," said Bláithín.

"And how old is he?" he asked then.

"Just ten months," replied Bláithín.

"Can he talk?" asked the giant.

"Not yet, but you should hear him roar!" At once, Fionn began to yell.

"Quick, quick," cried Bláithín. "Let him suck your little finger. If Fionn comes home and hears him, he'll be in such a temper."

With an anxious glance at the door, the giant gave Fionn his finger. Fionn bit off the giant's magic little finger. Screeching, the giant bolted from the house. Fionn leaped from the cradle in bib and bonnet and danced his Bláithín round the kitchen.

Activities

1. **THINK ABOUT IT** In many European myths and legends, the heroes are powerful and fearless. How does Fionn act in this story? What words does the author use to make clear Fionn's attitude toward the danger he faces?

2. **WRITE ABOUT IT** Often, myths are created in order to answer questions about or explain mysteries in the world. This legend explains why the causeway was never finished. Write an end to the story in which the causeway is finished.

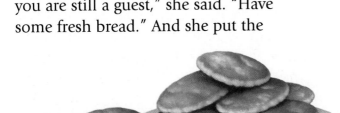

Europe at War

1900 1910 1920 1930 1940 1950

1908–1949

VOCABULARY

alliance
fascism
Holocaust
NATO

Vocabulary Strategy

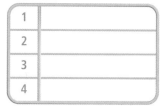

NATO

Notice that NATO is written in capital letters. **NATO** stands for **North Atlantic Treaty Organization**. It is an acronym, a shortened word made up of the first letters of the words in its full name.

READING SKILL

Sequence Take notes as you read to follow the sequence of events that led to the world wars in Europe.

1	
2	
3	
4	

Build on What You Know Was there ever a time when two of your friends were arguing? Each might have expected you to take his or her side. Other friends might have become involved as well. Suddenly, people were on different sides and angry with one another. This can happen between nations, too, and war can be the result.

The World at War

Main Idea World War I began between just two countries but spread to include all of Europe due to agreements between different European nations.

On June 28, 1914, Archduke of Austria-Hungary Franz Ferdinand and his wife were murdered by a nineteen-year-old Serb, Gavrilo Princip. The Serbians had been against Austria-Hungary since 1908, when the empire took over Serbia.

Because of the murder of Archduke Franz Ferdinand, the emperor of Austria-Hungary declared war on Serbia. When Russia sent troops to defend Serbia, Germany declared war on Russia. Russia supported Serbia because both Russians and Serbians share a similar ethnic background—they are both Slavic peoples. This was the beginning of World War I.

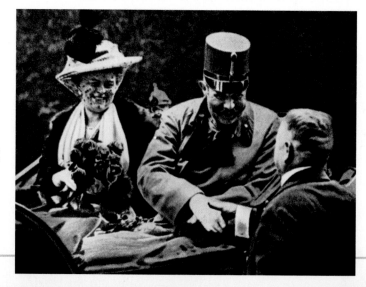

Archduke Franz Ferdinand
The Archduke and his wife, Duchess Sophie, were fatally shot in Sarajevo.

World War I Alliances

European rulers wanted other leaders to think twice before declaring war on their countries. To help defend themselves, several countries joined alliances (uh LY uhn sez). An **alliance** is an agreement among people or nations to unite for a common cause. Each member of an alliance agrees to help the other members in case one of them is attacked.

When Germany joined the war to support Austria-Hungary, France came in on the side of Russia. Germany then invaded Belgium, which was neutral, to attack France. Because Great Britain had promised to protect Belgium, it, too, declared war on Germany. After German submarines sank four American merchant ships, the United States joined the side of Russia, France, and Great Britain.

The chart above shows the major powers on both sides of World War I. Italy had originally been allied with Germany and Austria-Hungary but joined the Allies after the war began. Russia dropped out of the war completely after the revolution in that country in 1917.

REVIEW Why did Great Britain enter World War I?

World War I Alliances (1914-1918)

THE CENTRAL POWERS	THE ALLIES
Austria-Hungary	Russia (dropped out
Germany	in 1917)
Turkey	France
(Ottoman Empire)	United Kingdom
Bulgaria	Italy (joined 1915)
	United States
	(joined 1917)

Alliances Many powerful nations were brought in to World War I because of defense agreements.

Progress Cartoons are often used to criticize governmental policies. **SKILL** **Interpret a Political Cartoon** What does the artist mean by naming the figure "Progress"?

Trench Warfare World War I was primarily fought in trenches, which were dug by the armies for better defense against machines guns and cannons.

Post–World War I Europe Borders of Eastern European countries were redrawn after World War I.

SKILL **Interpret a Map** What body of water does the coast of Yugoslavia border?

Europe After World War I

World War I was costly in terms of human life. When it was over, nearly 22 million civilians and soldiers on both sides were dead. The Allies had won, and Europe had been devastated.

More people were killed during World War I than during all the wars of the 19th century combined. Afterward, people in many countries on both sides of the costly war—and even those not directly involved—were poor, homeless, and without work.

The Allies blamed Germany for much of the killing and damage during the war. In 1919, Germany and the Allies signed the Treaty of Versailles (vuhr SY).

The Treaty of Versailles demanded that Germany be punished by being forced to pay for the damage done to the Allied countries. Germany was also made to give up valuable territory.

A New Map of Europe

Additional treaties during the following year also altered the political boundaries of many European countries. As the map on this page shows, Austria-Hungary was divided as a result of the war, becoming two separate countries. This allowed several Eastern European ethnic groups that had been part of Austria-Hungary to gain their independence.

For decades, Germany was forced to pay for the damage done to the Allied countries during World War I. The German economy was in ruins, and the Germans greatly wished to rebuild their own country. In 1933, citizens elected Adolf Hitler and brought the National Socialist, or Nazi, Party to power.

World War II

Main Idea In the mid-20th century, European nations once again went to war over land and nationalist ideas.

The Nazi Party believed in fascism. **Fascism** (FASH ihz uhm) is a philosophy that supports a strong, central government controlled by the military and led by a powerful dictator. Germans believed that their new leader, Adolf Hitler, would help Germany recover and become powerful.

Fascists practiced an extreme form of patriotism and nationalism. Fascists also had racist beliefs.

In the 1930s, Hitler unjustly blamed the Jewish citizens of Germany, among other specific groups, for the country's problems. His Nazi followers seized Jewish property and began to send Jews, along with disabled people, political opponents, and others, to concentration camps. During this **Holocaust,** millions of people were deliberately killed, and others starved or died from disease.

World War II Alliances (1939-1945)

THE AXIS POWERS	THE ALLIES
Germany	United Kingdom
Italy	France (until June 1940)
Japan	Soviet Union (formerly "Russia")
	United States (joined in 1941)

Alliances Relationships between nations had slightly changed by World War II.

The War Begins

In 1934, Hitler took command of the armed forces. Then, in 1939, Hitler's army invaded Poland. World War II had begun. By June 1940, Hitler's army had swept through Western Europe, conquering Belgium, the Netherlands, Luxembourg, France, Denmark, and Norway. A year later, Germany invaded the Soviet Union.

The chart above shows the major powers on both sides of World War II. As in World War I, the United States at first tried to stay out of the conflict but entered the war after Japan bombed U.S. military bases at Pearl Harbor in Hawaii on December 7, 1941.

REVIEW What conditions led Germany to find hope in Adolf Hitler?

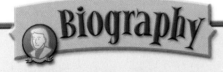
Biography

Anne Frank In July 1942, during World War II, Anne Frank and her family went into hiding in Amsterdam—a city in the Netherlands. The Frank family were Jewish and were afraid they would be sent to a concentration camp. Anne was only thirteen.

For two years, Anne, her father, mother, sister, and four other people lived in rooms in an attic. Their rooms were sealed off from the rest of the building. While in hiding, Anne kept a diary. Although the family was discovered and Anne died in a concentration camp, her diary was eventually published. Today, this famous book—translated into many languages and the basis for a play and a film—lives on.

Post–World War II Europe Germany was divided after World War II, and much of Eastern Europe fell under the control of the USSR. [SKILL] **Interpret a Map** In what country is Berlin located?

Europe After World War II

World War II turned much of Europe into a battleground. By the end of the war, the United States, France, and the United Kingdom occupied Western Europe. The Soviet Union occupied Eastern Europe, including the eastern part of Germany.

Once peace was established, the western allies helped to set up free governments in Western Europe. In 1949, the countries of Western Europe joined Canada and the United States to form a defense alliance called **NATO** (NAY toh). The members of this alliance, whose name stands for North Atlantic Treaty Organization, agreed to defend one another if they were attacked by the Soviet Union or any other country. Without a common enemy, political differences quickly separated the Soviet Union from Western Europe and the United States.

Kaiser Wilhelm Memorial Church Nearly destroyed by Allied bombs, this church in Berlin stands today as a World War II monument.

The Marshall Plan

United States Secretary of State George C. Marshall created the Economic Cooperation Act of 1948, also known as the Marshall Plan. This plan provided U.S. aid—agricultural, industrial, and financial—to countries of Western Europe. The Marshall Plan greatly benefited war-torn Europe. It may also have prevented economic depression or political instability.

REVIEW What agreement did the members of NATO make?

Lesson Summary

- During the first half of the 20th century, European countries had conflicts over country borders and colonies. World War I spread through Europe as a result of alliances.

- The hardships following World War I led to fascism and, ultimately, to the beginning of World War II, in which millions of people died.

- Allies from World War II were divided after the war, but Western Europe recovered thanks to the Marshall Plan, a program of economic assistance from the United States.

Why It Matters...

The changes brought about by the two world wars continue to affect Europe today.

Marshall Plan The United States sent food and other aid to help Europe recover from the war. This picture shows officials discussing aid from America.

Lesson Review

1914 World War I begins
1939 World War II begins
1949 NATO formed

1910 — 1920 — 1930 — 1940 — 1950

1. **VOCABULARY** Explain the relationship between **fascism** and the **Holocaust**.

2. **READING SKILL** Review the **sequence** of events in Europe from World War I to World War II. After which war was the dual monarchy of Austria-Hungary separated into two countries?

3. **MAIN IDEA: History** What event set off World War I?

4. **MAIN IDEA: History** When did World War II begin and end? Which countries won?

5. **MAIN IDEA: Economics** What happened at the end of World War II?

6. **EVENTS TO KNOW** What effect did the attack on Pearl Harbor by Japan have on the United States?

7. **TIMELINE SKILL** How many years separated the beginning of World War I and the beginning of World War II?

8. **CRITICAL THINKING: Infer** How did World War I change Europe?

WRITING ACTIVITY Look at the photographs in this lesson. Write a letter in which you describe what it might have been like to visit Europe just after World War I or World War II.

Skillbuilder

Read a Political Cartoon

Political cartoons—also known as editorial cartoons—express an opinion about a serious subject. A political cartoonist uses symbols, familiar objects, and people to make his or her point quickly and visually. Sometimes the caption and words in the cartoon help to clarify the meaning. Although a cartoonist may use humor to make a point, political cartoons are not always funny.

This political cartoon was created in the period between World War I and World War II. Europeans were already concerned about the rise of Hitler's Nazi Party in Germany.

Learn the Skill

Step 1: Read the cartoon's title and any other words. For example, some cartoons have labels, captions, and thought balloons. Then study the cartoon as a whole.

Step 2: If the cartoon has people in it, are they famous? Sometimes the cartoonist wants to comment on a famous person, such as a world leader. Look for symbols or details in the cartoon. For example, in this cartoon a German soldier who looks like Adolf Hitler is climbing out of the Versailles Treaty. Think about the relationships between the words and the images.

Step 3: Summarize the cartoonist's message. What is the cartoonist's point of view about the subject? What does this cartoonist think was the cause of Hitler's rise to power?

Practice the Skill

A chart can help you to analyze the information in a political cartoon. Once you understand the cartoon's elements, you can summarize its meaning. Use a chart such as this one to help you organize the information.

Important Words	Hitler Party; Versailles Treaty
Important Symbols/Images	German soldier with "Hitler Party" on his helmet crawling out of the Versailles Treaty that officially ended World War I.
Summary	The terms of the Versailles Treaty led to the rise of Hitler's party in Germany; Hitler's party, symbolized by a soldier, is war-like and threatens Europe.

Apply the Skill

Study the political cartoon in Chapter 12, Lesson 2, on page 337. Make a chart similar to the one above in which you list the important parts of the cartoon and write a summary of the cartoon's message.

The Soviet Union

Build on What You Know You know that countries use armies to fight wars. After World War II, Communist and non-Communist countries fought a war of words and ideas. The possibility of nuclear war was a constant threat.

VOCABULARY

Iron Curtain
puppet government
one-party system
collective farm
Cold War

Vocabulary Strategy

| puppet government |

Think about the meanings of the words **puppet** and **government** in the phrase **puppet government**. A puppet government is a government that is controlled by an outside force. It is the "puppet" of someone or something else.

READING SKILL

Classify As you read, take notes to list ideas and actions of the Soviet Union. Note each idea and action in the chart.

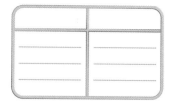

East Against West

Main Idea After World War II, Europe was divided between Western democracies and Eastern European nations that took orders from the Soviet Union.

After World War II, political differences divided the Soviet-controlled countries of Eastern Europe from those of Western Europe. These differences gave rise to an invisible wall known as the **Iron Curtain.** While there was no actual curtain, people of the East were restricted from traveling outside of their countries. Westerners who wished to visit the East also faced restrictions.

The Union of Soviet Socialist Republics, or USSR, was the official name of the Soviet Union. It included 15 republics, of which Russia was the largest. The Soviet Union entered World War II in 1941, when Germany invaded its borders. German troops destroyed much of the western Soviet Union and killed millions of people. This invasion brought the Soviet Union close to collapse. However, with the defeat of Germany, the Soviet Union rose to become the strongest nation in Europe.

Hammer and Sickle The symbol of Soviet Communism represents the unity of the peasants (sickle) with the workers (hammer).

Communism

After World War II, the Soviet Union established Communist governments in Eastern Europe. The Soviets made sure—either by politics or by force—that these new Eastern European governments were loyal to the Soviet Union.

The Soviet Union controlled the countries of Eastern Europe through puppet governments. A **puppet government** is one that does what it is told by an outside force. In this case, the Eastern European governments followed orders from Soviet leaders in Moscow.

Most Eastern Europeans had the chance to vote, but they only had one political party to choose from: the Communist Party. All other parties were outlawed. This meant that there was only one candidate to choose from for each government position. This is an example of a **one-party system.** Soviet citizens could not complain about the government. In fact, they could be jailed for expressing any view that the Soviet leaders did not like.

REVIEW How do you think the Soviet Union enforced a one-party system in Eastern Europe?

Shortages The government-controlled factories in the Soviet Union did not produce enough of certain items. When goods that were often in short supply—such as bread and shoes—finally became available, people had to wait in long lines to buy them.

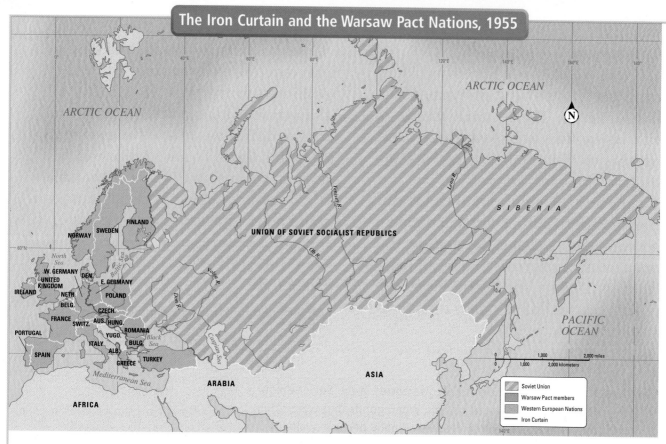

Iron Curtain The Soviet Union controlled all land east of the "Iron Curtain," which included much of Eastern Europe. **SKILL** **Interpret a Map** Which countries were behind the Iron Curtain but not in the Soviet Union?

Joseph Stalin

Main Idea Under Communist leader Joseph Stalin, the government controlled nearly every aspect of life in the Soviet Union.

Joseph Stalin (STAH lihn) (1879–1953) ruled the Soviet Union during World War II. Stalin took power after the death of Vladimir Lenin. Lenin was a Communist leader who had helped overthrow the czar and ruled the Soviet Union from 1917 until his death in 1924. The name Stalin is related to the Russian word for "steel." Stalin was greatly feared, and his rule was indeed as tough as steel. He controlled the government until his death.

Lenin and Stalin Vladimir Ilyich Lenin (1870–1924) founded the Soviet state and was succeeded by Joseph Stalin (1879–1953), who used dictatorial methods to govern.

Five-Year Plans

Under Stalin, the government controlled every aspect of Soviet life. Stalin hoped to strengthen the country with his five-year plans, which were sets of economic goals. For example, Stalin ordered many new factories to be built. The Soviet government decided where and what types of factories to build, how many goods to produce, and how to distribute them. These decisions were based on the Communist theory that this would benefit the most people.

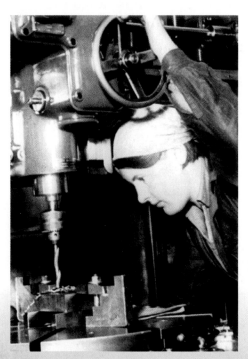

Soviet Workers The Soviet government managed the factories while citizens provided the actual labor. Russian peasants labored on government-controlled collective farms, and urban workers labored in government-controlled factories.

Soviet Agriculture

Stalin also hoped to strengthen the Soviet Union by controlling the country's agriculture. During the 1930s, peasants were forced to move to collective farms. A **collective farm** was government-owned and employed large numbers of workers. All the crops produced by the collective farms were distributed by the government. Sometimes farm workers did not receive enough food to feed themselves and their families.

Stalin used his secret police to get rid of citizens he did not trust. The secret police arrested those who did not support the Soviet government. Suspects were transported to slave-labor camps in Siberia. Millions of men and women were sent to this remote and bitterly cold region of northeastern Russia. Many never returned home.

REVIEW How did Joseph Stalin maintain control of the huge Soviet Union?

The Cold War

Main Idea After World War II, NATO and the Communist Eastern European countries refused to trade or cooperate with one another.

From 1941 to 1945, the United Kingdom, the United States, and the Soviet Union shared a goal: to defeat the Axis Powers. They became allies to make that happen. Once the war ended, however, these countries no longer had a common enemy—and had little reason to work together. Most Western European countries were constitutional monarchies or democracies, and most Eastern European countries had Communist, largely Soviet-controlled, governments.

In 1946, Winston Churchill, former prime minister of Great Britain, described the situation in Europe. He said that an "iron curtain" had descended across the continent. This iron curtain shut off the Communist countries in the east from the freedoms of countries in Western Europe.

The members of NATO and the nations in the Warsaw Pact—the alliance of Eastern European countries behind the Iron Curtain—refused to trade or cooperate with each other. The countries never actually fought, so this period of political noncooperation is called the **Cold War.** Both sides in the Cold War were hesitant to start a war that would involve the use of newly developed nuclear weapons, which could cause destruction on a global scale.

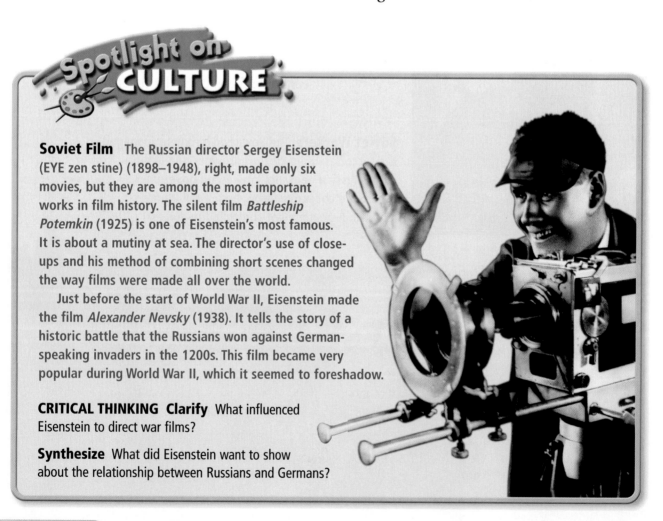

Spotlight on CULTURE

Soviet Film The Russian director Sergey Eisenstein (EYE zen stine) (1898–1948), right, made only six movies, but they are among the most important works in film history. The silent film *Battleship Potemkin* (1925) is one of Eisenstein's most famous. It is about a mutiny at sea. The director's use of close-ups and his method of combining short scenes changed the way films were made all over the world.

Just before the start of World War II, Eisenstein made the film *Alexander Nevsky* (1938). It tells the story of a historic battle that the Russians won against German-speaking invaders in the 1200s. This film became very popular during World War II, which it seemed to foreshadow.

CRITICAL THINKING Clarify What influenced Eisenstein to direct war films?

Synthesize What did Eisenstein want to show about the relationship between Russians and Germans?

The United States and Western Europe feared that the Soviet Union would influence other countries to become Communist. At the same time, the Soviet Union wanted to protect itself against invasion. This led the countries on either side of the Iron Curtain to view and treat each other as possible threats. The tense international situation caused by the Cold War would continue for more than 40 years.

REVIEW Compare the Soviet Union's fears during the Cold War with those of the United States and Western Europe.

The Brandenburg Gate This monument was a part of the Berlin Wall that once separated East Berlin from West Berlin.

Lesson Summary

```
                    ┌──────────────────────────────┐
                    │ Communists controlled        │
                    │ people's lives and the economy.│
                    └──────────────────────────────┘
┌──────────────┐    ┌──────────────────────────────┐
│ Soviet Union │────│ controlled Eastern Europe    │
└──────────────┘    └──────────────────────────────┘
                    ┌──────────────────────────────┐
                    │ fought Cold War with the     │
                    │ United States and former allies│
                    └──────────────────────────────┘
```

Why It Matters...

Russia, the largest country in the former Soviet Union, remains powerful and is currently experiencing great change.

Lesson Review

1. **VOCABULARY** Explain how the words **puppet government** and **one-party system** are related.

2. **READING SKILL** Would you **classify** Joseph Stalin's creation of collective farms as an idea or action? Explain your answer.

3. **MAIN IDEA: History** What happened to the Soviet Union during World War II?

4. **MAIN IDEA: Government** How did the governments of most Western and Eastern European countries differ?

5. **MAIN IDEA: Geography** What were the eastern and western borders of the Soviet Union?

6. **EVENTS TO KNOW** When did the Soviet Union establish Communist governments in Eastern Europe? How did it keep their loyalty?

7. **CRITICAL THINKING: Analyze** Why do you think the Soviet Union wanted to control the countries of Eastern Europe?

MAP ACTIVITY Using the map on page 346, create an illustrated map of Eastern and Western Europe divided by an iron curtain.

Review and Test Prep

Visual Summary

1–3. ✏️ Write a description for each image below.

European Empires

_____
_____
_____
_____

Europe at War

_____
_____

The Soviet Union

_____
_____

Facts and Main Ideas

Answer the following questions.

4. **Geography** What was the largest empire in Eastern Europe in 1900?

5. **Economics** What did the Treaty of Versailles require Germany to do?

6. **History** What country did Germany invade to begin World War II?

7. **Government** Why did most Eastern European voters have only one political party to choose from?

8. **History** Why were both sides in the Cold War hesitant to start a war?

Vocabulary

Choose a word from the list to complete each sentence below.

colonialism, p. 332
alliance, p. 337
Iron Curtain, p. 344

9. During the period of _____, Western European nations controlled large portions of the world.

10. World War I spread rapidly as countries in _____ with one another joined the hostilities.

11. The _____ was an invisible line that divided Communist Eastern and democratic Western European nations.

1914
World War I begins

1933
Hitler elected in Germany

1939
World War II begins

1949
NATO formed

1910 — 1920 — 1930 — 1940 — 1950

Apply Skills

 TEST PREP Read a Political Cartoon
Look at the cartoon, then apply what you learned about reading political cartoons to answer the questions.

A Toast
to Next Thanksgiving:
"Here's hoping we're not the bird!"

Dr. Seuss ©⁹ᵐ

12. Who are the subjects of this cartoon?
    A. Adolf Hitler and Uncle Sam
    B. Joseph Stalin and the Slavic people
    C. Adolf Hitler and Archduke Franz Ferdinand
    D. George C. Marshall and Uncle Sam

13. What do you think the cartoonist, Dr. Seuss, was worried about?
    A. A war starting on Thanksgiving
    B. Hitler and Germany harming America
    C. Hitler and Germany stealing food
    D. The Holocaust spreading beyond Europe

Critical Thinking

 TEST PREP Write a short paragraph to answer each question below.

14. **Infer** Why might a citizen who has helped elect a government be more willing to fight to defend it?

15. **Draw Conclusions** How do you think Soviet peasants felt about collective farms? Why?

Timeline

Use the Chapter Summary Timeline above to answer the question.

16. Which came second, the beginning of World War II or the formation of NATO?

Activities

HANDS ON **ART ACTIVITY** Design a monument to commemorate an event in 20th-century Europe, such as to memorialize the people who died in the Holocaust or the success of the Marshall Plan. Sketch the monument and explain its meaning.

WRITING ACTIVITY Write a diary entry from the perspective of a young person in the Soviet Union just after World War II. Describe what it is like to live with secret police and the risk that a person could be arrested for criticizing the government.

 Technology

Writing Process Tips
Get help with your diary entry at www.eduplace.com/kids/hmss05/

Chapter 13

Modern Europe

Technology

e • **glossary**
e • **word games**
www.eduplace.com/kids/hmss05/

Vocabulary Preview

propaganda

Propaganda is material designed to spread certain beliefs. When used as propaganda, facts are presented in a way that can distort the truth. In the Soviet Union, even artwork was used as propaganda. **page 356**

deposed

When the leader of a government is removed from power against his or her will, he or she has been **deposed.** Nikita Khrushchev led the Soviet Union and tried to give more freedom to its citizens, but he was deposed in 1964. **page 358**

Chapter Timeline

1964
Nikita Khrushchev deposed

1955   1965   1975

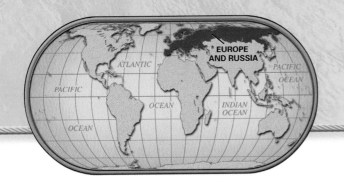

EUROPE
AND RUSSIA

ATLANTIC
OCEAN
PACIFIC
OCEAN
PACIFIC
OCEAN
INDIAN
OCEAN
OCEAN

Reading Strategy

Summarize Use this strategy to help you understand important information in this chapter.

Quick Tip Take notes as you read. Then highlight the most important information.

parliamentary republic

The head of a political party that wins a majority of seats in parliament will be the head of government in a **parliamentary republic.** A parliamentary republic is different from a federal republic, such as the United States. **page 365**

currency

A country's system of money is its **currency.** For example, the currency of the United States is based on the dollar. Before 2002, there was no common currency among the many nations of Europe. Today, there is the euro. **page 372**

1991
Soviet Union collapses

2002
European Union adopts the euro

1985   1995   2005

Eastern Europe Under Communism

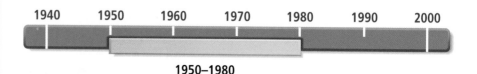

| 1940 | 1950 | 1960 | 1970 | 1980 | 1990 | 2000 |

1950–1980

Build on What You Know Have you ever met a person whose family immigrated to the United States? People leave their home countries to come here in search of a better life. But for about 40 years, many people in Communist Eastern Europe could not make that choice.

Soviet Culture

Main Idea The Communist government of the Soviet Union controlled the lives of its citizens.

Daily life for citizens of the Soviet Union and of the Eastern European countries under its control was difficult. Most people were poor and had little, if any, say in their government. Officials in the Communist Party, on the other hand, usually had more power and more consumer goods.

The Soviet government was fearful that some ethnic groups might want to break away from the Soviet Union. To keep this from happening, Soviet leaders tried to create a strong national identity. They wanted people in the republic of Latvia, for example, to think of themselves as Soviets, not as Latvians.

ARCTIC OCEAN

Bering Sea

RUSSIA ESTONIA
LITHUANIA LATVIA
BYELORUSSIA
MOLDAVIA UKRAINE

R U S S I A

Sea of Okhotsk

Baltic Sea

Black Sea

GEORGIA
ARMENIA
AZERBAIJAN

Caspian Sea

KAZAKHSTAN

UZBEKISTAN

TURKMENIA KIRGHIZIA

TAJIKISTAN

| 0 | 250 | 500 miles |
| 0 | 250 | 500 kilometers |

Caucasian peoples
Indo-European peoples
Uralic and Altaic peoples
Sparsely populated

Soviet Empire The Soviet Union included people of many different ethnic and cultural backgrounds. **SKILL** **Interpret a Map** Where in the Soviet Union do most Uralic and Altaic people live?

Soviet Control of Daily Life

To prevent different ethnic groups from identifying with their individual cultures rather than with the Soviet Union, the Soviet government outlawed many cultural celebrations. It destroyed churches and other religious buildings and killed thousands of religious leaders. The members of many ethnic groups were not allowed to speak their native languages or celebrate certain holidays.

The leaders of the Soviet Union wanted their country to be seen as equal to, if not better than, other powerful nations. One way to achieve this goal was to become a strong competitor in the Olympics and in other international sports competitions.

The Soviet government supported its top athletes and provided for all their basic needs. It even hired and paid for the coaches and paid for all training. The hockey teams and gymnasts of the Soviet Union were among the best in the world.

REVIEW What actions did the Soviet government take to try to establish a national identity?

State-Sponsored Sports Soviet countries trained and supported their athletes. Romanian gymnasts, like Nadia Comaneci, won many medals at the Olympics.

Soviet Control

The Soviet government also controlled communications media, such as newspapers, books, and radio. This meant that most Soviet citizens could not learn much about other nations around the world.

The works of many writers, poets, and other artists who lived during the Soviet era often were banned or censored. Soviet artists were forced to join government-run unions. These unions told artists what kinds of works they could create.

Artists who disobeyed the government were punished. Some were imprisoned or even killed. To help achieve its goals, the Soviet government created and distributed **propaganda** (prahp uh GAN duh), or material designed to spread certain beliefs. Soviet propaganda included pamphlets, posters, artwork, statues, songs, and films. It praised the Soviet Union, its leaders, and Communism.

Solzhenitsyn In 1945, army officer Aleksandr Solzhenitsyn (sohl zhuh NEET sihn), far right, called the Soviet leader Joseph Stalin "the boss." For this, he was sentenced to eight years in slave-labor camps. Later, Solzhenitsyn wrote books about his experiences in those camps. He also wrote a letter against censorship. The government called him a traitor, and in 1969 it forced Solzhenitsyn to leave the writers' union. Five years later, Solzhenitsyn left the country.

Although Solzhenitsyn's works were banned, many Soviet citizens read them in secret. Copies of his and other banned books were passed from person to person across the nation. Through such writings, Soviet citizens learned many things that the government had tried to hide from them.

CRITICAL THINKING Analyze Motives
Why would the Soviet government stop people from reading Solzhenitsyn's books?

Compare Compare the censorship of literature in the Soviet Union with freedom of speech and press in the United States.

The Soviet Economy

Main Idea The Communist government of the Soviet Union decided what would be produced, how it would be produced, and who would receive the goods.

In addition to controlling the governments of the Soviet Union and of those Eastern European countries under its influence, Soviet leaders also ran the economy. When the Soviets installed Communist governments in Eastern Europe after World War II, they promised to improve industry and to bring new wealth to be shared among all citizens. This did not happen.

Communism in the Soviet Union did not support **private property rights,** or the right of individuals to own land or an industry. The Soviets wanted all major industries to be owned by the government rather than by private citizens. So the government took over factories, railroads, and businesses.

The Soviet government decided what would be produced, how it would be produced, and who would get what was produced. These choices were made based on Soviet interests, not on the interests of the republics or of individuals. Communist countries of Eastern Europe were often unable to meet the needs—including bread, meat, and clothing—of their citizens.

Starting in the 1950s, Eastern Europeans began to demand more goods of better quality. They also wanted changes in the government. In 1956, Hungary and Poland tried to free their governments and economies from Soviet control. But the Communist army put an end to these attempts at change.

REVIEW Who benefited most from Soviet industry?

Worker and Farmer This statue, a form of propaganda, displays the Soviet belief in the unity of the worker (hammer) and the farmer (sickle).

Attempts at Change

Main Idea Even though people wanted change under Communist governments, the rulers of the Soviet Union refused to give up power or control.

From 1958 until 1964, Nikita Khrushchev (KRUSH chehf) ruled the Soviet Union. During this period, called "The Thaw," writers and other citizens began to have greater freedoms. Khrushchev even visited the United States in 1959, but the thaw in the Cold War did not last. In 1964, with the Soviet economy growing weaker, Khrushchev was **deposed,** or removed from power.

In January 1968 in Czechoslovakia, Alexander Dubček (DOOB chek) became the First Secretary of the Czechoslovak Communist Party. His attempts to lessen the Soviet Union's control over Czechoslovakia led to a period of improvement called the "Prague Spring." Czech citizens enjoyed greater freedoms, including more contact with Western Europe. In August of that year, however, the Soviet Union sent troops to force a return to strict Communist control. Dubček was later replaced, and Soviet controls were back in place.

Nikita Khrushchev The son of a miner and grandson of a peasant, Khrushchev lessened government control of Soviet citizens.

Protest Citizens of Czechoslovakia protested Soviet control in 1968.

In the 1970s leaders of the Soviet Union and the United States began to have more contact. This led to a period of **détente** (day TAHNT), or lessening tension, between the members of NATO and the Warsaw Pact nations.

By the 1980s, economic conditions in the Soviet Union and in those countries under its control had still not improved. Even after détente, the Soviet government continued to spend most of its money on the armed forces and nuclear weapons. In addition, people who lived in the non-Russian republics of the Soviet Union now wanted more control over their own affairs. Many citizens began to reject the Soviet economic system, but the Soviet leaders refused to give up any of their power or control.

REVIEW How did the Soviet Union maintain control over other Eastern European nations?

Lesson Summary

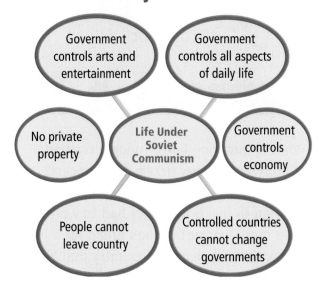

- Government controls arts and entertainment
- Government controls all aspects of daily life
- No private property
- **Life Under Soviet Communism**
- Government controls economy
- People cannot leave country
- Controlled countries cannot change governments

Why It Matters . . .

Today, many republics of the former Soviet Union have become independent nations.

Lesson Review

1964
Nikita Khrushchev deposed

1968
"Prague Spring"

1960   1962   1964   1966   1968   1970

❶ **VOCABULARY** How might **détente** have changed **propaganda** in the Soviet Union? Use these words in your answer.

❷ **READING SKILL Compare** the life of an athlete in the Soviet Union to that of an ordinary citizen.

❸ **MAIN IDEA: Government** Why did Soviet leaders try to create a strong national identity?

❹ **MAIN IDEA: History** What began to happen in Eastern Europe in the 1950s?

❺ **MAIN IDEA: Citizenship** Describe the significance of the "Prague Spring."

❻ **PEOPLE TO KNOW** Which leader of the Soviet Union visited the United States in 1959?

❼ **TIMELINE SKILL** Was Khrushchev in power during the "Prague Spring"?

❽ **CRITICAL THINKING: Analyze** Why do you think the works of many writers, poets, and artists were banned or censored during the Soviet era?

HANDS ON

SPEAKING ACTIVITY Reread the information about literature and arts and the Spotlight on Culture feature on page 356. Write and give a speech for or against censorship in the arts.

Command & Market Economies

What is that long line of people waiting for? Could it be to buy tickets to a concert? Or to get into a ball game? No, the people are waiting to buy bread. They had to wait because there was not enough bread for everyone. Yet they lived in a country that has millions of acres of fertile farmland and wheat fields. How could there be shortages of bread in a country that could produce so much wheat?

The answer is that although it could produce enough wheat, it didn't. The Soviet government's economic plan did not lead to enough wheat production or wheat processing.

The Soviet Union and other communist governments had a **command economy.** The government owned the means of producing goods, and they based their production decisions on government need, not what the people wanted or needed.

On the other hand, the United States has what is called a **free market economy.** In a free market economy, the government owns and plans very little. Instead, goods are produced depending on what people want (demand) and how much of it there already is (supply). Look at the chart on the right to see how a command economy differs from a free market economy.

Chronic Shortages Government planning led to chronic shortages of basic goods in the Soviet Union. Here, people wait in a long line to buy bread.

COMMAND ECONOMY (Communism)   **FREE MARKET ECONOMY (Capitalism)**

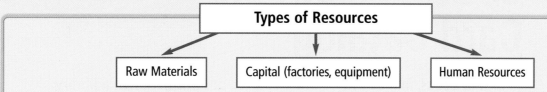

Types of Resources

Raw Materials   **Capital (factories, equipment)**   **Human Resources**

TOTAL STATE CONTROL

- Government owns and controls all resources.
- Government controls where people live and what their occupation will be according to needs of the state.

INDIVIDUAL CONTROL

- Individuals and businesses own and control most resources.
- Individuals decide where they live and their occupation according to intelligent self-interest.

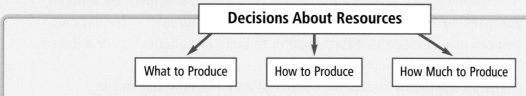

Decisions About Resources

What to Produce   **How to Produce**   **How Much to Produce**

GOVERNMENT PLANS

- Government plans what to produce, how much to produce, and how to produce it, based on what the government determines is the common good.

INDIVIDUAL DECISIONS

- Individuals and businesses look to consumer demand and the marketplace to decide what to produce, how much to produce, and how to produce it.

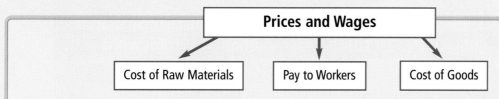

Prices and Wages

Cost of Raw Materials   **Pay to Workers**   **Cost of Goods**

GOVERNMENT SETS PRICES & REWARDS

- Government bureaucracies set the price of raw materials, pay to workers, and the cost of finished goods.
- Prices and wages do not reflect supply and demand, producing shortages and surpluses.
- Individual workers are not rewarded for increased productivity or new ideas, destroying initiative.

MARKETPLACE SETS PRICES & REWARDS

- The interaction of buyer and seller fixes the price of raw materials, labor, and finished goods.
- Prices and wages adjust according to supply and demand.
- Workers and businesses are rewarded for productivity and new ideas, creating initiative.

Activities

1. **TALK ABOUT IT** Look at the chart above. What are the main differences between a command economy and a free market economy? How might these differences affect production?

2. **EVALUATE IT** Discuss the benefits and drawbacks of a command economy and a free market economy, and then make a chart listing your conclusions.

Skillbuilder

Use an Electronic Card Catalog

To find books, magazines, or other sources of information in a library, you may use an electronic card catalog. This catalog is a computerized search program on the Internet that lists every book, periodical, or other resource found in the library. You can search for resources in the catalog in four ways: by title, by author, by subject, and by keyword. Once you have typed in your search information, the catalog will give you a list of every resource that matches it. This is called bibliographic information. You can use an electronic card catalog to build a bibliography, or a list of books, on the topic you are researching.

The screen below shows the results of an electronic search for information about the Danube River. To use the information on the screen, follow the steps listed to the right.

SEARCH REQUEST: Danube River

Subject	Title	Author	Keyword

Find   Options   Locations   Backup   Startover   Help

Lessner, Erwin Christian. The Danube; the dramatic history of the great river and the people touched by its flow. Westport, Conn.: Greenwood Press, 1961.

AUTHOR: Lessner, Erwin Christian

TITLE: The Danube; the dramatic history of the great river and the people touched by its flow

PUBLISHED: Westport, Conn., Greenwood Press, 1961

PAGING: 529 p.

NOTES: Includes maps, bibliography

CALL NO: 914.9603 L Book Available

Learn the Skill

Step 1: To begin your search, choose Subject, Title, Author, or Keyword. The student doing this search chose "Subject" and then typed in "Danube River."

SEARCH REQUEST: Danube River			
Subject	Title	Author	Keyword

Step 2: Based on your search, the catalog will give you a list of records that match that subject. You must then select one of the records to view the details about the resource. The catalog will then give you a screen like the one to the right. This detailed record lists the author, title, and information about where and when the resource was published, and by whom.

Lessner, Erwin Christian. The Danube; the dramatic history of the great river and the people touched by its flow. Westport, Conn.: Greenwood Press, 1961.

> **AUTHOR:** Lessner, Erwin Christian
> **TITLE:** The Danube; the dramatic history of the great river and the people touched by its flow
> **PUBLISHED:** Westport, Conn., Greenwood Press, 1961
> **PAGING:** 529 p.
> **NOTES:** Includes maps, bibliography
> **CALL NO: 914.9603 L** Book Available

Step 3: Locate the call number for the book. The call number indicates the section in the library where you will find the book. You can also find out if the book is available in the library you are using. If not, it may be available in another library in the network.

Practice the Skill

Based on the information you've learned about using an electronic card catalog, answer the questions below.

1. What keywords might you use to find a book about the Soviet economy?
2. What would you do if you wanted to find other books by the author of a book you enjoyed?

Apply the Skill

Review the text in Chapter 13, Lesson 1, to find a topic that interests you. Use the Subject search on an electronic card catalog to find information about your topic. Make a bibliography about the subject. Organize your bibliography alphabetically by author. For each book you list, also include the title, city, publisher, and date of publication.

Eastern Europe and Russia

VOCABULARY

parliamentary
republic
coalition government
ethnic cleansing

Vocabulary Strategy

coalition government

You know what **government** means. A **coalition** is two or more groups that have joined forces. A **coalition government** is formed by small political parties joining together to form a government.

READING SKILL

Sequence Use a flow chart to outline the changes that took place in Eastern Europe and Russia from 1991 through 2000.

Build on What You Know What would happen if one day you suddenly had a different teacher in a class? Your classroom would be the same, but many things would be different. This is what happened on a much larger scale to the people of the Soviet Union and Eastern Europe when Communism collapsed and new leaders and governments came to power.

The Breakup of the Soviet Union

Main Idea The Soviet republics gained independence and, along with the Eastern European countries, chose new governments.

Mikhail Gorbachev (GAWR buh chawf) became leader of the Soviet Union in 1985 and began to make changes. Although Gorbachev believed in the ideals of the Soviet system, he thought that change was necessary to help solve the country's economic and political problems. Beginning in 1985, Gorbachev reduced Cold War tensions with the United States. At home in the Soviet Union, he allowed more political and economic freedom. He also removed large numbers of troops and arms from Eastern Europe.

Mikhail Gorbachev's reforms, however, did not solve the problems of the Soviet Union. The economy continued to get worse. When Gorbachev did not force the countries of Eastern Europe to remain Communist, this further displeased many Communists.

In 1991, a group of more traditional Soviet leaders tried to take over the Soviet government. Thousands of people opposed this move and those leaders failed. Then, one by one, the Soviet republics declared independence. The Warsaw Pact was dissolved. By the end of 1991, the Soviet Union no longer existed. The huge country had become 15 different nations.

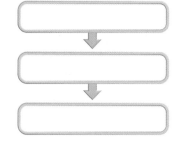

Mikhail Gorbachev
He helped lead the Soviet Union toward a freer society.

R U S S I A

ESTONIA
LATVIA
LITHUANIA
RUSSIA
EAST
GERMANY
POLAND
BELARUS
SLOVAKIA
CZECH REP.
UKRAINE
KAZAKHSTAN
AUSTRIA
HUNGARY
MOLDOVA
SLOVENIA
ROMANIA
CROATIA
GEORGIA
BOSNIA-HERZEGOVINA
BULGARIA   Black Sea
YUGOSLAVIA
UZBEKISTAN
ALBANIA   MACEDONIA   ARMENIA
KYRGYZSTAN
TURKMENISTAN
TAJIKISTAN
AZERBAIJAN

Baltic Sea

Caspian Sea

Mediterranean Sea

0   1,000   2,000 miles
0   1,000   2,000 kilometers

60°N

Post-Communist Europe After the Soviet Union dissolved, this once large empire became 15 different nations. **SKILL** **Interpret a Map** On which continent are most of these countries located?

Modern Eastern Europe

Each former Soviet republic set up its own non-Communist government. The countries of Eastern Europe that had been under Soviet control held democratic elections, and many wrote or revised their constitutions.

In some countries, such as the Czech Republic, former Communists were banned from important government posts. In other countries, such as Bulgaria, the former Communists reorganized themselves into a new political party and have won elections. Many different ethnic groups also tried to create new states within a nation or to reestablish old states that had not existed in many years.

Today, most of the countries of Eastern Europe are parliamentary republics. A **parliamentary republic** is a form of government led by the head of the political party with the most members in parliament. The head of government, usually a prime minister, proposes the programs that the government will undertake. Most of these countries also have a president who has ceremonial, rather than political, duties.

In some countries, small political parties have joined forces to work together to form a government. This is called a **coalition government.**

REVIEW How did Eastern European governments change after the fall of the Soviet Union?

Easter in Ukraine In Ukraine, most Christians belong to the Orthodox Church. These Ukrainians are known for the special way in which they celebrate the Easter holiday. They create beautiful Easter eggs, which are dyed bright colors and covered with intricate designs. These eggs are so beautiful that people around the world collect them.

Ukrainians also bake a special bread for Easter. They decorate it with designs made from pieces of dough. Families bring the bread and other foods to church to be blessed on Easter. Then they eat the foods for the holiday feast.

CRITICAL THINKING Analyze Issues Why were Ukrainian Easter eggs not common during the Soviet era?

Compare Are any of the Ukrainian Easter holiday customs similar to your family's holiday customs?

New Economies

Under Soviet rule, Eastern Europe struggled economically and its people's freedoms were severely restricted. Although Eastern Europeans gained their freedom, they also faced problems such as inflation and unemployment.

Eastern Europe's countries are changing from command economies to free-market economies. Some countries, such as Slovakia, made this change slowly. Others, such as Poland, reformed their economic system and achieved economic success.

Many former Soviet republics, which did not quickly reform their economic systems, are in bad economic shape. Some of these nations are terribly poor. Struggles for power have led to violence and sometimes civil war. Pollution from the Soviet era threatens people's health. Still, some republics, including Ukraine, Latvia, Lithuania, and Estonia, are making progress as independent nations.

After the breakup of the Soviet Union, Eastern European nations no longer looked to the Soviet government to defend them. Many wanted to become members of NATO. Belonging to NATO would help assure them of protection in case of invasion.

In 1999 three new members joined NATO: Poland, Hungary, and the Czech Republic. In 2001 Bulgaria, Romania, Slovakia, Slovenia, and the Baltic states were also working to become NATO members.

Pollution Developing industry has caused massive pollution in Eastern Europe.

War in the Balkan Peninsula

Main Idea Once freed from the control of Communist armies, ancient enemies in the former nation of Yugoslavia engaged in terrible wars.

Since the late 1980s, much of Eastern Europe has been a place of turmoil and struggle. Yugoslavia, one of the countries located on Europe's Balkan Peninsula, has experienced terrible wars, extreme hardships, and great change.

After World War II, Yugoslavia came under Marshal Tito's (TEE toh) dictatorship. Tito controlled all the country's many different ethnic groups, which included Serbs, Croats, and Muslims. His rule continued until his death in 1980. Slobodan Milošević (sloh boh DON muh LAW shuh vich) became Yugoslavia's president in 1989, after years of political turmoil.

Slobodan Milošević, a Serb, wanted the Serbs to rule Yugoslavia. The Serbs in Bosnia began fighting the Croats and Muslims living there. The Bosnian Serbs murdered many Muslims so that Serbs would be in the majority. The Serbs called these killings of members of minority ethnic groups **ethnic cleansing.** Finally, NATO attacked the Bosnian Serbs and ended the war.

In 1995 the Serbs, Croats, and Muslims of Bosnia signed a peace treaty. In 1999 Milošević began using ethnic cleansing against the Albanians in Kosovo, a region of Serbia. NATO launched an air war against Yugoslavia that ended with the defeat of the Serbs. In 2000, public protests led to Milošević's removal. He was subsequently arrested and brought to trial for war crimes by the United Nations.

REVIEW What were the causes of ethnic cleansing in former Yugoslavia?

The Balkan States, 1991 and 2001

Legend:
- National boundaries, 2001
- Yugoslavia, 1991
- Autonomous province boundaries, 2001
- ★ National capital

The Balkans
Inner turmoil caused the former country of Yugoslavia to break up into independent nations.

SKILL Interpret a Map Which former Yugoslavian state borders Greece?

367

Modern Russia

Main Idea Although it still faces difficulties, Russia has made great progress since the breakup of the Soviet Union.

Life in Russia has improved since the breakup of the Soviet Union. Russian citizens can elect their own leaders. They enjoy more freedom of speech. New businesses have sprung up, and some Russians have become wealthy.

Unfortunately, Russia still faces serious problems. Many leaders are dishonest. The nation has been slow to reform its economic system. Most of the nation's new wealth has gone to a small number of people, so that many Russians remain poor. The crime rate has grown tremendously. The government has also fought a war against Chechnya (CHECH nee yah), a region of Russia that wants to become independent.

Russia's Government

Russia has a democratic form of government. The president is elected by the people. The people also elect members of the Duma (DOO muh), which is part of the legislature.

Democracy is still new to the Russian people. Some citizens are working to improve the system to reduce corruption and to ensure that everyone receives fair treatment. Even the thought of changing the government is new to most Russians. Under the Soviets, people had to accept things the way they were.

Russia Today Shoppers, such as these in this Moscow store (left), can find a wide variety of consumer goods, and voters (below) can participate in democratic elections.

Russia's Natural Resources Today

Forest
Grassland
Desert
Tundra
Farmland
Fishing
Natural gas
Coal
Oil
Iron
Gold
Lead

ARCTIC OCEAN

Bering Sea

Sea of Okhotsk

RUSSIA

80°N 60°N 180° 160°E 140°E 40°N

0   250   500 miles
0   250   500 kilometers

Natural Resources Russia is a huge country with many natural resources to support its economy. **SKILL** **Interpret a Map** Name three of Russia's more common natural resources.

Economics

The map above shows Russia's major natural resources. The country is one of the world's largest producers of oil. Russia also contains the world's largest forests. Its trees are made into lumber, paper, and other wood products.

Russian factories produce steel from iron ore. Other factories use that steel to make tractors and other large machines. Since Russian ships can reach both the Pacific and Atlantic oceans, Russia also has a large fishing industry.

Following the lead of Eastern European countries, Russia has been moving toward a free-market economy. Citizens can own land, and foreign companies are encouraged to do business in Russia. These changes have given many Russians more opportunities, but they have also brought difficulties.

Prices are no longer controlled by the government. This means that companies can charge a price that is high enough for them to make a profit. At the beginning of the 21st century, however, people's wages have not risen as fast as prices. Many people cannot afford to buy new products.

Some Russians have done well in the new economy. On the other hand, people with less education and less access to power have not done as well. Also, today most new businesses and jobs are in the cities, which means that people in small towns have fewer job opportunities.

REVIEW What are the main problems that face Russia today?

Russian Culture

The fall of Communism helped most Russians to follow their cultural practices more freely. Russians gained the freedom to practice the religion of their choice. They can also buy and read the great works of Russian literature that once were banned. At the beginning of the 21st century, writers and other artists also have far more freedom to express themselves.

New magazines and newspapers are being published. Even new history books are being written. For the first time in decades, these publications are telling more of the truth about the Soviet Union.

Russian Icons Russian Orthodox religious paintings usually depict biblical figures and scenes. This painting, by Andrei Rublev (AHN dray ruhb LYAWF), is brightly colored and highlighted in gold.

Lesson Summary

As its command economy failed, the Soviet Union broke apart. Eastern European nations were free to choose new governments. Many problems, including wars, had to be overcome, but many former Soviet republics and countries of Eastern Europe are now independent.

Why It Matters...

Nations that were once under Soviet rule are working hard to build new economies and stable democratic governments.

Lesson Review

① **VOCABULARY** Write two sentences using **parliamentary republic** and **coalition government.**

② 🕐 **READING SKILL** In the **sequence** of events before and after the breakup of the Soviet Union, which came first, freedom for Eastern European countries or independence for former republics of the Soviet Union?

③ **MAIN IDEA: Government** What happened to the governments of the former Soviet republics after independence?

④ **MAIN IDEA: Economics** How have the economies of Eastern European countries changed now that those countries are free?

⑤ **MAIN IDEA: Culture** In what ways has life in Russia improved since the breakup of the Soviet Union?

⑥ **FACTS TO KNOW** Why was Slobodan Milošević arrested and put on trial?

⑦ **CRITICAL THINKING: Infer** Why do you think many Eastern European countries wanted to join NATO?

✏️ **WRITING ACTIVITY** Reread the information in the Spotlight on Culture feature on page 366. Write a short, personal essay that describes a special family, school, neighborhood, or holiday celebration in which you participated.

The European Union

Build on What You Know What would it be like if every state in the United States had its own system of money? Every time you went from one state to another, you might have to exchange your state's money for that state's money. That's how it was across Europe until 2002.

Western Europe Today

Main Idea Europeans want to cooperate to maintain a high quality of life for all citizens.

Today, in Western Europe, all national leaders share their power with elected lawmakers. Citizens take part in government by voting and through membership in a variety of political parties.

Many countries of Western Europe belong to a group called the **European Union** (EU). At first, countries joined the EU to encourage trade. This economic group, however, is becoming a loose political union.

Trains High-speed trains, like this one in France, make travel in Europe very convenient.

VOCABULARY

European Union
currency
euro
tariff
standard of living

Vocabulary Strategy

curren**cy**

The words **currency** and **current** both contain **curren-**. A current is a flow of water, and currency, a country's system of money, helps goods flow between buyers and sellers.

READING SKILL

Main Idea and Details As you read, use a chart to outline details that support ideas about the European Union.

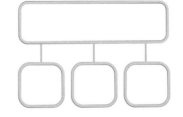

371

Members of the European Union, 2001

Austria		Italy	
Belgium		Luxembourg	
Denmark		Netherlands	
Finland		Portugal	
France		Spain	
Germany		Sweden	
Greece		United Kingdom	
Ireland			

European Union
After centuries of war and often bitter rivalry, the nations of Europe hope that the EU will unite the countries of Europe and bring peace and prosperity.

The European Union

Many former Communist countries of Eastern Europe want to join the Union too. They know that membership will help them economically and politically. Eastern European countries, however, cannot automatically join the EU. Many must first make legal, economic, and environmental improvements. The EU has agreed to include them over time. With 25 member nations in 2004, and more applying for membership, the EU may be the best hope for European peace and prosperity.

In Western Europe, each nation also has regional governments, similar to those of individual states in the United States. Regional governments are demanding—and receiving—greater power. As a result, many people in Western Europe enjoy increased self-rule and participation in the political process.

Euros This new form of currency was introduced to the European market in January 2002.

EU Economies

Traditionally, each European nation has had its own **currency,** or system of money. The EU is meant to make international trade much simpler. With more Europeans using the **euro,** the currency of the EU, currency no longer has to be exchanged every time a payment crosses a border.

To encourage trade, members have also done away with tariffs on the goods they trade with one another. A **tariff** is a duty or fee that must be paid on imported or exported goods, making them more expensive. EU members have lifted border controls as well. This means that goods, services, and people flow freely among these member nations.

A Higher Standard of Living

Another goal of the EU is to achieve economic equality among its members. To reach this goal, EU members are sharing their wealth. For example, poorer countries receive money to help them build businesses.

Member nations hope that increased trade and shared wealth will help give all citizens of the EU a high standard of living. A person's **standard of living,** or quality of life, is based on the availability of goods and services.

People who have a high standard of living have enough food and housing, good transportation and communications, and access to schools and health care. They also have a high rate of literacy, meaning that most adults are able to read.

The members of the EU are helping the countries of Eastern Europe to raise their environmental standards. They are willing to pay up to 75 percent of the cost for a new waste treatment system in Romania, for example. The program includes recycling centers for paper, glass, and plastics. It will clean up and close old dumping grounds, which were leaking pollution into the ground water.

The EU also runs programs that train people for jobs. As citizens of a member nation, people are not limited to a job in their own country. They may work in any part of the EU. They can even vote in local elections wherever they live. In addition, the Council of Europe's Court of Human Rights protects the rights of all its citizens in whichever member country they live.

REVIEW How would improved trade raise the standard of living?

Bank The headquarters (below) of the European Central Bank is located in Frankfurt, Germany. The sign shows the member nations and their flags.

Cultural Diversity

Main Idea Europeans want to share in prosperity, cooperate to avoid conflicts, and preserve their unique cultural identities.

Although many European nations are part of the EU, they still have their own distinct cultural traditions. These traditions may include different languages, unique foods, certain ways of doing business, and even special games and celebrations. Many of these traditions developed over hundreds of years.

Some nations are a mix of several cultures. In Belgium, for example, Flemings live in the north and speak Dutch. Another major group, the Walloons, lives in the south. They speak French. A third group, of German-speaking Belgians, lives in the eastern part of the country. Many Belgian cities include people from all three groups.

Many of the world's famous and exciting cities are located in Western Europe. London, Madrid, Paris, Amsterdam, and Rome are just a few of the major centers for the arts, business, and learning. These cities are centuries old, and Europeans work hard to preserve them.

Europeans also take pride in the conveniences that their cities offer. Most major urban areas have excellent public transportation, including subways, buses, and trains. Sidewalk cafés are also popular, where people come to meet friends, eat, and relax.

European cities have much to offer, but the countryside is also popular— especially for vacationers. The Italian region of Tuscany (TUHS kuh nee) and the French region of Provence (pruh VAHNS) are two of the best-known examples of the many beautiful rural areas.

Social Meeting Places Many Europeans center their social lives around urban sidewalk cafés, such as this one in Italy.

Small European villages may have only a café, a grocery store, a post office, a town square, and a collection of houses. Many families who live in such areas have been farming or raising animals on the same land for generations. Some even live in houses that their families have owned for hundreds of years.

REVIEW Why do European nations who have decided to join the EU still choose to preserve their own cultures and traditions?

Lesson Summary

- The European Union was formed among Western European countries to encourage trade, but it has become a political union.

- As European nations cooperate more politically and economically, they still try to preserve their diverse cultural traditions.

Why It Matters...

A prosperous and culturally diverse Europe provides goods and markets for the rest of the world.

Tourist Destinations Small European villages that maintain their old traditions are popular tourist attractions.

Lesson Review

1 VOCABULARY Explain how the words **currency, euro,** and **tariff** are related.

2 READING SKILL The European Union wants equality among its members. List two details that support this idea.

3 MAIN IDEA: Economics Describe the importance of the new shared currency that is based on the euro.

4 MAIN IDEA: Government Can any European country automatically join the EU? Why or why not?

5 MAIN IDEA: Citizenship List at least two benefits, other than a shared currency, for countries that are members of the EU.

6 FACTS TO KNOW Would a person from Belgium be allowed to work in Germany or France? Why or why not?

7 CRITICAL THINKING: Synthesize Why may the EU be the best hope for European peace and prosperity?

WRITING ACTIVITY Choose one photograph from this lesson that shows a place in Europe. Write a postcard or e-mail to a friend or family member as if you were there. What sights and sounds will you describe?

Visual Summary

1–3. 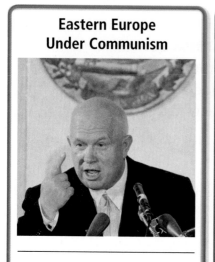 Write a description for each image below.

Eastern Europe Under Communism	Eastern Europe and Russia	The European Union
	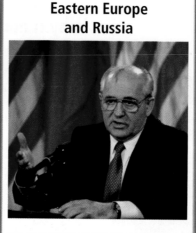	

Facts and Main Ideas

Answer the following questions.

4. **Citizenship** Explain why most Soviet citizens learned little about other nations around the world.

5. **History** How did the Soviet Union change during 1991?

6. **Economics** List at least three of Russia's natural resources.

7. **Government** What is the importance of the European Union?

8. **Geography** Identify at least three of Europe's major centers of the arts, business, and learning.

Vocabulary

Choose the correct term from the list to complete each sentence below.

> **private property rights,** p. 357
> **parliamentary republic,** p. 365
> **standard of living,** p. 373

9. One goal of the European Union is to raise the _____, or quality of life, for citizens in all of its member nations.

10. Under the Soviet system, the government owned everything, and no _____ were recognized.

11. In a _____, the head of the political party with the most seats in parliament is the leader of the government.

1964
Nikita Khrushchev deposed

1991
Soviet Union collapses

2002
European Union adopts the euro

1960 1970 1980 1990 2000 2010

Apply Skills

 TEST PREP **Use an Electronic Card Catalog** Look at the card catalog screen. Apply what you learned about using an electronic card catalog to answer the questions.

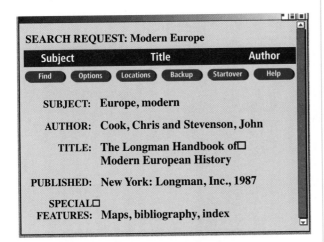

SEARCH REQUEST: Modern Europe

Subject   Title   Author

Find   Options   Locations   Backup   Startover   Help

SUBJECT: Europe, modern

AUTHOR: Cook, Chris and Stevenson, John

TITLE: The Longman Handbook of
Modern European History

PUBLISHED: New York: Longman, Inc., 1987

SPECIAL
FEATURES: Maps, bibliography, index

12. What is the title of this book?

 A. Chris Cook and John Stevenson

 B. Modern Europe, Longman, 1987

 C. The Longman Handbook of Modern European History

 D. Maps, bibliography, index

13. How was the book probably found?

 A. A search for the subject, "Modern Europe"

 B. A search for the author, "Chris Cook"

 C. A search for the title, "Longman Handbook"

 D. A search for the feature, "Maps"

Critical Thinking

 TEST PREP Write a short paragraph to answer each question below.

14. **Compare** Compare Eastern Europe under Communism with Eastern Europe after Communism.

15. **Summarize** Outline the changes to the Russian economy since the breakup of the Soviet Union.

Timeline

Use the Chapter Summary Timeline above to answer the question.

16. Did the European Union adopt the euro before or after the fall of the Soviet Union?

Activities

 ART ACTIVITY Design a new flag or seal for the European Union that reflects both the diversity of Europe and the unity of the nations joining together.

 WRITING ACTIVITY Write a journal entry that might have been written by a Soviet citizen after he or she gained and then lost freedoms after Khrushchev was deposed.

 Technology

Writing Process Tips
Get help with your journal entry at
www.eduplace.com/kids/hmss05/

Technology

e • **glossary**
e • **word games**
www.eduplace.com/kids/hmss05/

Vocabulary Preview

acid rain

When the air is polluted, pollutants often return to Earth in the form of precipitation called **acid rain.** This water poisons the environment, particularly trees. Countries such as France have turned to nuclear power, which reduces air pollution.
page 387

impressionism

A completely new way of painting was created in France toward the end of the 19th century. Called **impressionism,** it is an art style that uses light and color to give the viewer an impression of a scene, rather than a carefully realistic painting.
page 391

Reading Strategy

Question Use this strategy as you read the lessons in this chapter.

Quick Tip Stop and ask yourself questions. Do you need to go back and reread?

reunification

After 45 years as a divided country, West Germany and East Germany were reunited in 1990. This **reunification** of the country set off celebrations that lasted for days.

page 395

dissident

The Communist government of Poland did not allow anyone to disagree openly with its policies. Courageous individuals called **dissidents,** or open opponents of the government, worked for change.

page 400

The United Kingdom

VOCABULARY

secede

Vocabulary Strategy

secede

You may know the word **recede**, which means to "move away from." **Secede** has the same root word, but it means to "withdraw from." To secede is to formally withdraw from an organization or union.

READING SKILL

Classify As you read, take notes to categorize the major aspects of the United Kingdom's modern government, economy, and culture.

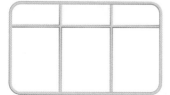

Build on What You Know What language is this textbook written in? Though it was written and printed in the United States, it is in English. Language is just one example of an important area where the small island of the United Kingdom has had a big impact in America and elsewhere.

A Kingdom of Four Political Regions

Main Idea The United Kingdom is made up of four different regions: England, Scotland, Wales, and Northern Ireland.

The United Kingdom is a small island nation of Western Europe. Its culture has had an enormous impact on the world. The nation's official name is the United Kingdom of Great Britain and Northern Ireland. London, located in southeastern England, is the capital.

Four different political regions make up the United Kingdom: Scotland, England, Wales, and Northern Ireland (see the map on page 381). The British monarchy has ruled over the four regions for hundreds of years.

Political Regions Each political region of the United Kingdom has its own flag, and they all share the United Kingdom flag, also called the Union Jack.

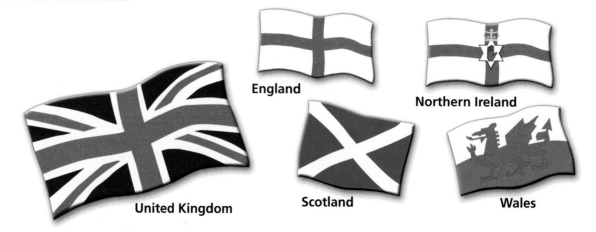

England

Northern Ireland

United Kingdom

Scotland

Wales

National Government

Today, the government of the United Kingdom is a constitutional monarchy. The British monarch is a symbol of power rather than an actual ruler. The power to govern belongs to Parliament, which is the national lawmaking body.

The British Parliament has two parts. The House of Lords is made up of nobles. Elected representatives make up the House of Commons. The House of Commons is the more powerful of the two houses.

The prime minister leads the government. He or she is usually the leader of the political party that wins the most seats in the House of Commons. The other political parties go into "opposition," which means their role is to question government policies.

REVIEW Who is the head of government in the United Kingdom?

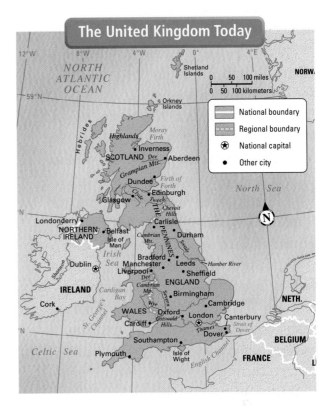

The United Kingdom Today

The United Kingdom Different regions make up this union. **SKILL** **Interpret a Map** Which region of the United Kingdom is on a different island?

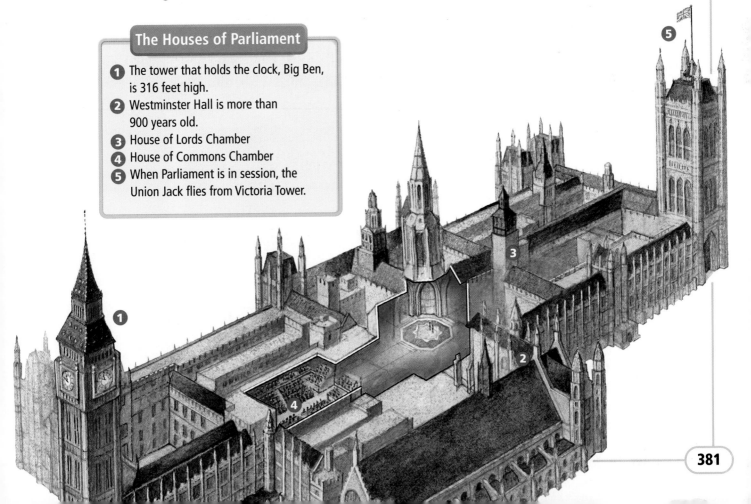

The Houses of Parliament

1. The tower that holds the clock, Big Ben, is 316 feet high.
2. Westminster Hall is more than 900 years old.
3. House of Lords Chamber
4. House of Commons Chamber
5. When Parliament is in session, the Union Jack flies from Victoria Tower.

Governing Regions

Recently, the national government of the United Kingdom has returned some self-rule to some regions of Great Britain. In the late 1990s, voters in Wales approved plans for their own assembly, or body of lawmakers. Also at this time, the Scots voted to create their own parliament. Both Wales's assembly and Scotland's parliament met for the first time in 1999.

Throughout the 20th century, there were conflicts in Northern Ireland between Irish Catholic nationalists and Irish Protestants who supported the government of the United Kingdom. In fact, during the 1960s, many Irish Catholics wanted Northern Ireland to **secede,** or withdraw from, the United Kingdom. They hoped to unite Northern Ireland with the Republic of Ireland. Irish Protestants—a majority in the region—generally wanted to remain part of the United Kingdom.

In 1969, riots broke out, and the British government sent in troops to stop them. Violence between groups of Protestants and Catholics continued for almost 30 years. In 1998, representatives from both sides signed the Good Friday Accord. This agreement set up the Northern Ireland Assembly, which represents both Catholic and Protestant voters. For this government to succeed in Northern Ireland, however, the former enemies will need to work together.

Cultural Heritage

Main Idea The United Kingdom has been making important contributions to world culture for more than 500 years.

The United Kingdom has a rich cultural heritage that includes the great Renaissance playwright William Shakespeare. With a long history as an imperial power, the nation has been exporting its culture around the world for hundreds of years. For example, India, Canada, and other former British colonies modeled their governments on the British parliamentary system. British culture has also set trends in sports, music, and literature.

Globe Theatre London's New Globe Theatre is a replica of the 17th-century playhouse that originally hosted William Shakespeare's works.

Music and Literature

British music influenced the early music of Canada and the United States, both former British colonies. One British tune long familiar to people in the United States is "God Save the Queen." You probably know it as "My Country, 'Tis of Thee." Several countries have put the words of their national anthems to this traditional British melody.

During the 1960s, many British musical groups—including the Beatles and the Rolling Stones—dominated music charts around the world. In later decades, other British singers, including Elton John, Sting, and Eric Clapton, became popular favorites.

The best-known cultural export of the United Kingdom, aside from the English language itself, may be literature. In the 19th century, Mary Shelley dreamed up Frankenstein's monster, and Sir Arthur Conan Doyle first wrote about Sherlock Holmes. Another popular author of the time was Charles Dickens (1812–1870), who wrote *Oliver Twist* and *A Christmas Carol*.

Two gifted British writers of the 20th century are Virginia Woolf and George Orwell. Modern British authors have also given the world many popular stories for young people. They include C. S. Lewis, who wrote *The Chronicles of Narnia*, and J. K. Rowling, who created the *Harry Potter* books.

REVIEW Why was the United Kingdom able to spread British culture across the world?

The Beatles In the early 1960s, the Beatles became wildly popular, not only in the United Kingdom, but also around the world.

J. K. Rowling Her *Harry Potter* books have captured the imaginations of children worldwide.

The British Economy

The United Kingdom is an important trading and financial center. Many British citizens also make their living in mining and manufacturing. Factories in the United Kingdom turn out a variety of products ranging from china to sports cars. The nation has plenty of coal, natural gas, and oil to fuel its factories, but it has few other natural resources.

The need for imported goods makes trade another major industry of the United Kingdom. The nation imports many raw materials used in manufacturing. It also imports food, because the farms of this nation produce only enough to feed about two-thirds of its large population.

Lesson Summary

The United Kingdom

↓

The United Kingdom is a small island nation that consists of four regions: England, Scotland, Wales, Northern Ireland.

↓

The United Kingdom has a long history of colonization. Its government and culture have spread throughout the world.

↓

For centuries, the United Kingdom has been an important center of finance and trade.

Why It Matters . . .

British economic, political, and cultural traditions have influenced nations around the world.

Lesson Review

1 VOCABULARY Explain who would like to **secede** from the United Kingdom.

2 🖐 READING SKILL How would you **classify** the widespread use of a British melody as the tune for national anthems and national songs? Is it an example of economic or cultural influence?

3 MAIN IDEA: **Geography** Identify the four regions that make up the United Kingdom.

4 MAIN IDEA: **Government** What role does the British monarchy play in the government of the modern United Kingdom?

5 MAIN IDEA: **Culture** What impact has the culture of the United Kingdom had on its colonies and on other parts of the world?

6 EVENTS TO KNOW What agreement established the **Northern Ireland Assembly**, and what is the assembly's purpose?

7 CRITICAL THINKING: **Analyze** Why do you think the conflict in Northern Ireland is so difficult to resolve?

HANDS ON

MUSIC ACTIVITY Use the melody of "God Save the Queen" and "My Country 'Tis of Thee" to write your own patriotic lyrics. Your song can be about your school, your community, or even about the entire world.

Sweden

Build on What You Know You probably have seen TV awards programs, such as the Oscars for movies, or the Grammy awards for music. Your school may have awards ceremonies as well. Some of the most important awards in the world—the Nobel Prizes—are given in Sweden each year.

Sweden's Government

Main Idea Sweden, a neutral country, is a constitutional monarchy, but the monarch makes no laws and power rests with parliament.

Sweden shares the Scandinavian Peninsula with Norway in Northern Europe (see the map on page 386). The country is a constitutional monarchy; the Swedish monarch has only ceremonial powers and cannot make laws. Instead, the people elect representatives to four-year terms in the Swedish parliament, called the Riksdag (REEKS dahg).

The 349 members of the Riksdag nominate Sweden's prime minister. They also appoint ombudsmen. **Ombudsmen** are officials who protect citizens' rights and make sure that the Swedish courts and civil service follow the law.

Swedish citizens vote to determine how many members of each political party serve in the Riksdag. Before 1976, the Social Democratic Labour Party had been in power for nearly 44 years. Today, the Swedish government includes four other parties.

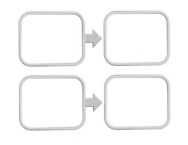

Lawmakers Women are active in Swedish government.

Sweden Today

Legend:
- National boundary
- ⊛ National capital
- • Other city

Sweden This country is on the Scandinavian Peninsula. **SKILL** **Interpret a Map** Which country shares the Scandinavian Peninsula with Sweden?

Foreign Policy

Since World War I, Sweden's foreign policy has been one of **armed neutrality.** This means that in times of war, the country has its own military forces but does not take sides in other nations' conflicts.

Even during peacetime, the Swedish government tries not to form military alliances. Unless Sweden is directly attacked, it will not become involved in war. The country is a strong supporter of the United Nations.

High-tech Industry Many in Sweden's highly educated labor force work in the high-tech and engineering industries.

The Economy and Daily Life

Main Idea Sweden has a highly educated workforce that enjoys a very high standard of living.

Privately owned businesses and international trade are important to Sweden's economy. It exports many goods, including metals, minerals, and wood. Engineering and communications are major industries. The automobile industry also provides many jobs.

After World War II, many Swedes left their towns and villages to find work in the large cities in the south. Today, more than 80 percent of the population lives in these urban areas. Much of Sweden's labor force is highly educated and enjoys a high standard of living.

Power Source

Hydroelectricity, or power generated by water, is the main source of electrical power in Sweden. Nuclear power is also widely used. The Swedish government is looking into other, safer sources of energy, which include solar- and wind-powered energy.

Sweden and its neighboring countries share similar environmental problems. One of the most severe problems is **acid rain.** Acid rain occurs when air pollutants come back to Earth in the form of precipitation. These pollutants may soon poison many trees throughout the region.

Sweden and neighboring countries are working to clean up the environment by trying to control air pollutants produced by cars and factories.

Winter Sports Sweden's cold winters have made downhill and cross-country skiing popular.

Daily Life and Culture

Culturally and ethnically, Sweden is primarily a homogeneous country. Ninety percent of the population are native to Sweden and are members of the Lutheran Church of Sweden. The majority of people speak Swedish.

Since World War II, immigrants from Turkey, Greece, and other countries have brought some cultural diversity to Sweden's population. Today, about one in nine people living in Sweden is an immigrant or the child of an immigrant.

Workers in Sweden have many benefits, including long vacations. The Swedes love taking time to enjoy both winter and summer sports. Sweden, with its cold weather and many hills and mountains, is a great place for cross-country and downhill skiing. Skating, hockey, and ice fishing are also popular.

Many small islands, called **skerries,** dot the Swedish coast. In the summer, many people visit these islands to hike, camp, and fish. Tennis, soccer, and outdoor performances such as concerts are popular as well.

REVIEW What causes acid rain?

Sweden is well known for its contributions to drama, literature, and film. The late 19th-century and early 20th-century plays of August Strindberg are produced all over the world. Astrid Lindgren's children's books, including *Pippi Longstocking* (1945), still delight readers everywhere. Ingmar Bergman is famous for the many great films he directed.

Stockholm The capital of Sweden hosts the Nobel Prize ceremonies.

Lesson Summary

Sweden is a Northern European constitutional monarchy that is governed by an elected parliament called the Riksdag. Its foreign policy is one of armed neutrality, which means it has an army, but will not participate in a war between other nations. The country is ethnically homogeneous, for the most part, with a highly educated workforce and a high standard of living, but it also faces environmental problems. Outdoor activities are popular throughout the country, and Sweden is noted for its contributions to drama, literature, and film.

Why It Matters . . .

Modern Sweden is dealing with environmental issues that affect many countries around the world.

Lesson Review

1 VOCABULARY Use these words to complete each sentence.

  acid rain   armed neutrality

Sweden has a policy of _____ that states it will not enter a war between other countries.
One of Sweden's biggest environmental concerns is _____, which kills its forests.

2 READING SKILL What is the **effect** of ombudsmen in Swedish society?

3 MAIN IDEA: Geography On which European peninsula is Sweden located? What other country shares this peninsula?

4 MAIN IDEA: Economics What happened to the Swedish labor force after World War II?

5 MAIN IDEA: Culture How has immigration since World War II changed the population of Sweden?

6 PLACES TO KNOW Why are **skerries** popular vacation spots in Sweden?

7 CRITICAL THINKING: Evaluate What do you think might be the advantages and disadvantages of armed neutrality for Sweden?

WRITING ACTIVITY The Nobel Prize is given for peace, literature, physics, chemistry, economics, and medicine. Write a short description of which category you would like to earn a Nobel Prize in and why.

France

Build on What You Know Have you ever visited an art museum? The largest, most famous art museum in the world, the Louvre (loove), is in Paris, France.

The Fifth Republic

Main Idea Conquered by Germany in World War II, France took its own approach to rebuilding its ruined economy.

During World War II, Charles de Gaulle (1890–1970) was a general in the French army. After Germany conquered France in 1940, de Gaulle fled to the United Kingdom. There, he became the leader of the French in exile and stayed in contact with the French Resistance. The French Resistance established communications for the Allied war effort, spied on German activity, and sometimes assassinated high-ranking German officers.

On December 21, 1958, Charles de Gaulle was elected president of France. He reorganized the French constitution and instituted the Fifth Republic of France.

France is a parliamentary republic. Governmental power is split between the president and parliament. The president is elected by the public to a five-year term. The president's primary responsibilities are to act as guardian of the constitution and to ensure proper functioning of other authorities.

Parliament has two parts: the Senate and the National Assembly. The president chooses a prime minister, who heads parliament and is largely responsible for the internal workings of the government. The French government is very active in the country's economy.

▶ **VOCABULARY**

socialism
European Community
impressionism

Vocabulary Strategy

socialism

Look at the word **socialism.** Think of other words that describe ideas that end with **-ism,** such as capitalism or communism. Socialism is an economic system in which some businesses and industries are controlled by the government.

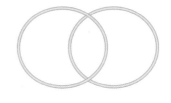

READING SKILL

Compare and Contrast As you read, compare the political and economic condition of France at the end of World War II with today.

Charles de Gaulle A hero of World War II, he served as president of France from 1958 to 1969.

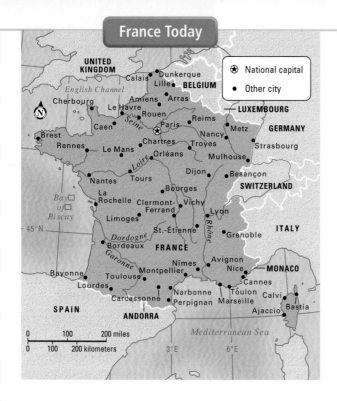

France The country stretches from the English Channel to the Mediterranean Sea.

SKILL Interpret a Map Name three countries that border France.

Nuclear Power Nuclear power plants such as these are a common sight in the French countryside.

A Centralized Economy

World War II left France poor and in need of rebuilding. The National Planning Board, established by Jean Monnet (moh NAY) in 1946, launched a series of five-year plans to modernize France and set economic goals for the country.

The result of these plans was a mixed economy, with both public and private sectors. The French government nationalized, or took over, major banks; insurance companies; the electric, coal, and steel industries; schools; universities; hospitals; railroads; airlines; and even an automobile company.

This nationalization of industry is a form of socialism. **Socialism** is an economic system in which some businesses and industries are controlled by the government. The government also provides many health and welfare benefits, such as health care, housing, and unemployment insurance. However, today the French government is slowly placing more of the economy under the control of private companies.

Most famous for its wines, France also exports grains, automobiles, electrical machinery, and chemicals. Although only about 7 percent of the labor force works on farms, France exports more agricultural products than any other nation in the European Community.

The French economy grew rapidly after 1946, and the country's industry was powered mainly by coal, oil, and gas. When worldwide oil prices rose in the 1970s, the French economy suffered. In the 1980s, France turned to nuclear power so that its economy would be less dependent on oil. Today, France draws 75 percent of its power from nuclear energy, a higher percentage than any other nation in the world.

The **European Community** is an association developed after World War II to promote economic unity among the countries of Western Europe. Its success gave rise to greater unity, both politically and economically, in the European Union.

The Culture of Paris

Main Idea France's capital city has been and remains an important artistic and cultural center.

Paris, the capital city of France, is famous for its contributions to world culture, most especially in the arts. Nicknamed "City of Light," Paris has long been an intellectual and artistic center.

Edouard Manet (muh NAY) (1832–1883) helped influence one of the most important art movements of modern times, impressionism. **Impressionism** is an art style that uses light to create an impression of a scene rather than a strictly realistic picture. Manet inspired such artists as Claude Monet (moh NAY), Pierre Renoir (ruhn WAHR), and Paul Cézanne (say ZAHN). This group of artists worked together in Paris and shared their thoughts and opinions of art.

Paris's Musée d'Orsay and the Louvre (loove) house two of the greatest collections of fine art in the world. The School of Fine Arts leads a tradition of education and art instruction that has produced artists such as Pierre Bonnard (baw NAHR) (1867–1947) and Balthus (1908–2001).

REVIEW What is the nickname of Paris? How do you think it was given that nickname?

Impressionism The artist Monet and his family often modeled for his fellow impressionist painter, Manet, as in this 1874 painting, *Monet Working on His Boat in Argenteuil.*

France has a rich tradition of literature as well. Marcel Proust, who wrote *Remembrance of Things Past*, was an influential writer in the early 20th century. Other significant writers include Albert Camus (kah MOO), who wrote *The Stranger*, and Simone de Beauvoir (boh VWAHR), author of *The Mandarins*.

Simone de Beauvoir This French author wrote about the meaning of human existence and the place and role of women in society.

Lesson Summary

- France was conquered by Germany in World War II. People in the country fought against the German army in an organization called the French Resistance.

- After the war, the French had to rebuild their government and economy. France is a parliamentary republic with many nationalized industries.

- France uses more nuclear power than any other country, and it exports more agricultural goods than any other nation in the European Community.

- Paris, the capital of France, has long been a center of artistic and cultural activity.

Why It Matters . . .

France is an important member of the European Union and continues to influence the world's economy and cultures.

Lesson Review

1 VOCABULARY Explain the importance of **impressionism** and the **European Community** to France.

2 READING SKILL Contrast the condition of France's economy following World War II and its condition today.

3 MAIN IDEA: Government What role does the French government play in the country's economy?

4 MAIN IDEA: Economics What is France's primary source of power?

5 MAIN IDEA: Culture Name three contributions of French culture to the world.

6 PEOPLE TO KNOW Who was **Charles de Gaulle?**

7 CRITICAL THINKING: Draw Conclusions Do you think the French Resistance was an open movement or a secret movement? Why?

ART ACTIVITY Reread the text about Edouard Manet. Draw an impressionist portrait of a classmate, friend, or family member.

Germany

Build on What You Know Was there ever a time when you were separated from people or places you love? You might have thought constantly about getting together again. That's how it was for the German people, but Germany was divided for 45 years!

A Divided Germany

Main Idea At the end of World War II, Germany was divided into two countries, Communist East Germany and democratic West Germany.

Today, the reunified nation of Germany is one of the largest countries in Europe. When World War II ended in 1945, however, Germany was divided. United States, French, and British soldiers occupied the new West German nation, and Soviet soldiers occupied the new East Germany.

The Dividing Wall The Berlin Wall, built in 1961, divided neighborhoods and families. Few East Berliners managed to escape after it was built.

VOCABULARY

reunification

Vocabulary Strategy

reunification

When you read the word **reunification,** think of its parts. The base word is **unify**, and **reunify** means to put together again; the suffix *-ation* means the act of doing something. **Reunification** means reuniting, or making into one again.

READING SKILL

Draw Conclusions As you read, note facts that help you draw conclusions about Germany and its importance in modern Europe.

393

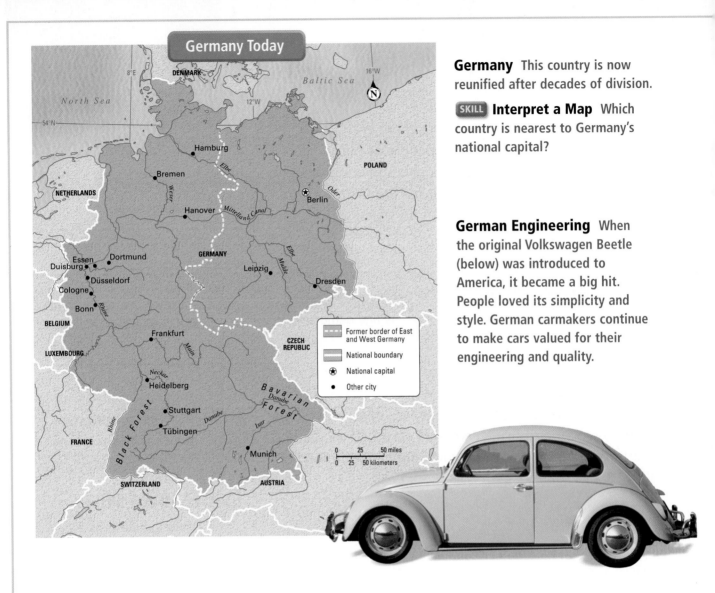

Germany Today

Germany This country is now reunified after decades of division.

SKILL **Interpret a Map** Which country is nearest to Germany's national capital?

German Engineering When the original Volkswagen Beetle (below) was introduced to America, it became a big hit. People loved its simplicity and style. German carmakers continue to make cars valued for their engineering and quality.

Map legend:
- Former border of East and West Germany
- National boundary
- ⊛ National capital
- • Other city

West Germany

The United States helped West Germany set up a democratic government. In part, the United States supported the new nation because it was located between the Communist countries of Eastern Europe and the rest of Western Europe.

With the help of U.S. loans, West Germany experienced a so-called economic miracle. In 20 years, it rebuilt its factories and became one of the world's richest nations. It was its economy that later became the driving force behind the European Union.

East Germany

In contrast to West Germany, East Germany remained poor. Most East Germans saw West Germany, and Western Europe in general, as a place where people had better lives. East Germany's Communist government, however, discouraged contact between east and west.

By 1989, the Soviet Union's control of Eastern Europe was weakening. Hungary, a Soviet ally, relaxed control over its borders with Western Europe. East Germans began crossing the Hungarian border into Austria and eventually made their way into West Germany. After the Berlin Wall came down in 1989, more East Germans fled to West Germany.

Reunified Germany

Main Idea In 1990, Germany once again became a single nation, united by pride in the nation's rich cultural traditions.

Since the 1990 **reunification,** or the reuniting of East and West Germany, the German government has spent billions of dollars rebuilding the eastern part of the country. The effort has included roads, factories, housing, and hospitals. The city of Berlin, once again the nation's capital, was also rebuilt. The newly reunified nation also restored the Reichstag (RYK shtahg), where the Federal Assembly meets.

However, reunification has also caused tensions between "Ossies" (OSS eez) and "Wessies" (VEHSS eez). Many Ossies complain about the lack of jobs and the cost of housing. Many Wessies complain about paying taxes to rebuild the nation and to help support the former East Germans.

German Culture

Germany's rich cultural traditions may help to unite its people, who are especially proud of their music and literature. Germans are also famous for designing high-quality products, such as cars, electronic appliances, and other complex machinery.

Three of Germany's best-known composers are Johann Sebastian Bach (bahck) (1685–1750), George Frederick Handel (HAHN duhl) (1685–1759), and Ludwig van Beethoven (LOOD vig vahn BAY toh vuhn) (1770–1827). Their music is still performed and recorded all over the world. German composer Richard Wagner (VAHG nuhr) (1813–1883) wrote many operas, including a series based on German myths and legends known as the Ring Cycle.

REVIEW Why did East Germany need to be rebuilt and not West Germany?

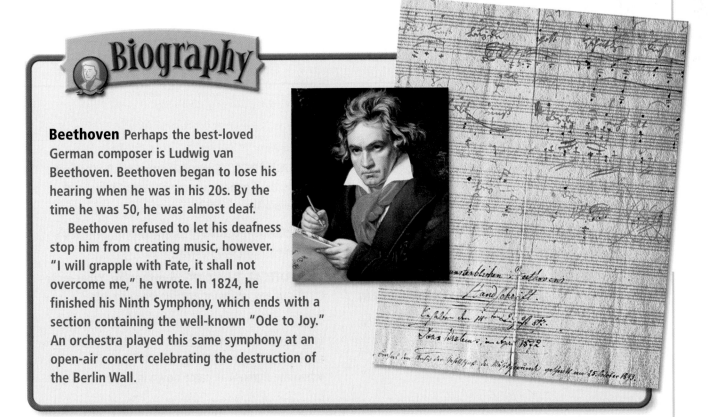

Biography

Beethoven Perhaps the best-loved German composer is Ludwig van Beethoven. Beethoven began to lose his hearing when he was in his 20s. By the time he was 50, he was almost deaf.

Beethoven refused to let his deafness stop him from creating music, however. "I will grapple with Fate, it shall not overcome me," he wrote. In 1824, he finished his Ninth Symphony, which ends with a section containing the well-known "Ode to Joy." An orchestra played this same symphony at an open-air concert celebrating the destruction of the Berlin Wall.

Literature

One of the greatest writers in the German language was Rainer Maria Rilke (RIHL kuh) (1875–1926). His poems, which are still admired and studied today, were a way for Rilke to communicate his feelings and experiences.

Other important 20th-century German authors include Günter Grass (grahs) (b. 1927) and Thomas Mann (man) (1875–1955). Grass has written about the horrors of World War II, the setting for his novel *The Tin Drum*. Both writers were awarded the Nobel Prize in Literature—Mann in 1929 and Grass in 1999.

Lesson Summary

> After World War II, Germany was divided into West Germany, occupied by British, French, and American troops, and East Germany, occupied by Soviet troops.

> With United States help, West Germany established a stable democracy and rebuilt its economy.

> In East Germany, the Soviet Union installed a Communist puppet government.

> In 1990, the two German countries were reunited as a single nation. The German people are also united by pride in their cultural heritage.

Why It Matters . . .

Germany has helped to shape recent European history and contemporary Western culture.

Traditional Design Half-timber architecture, shown here, is common throughout Germany.

Lesson Review

1 VOCABULARY Explain the significance of **reunification** in the history of Germany.

2 READING SKILL Draw a **conclusion** about the obstacles Germans have overcome in recent years.

3 MAIN IDEA: Economics Describe the economic miracle that occurred in West Germany.

4 MAIN IDEA: Citizenship Why has there been tension between the Ossies and the Wessies?

5 MAIN IDEA: Government On what projects has the German government spent billions of dollars since 1990?

6 PEOPLE TO KNOW Name two of Germany's best-known composers.

7 CRITICAL THINKING: Synthesize What makes Germany an important European country?

WRITING ACTIVITY Think about what it was like when Germany was reunified. Write a short story describing how it might have felt to be there when the Berlin Wall came down in 1989.

Poland

Build on What You Know Like most people, you have probably encountered a situation that was unfair or unjust. It takes a lot of courage to speak out against injustice. Time after time, following World War II, the people of Poland courageously tried to free themselves from a Communist government they did not want.

Political and Economic Struggles

Main Idea It took 35 years of struggle for the Polish people to replace the Communist government with a parliamentary republic.

There have been political and economic struggles in Poland since World War II ended in 1945. At that time, Communists took over the government and set strict wage and price controls. In 1956, Polish workers rioted to protest their low wages. In the 1970s and 1980s, citizens also led protests against increased food prices, and won the right to form labor unions.

Core Lesson 5

▶ **VOCABULARY**

censorship
dissident

Vocabulary Strategy

dissident

Another word for **dissident** is **rebel**. The two words can be synonyms. A **dissident** is a person who openly disagrees with a government's policies.

 READING SKILL

Compare and Contrast As you read, compare and contrast Poland today with its history under Communist leaders.

Brave Protest Polish workers united to protest poor conditions under the Communist government.

Poland Today

Poland This country's location made it difficult to resist Soviet domination.

SKILL **Interpret a Map** How many different countries border Poland?

Solidarity

In 1980, labor unions throughout Poland joined an organization called Solidarity. This trade union was led by Lech Walesa (LEK wah LEHN suh), an electrical worker from the shipyards of Gdańsk (guh DAHNSK).

In the beginning, Solidarity's goals were to increase pay and improve working conditions. Before long, however, the organization set its sights on bigger goals. In late 1981, members of Solidarity were calling for free elections and an end to Communist rule. Even though Solidarity had about 10 million members, the government fought back. It suspended the organization, cracked down on protesters, and arrested thousands of members, including Walesa.

A Free Poland

In the late 1980s, economic conditions continued to worsen in Poland. The government asked Solidarity leaders to help them solve the country's economic difficulties. Finally, the Communists agreed to Solidarity's demand for free elections.

When the elections were held in 1989, many Solidarity candidates were elected, and the Communists lost power. In 1990, Lech Walesa became the president of a free Poland.

Today, Poland is a parliamentary republic. The country approved a new constitution in 1997. This constitution guarantees civil rights such as free speech. It also helps to balance the powers held by the president, the prime minister, and parliament.

Lech Walesa In 1980, Solidarity leader Lech Walesa gained the support of labor unions. Ten years later, he became Poland's first democratically elected president.

Parliament Poland's senate helps ensure that all the country's citizens have representation.

A Changing Economy

Main Idea Along with a new government, Poland struggled to adapt to a completely new economic system.

Besides a new government, the Poles have also had to deal with a changing economy. In 1990, Poland's new democratic government quickly switched from a command economy to a free market economy. Prices were no longer controlled by the government, and trade suddenly faced international competition.

Although Polish shops were able to sell goods that had not been available before, prices rose quickly—by almost 80 percent. With this inflation, or a continual rise in prices, people's wages could not keep up with the cost of goods.

Many Polish companies, which could not compete with high-quality foreign goods, went out of business. This, in turn, resulted in high unemployment. As more and more people lost their jobs, Poland's overall standard of living fell.

REVIEW What led to free elections in Poland?

Parliament

Poland's parliament is made up of two houses. The upper house, or senate, has 100 members. The lower house, which has 460 members, chooses the prime minister. Usually, as in the United Kingdom, the prime minister is a member of the largest party or alliance of parties within parliament.

A number of seats in parliament are reserved for representatives of the small German and Ukrainian ethnic groups in Poland. In this way, all Polish citizens are ensured a voice in their government.

Economic Success

In time, new Polish businesses found success, giving more people work. Inflation started to drop. By 1999, inflation was down to around 7 percent. By 2000, Poland no longer needed the economic aid it had been receiving from the United States.

One way to measure the strength of a country's economy is to look at consumer spending. Between 1995 and 2000, Poles bought new cars at a high rate of half a million each year. Today, Poland has 2 million small and medium-sized businesses. The success of these businesses is another sign of Poland's healthy economy.

Worker With Poland's economy on the rise, unemployment has decreased.

Poland's Culture

Main Idea Despite hundreds of years of foreign domination, Poland developed a rich culture of its own.

The history of Poland has been one of ups and downs. In the 1500s and 1600s, Poland was a large and powerful kingdom. By 1795, Russia, Prussia, and Austria had taken control of its land, and Poland ceased to exist as an independent country. Poland did not become a republic until 1918, after World War I. Throughout the centuries, however, Poland has had a rich culture.

Polish literature is full of accounts of struggles for national independence and stories about glorious kingdoms won and lost by heroic patriots.

One of Poland's best-known writers of recent times is Czeslaw Milosz (CHEH slawv MEE lawsh) (b. 1911). Milosz published his first book of poems in the 1930s. After World War II, he worked as a diplomat in the United States and then France. Milosz, who became a professor at the University of California at Berkeley, won the Nobel Prize in Literature in 1980.

Under Communist rule, the Polish media were controlled by the government. The government decided what the media could and could not say. It outlawed any information that did not support and praise the accomplishments of Communism. As a result of this **censorship,** many writers could not publish their works. Some of them became dissidents. A **dissident** is a person who openly disagrees with a government's policies.

In order to help Polish writers, the government now allows publications printed in Poland to be sold tax-free. To help Polish actors, screenwriters, and directors, movie theaters are repaid their costs for showing Polish movies. Public-sponsored television stations are supported not only by free-market advertising but also by fees the public pays to own television sets.

REVIEW Why did the Communist government control the media?

John Paul II In 1978, Poland's pride was greatly boosted when Polish-born John Paul II was elected Pope of the Roman Catholic Church. He was the first non-Italian to be elected Pope in 456 years.

Lesson Summary

- At the end of World War II, a Communist government took power in Poland. The Polish people resisted and protested time after time. In 1981, a union called Solidarity had 10 million members who were calling for free elections.

- Elections were finally held in 1989, and Poland became a parliamentary republic. The next year, the new government switched from a command economy to a free-market economy.

- The Polish people worked through all the difficulties of establishing a new democratic government and a new economic system. The country's long struggle for independence has finally been rewarded.

Why It Matters...

Poland is an excellent example of the success that has been achieved by the recently independent Eastern European nations.

Lesson Review

1. **VOCABULARY** Explain the significance of **censorship** and **dissidents** in Poland's long struggle for freedom.

2. **READING SKILL** **Compare** the media of Poland under Communism with Poland's media today.

3. **MAIN IDEA: Government** How did the Polish government respond to Solidarity's goals?

4. **MAIN IDEA: Citizenship** What was the outcome of Poland's free election in the late 1980s?

5. **MAIN IDEA: Economics** Describe the recent changes in the economy of Poland.

6. **EVENTS TO KNOW** In what year did Poland, once a large and powerful kingdom, cease to be an independent country?

7. **CRITICAL THINKING: Generalize** How would you describe what life was like in Poland before the changes of 1990?

HANDS ON

SPEAKING ACTIVITY Reread the information about Solidarity. Write and deliver a short speech that might have been given to gain support for the organization in the 1980s.

Telecommunications Satellites
These help bring television and telephone services to Polish homes and businesses. Most telecommunication satellites are geostationary, meaning that they stay in place over one location, moving with Earth as it rotates.

TELECOMMUNICATIONS

How many television channels do you get at home? How many telephones do you have? In the United States, many people can choose from hundreds of television channels because their television sets are linked to cable television or satellite networks. Nearly everyone uses cord phones, cordless phones, or cellular phones.

When Poland was a Communist nation, the government controlled television and the telephone industry. Until 1990, the government did little to invest in communication devices that served the people. The nationwide system of telephones was underdeveloped and outdated. Even by the mid-1990s, only about one out of every ten Poles had a telephone. Since then, Poland has worked to update and modernize its telecommunications services.

Types of Telephones In the late 1990s, many Poles were on waiting lists to get main-line phone service. Today there are more cell phone users than cord-phone users.

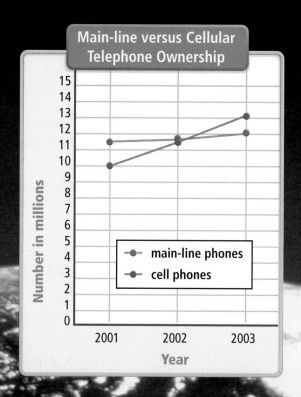

Main-line versus Cellular Telephone Ownership

Number in millions (0–15)

- main-line phones
- cell phones

Year: 2001, 2002, 2003

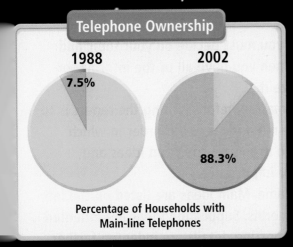

Telephone Ownership

1988

7.5%

2002

88.3%

Percentage of Households with
Main-line Telephones

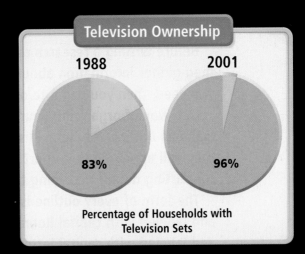

Television Ownership

1988

83%

2001

96%

Percentage of Households with
Television Sets

Telephones Since the fall of Communism in Poland in 1989, telephone ownership has increased over 80%.

Television In 1988, before the fall of Communism, Poland only had about 10 million television sets. Now, almost every household has one, and more than half of those households with television also have satellite television access.

Growing Television Industry The first privately owned television station in Poland began broadcasting in 1990. Today, the people watch Polish television stations as well as shows from Western Europe by satellite. Young Poles can even watch America's popular music channel, MTV.

Activities

1. **IMAGINE IT** Tell how life would change if you had no phone service.

2. **DISCUSS IT** Discuss and list the effects poor communications technology would have on business and on people's personal lives.

Skillbuilder

Make an Outline

Before writing a research report, you must decide on your topic and then gather information about it. When you have all of the information you need, then you begin to organize it.

One way of organizing your information before writing the report is to make an outline. An outline lists the main ideas in the order in which they will appear in the report. It also organizes the main ideas and supporting details according to their importance.

The form of every outline is the same. Main ideas are listed on the left and labeled with capital Roman numerals. Supporting ideas are indented and labeled with capital letters. Supporting details are indented farther and labeled with numerals.

The outline below is for a biography of Marie Curie, one of the great physicists of all time. Use the steps listed to the right to help you learn how to make an outline.

I. Who Was She?
  A. Polish-born physicist
  B. Birth and early life
  C. Schooling
    1. In secret in Poland (women were not allowed to enter higher education)
    2. In France at the Sorbonne
      a. license of physical sciences, 1893
      b. license of mathematical sciences, 1894

II. The Physicist
  A. Life and work with husband, Pierre Curie
    1. Discoveries
      a. polonium, summer 1898
      b. radium, fall 1898
    2. Nobel Prize in Physics, 1903
      a. shared with Henri Becquerel
      b. Marie was the first woman ever to be awarded a Nobel Prize
  B. Her own accomplishments
    1. Became the first female professor at the Sorbonne
      a. took over Pierre's position after his death, 1906
    2. Her research on radioactivity was published, 1910
    3. Nobel Prize in Chemistry, 1911

Step 1: Read the main ideas of this report. They are labeled with capital Roman numerals. Each main idea will need at least one paragraph.

I. Who Was She?

Step 2: Read the supporting ideas for each main idea. These are labeled with capital letters. Notice that some of the main ideas require more supporting ideas than others.

A. Polish-born physicist

Step 3: Read the supporting details that are included in this outline. These are labeled with numerals. The writer of this outline did not include the supporting details for some of the supporting ideas. It is not necessary to include every piece of information that you have. An outline is intended merely as a guide for you to follow as you write the report.

2. In France at the Sorbonne

Step 4: A report can be organized in different ways. This biography is organized chronologically, that is, according to time. It starts with Curie's birth and ends with her legacy after death. The outline follows the order of events in her life. A report can be organized in other ways, such as comparing and contrasting or according to advantages and disadvantages. The outline should clearly reflect the way the report is organized.

Practice the Skill

Use the outline to answer these questions.
1. How many main ideas does this outline have? How many supporting ideas?
2. Are the ideas and details written as complete sentences or as phrases?

Apply the Skill

Look through Chapter 14 and find a topic that interests you. Gather information about that topic and then write an outline for a report about that topic. Be sure to use the correct outline form.

Visual Summary

1–5. ✏️➤ Write a description for each image below.

The United Kingdom	Sweden	France	Germany	Poland

_____	_____	_____	_____	_____
_____	_____	_____	_____	_____

Facts and Main Ideas

Answer the following questions.

6. **Government** What are the two houses that form the British Parliament? Which is more powerful?

7. **Citizenship** What role do ombudsmen play in the Swedish government?

8. **Culture** Identify at least three impressionist painters.

9. **Economics** What role did the United States play in West Germany after World War II?

10. **History** Describe the new constitution that Poland approved in 1997.

Vocabulary

Choose a word from the list to complete each sentence below.

socialism, p. 390
reunification, p. 395
censorship, p. 400

11. The moment of _____, when Germany again became a single nation, was a time of great joy for the German people.

12. Under _____, the government partly controls businesses and industries.

13. Because of government _____, many Polish writers could not publish their works.

Apply Skills

 TEST PREP **Make an Outline** Read the passage. Then apply what you learned about making an outline to answer the questions.

Jacques Cousteau (koo STOH) (1910–1997) was the most famous undersea explorer of the 20th century. While serving in the French navy in 1943, Cousteau invented the Aqua-Lung, also known as scuba gear. *Scuba* stands for "self contained underwater breathing apparatus." Scuba gear allowed divers to more freely explore the depths of the oceans, which cover more than three-fifths of Earth's surface. Cousteau became a household name after he popularized underwater exploration through books, films, and a television series.

14. In an outline of this passage about Jacques Cousteau, which of the following would be a main idea?
   A. Cousteau's date of birth
   B. Cousteau's fame as an explorer
   C. the meaning of *scuba*
   D. Cousteau's TV series

15. Which of the following is an important detail that should be included under the main idea of an outline of the passage?
   A. Cousteau's name is pronounced (koo STOH).
   B. Cousteau was in the French Navy.
   C. Cousteau invented the Aqua-Lung.
   D. Oceans cover three-fifths of Earth's surface.

Critical Thinking

 TEST PREP Write a short paragraph to answer each question below.

16. **Compare** Compare the governments and economies of the United Kingdom, Sweden, France, Germany, and Poland.

17. **Infer** Why do you think it was important to the United States that West Germany have a democratic government?

Activities

 DRAMA ACTIVITY Try to imagine what it felt like to be in East Germany or Poland when your country finally gained freedom in 1990. Create a short play with two characters that shows how you think the people in those countries reacted to the historic change.

 WRITING ACTIVITY Write a headline and a feature article that might have appeared in a newspaper on November 10, 1989, the day after people tore down the Berlin Wall. Include "quotations" from people who were there when the wall came down.

 Technology
Writing Process Tips
Get help with your article at
www.eduplace.com/kids/hmss05/

Review and Test Prep

Vocabulary and Main Ideas

Answer each question below.

1. Why is the **republic** of ancient Rome important to modern history?

2. What impact did the **Renaissance** have on European society?

3. How did the **Industrial Revolution** change European society?

4. How is Europe today still influenced by the rise of **nationalism** in the 19th century?

5. In what way might the European Union affect the **standard of living** throughout Europe?

6. Why was **reunification** a cause for celebration in Germany?

Critical Thinking

 TEST PREP Write a short paragraph to answer each question below.

7. **Draw Conclusions** A severe environmental problem facing Sweden and other European countries is acid rain. Why might it be difficult for any one country to solve this problem?

8. **Synthesize** Why are peninsulas important to the history of Europe?

Apply Skills

TEST PREP Look at the political cartoon below and use what you learned about reading political cartoons to answer each question.

The countries represented are, from left to right, Serbia, Austria-Hungary, Russia, Germany, France, and Britain.

9. What is this cartoon about?

   A. geographic locations of European countries
   B. the Cold War
   C. interconnectedness of the European economy
   D. international alliances during World War I

10. Which country does Germany say it will defend?

    A. Serbia
    B. Austria-Hungary
    C. Russia
    D. France

Unit Activity

The Big Idea

Make a Democratic Government Poster

- Create a list of basic freedoms you feel the citizens of a democracy should enjoy. Then add a list of laws that you feel a government should enforce.

- Use your ideas to design a poster that presents the ways a democratic government protects the freedoms of its citizens.

- Give your poster a title, and include an eye-catching illustration.

- List the benefits of democracy and what citizens should do to defend their freedoms.

- Display your poster in the room.

At the Library

Go to your school's library or a public library to find the following books.

The Fall of the Berlin Wall: The Cold War Ends
by Nigel Kelly
Readers learn how the destruction of the Berlin Wall symbolized the fall of the Iron Curtain.

Ten Queens: Portraits of Women of Power
by Milton Meltzer
This book portrays ten queens throughout Europe, as well as in Africa and the East.

CURRENT EVENTS
WEEKLY (WR) READER

Connect to Today

Create a magazine article about the challenges facing democracy in Europe.

- Choose two countries from this unit and find articles that tell about their governmental or political challenges.

- Make charts, graphs, and maps to compare the two countries.

- Write an article that compares democracy in the two countries. Illustrate your article with your charts, graphs, and maps.

Technology

Get your information for the magazine article from the Weekly Reader at **www.eduplace.com/kids/hmss05/**

Read About It

Look for these Social Studies books in your classroom.

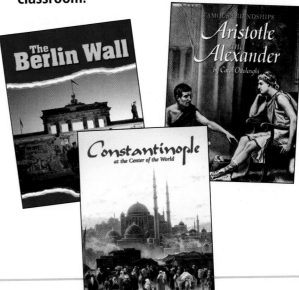

Resources

RAND McNALLY
World Atlas

SEA LEVEL
the level of the ocean's surface, used as a reference point when measuring heights and depths on Earth's surface

VOLCANO
an opening in Earth's surface through which gases and lava escape from Earth's interior

BAY
part of an ocean or a lake partially enclosed by land

(RIVER) MOUTH
the place where a river flows into a lake or an ocean

CAPE
a pointed piece of land extending into an ocean or a lake

HARBOR
a sheltered area of water, deep enough for docking ships

STRAIT
a narrow strip of water connecting two large bodies of water

MARSH
a soft, wet, low-lying, grassy area located between water and dry land

ISLAND
a body of land surrounded by water

DELTA
a triangular area of land formed from deposits at the mouth of a river

FLOOD PLAIN
flat land alongside a river, formed by mud and silt deposited by floods

SWAMP
an area of land that is saturated by water

DESERT
a dry area where few plants grow

OASIS
a spot of fertile land in a desert, supplied with water by a well or spring

BUTTE
a raised, flat area of land with steep sides, smaller than a mesa

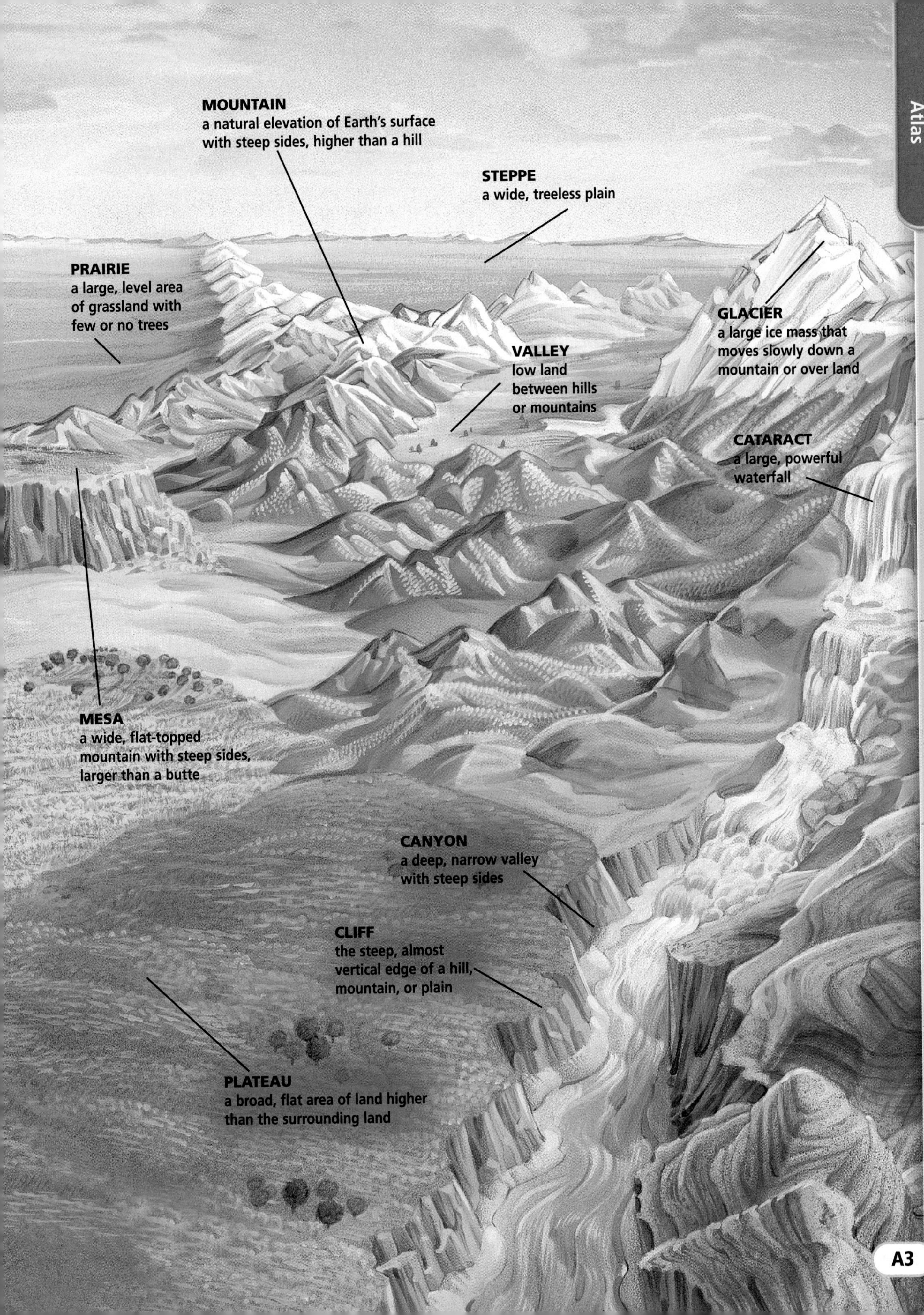

MOUNTAIN
a natural elevation of Earth's surface
with steep sides, higher than a hill

STEPPE
a wide, treeless plain

PRAIRIE
a large, level area
of grassland with
few or no trees

GLACIER
a large ice mass that
moves slowly down a
mountain or over land

VALLEY
low land
between hills
or mountains

CATARACT
a large, powerful
waterfall

MESA
a wide, flat-topped
mountain with steep sides,
larger than a butte

CANYON
a deep, narrow valley
with steep sides

CLIFF
the steep, almost
vertical edge of a hill,
mountain, or plain

PLATEAU
a broad, flat area of land higher
than the surrounding land

World: Physical

ARCTIC OCEAN

Baffin Bay · Greenland · Jan Ma... · Arctic Circ... · Iceland · Faroe Is.

Baffin Island · Hudson Bay · Newfoundland · British · Lond...

Mt. McKinley △ 20,320 Ft. 6,194m · Yukon · Mackenzie · Canadian Shield

Aleutian Islands · Vancouver · NORTH AMERICA · St. Lawrence · Azores · Iberian Penins...

Rocky Mountains · Great plains · Appalachian Mts. · Washington D.C. · ATLANTIC

Los Angeles · Colorado · Mississippi · Cape Hatteras · Canary Islands · Atlas Mts.

Midway Is. · Baja California · Gulf of Mexico

Tropic of Cancer · Hawaiian Islands · Yucatan Peninsula · Cuba · Hispaniola · Cape Verde Islands

PACIFIC · Jamaica · Puerto Rico · Caribbean Sea · Cape Verde · Niger

Palmyra · Trinidad · OCEAN · Orinoco

Equator · Galapagos Islands · Amazon · Amazon · St. Helena

Kiribati · OCEAN · SOUTH · Basin · Amazon

Marquesas Is. · AMERICA · Andes

Samoa Islands · Mato Grosso Plateau · St. Helena

Tonga Is. · Cook Islands · Tahiti · Rio de Janeiro

Tropic of Capricorn · Paraguay · Andes

Easter Island

△ Mt. Aconcagua 22,681 Ft. 6,959m · Buenos Aires · N

Chatham Is. · Archipiélago Juan Fernández · Patagonia

Falkland Is. · South Georgia

Tierra del Fuego · South Sandwich Is.

Cape Horn · South Orkney Is.

South Shetland Is.

Antarctic Circle · Antarctic Peninsula · Weddell Sea

Ross Sea · Marie Byrd Land · △ Vinson Massif 16,066 Ft. 4,897m

0 ... 1000 ... 2000 Miles
0 ... 1000 ... 2000 ... 3000 Kilometers
Copyright by Rand McNally & Co.
Robinson Projection

⊛ RAND M℠NALLY

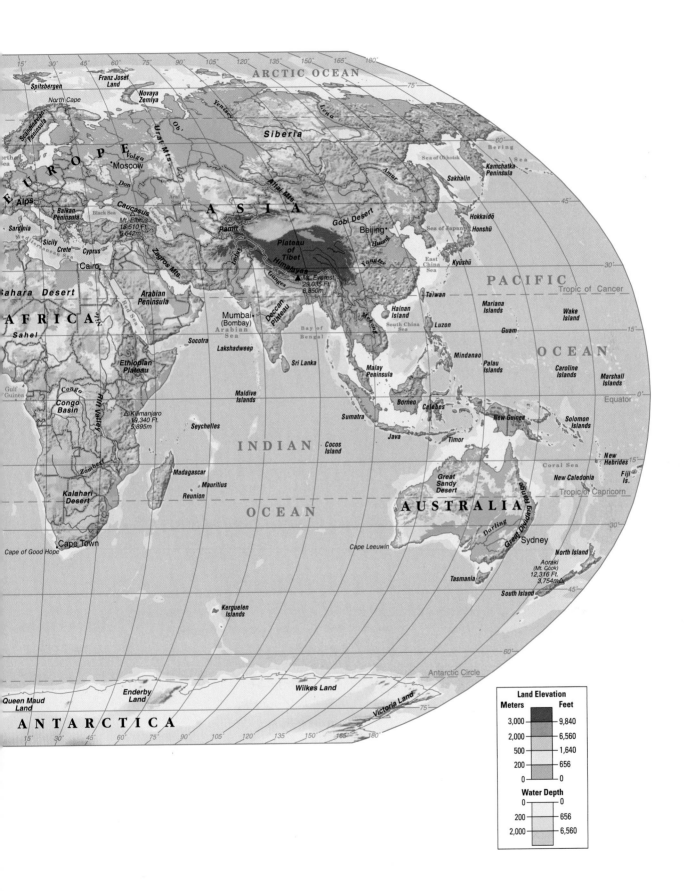

ARCTIC OCEAN

Spitsbergen
Franz Josef Land
North Cape
Novaya Zemlya
Scandinavian Peninsula
EUROPE
Moscow
Volga
Ural Mts.
Ob'
Yenisey
Lena
Siberia
Bering Sea
Sea of Okhotsk
Kamchatka Peninsula
Sakhalin
Amur
Alps
Balkan Peninsula
Caucasus
Don
Aral Sea
Black Sea
Mt. Elbrus 18,510 Ft. 5,642m
Sardinia
Sicily
Crete
Cyprus
Mediterranean Sea
Cairo
Zagros Mts.
Red Sea
ASIA
Pamir
Altai Mts.
Plateau of Tibet
Himalayas
Indus
Ganges
Mt. Everest 29,035 Ft. 8,850m
Gobi Desert
Beijing
Huang
Yangtze
Mekong
Hokkaidō
Honshū
Sea of Japan
Kyūshū
East China Sea
Taiwan
PACIFIC
Tropic of Cancer
Hainan Island
South China Sea
Luzon
Mariana Islands
Guam
Wake Island
Sahara Desert
AFRICA
Sahel
Nile
Arabian Peninsula
Mumbai (Bombay)
Arabian Sea
Deccan Plateau
Bay of Bengal
Lakshadweep
Sri Lanka
Socotra
Maldive Islands
Malay Peninsula
Mindanao
Palau Islands
Caroline Islands
OCEAN
Marshall Islands
Gulf of Guinea
Ethiopian Plateau
Congo
Congo Basin
Rift Valley
Kilimanjaro 19,340 Ft. 5,895m
Seychelles
Sumatra
Borneo
Celebes
Java
Timor
New Guinea
Solomon Islands
Equator
Zambezi
INDIAN
Cocos Island
Madagascar
Mauritius
Reunion
New Hebrides
Coral Sea
New Caledonia
Fiji Is.
Kalahari Desert
Great Sandy Desert
AUSTRALIA
Tropic of Capricorn
Cape Town
Cape of Good Hope
OCEAN
Darling
Great Dividing Range
Sydney
North Island
Cape Leeuwin
Aoraki (Mt. Cook) 12,316 Ft. 3,754m
Tasmania
South Island
Kerguelen Islands
Antarctic Circle
Queen Maud Land
Enderby Land
Wilkes Land
Victoria Land
ANTARCTICA

Land Elevation	
Meters	Feet
3,000	9,840
2,000	6,560
500	1,640
200	656
0	0

Water Depth	
0	0
200	656
2,000	6,560

ARCTIC OCEAN

GREENLAND
(Den.)

Baffin
Bay

Arctic Circle

ICELAND

FAROE IS.
(Den.)

RUSSIA   ALASKA
Yukon (U.S.)

UNITED
KINGDOM

Anchorage

Hudson
Bay

IRELAND

Londo

Aleutian Islands

C A N A D A

Newfoundland

FRANC

Missouri

Vancouver

PORTUGAL   Madri

Chicago

Montréal
Ottawa

Azores
(Port.)

SPA

UNITED STATES   *Colorado*

New York
Washington D.C.

Casablanca

MAROCCO

Los Angeles

Mississippi

ATLANTIC

Houston

MIDWAY IS.
(U.S.)

Canary
Islands
(Sp.)

Tropic of Cancer

MEXICO

Gulf of Mexico

BAHAMAS

W. SAHARA

Hawaiian
Islands
(U.S)

CUBA

DOM. REP.

MAURITANIA   MA

PACIFIC

Mexico City

HAITI
JAMAICA

PUERTO RICO (U.S.)

Niger

CAPE
VERDE

SENEGAL

BELIZE

Caribbean
Sea

GAMBIA

BURK
FASO

GUAT. HOND.
EL SAL. NIC.

Caracas

TRINIDAD AND TOBAGO

GUINEA-BISSAU   GUINEA

COSTA
RICA

VENEZUELA

GUYANA

SIERRA LEONE

COTE
D'IVOIRE

PANAMA

SURINAME
FRENCH GUIANA

LIBERIA

COLOMBIA

Galapagos Islands
(Ecuador)

ECUADOR

Amazon

BRAZIL

Equator

KIRIBATI

PERU

O C E A N

O C E A N

Lima

SAMOA

ST. HELENA
(U.K.)

AMERICAN
SAMOA

COOK
ISLANDS (N.Z.)

BOLIVIA

TONGA

FRENCH POLYNESIA

Tropic of Capricorn

PARAGUAY

Rio de Janeiro

Easter Island
(Chile)

ARGENTINA

N

Santiago

URUGUAY

Buenos
Aires

CHILE

0   1000   2000 Miles

0   1000   2000   3000 Kilometers

Copyright by Rand McNally & Co.
Robinson Projection

FALKLAND IS.
(U.K.)

South
Georgia
(U.K.)

South
Orkney Is.
(U.K.)

Antarctic Circle

South
Shetland Is.
(U.K.)

W e d d e l l
S e a

⊛ RAND M^cNALLY

⊛ National Capital

• Major Cities

World: Climate

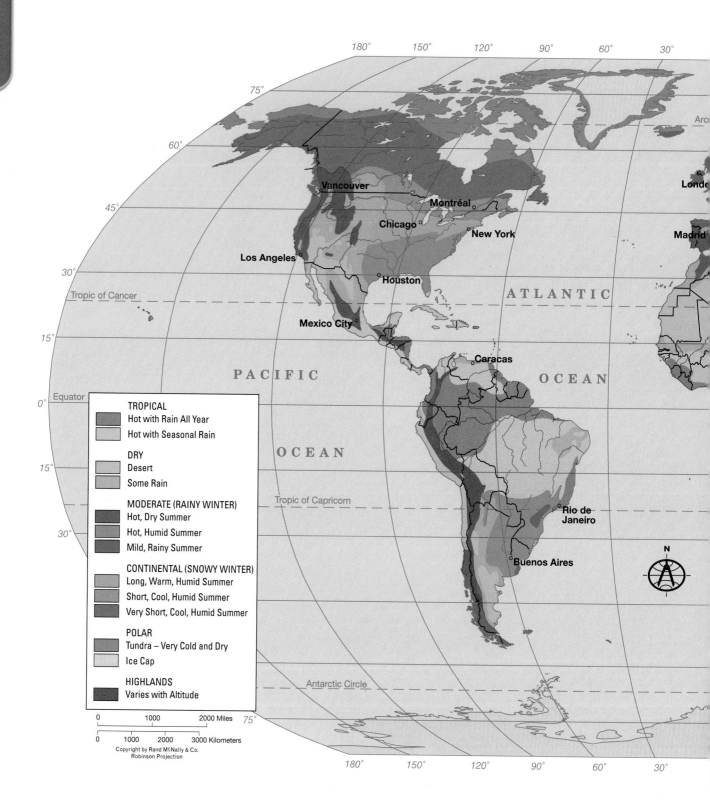

TROPICAL
- Hot with Rain All Year
- Hot with Seasonal Rain

DRY
- Desert
- Some Rain

MODERATE (RAINY WINTER)
- Hot, Dry Summer
- Hot, Humid Summer
- Mild, Rainy Summer

CONTINENTAL (SNOWY WINTER)
- Long, Warm, Humid Summer
- Short, Cool, Humid Summer
- Very Short, Cool, Humid Summer

POLAR
- Tundra – Very Cold and Dry
- Ice Cap

HIGHLANDS
- Varies with Altitude

0   1000   2000 Miles
0   1000   2000   3000 Kilometers
Copyright by Rand McNally & Co.
Robinson Projection

RAND McNALLY

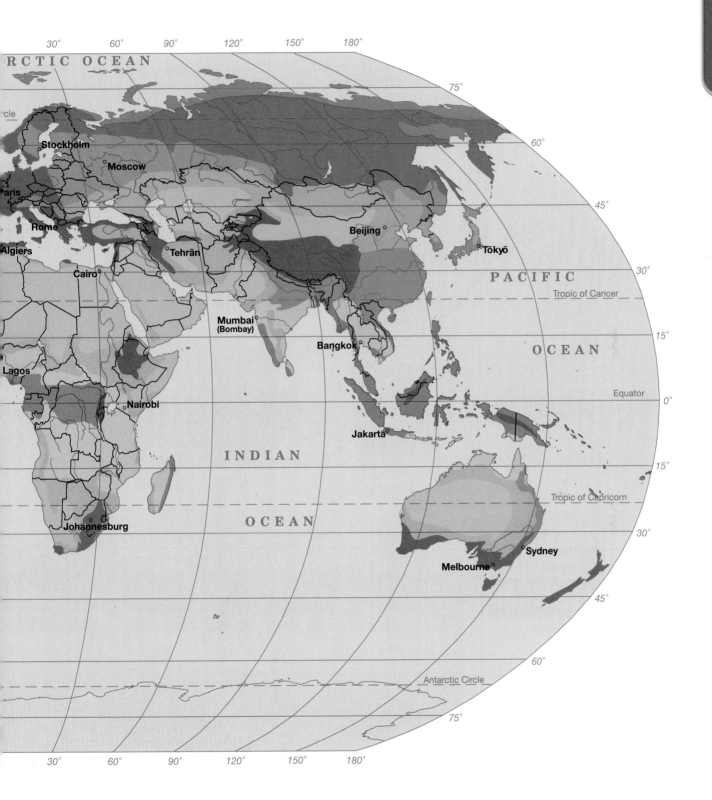

World: Environments

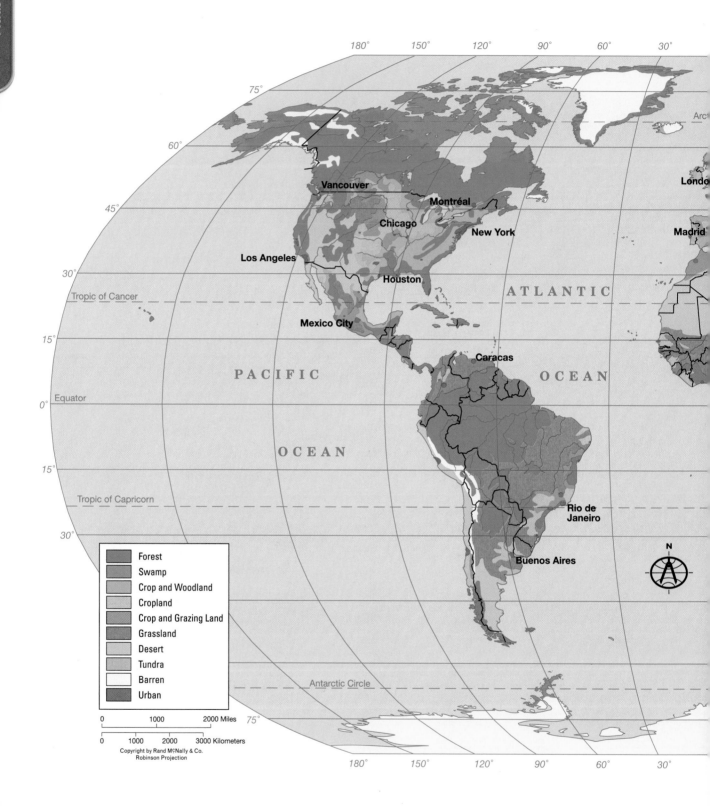

Legend:
- Forest
- Swamp
- Crop and Woodland
- Cropland
- Crop and Grazing Land
- Grassland
- Desert
- Tundra
- Barren
- Urban

0   1000   2000 Miles

0   1000   2000   3000 Kilometers

Copyright by Rand McNally & Co.
Robinson Projection

RAND M°NALLY

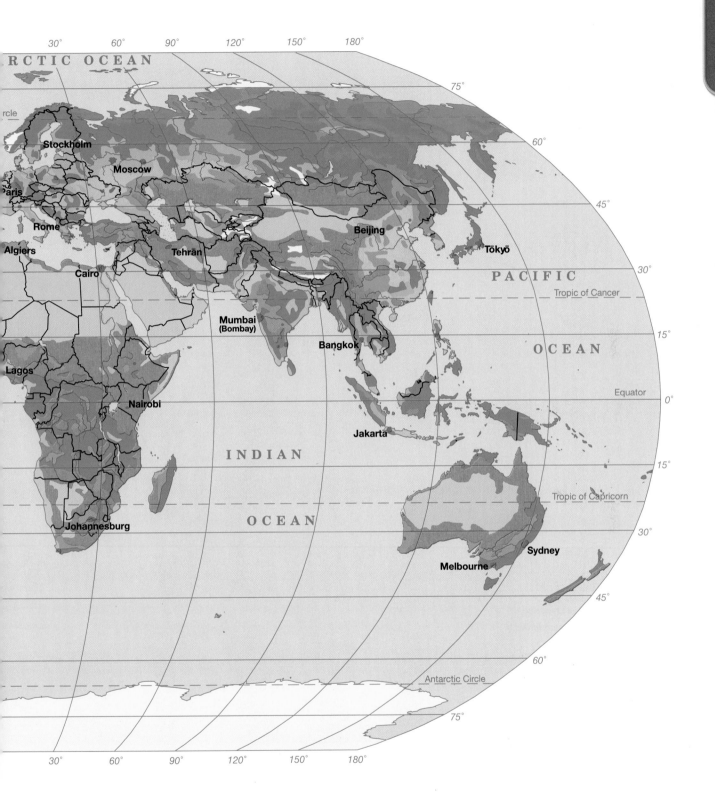

30° 60° 90° 120° 150° 180°

ARCTIC OCEAN

75°

60°

Stockholm

Moscow

45°

Paris

Rome

Tehrān

Beijing

Tōkyō

PACIFIC

30°

Algiers

Cairo

Tropic of Cancer

Mumbai
(Bombay)

Bangkok

15°

OCEAN

Lagos

Nairobi

Equator 0°

Jakarta

INDIAN

15°

Johannesburg

Tropic of Capricorn

OCEAN

30°

Sydney

Melbourne

45°

Antarctic Circle

60°

75°

30° 60° 90° 120° 150° 180°

World: Population

75°
60°
45°
30°
Tropic of Cancer
15°
Equator
15°
Tropic of Capricorn
30°

180° 150° 120° 90° 60° 30°

Vancouver
Montréal
Chicago
New York
Los Angeles
Houston
Mexico City
Caracas
Rio de Janeiro
Buenos Aires

London
Madrid

PACIFIC

OCEAN

ATLANTIC

OCEAN

N

Per square mile
(per square kilometer)

	Under 2 *(Under 1)*
	2-60 *(1-25)*
	60-125 *(25-50)*
	125-250 *(50-100)*
	Over 250 *(Over 100)*

0   1000   2000 Miles
0   1000   2000   3000 Kilometers
Copyright by Rand McNally & Co.
Robinson Projection

Antarctic Circle
75°

180° 150° 120° 90° 60° 30°

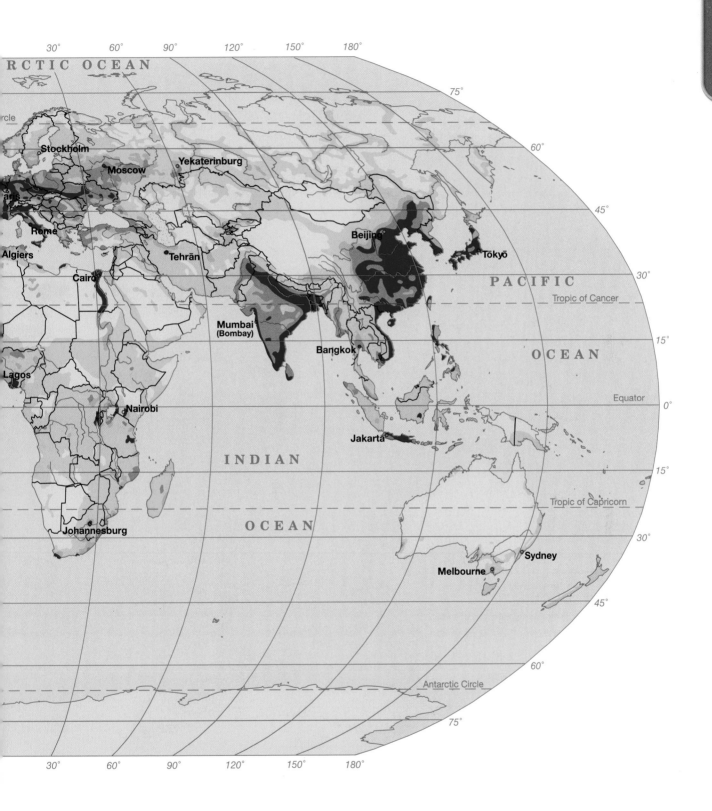

World: Economies

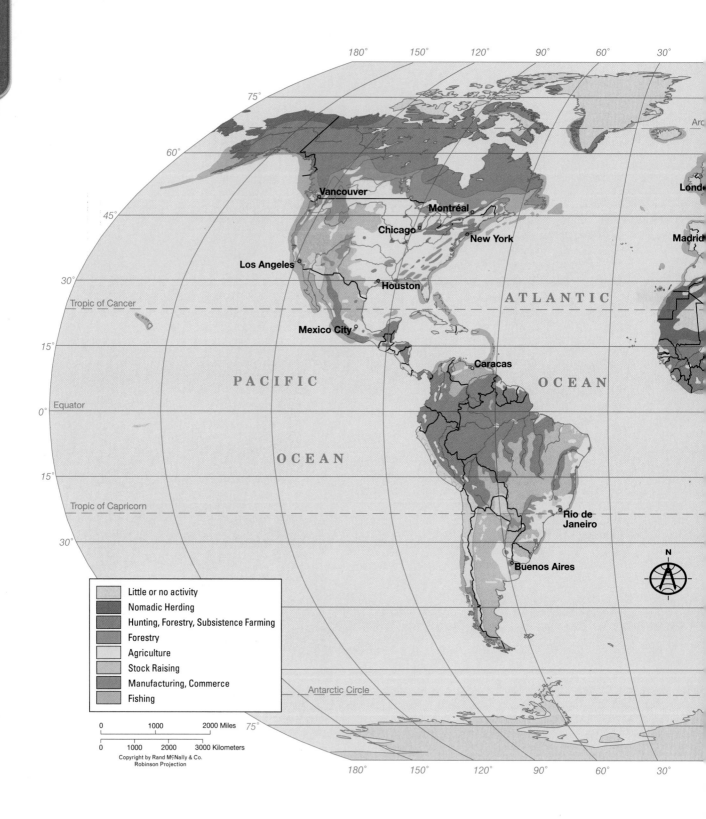

Vancouver

Montréal

Chicago

New York

Los Angeles

Houston

Mexico City

Caracas

Rio de Janeiro

Buenos Aires

London

Madrid

ATLANTIC

OCEAN

PACIFIC

OCEAN

OCEAN

Equator

Tropic of Cancer

Tropic of Capricorn

Antarctic Circle

75°

60°

45°

30°

15°

0°

15°

30°

180°   150°   120°   90°   60°   30°

N

Legend:
- Little or no activity
- Nomadic Herding
- Hunting, Forestry, Subsistence Farming
- Forestry
- Agriculture
- Stock Raising
- Manufacturing, Commerce
- Fishing

0   1000   2000 Miles
0   1000   2000   3000 Kilometers
Copyright by Rand McNally & Co.
Robinson Projection

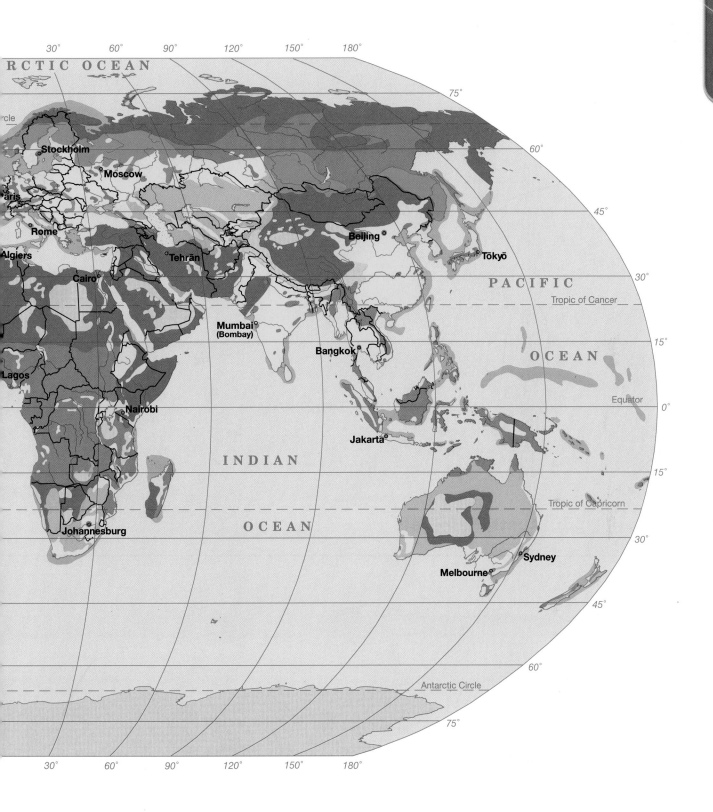

RCTIC OCEAN

75°

60°

45°

Stockholm

Moscow

ris

Rome

Algiers

Tehrān

Beijing

Tōkyō

PACIFIC

30°

Cairo

Tropic of Cancer

Mumbai
(Bombay)

Bangkok

15°

OCEAN

Lagos

Equator 0°

Nairobi

Jakarta

INDIAN

15°

Tropic of Capricorn

Johannesburg

OCEAN

30°

Sydney

Melbourne

45°

60°

Antarctic Circle

75°

30°   60°   90°   120°   150°   180°

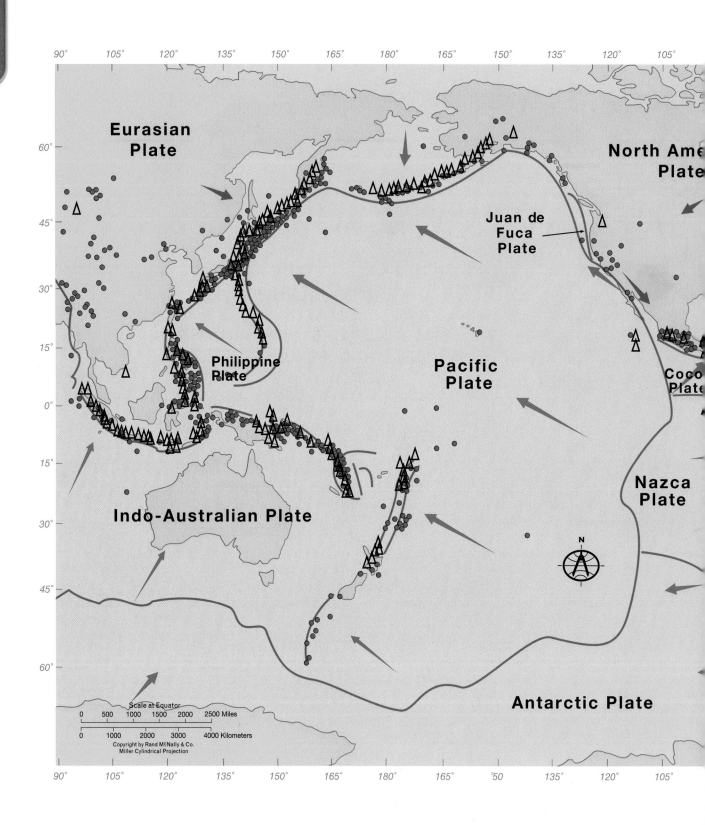

Eurasian
Plate

North Ame
Plate

Juan de
Fuca
Plate

Philippine
Plate

Pacific
Plate

Coco
Plate

Nazca
Plate

Indo-Australian Plate

N

Antarctic Plate

Scale at Equator

| 0 | 500 | 1000 | 1500 | 2000 | 2500 Miles |

| 0 | 1000 | 2000 | 3000 | 4000 Kilometers |

Copyright by Rand McNally & Co.
Miller Cylindrical Projection

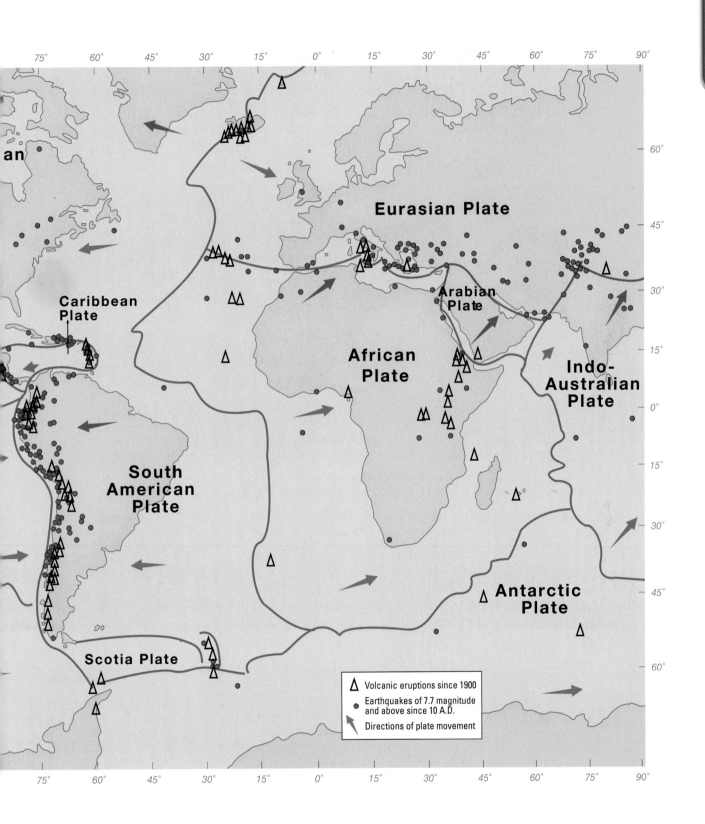

Eurasian Plate

Caribbean
Plate

Arabian
Plate

African
Plate

Indo-
Australian
Plate

South
American
Plate

Antarctic
Plate

Scotia Plate

△	Volcanic eruptions since 1900
•	Earthquakes of 7.7 magnitude and above since 10 A.D.
➔	Directions of plate movement

World: Time Zones

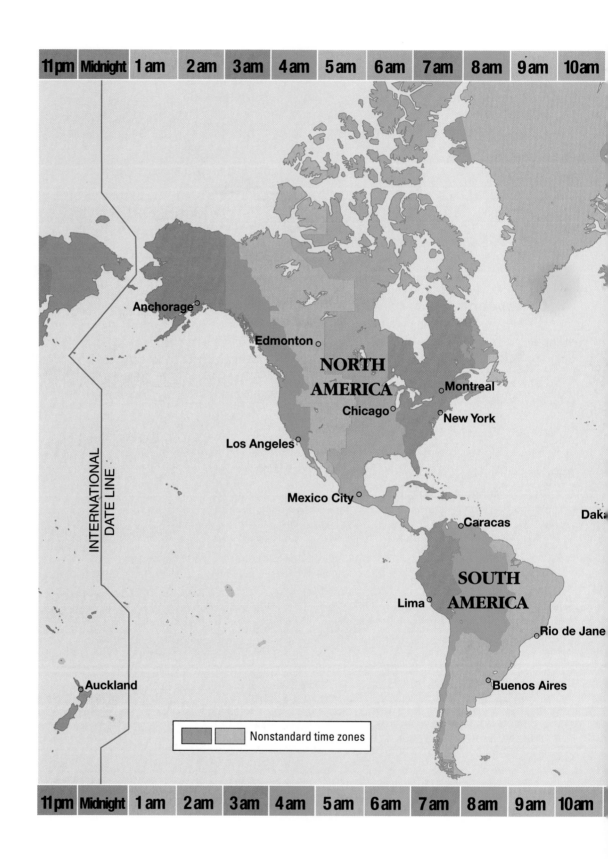

11pm	Midnight	1 am	2 am	3 am	4 am	5 am	6 am	7 am	8 am	9 am	10 am

Anchorage

Edmonton

NORTH AMERICA

Montreal

Chicago

New York

Los Angeles

INTERNATIONAL DATE LINE

Mexico City

Daka

Caracas

SOUTH AMERICA

Lima

Rio de Jane

Auckland

Buenos Aires

Nonstandard time zones

11pm	Midnight	1 am	2 am	3 am	4 am	5 am	6 am	7 am	8 am	9 am	10 am

RAND M℃NALLY

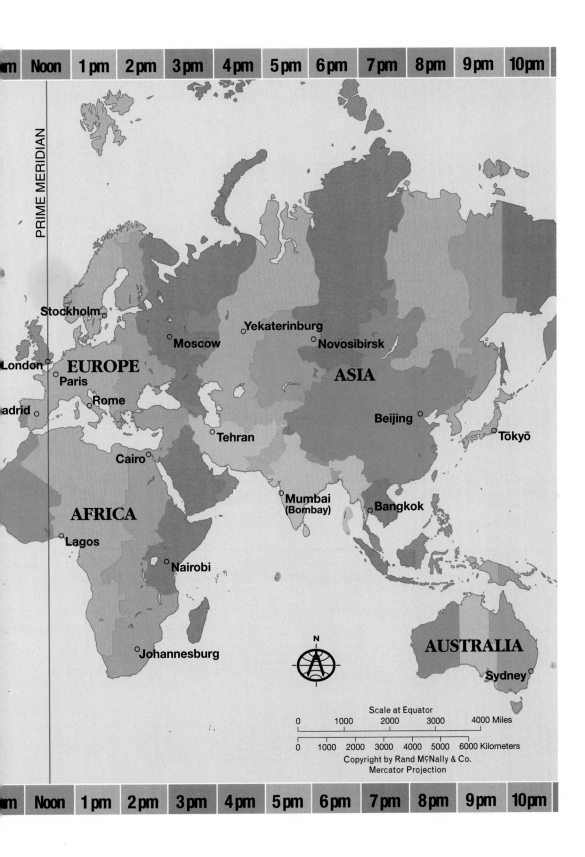

PRIME MERIDIAN

Stockholm
Moscow
Yekaterinburg
Novosibirsk
London
EUROPE
Paris
ASIA
Rome
adrid
Tehran
Beijing
Tōkyō
Cairo
Mumbai
(Bombay)
Bangkok
AFRICA
Lagos
Nairobi
N
AUSTRALIA
Johannesburg
Sydney

Scale at Equator

0 | 1000 | 2000 | 3000 | 4000 Miles

0 | 1000 | 2000 | 3000 | 4000 | 5000 | 6000 Kilometers

Copyright by Rand McNally & Co.
Mercator Projection

United States: Physical

PACIFIC OCEAN

CANADA

SASKATCHEWAN
ALBERTA
BRITISH COLUMBIA
MANITOBA

WASHINGTON

Cape Flattery
Olympic Mts.
Mt. Olympus△
7,965 Ft.
2,428m
Seattle
Puget Sound
Mt. Rainier△
14,410 Ft.
4,392m
Mt. Saint Helens△
8,364 Ft.
2,549m

Columbia

Cascade Range

Coast Ranges

OREGON

Mt. Hood△
11,239 Ft.
3,426m

Willamette
Deschutes

Blue Mts.

Clark Fork

Bitterroot Range

ROCKY MOUNTAINS

Flathead Lake

Marias
Milk
Missouri

MONTANA

Fort Peck Lake

NORTH DAKOTA

Lake Sakakawea
Sheyenne

Yellowstone

Tongue
Powder

Moreau
Lake Oahe

Cheyenne

SOUTH DAKOTA

Harney Peak△
7,242 Ft.
2,207m

White Lake
Francis Case

Niobrara
North Loup
Missouri

NEBRASKA

North Platte
South Platte
Platte
Republican

△Mt. McLoughlin
9,495 Ft.
2,894m

Cape Blanco

Goose Lake

Harney Basin

Salmon
Salmon River Mountains

IDAHO

Snake
△Borah Peak
12,662 Ft.
3,859m

American Falls Res.
Snake

Grand Teton△
13,770 Ft.
4,197m

Absaroka Range
△Granite Peak
12,799 Ft.
3,901m
Yellowstone Lake

Bighorn
Bighorn Mts.
△Cloud Peak
13,167 Ft.
4,013m

WYOMING

Black Hills

Cape Mendocino

△Mt. Shasta
14,162 Ft.
4,317m
Shasta Lake

Humboldt

Pyramid Lake

Great
NEVADA Basin

Great Salt Lake

Utah Lake

Flaming Gorge Res.

Great Divide Basin

Great Plains

△Mt. Whitney
14,494 Ft.
4,418m

Lake Tahoe

Sierra Nevada

Wheeler Peak△
13,064 Ft.
3,982m

Wasatch Range

UTAH

Kings Peak△
13,528 Ft.
4,123m
Uinta Mts.

Green

Colorado

Longs Peak△
14,255 Ft.
4,345m
Front Range

Denver

COLORADO

San Joaquin

Central Valley

San Francisco

Sacramento

CALIFORNIA

Death Valley
△Telescope Peak
11,050 Ft.
3,368m

Lake Mead

Lake Powell

Colorado Plateau

Colorado
Little Colorado

San Juan

△Mt. Elbert
14,433 Ft.
4,399m
△Pikes Pk.
14,110 Ft.
4,301m

Sangre de Cristo Mountains

San Juan Mts.

Wheeler Peak△
13,161 Ft.
4,011m

Smoky Hill

KANSAS

Arkansas

Point Arguello

Los Angeles

Channel Islands

Mojave Desert

Salton Sea

Grand Canyon
Humphreys Peak△
12,633 Ft.
3,851m

ARIZONA

Colorado

Gila

Salt
★Phoenix

Peloncillo Mts.

△Baldy Peak
11,404 Ft.
3,476m

△Mt. Taylor
11,301 Ft.
3,445m

NEW MEXICO

Sacramento Mts.

Rio Grande

Llano Estacado

OKLAHOMA

Cimarron

Canadian

Red

Lake Texoma

Pecos

△Guadalupe Pk.
8,749 Ft.
2,667m

Stockton Plateau

Edwards Plateau

TEXAS

Dallas

Brazos

Colorado

Nueces

Rio Grande

MEXICO

△Emory Peak
7,825 Ft.
2,385m

Padre Island

Hawaii inset:

Niihau
Kauai
Kalaheo
Kauai Channel
Oahu
Wahiawa
Honolulu
Molokai
Lanai
Kahoolawe
Maui
Hawaiian Islands
Mauna Kea
13,796 Ft.
4,205m
Hawaii
Mauna Loa
13,679 Ft.
4,169m
Hilo

HAWAII

PACIFIC OCEAN

N
0 50 Miles
0 50 Kilometers
20°
160°
155°

Alaska inset:

ARCTIC OCEAN
Chukchi Sea
Arctic Circle
RUSSIA
Bering Strait
Point Barrow
Prudhoe Bay
Beaufort Sea
NORTHWEST TERRITORIES
Brooks Range

ALASKA
Yukon
Fairbanks
Yukon
Tanana
Alaska Range
Mt. McKinley
20,320 Ft.
6,194m
Nome
Saint Lawrence Island
Kuskokwim

YUKON

CANADA

Valdez
Anchorage
Kenai Pen.
Gulf of Alaska
Juneau
BRITISH COLUMBIA

Bering Sea

Bristol Bay
Kodiak Island
Alaska Peninsula
Aleutian Islands

PACIFIC OCEAN

N
0 100 200 300 Miles
0 200 400 Kilometers

Land Elevation

Meters		Feet
3,000		9,840
2,000		6,560
500		1,640
200		656
0		0

Water Depth

0		0
200		656
2,000		6,560

0   100   200   300 Miles
0   100   200   300   400 Kilometers

Copyright by Rand McNally & Co.
Alber's Conic Equal Area Projection

ATLANTIC
OCEAN

San
Juan

Arecibo
Mayagüez
Ponce   Caguas

**PUERTO RICO
(U.S.)**

0   25   50 Miles
0   25   50 Kilometers

Caribbean
Sea

Atlas

RAND McNALLY

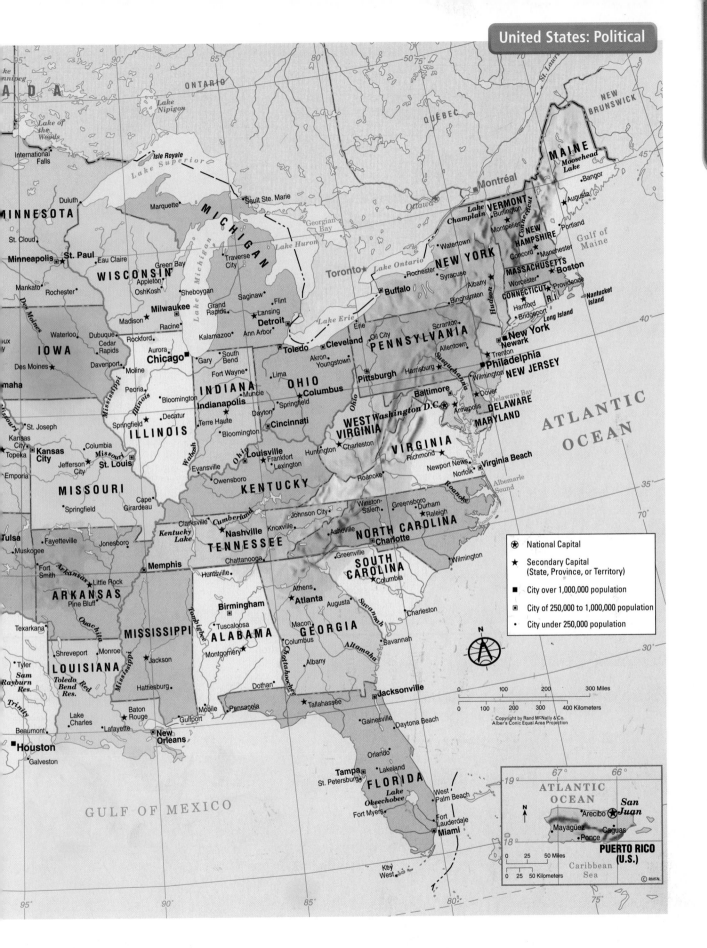

National Capital

Secondary Capital
(State, Province, or Territory)

City over 1,000,000 population

City of 250,000 to 1,000,000 population

City under 250,000 population

Copyright by Rand McNally & Co.
Alber's Conic Equal Area Projection

PUERTO RICO
(U.S.)

North America: Physical

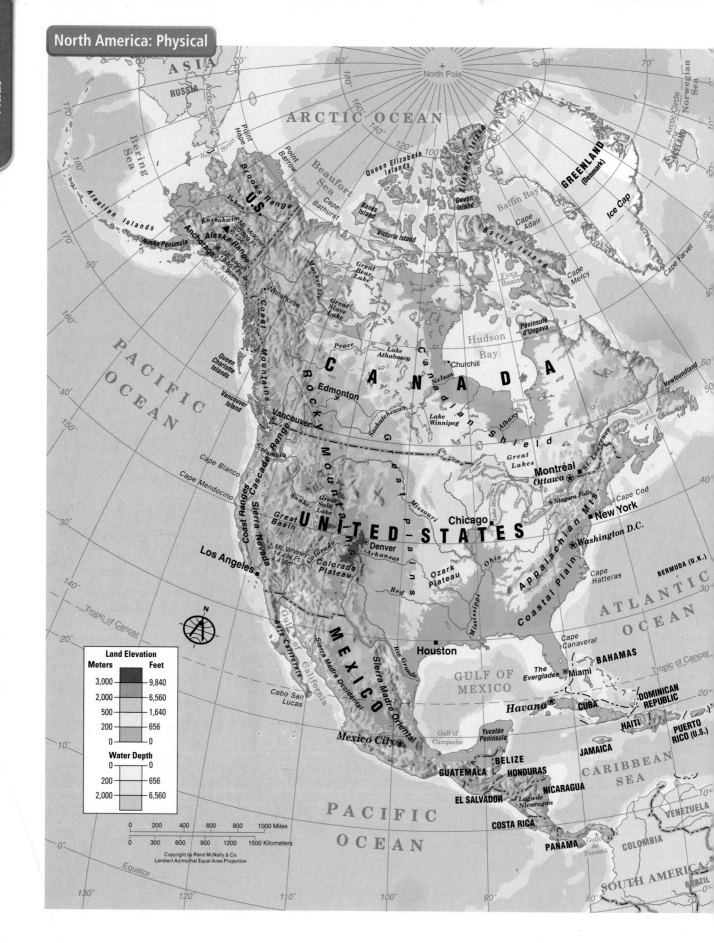

ASIA
RUSSIA

ARCTIC OCEAN

North Pole

GREENLAND
(Denmark)

Ice Cap

Arctic Circle

ICELAND

Norwegian Sea

Bering Sea

Point Hope
Point Barrow
Prudhoe Bay
Cape Bathurst

Beaufort Sea

Queen Elizabeth Islands

Ellesmere Island

Devon Island

Baffin Bay

Cape Adair

Aleutian Islands

Brooks Range

U.S.

Yukon
Kuskokwim
Mt. McKinley 20,320 Ft. 6,194m
Alaska Range
Anchorage 18,551 Ft.
Mt. Logan 5,959m
Gulf of Alaska

Banks Island

Victoria Island

Baffin Island

Foxe Basin

Cape Mercy

Cape Farvel

Whitehorse

Mackenzie

Great Bear Lake

Great Slave Lake

Peace

Hudson Bay

Péninsule d'Ungava

PACIFIC OCEAN

Queen Charlotte Islands

Vancouver Island

Coast Mountains

Columbia

Cape Blanco

Cape Mendocino

Vancouver

Edmonton

C A N A D A

Rocky Mountains

Saskatchewan

Lake Athabasca

Nelson

Churchill

Lake Winnipeg

James Bay

Albany

Canadian Shield

Newfoundland

Gulf of St. Lawrence

Great Lakes

Lake Superior

Montréal
Ottawa

St. Lawrence

Cape Cod

Niagara Falls

New York

Appalachian Mts.

Washington D.C.

BERMUDA (U.K.)

Cascade Range

Coast Ranges

Sierra Nevada

Snake

Great Salt Lake

Great Basin

U N I T E D   S T A T E S

Mt. Whitney 14,494 Ft. 4,418m

Colorado

Colorado Plateau

Los Angeles

Denver

Arkansas

Missouri

Chicago

Lake Michigan

Lake Huron

Lake Erie

Lake Ontario

Ohio

Red

Ozark Plateau

Mississippi

Coastal Plain

Cape Hatteras

ATLANTIC OCEAN

Gulf of California

Baja California

Sierra Madre Occidental

Rio Grande

Houston

Cabo San Lucas

M E X I C O

Sierra Madre Oriental

Mexico City

Tropic of Cancer

Cape Canaveral

The Everglades
Miami

BAHAMAS

Tropic of Cancer

GULF OF MEXICO

Gulf of Campeche

Yucatán Peninsula

Havana

CUBA

HAITI

DOMINICAN REPUBLIC

PUERTO RICO (U.S.)

JAMAICA

BELIZE

GUATEMALA
HONDURAS

EL SALVADOR

NICARAGUA

Lago de Nicaragua

CARIBBEAN SEA

VENEZUELA

COSTA RICA

PANAMA

Golfo de Panamá

COLOMBIA

PACIFIC OCEAN

SOUTH AMERICA

BRAZIL

Equator

Land Elevation

Meters	Feet
3,000	9,840
2,000	6,560
500	1,640
200	656
0	0

Water Depth

0	0
200	656
2,000	6,560

0   200   400   600   800   1000 Miles

0   300   600   900   1200   1500 Kilometers

Copyright by Rand McNally & Co.
Lambert Azimuthal Equal Area Projection

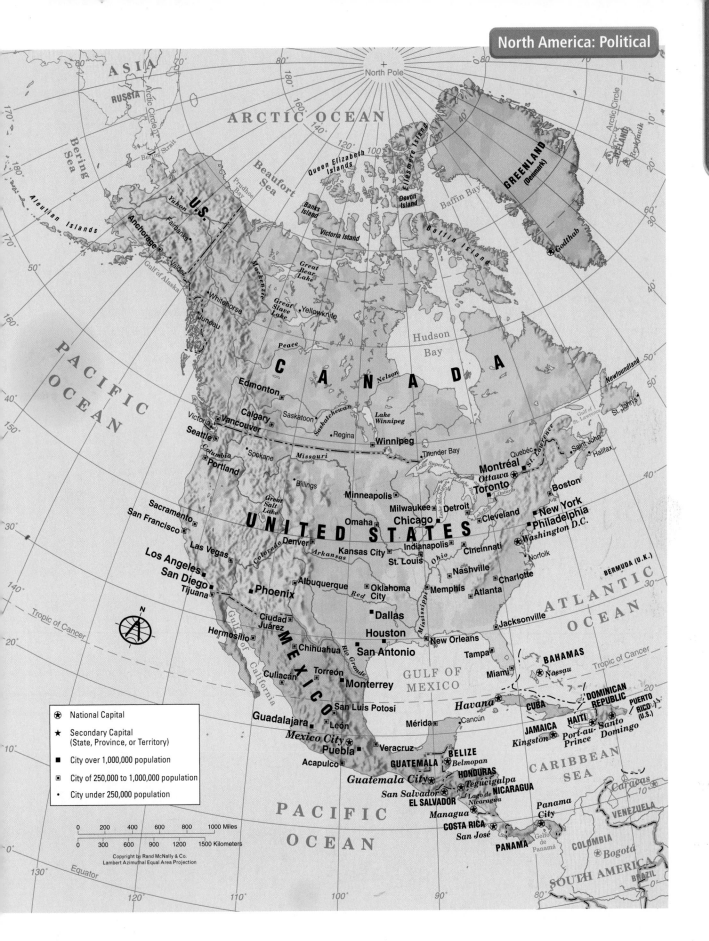

ASIA
RUSSIA
Bering Sea
Arctic Circle
Aleutian Islands
PACIFIC OCEAN

ARCTIC OCEAN
North Pole
Beaufort Sea
Prudhoe Bay
Queen Elizabeth Islands
Ellesmere Island
Devon Island
Banks Island
Victoria Island
Baffin Island
Baffin Bay
GREENLAND (Denmark)
ICELAND
Reykjavik
Arctic Circle
Godthab

U.S.
Anchorage
Fairbanks
Valdez
Gulf of Alaska
Whitehorse
Juneau
Mackenzie
Great Bear Lake
Great Slave Lake
Yellowknife
Peace

C A N A D A
Edmonton
Calgary
Saskatoon
Saskatchewan
Nelson
Lake Winnipeg
Regina
Winnipeg
Hudson Bay
Newfoundland
St. John's
Gulf of St. Lawrence
Halifax

Victoria
Vancouver
Seattle
Columbia
Portland
Spokane
Missouri
Billings
Thunder Bay
Lake Superior
Lake Michigan
Quebec
St. Lawrence
Saint John
Montréal
Ottawa
Toronto
Lake Ontario
Boston

Sacramento
San Francisco
Great Salt Lake
Minneapolis
Milwaukee
Chicago
Detroit
Cleveland
New York
Philadelphia
Washington D.C.

UNITED STATES
Las Vegas
Denver
Colorado
Arkansas
Omaha
Kansas City
St. Louis
Indianapolis
Ohio
Cincinnati
Nashville
Charlotte
Norfolk

Los Angeles
San Diego
Tijuana
Phoenix
Albuquerque
Oklahoma City
Red
Memphis
Atlanta
BERMUDA (U.K.)
ATLANTIC OCEAN

Gulf of California
Hermosillo
Ciudad Juárez
MEXICO
Chihuahua
San Antonio
Dallas
Houston
Rio Grande
New Orleans
Mississippi
Jacksonville
Tampa
Tropic of Cancer

Culiacán
Torreón
Monterrey
San Luis Potosí
Guadalajara
León
Mérida
Cancún
Miami
BAHAMAS
Nassau
Havana
CUBA
JAMAICA
Kingston
HAITI
Port-au-Prince
DOMINICAN REPUBLIC
Santo Domingo
PUERTO RICO (U.S.)

Mexico City
Puebla
Veracruz
Acapulco
BELIZE
Belmopan
GUATEMALA
Guatemala City
HONDURAS
Tegucigalpa
NICARAGUA
Lago de Nicaragua
CARIBBEAN SEA
Caracas
VENEZUELA

San Salvador
EL SALVADOR
Managua
COSTA RICA
San José
PANAMA
Panama City
Golfo de Panamá
COLOMBIA
Bogotá
SOUTH AMERICA
BRAZIL

PACIFIC OCEAN

Legend:
- ⊛ National Capital
- ★ Secondary Capital (State, Province, or Territory)
- ■ City over 1,000,000 population
- ◲ City of 250,000 to 1,000,000 population
- • City under 250,000 population

Scale:
0 200 400 600 800 1000 Miles
0 300 600 900 1200 1500 Kilometers

Copyright by Rand McNally & Co.
Lambert Azimuthal Equal Area Projection

Equator

⊛ RAND MCNALLY

South America: Physical

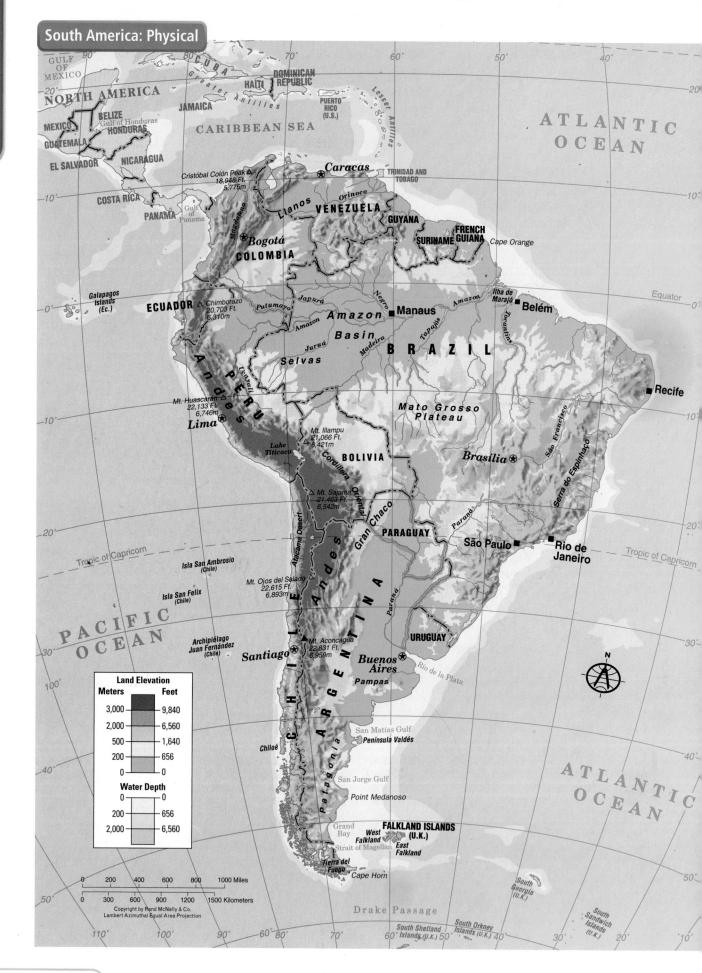

GULF OF MEXICO

NORTH AMERICA

MEXICO

GUATEMALA
BELIZE
Gulf of Honduras
HONDURAS

EL SALVADOR
NICARAGUA

COSTA RICA

PANAMA
Gulf of Panama

CUBA

Greater Antilles

JAMAICA

HAITI
DOMINICAN REPUBLIC

PUERTO RICO (U.S.)

CARIBBEAN SEA

Lesser Antilles

Cristóbal Colón Peak △
18,948 Ft.
5,775m

Caracas ✪

TRINIDAD AND TOBAGO

ATLANTIC OCEAN

Llanos
Orinoco
VENEZUELA
GUYANA
SURINAME
FRENCH GUIANA
Cape Orange

Magdalena

Bogotá ✪
COLOMBIA

Galapagos Islands (Ec.)

ECUADOR
△ Chimborazo
20,703 Ft.
6,310m

Putumayo
Japurá
Amazon
Negro
Amazon
Manaus ■
Ilha de Marajó
Belém ■

Equator

Juruá
Ucayali
Amazon
Selvas
Amazon Basin
Madeira
Tapajós
Tocantins

B R A Z I L

A
n
d
e
s

P E R U

Mt. Huascarán △
22,133 Ft.
6,746m

Lima ✪

Lake Titicaca

Mt. Illampu △
21,066 Ft.
6,421m

BOLIVIA

Cordillera Oriental

Mato Grosso Plateau

Brasília ✪

Serra do Espinhaço
São Francisco

Recife ■

△ Mt. Sajama
21,463 Ft.
6,542m

Gran Chaco

PARAGUAY

Paraná

São Paulo ■

Rio de Janeiro ■

Tropic of Capricorn

Isla San Ambrosio (Chile)

Mt. Ojos del Salado △
22,615 Ft.
6,893m

Isla San Félix (Chile)

P A C I F I C
O C E A N

Archipiélago Juan Fernández (Chile)

A
t
a
c
a
m
a

D
e
s
e
r
t

C
H
I
L
E

A
n
d
e
s

A
R
G
E
N
T
I
N
A

Paraná

URUGUAY

Santiago ✪

△ Mt. Aconcagua
22,831 Ft.
6,959m

Buenos Aires ✪

Pampas

Río de la Plata

N

San Matías Gulf

Chiloé

Península Valdés

P
a
t
a
g
o
n
i
a

San Jorge Gulf

Point Medanoso

ATLANTIC OCEAN

Grand Bay

West Falkland

FALKLAND ISLANDS (U.K.)

East Falkland

Strait of Magellan

Tierra del Fuego

Cape Horn

South Georgia (U.K.)

Drake Passage

South Shetland Islands (U.K.)
South Orkney Islands (U.K.)

South Sandwich Islands (U.K.)

Land Elevation

Meters		Feet
3,000		9,840
2,000		6,560
500		1,640
200		656
0		0

Water Depth

0		0
200		656
2,000		6,560

0   200   400   600   800   1000 Miles

0   300   600   900   1200   1500 Kilometers

Copyright by Rand McNally & Co.
Lambert Azimuthal Equal Area Projection

GULF OF MEXICO

Havana CUBA

NORTH AMERICA

MEXICO
BELIZE
HONDURAS
GUATEMALA
EL SALVADOR
NICARAGUA
COSTA RICA
PANAMA

JAMAICA
HAITI
DOMINICAN REPUBLIC
PUERTO RICO (U.S.)

CARIBBEAN SEA

Lesser Antilles

TRINIDAD AND TOBAGO

ATLANTIC OCEAN

Barranquilla
Cartagena
Maracaibo
Caracas
Barquisimeto
Valencia
Cúcuta
Bucaramanga
Medellín
Bogotá
COLOMBIA
Cali

Orinoco
Ciudad Guayana
VENEZUELA
Georgetown
GUYANA
Paramaribo
SURINAME
Cayenne
FRENCH GUIANA

Magdalena

Macapá

Galapagos Islands (Ec.)

Quito
ECUADOR
Guayaquil

Iquitos

Putumayo
Japurá
Negro
Amazon

Manaus
Santarém

Amazon

Belém
São Luís
Fortaleza

Chiclayo
Trujillo

PERU

Ucayali

Amazon

Juruá

Madeira

Tapajós

Tocantins

BRAZIL

Imperatriz
Teresina

Natal
Recife
Maceió

Lima

Cusco
Lake Titicaca
Arequipa

Pôrto Velho

BOLIVIA
La Paz
Cochabamba
Santa Cruz
Sucre

Cuiabá

Goiânia

Feira de Santana
Salvador

Aracaju

Brasília
Montes Claros

Uberlândia

Campo Grande

Paraná

Belo Horizonte
Vitória

PARAGUAY

Campinas
São Paulo
Rio de Janeiro

Antofagasta

Salta
San Miguel de Tucumán

Asunción

Curitiba

Caxias do Sul
Pôrto Alegre

Isla San Ambrosio (Chile)

Isla San Félix (Chile)

Tropic of Capricorn

Paraná

Córdoba
Santa Fe
Rosario
URUGUAY

Archipiélago Juan Fernández (Chile)

Valparaíso
Santiago

Mendoza
Buenos Aires
La Plata
Montevideo

Río de la Plata

CHILE

ARGENTINA

Concepción
Bahía Blanca
Mar del Plata

PACIFIC OCEAN

ATLANTIC OCEAN

N

Chiloé

Archipiélago de los Chonos
Comodoro Rivadavia

National Capital

Secondary Capital (State, Province, or Territory)

■ City over 1,000,000 population

▣ City of 250,000 to 1,000,000 population

• City under 250,000 population

FALKLAND ISLANDS (U.K.)
West Falkland
East Falkland

Punta Arenas
Strait of Magellan
Tierra del Fuego

South Georgia (U.K.)

Drake Passage
South Orkney Islands (U.K.)
South Shetland Islands (U.K.)

South Sandwich Islands (U.K.)

0 200 400 600 800 1000 Miles
0 300 600 900 1200 1500 Kilometers

Copyright by Rand McNally & Co.
Lambert Azimuthal Equal Area Projection

Europe: Physical

ICELAND

Surtsey

Horn

Fontur

ATLANTIC

OCEAN

Arctic Circle

NORWEGIAN SEA

Lofoten Islands

Kebnekaise
6,926 Ft.
2,111m

Scandinavian
Peninsula

FAROE ISLANDS
(Den.)

Umeälven

NORWAY   SWEDEN

Galdhøpiggen △
8,100 Ft.
2,469m

Glåma

Klarälven

Dalälven

Gulf of Bothnia

Hebrides

Grampian
Mts.

Cheviot
Hills

UNITED

KINGDOM

Orkney
Islands

NORTH SEA

Skagerrak

DENMARK

Stockholm ✪

Vänern   Vättern

Öland

BALTIC SEA

Land Elevation

Meters		Feet
3,000		9,840
2,000		6,560
500		1,640
200		656
0		0

Water Depth

0		0
200		656
2,000		6,560

N

IRELAND

Irish
Sea

Great
Britain

St. George's Channel

Thames

London ✪

NETHERLANDS

Bornholm
(Den.)

RUSS

Northern Europ

Berlin ✪

Elbe

Oder

GERMANY

POLAND

Wisła

0	100	200	300	400 Miles

0	200	400	600 Kilometers

Copyright by Rand McNally & Co.
Lambert Conformal Conic Projection

English Channel

Strait of Dover

BELGIUM

Rhine

LUX.

✪ Paris

Paris
Basin

Loire

Seine

Saône

Jura

Black
Forest

Bohemian
Forest

CZECH
REPUBLIC

Danube

SLOVAKIA

FRANCE

SWITZERLAND   LIECH.

AUSTRIA

HUNGARY

Great Hungarian
Plain

Bay of Biscay

Cantabrian Mts.

Douro

Dordogne

Massif
Central

Mt. Blanc
15,771 Ft.
4,808m

Rhône

A   l   p   s

Drava

SLOVENIA

CROATIA

Po

Apennines

Dinaric Alps

BOSNIA AND
HERZEGOVINA

Balka

Duero

Ebro

Pyrenees

ANDORRA

MONACO

SAN
MARINO

ADRIATIC SEA

YUGOSLAV

Lisbon ✪

PORTUGAL

Iberian
Peninsula

Tagus

Iberian Mts.

SPAIN

Sierra Morena

Corsica
(Fr.)

Rome ✪

ITALY

ALBANIA

MAC.
DON.

Balearic Islands

Minorca

Ibiza   Majorca

Sardinia
(It.)

TYRRHENIAN
SEA

△Vesuvius
4,190 Ft.
1,277m

Pindus M

Strait of Gibraltar

GIBRALTAR
(U.K.)

M   E   D   I   T   E   R   R   A   N   E

IONIAN
SEA

Algiers ✪

AFRICA

ALGERIA

Mt. Etna
10,902 Ft.
3,323m △

Sicily

MOROCCO

TUNISIA

MALTA

20°

Murmansk
Kola Peninsula
Ponoy
WHITE SEA
Timan Ridge
Pechora
Mezen
Ural Mountains
Ob'
Irtysh

INLAND
Northern Dvina
Onega
Lake Onega
Sukhona
Northern Uvals (Uplands)
Kama

Helsinki
Gulf of Finland
ESTONIA
Lake Peipus
Lake Ladoga
Rybinsk Res.
Valdai Hills
Moscow
Oka
RUSSIA
ASIA

LATVIA
Khopër
KAZAKHSTAN
Syr Darya

LITHUANIA
Plain
Central Russian Upland
Don
Ural
Aral Sea

Neman
BELARUS
Caspian Depression
UZBEKISTAN

Pripyat
Dnieper
Lowland
Volga
Amu Darya

Kiev
UKRAINE
Dnieper
Donets Basin
Dniester

Dniester
MOLDOVA
Sea of Azov
CASPIAN
TURKMENISTAN

Carpathian Mts.
Crimean Peninsula
Mt. Elbrus 18,510 Ft. 5,642m
Caucasus
Baku

ROMANIA
ansylvanian Alps
GEORGIA
SEA

BLACK SEA
ARMENIA
AZERBAIJAN

Peninsula
Danube
AZER.
Tehran

BULGARIA
Istanbul
IRAN

Mt. Olympus 9,570 Ft. 2,917m
TURKEY
IRAQ

GREECE
SYRIA

AEGEAN SEA
Euphrates

Rhodes
NORTH CYPRUS
LEBANON
Tigris

Crete
SEA
CYPRUS

National Capital

★ Secondary Capital
(State, Province, or Territory)

■ City over 1,000,000 population

▣ City of 250,000 to 1,000,000 population

• City under 250,000 population

0   100   200   300   400 Miles

0   200   400   600 Kilometers

Copyright by Rand McNally & Co.
Lambert Conformal Conic Projection

✦ RAND McNALLY

Murmansk

Oulu

FINLAND

WHITE SEA

Arkhangel'sk

Northern Dvina

Syktyvkar

R U S S I A

Pechora

Ob'

Irtysh

Petrozavodsk
Lake
Onega

Lake Ladoga

Helsinki
Gulf of Finland

St. Petersburg

Tallinn
ESTONIA

Lake Peipus

Cherepovets
Rybinsk Res.

Kirov

Perm'

Izhevsk

Ufa

A S I A

Riga
LATVIA

Vilnius

Vitsyebsk

Minsk

BELARUS

Homyel'

Chernobyl

Kiev

L'viv

Dniester

Vinnytsya

UKRAINE

Kryvyy Rih
Zaporizhzhya

Tver'

Moscow

Tula

Bryansk

Dnieper

Dnipro-
petrovs'k

Yaroslavl'

Oka

Ryazan'

Don

Lipetsk

Voronezh

Kharkiv

Luhans'k

Donets'k

Mariupol'

Rostov

Nizhniy
Novgorod

Kazan'

Penza

Saratov

Samara

Ural

Volgograd

Volga

Astrakhan'

KAZAKHSTAN

Aral Sea

UZBEKISTAN

Syr Darya

Amu Darya

MOLDOVA

Iaşi

Chişinău

Cluj-Napoca

ROMANIA

Craiova

Galaţi

Bucharest

Danube

BULGARIA

Sofia

Plovdiv

Varna

Odesa

Simferopol'

Sevastopol'

Sea of Azov

Krasnodar

Stavropol'

Grozny

BLACK SEA

GEORGIA

Tbilisi

ARMENIA

Yerevan

AZER.

AZERBAIJAN

Baku

CASPIAN SEA

TURKMENISTAN

Ashgabat

Tehran

IRAN

Istanbul

Thessaloniki

GREECE

Athens

AEGEAN SEA

Crete

N

Ankara

TURKEY

NORTH
CYPRUS
Nicosia

CYPRUS

Beirut LEBANON

SYRIA

IRAQ

Euphrates

Baghdad

Tigris

Africa: Physical

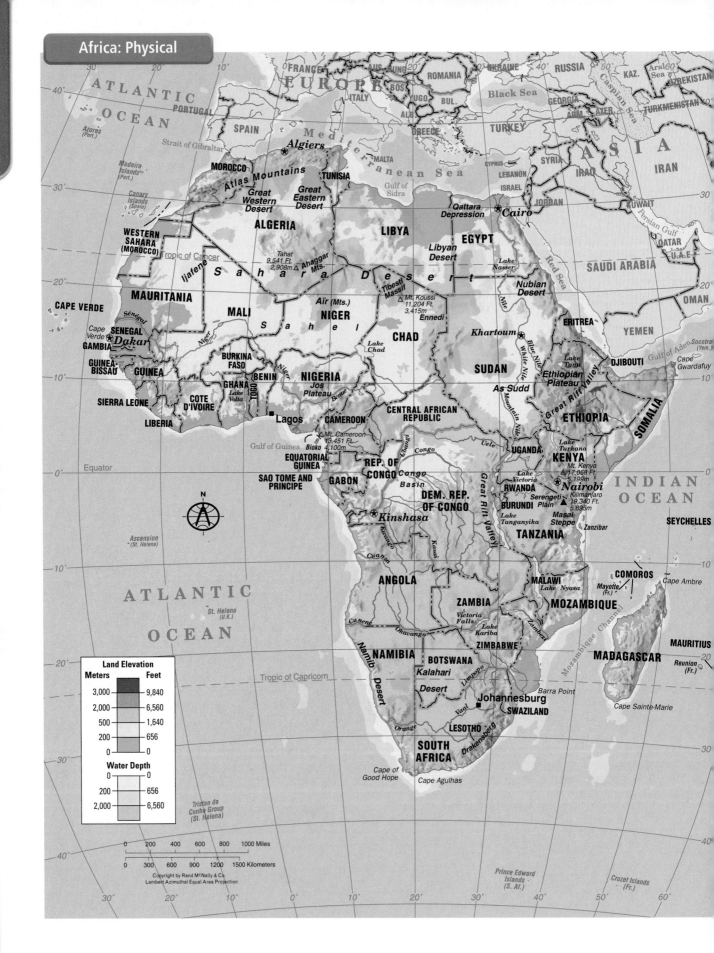

Land Elevation

Meters	Feet
3,000	9,840
2,000	6,560
500	1,640
200	656
0	0

Water Depth

0	0
200	656
2,000	6,560

0   200   400   600   800   1000 Miles
0   300   600   900   1200   1500 Kilometers
Copyright by Rand McNally & Co.
Lambert Azimuthal Equal Area Projection

✦ RAND McNALLY

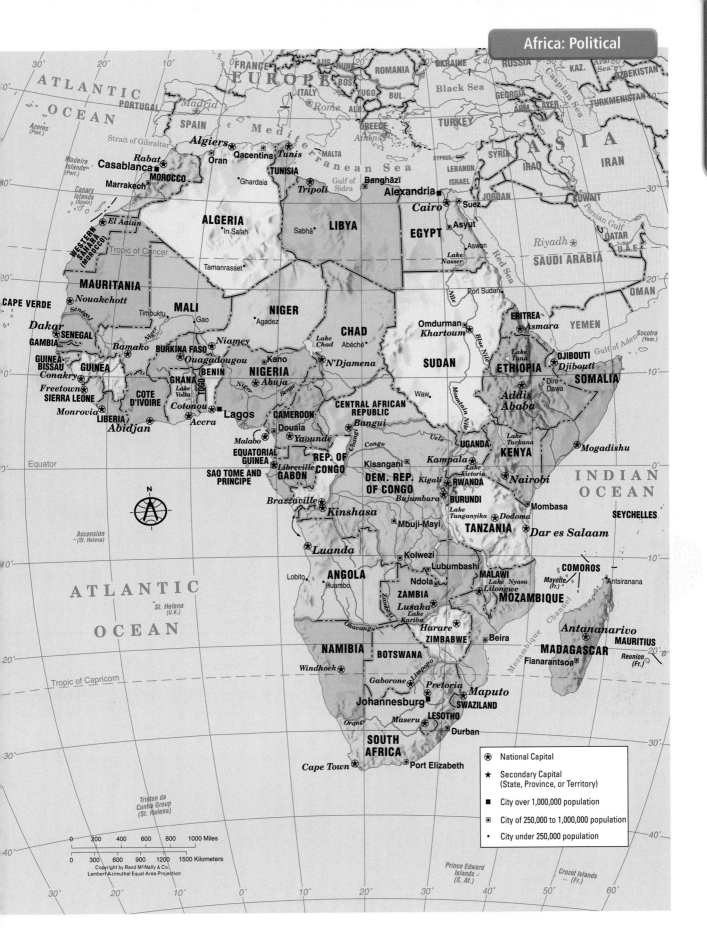

ATLANTIC OCEAN

Azores (Port.)

EUROPE

FRANCE
PORTUGAL
SPAIN
Madrid
ITALY
Rome
ROMANIA
BOS.
YUGO.
BUL.
ALB.
GREECE
Athens
MALTA

Strait of Gibraltar

Mediterranean Sea

Black Sea
UKRAINE
RUSSIA
KAZ.
Aral Sea
Caspian Sea
UZBEKISTAN
TURKMENISTAN
GEORGIA
ARM. AZER.

ASIA

TURKEY
CYPRUS
SYRIA
LEBANON
ISRAEL
IRAQ
IRAN
JORDAN
KUWAIT
Persian Gulf
QATAR
U.A.E.
SAUDI ARABIA
Riyadh ⊛
OMAN
YEMEN

Algiers ⊛
Oran
Qacentina
Tunis ⊛
TUNISIA
Rabat ⊛
Casablanca
Ghardaia
Tripoli ⊛
Gulf of Sidra
Banghāzī
Alexandria
MOROCCO
Marrakech

Madeira Islands (Port.)

Canary Islands (Spain)

El Aaiún ⊛

WESTERN SAHARA (MOROCCO)

ALGERIA
In Salah
Sabhā
LIBYA
Cairo ⊛ *Suez*
EGYPT
Asyut
Aswan
Lake Nasser

Tropic of Cancer

Tamanrasset

MAURITANIA
Nouakchott ⊛

CAPE VERDE

Dakar ⊛ SENEGAL
GAMBIA
Timbuktu
MALI
Gao
Senegal
Niger
NIGER
Agadez
CHAD
Lake Chad
Abéché
N'Djamena
Omdurman
Khartoum ⊛
SUDAN
Port Sudan
Nile
Blue Nile
ERITREA
Asmara ⊛
YEMEN
Socotra (Yem.)
Gulf of Aden
DJIBOUTI
Djibouti ⊛

GUINEA-BISSAU
Conakry ⊛
GUINEA
Bamako ⊛
Niamey ⊛
BURKINA FASO
Ouagadougou ⊛
Kano
NIGERIA
BENIN
Abuja ⊛
Benue
CENTRAL AFRICAN REPUBLIC
Bangui ⊛
Waw
Mountain Nile
ETHIOPIA
Addis Ababa ⊛
Dire Dawa
SOMALIA

Freetown ⊛
SIERRA LEONE
GHANA
Lake Volta
TOGO
COTE D'IVOIRE
Cotonou
Accra ⊛
Lagos
Niger
CAMEROON
Douala
Yaoundé ⊛
Uele
Congo
UGANDA
Kampala ⊛
Lake Turkana
Mogadishu ⊛

Monrovia ⊛
LIBERIA
Abidjan
Malabo
EQUATORIAL GUINEA
SAO TOME AND PRINCIPE
GABON
Libreville ⊛
REP. OF CONGO
Kisangani
DEM. REP. OF CONGO
Kigali ⊛ RWANDA
Lake Victoria
KENYA
Nairobi ⊛
Mombasa

INDIAN OCEAN

Equator

N

Brazzaville ⊛
Kinshasa ⊛
Mbuji-Mayi
Bujumbura ⊛
BURUNDI
Lake Tanganyika
Dodoma ⊛
TANZANIA
Dar es Salaam ⊛
SEYCHELLES

Ascension (St. Helena)

Luanda ⊛

Kolwezi
Lubumbashi
Ndola
MALAWI
Lake Nyasa
Lilongwe ⊛
COMOROS
Mayotte (Fr.)
Antsiranana

ATLANTIC

St. Helena (U.K.)

ANGOLA
Huambo
Lobito
Zambezi
ZAMBIA
Lusaka ⊛
Lake Kariba
MOZAMBIQUE
Okavango
Harare ⊛
ZIMBABWE
Beira
Mozambique Channel

OCEAN

Antananarivo ⊛
MAURITIUS
MADAGASCAR
Fianarantsoa
Reunion (Fr.)

Windhoek ⊛
NAMIBIA
BOTSWANA
Limpopo
Gaborone ⊛
Pretoria ⊛
Johannesburg
SWAZILAND
Maputo ⊛
Maseru ⊛ LESOTHO
Durban

Tropic of Capricorn

Orange

SOUTH AFRICA

Cape Town ⊛
Port Elizabeth

Tristan da Cunha Group (St. Helena)

	National Capital
★	Secondary Capital (State, Province, or Territory)
■	City over 1,000,000 population
▫	City of 250,000 to 1,000,000 population
•	City under 250,000 population

0 200 400 600 800 1000 Miles
0 300 600 900 1200 1500 Kilometers
Copyright by Rand McNally & Co.
Lambert Azimuthal Equal Area Projection

Prince Edward Islands (S. Af.)

Crozet Islands (Fr.)

Asia: Physical

ATLANTIC OCEAN

ARCTIC OCEAN

ICELAND

IRELAND

UNITED KINGDOM

London ⊕

FAROE ISLANDS (Den.)

NORWAY

SWEDEN

FINLAND

DENMARK

North Sea

Arctic Circle

Barents Sea

Severna Zem

Kara Sea

Novaya Zemlya

Yamal Pen.

PORTUGAL

SPAIN

MOROCCO

GIBRALTAR (U.K.)

FRANCE

NETH.

GERMANY

POLAND

BELARUS

ESTONIA

LATVIA

LITH.

Moscow ⊕

Ural Mountains

Ob

West

Siberian

Lowland

Novosibirs

ALGERIA

ITALY

AUSTRIA

CZECH

SLOVAKIA

HUNGARY

CROATIA

BOS.

YUGO.

ALB.

MAC.

ROMANIA

BULGARIA

UKRAINE

MOLD.

Ishim

Volga

Irtysh

Ob

TUNISIA

GREECE

Black Sea

Ankara ⊕

Caucasus

Caspian Depression

Astana ⊕

KAZAKHSTAN

Mediterranean Sea

LIBYA

TURKEY

GEORGIA

Mount Ararat 16,940 Ft. 5,165 m

ARM.

AZER.

Caspian Sea

Aral Sea

Ust-Urt Plateau

Syr Darya

Lake Balkhash

N. CYPRUS

CYPRUS

LEBANON

SYRIA

Kara Kum (Desert)

UZBEKISTAN

Amu Darya

Tian Shan

KYRGYZSTAN

Cairo ⊕

ISRAEL

Nile

Sinai Pen.

JORDAN

IRAQ

Tigris

Euphrates

Tehran ⊕

Dasht-e Kavir

TURKMENISTAN

TAJIKISTAN

Pamirs

Tarim Basin

K2 (Qogir Feng) 28,250 Ft. 8,611m

Altun S

EGYPT

An-Nafud

SAUDI ARABIA

Zagros Mts.

IRAN

Dasht-e Lut

AFGHANISTAN

Hindu Kush

Kunlun M

CHAD

SUDAN

Red Sea

KUWAIT

Persian Gulf

BAHRAIN

QATAR

PAKISTAN

Indus

Great Indian Desert

New Delhi ⊕

NEPAL

Ganges

HIMALAYA MT.

Mt. Evere 29,035 8,850

Arabian Peninsula

U.A.E.

Gulf of Oman

ERITREA

Rub Al-Khali

OMAN

Great Indian Desert

INDIA

YEMEN

DJIBOUTI

ETHIOPIA

Gulf of Aden

Mumbai (Bombay)

Godavari

Deccan Plateau

Western Ghats

Eastern Ghats

Bay Beng

DEM. REP. OF THE CONGO (ZAIRE)

Socotra (Yem.)

Arabian Sea

SOMALIA

UGANDA

KENYA

N

Lakshadweep (India)

SRI LANKA

RWANDA

BURUNDI

TANZANIA

MALDIVES

INDIAN OCEAN

ZAMBIA

MALAWI

MOZAMBIQUE

0   200   400   600   800 Miles

0   200   400   600   800 1000 Kilometers

Copyright by Rand McNally & Co.
Lambert Azimuthal Equal Area Projection

⊛ RAND M℃NALLY

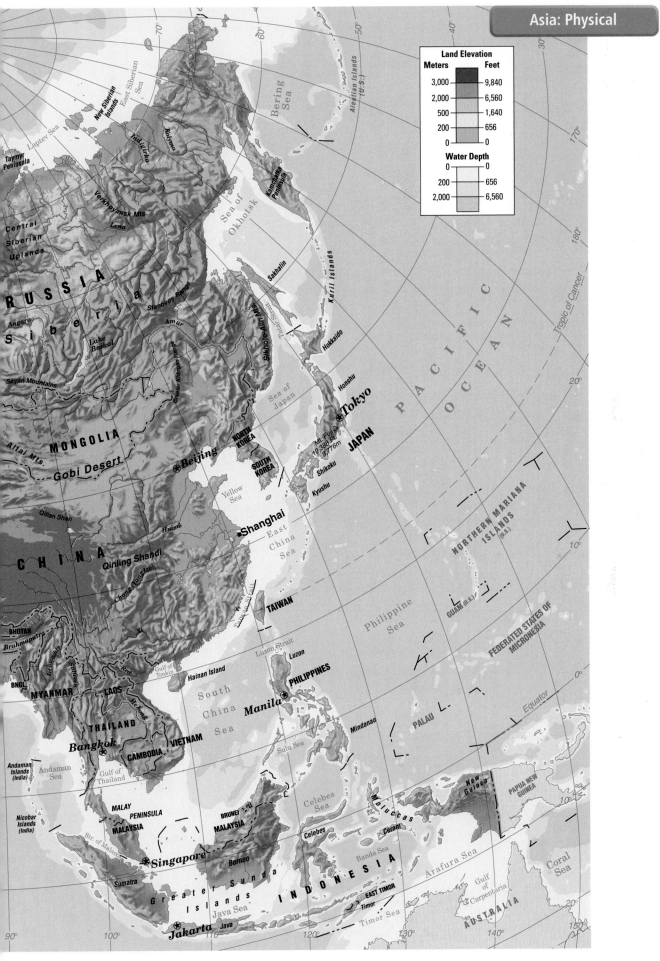

Land Elevation

Meters	Feet
3,000	9,840
2,000	6,560
500	1,640
200	656
0	0

Water Depth

0	0
200	656
2,000	6,560

Taymyr
Peninsula

Laptev Sea

New Siberian
Islands

East Siberian
Sea

Indigirka

Kolyma

Bering
Sea

Aleutian Islands
(U.S.)

70°

60°

50°

40°

30°

Central
Siberian
Uplands

RUSSIA

Verkhoyansk Mts.

Lena

Sea of
Okhotsk

Kamchatka
Peninsula

Siberia

Angara

Lake
Baikal

Stanovoy Range

Amur

Sakhalin

Kuril Islands

Sayan Mountains

Altai Mts.

Greater Khingan Range

Sikhote Alin Mts.

Sea of
Japan

Hokkaido

PACIFIC

OCEAN

Tropic of Cancer

180°

20°

MONGOLIA

Gobi Desert

Beijing

NORTH
KOREA

SOUTH
KOREA

Honshu

Tokyo

Mt. Fuji
12,388 Ft.
3,776m

JAPAN

Shikoku

Kyushu

NORTHERN MARIANA
ISLANDS
(U.S.)

10°

Qilian Shan

Yellow
Sea

Shanghai

East
China
Sea

CHINA

Qinling Shandi

Chang (Yangtze)

Huang

TAIWAN

Taiwan Strait

Philippine
Sea

GUAM (U.S.)

FEDERATED STATES OF
MICRONESIA

BHUTAN

Brahmaputra

Xi

Luzon Strait

Luzon

BNGL

MYANMAR

LAOS

Irrawaddy

Salween

Red

Mekong

Gulf of
Tonkin

Hainan Island

South
China
Sea

Manila

PHILIPPINES

Mindanao

PALAU

Equator

THAILAND

Bangkok

CAMBODIA

VIETNAM

Sulu Sea

Andaman
Islands
(India)

Andaman
Sea

Gulf of
Thailand

Celebes
Sea

Moluccas

New
Guinea

PAPUA NEW
GUINEA

10°

Nicobar
Islands
(India)

MALAY
PENINSULA

MALAYSIA

Str. of Malacca

BRUNEI

MALAYSIA

Celebes

Ceram

Banda Sea

Arafura Sea

Coral
Sea

Singapore

Borneo

Greater Sunda
Islands

INDONESIA

Gulf
of
Carpentaria

Sumatra

Jakarta

Java

Java Sea

EAST TIMOR

Timor

Timor Sea

AUSTRALIA

90°

100°

110°

120°

130°

140°

150°

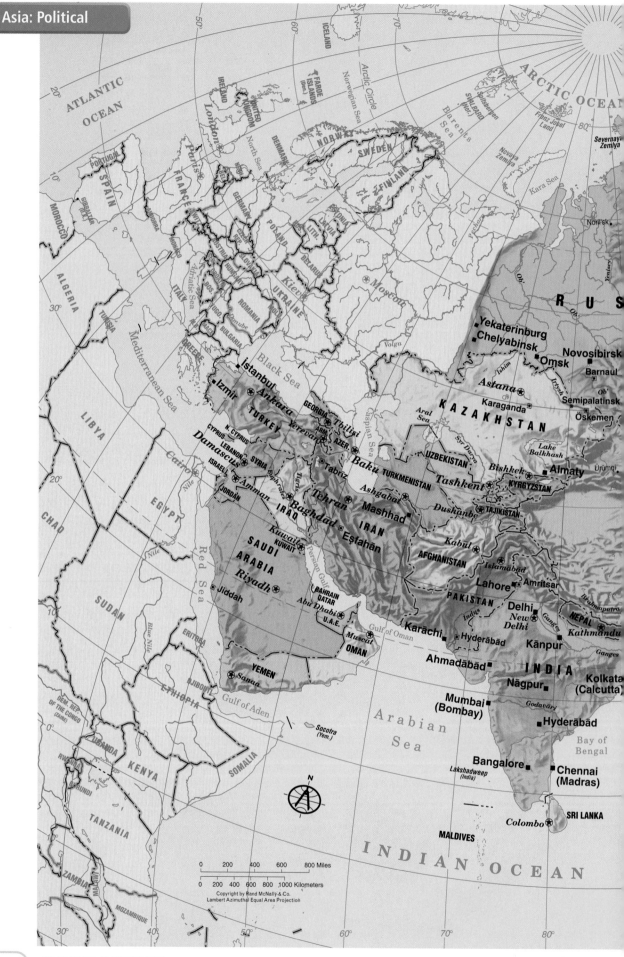

RAND MCNALLY

National Capital

Secondary Capital
(State, Province, or Territory)

City over 1,000,000 population

City of 250,000 to 1,000,000 population

City under 250,000 population

PACIFIC OCEAN

East Siberian Sea

New Siberian Islands

Laptev Sea

ASIA

Angara

Kraynoyarsk

Irkutsk

Enisej

Lena

Yana

Yakutsk

Lake Baikal

Chita

Ulaanbaatar

MONGOLIA

Changchun

Shenyang

Beijing

Tianjin

Taiyuan

Jinan

Huang (Yellow)

Lanzhou

Xi'an

Nanjing

Shanghai

Wuhan

Hangzhou

Chengdu

Chongqing

Chang (Yangtze)

Guiyang

CHINA

Kunming

Nanning

Guangzhou

Hong Kong

Lhasa

BHUTAN

Brahmaputra

BNGL.

Dhaka

Chittagong

MYANMAR

Yangon

THAILAND

Bangkok

LAOS

Vientiane

Mekong

Hanoi

Da Nang

VIETNAM

CAMBODIA

Phnom Penh

Ho Chi Minh City

Gulf of Tonkin

Hainan Island

South China Sea

Andaman Islands (India)

Andaman Sea

Gulf of Thailand

Nicobar Islands (India)

Medan

MALAYSIA

Kuala Lumpur

Singapore

Sumatra

Palembang

Jakarta

Bandung

Surabaya

Java

Java Sea

Banjarmasin

Borneo

Celebes

INDONESIA

Bandar Seri Begawan

BRUNEI

MALAYSIA

Ceram

Celebes Sea

Manado

Banda Sea

EAST TIMOR

Timor

Timor Sea

Arafura Sea

Gulf of Carpentaria

AUSTRALIA

Coral Sea

New Guinea

PAPUA NEW GUINEA

Sulu Sea

Mindanao

Davao

Cebu

Samar

PHILIPPINES

Manila

Luzon

Luzon Strait

PALAU

FEDERATED STATES OF MICRONESIA

GUAM (U.S.)

NORTHERN MARIANA ISLANDS (U.S.)

Philippine Sea

Equator

Taipei

TAIWAN

Kaohsiung

Fuzhou

Taiwan Strait

East China Sea

Qiqihar

Harbin

Vladivostok

Sapporo

Hokkaido

Khabarovsk

Amur

Sea of Japan

Honshu

Tokyo

Nagoya

Osaka

JAPAN

Kyushu

Shikoku

Seoul

SOUTH KOREA

NORTH KOREA

Pusan

Yellow Sea

Sea of Okhotsk

Sakhalin

Kuril Islands

Kamchatka Peninsula

Petropavlovsk-Kamchatskiy

Palana

Magadan

ALEUTIAN ISLANDS (U.S.)

Bering Sea

Anadyr

Tropic of Cancer

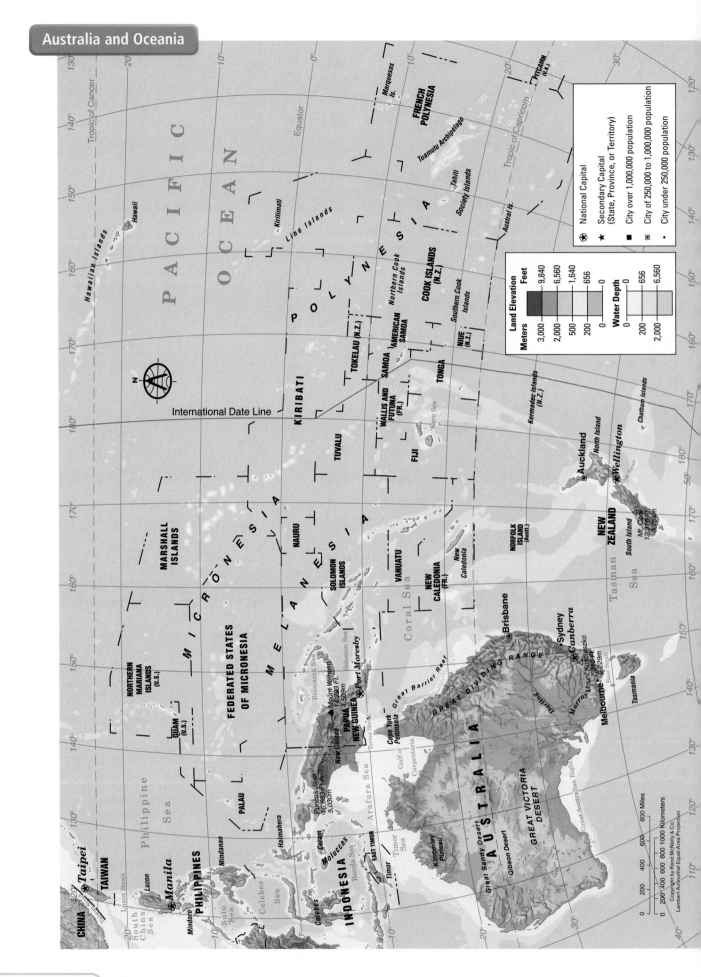

RAND MᶜNALLY

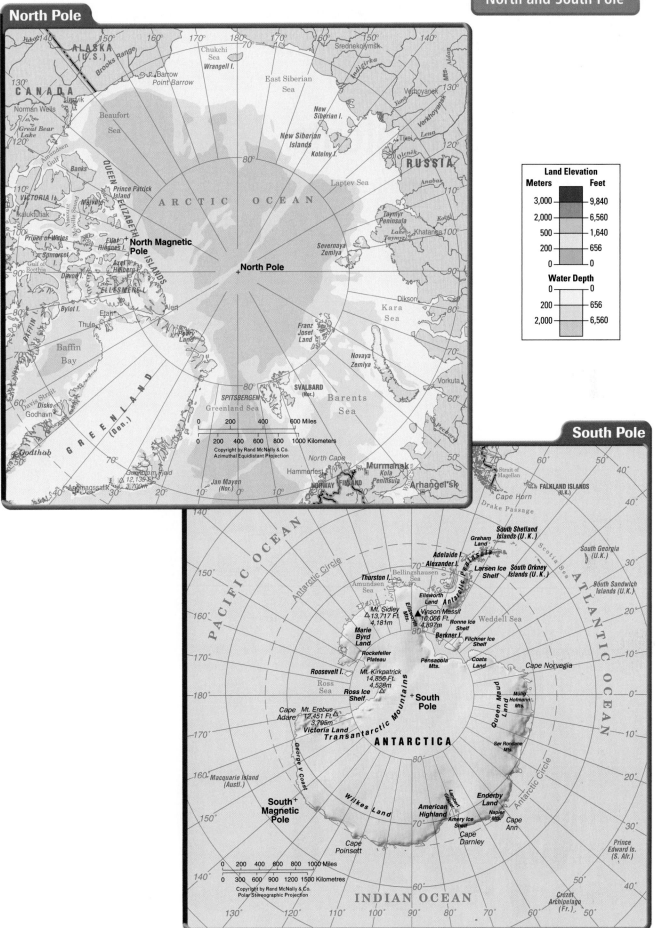

North Pole

ALASKA (U.S.)

Hkot 140° 150° 160° 170° 180° 70° 170° 160° 150° 140°

Chukchi Sea
Wrangell I.
Srednekolymsk
Indigirka
Barrow Point Barrow
East Siberian Sea
Brooks Range
CANADA
Imuvik
Norman Wells
Great Bear Lake
120°
New Siberian I.
New Siberian Islands
Kotelny I.
Verhoyansk
Yana
Mts.
Lena
RUSSIA
130°
Amundsen Gulf
Banks
Queen
110°
Prince Patrick Island
Melville I.
ARCTIC OCEAN
Laptev Sea
Anabar
110°
VICTORIA I.
Kalukfutiak
Prince of Wales
Elizabeth
Somerset
North Magnetic Pole
Axel Heiberg I.
ELLESMERE I.
ISLANDS
North Pole
Severnaya Zemlya
Taymyr Peninsula
Lake Taymyr
Khatanga
100°
Gulf of Boothia
Devon I.
Baffin I.
Bylot I.
Etah
Alert
Dikson
Kara Sea
80°
Thule
Pearl Land
Franz Josef Land
BAFFIN I.
Baffin Bay
GREENLAND
Novaya Zemlya
70°
Davis Strait
Disko
Godhavn
80° SVALBARD (Nor.)
SPITSBERGEN
Greenland Sea
Barents Sea
Vorkuta
60°
Godthab
Angmagssalik
Gunnbjorn Fjeld 12,139 Ft. 3,700m
Jan Mayen (Nor.)
North Cape
Hammerfest
Murmansk
Kola Peninsula
Arhangel'sk
NORWAY FINLAND
50°

Copyright by Rand McNally & Co.
Azimuthal Equidistant Projection

0 200 400 600 Miles
0 200 400 600 800 1000 Kilometers

Land Elevation

Meters		Feet
3,000		9,840
2,000		6,560
500		1,640
200		656
0		0

Water Depth

0		0
200		656
2,000		6,560

South Pole

Strait of Magellan
FALKLAND ISLANDS (U.K.)
Cape Horn
Drake Passage
60° 50° 40°
South Georgia (U.K.)
South Shetland Islands (U.K.)
Graham Land
Adelaide I.
Alexander I.
Larsen Ice Shelf
South Orkney Islands (U.K.)
Scotia Sea
30°
South Sandwich Islands (U.K.)
PACIFIC OCEAN
150°
Antarctic Circle
Thurston I.
Bellingshausen Sea
Amundsen Sea
70°
Ellsworth Land
Ellsworth Mts.
Vinson Massif 16,066 Ft. 4,897m
Ronne Ice Shelf
Berkner I.
Weddell Sea
ATLANTIC OCEAN
160°
Mt. Sidley 13,717 Ft. 4,181m
Marie Byrd Land
Rockefeller Plateau
Pensacola Mts.
Filchner Ice Shelf
Coats Land
Cape Norvegia
10°
170°
Roosevelt I.
Ross Sea
Mt. Kirkpatrick 14,856 Ft. 4,528m
Ross Ice Shelf
South Pole
Queen Maud Land
Mühlig Hofmann Mts.
0°
180°
Cape Adare
Mt. Erebus 12,451 Ft. 3,795m
Victoria Land
Transantarctic Mountains
ANTARCTICA
Ser Rondane Mts.
10°
170°
George V Coast
80°
20°
160°
Macquarie Island (Austl.)
South Magnetic Pole
Wilkes Land
70°
Lambert Glacier
American Highland
Amery Ice Shelf
Enderby Land
Napier Mts.
Cape Ann
Antarctic Circle
20°
150°
Cape Poinsett
Cape Darnley
Prince Edward Is. (S. Afr.)
30°
140°
INDIAN OCEAN
60°
Crozet Archipelago (Fr.)
40°
130° 120° 110° 100° 90° 80° 70° 60° 50°

0 200 400 600 800 1000 Miles
0 300 600 900 1200 1500 Kilometres
Copyright by Rand McNally & Co.
Polar Stereographic Projection

Rand McNally   A39

Table of Contents

Reading and Communication Skills

Critical Thinking Skills

Print and Visual Sources

Technology Sources

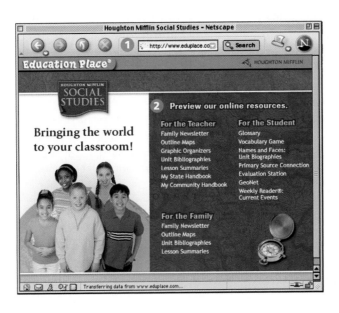

Summarize

When you **summarize**, you restate a paragraph, passage, or chapter in fewer words. You include only the main ideas and most important details. It is important to use your own words when summarizing.

The passage below and to the right describes the origins of several state names in the United States. Use the steps listed below to help you summarize the passage.

Learn the Skill

Step ❶ Look for topic sentences stating the main idea or ideas. These are often at the beginning of a section or paragraph. Briefly restate each main idea—in your own words.

Step ❷ Include key facts and any names, dates, numbers, amounts, or percentages from the text.

Step ❸ After writing your summary, review it to see that you have included only the most important details.

Practice the Skill

You should be able to write your summary in a short paragraph. The paragraph below right summarizes the passage you just read.

Apply the Skill

Turn to Chapter 4, Lesson 2, "A Constitutional Democracy." Read pages 92 and 93 and write a paragraph summarizing the three branches of government.

STATES' NAMES

❶ The name of a state often comes from that state's geography. For example, ❷ the name for Montana comes from a Latin word that means "mountainous."

❶ Other states are named after people who were in power at the time the area was explored or settled. Present-day Louisiana was explored by a Frenchman named La Salle. ❷ He named the area Louisiana after the French king at the time, Louis XIV. The state of ❷ Georgia was named after King George II of England, who granted the right to start the colony.

❶ Still other states get their names from Native American tribes living in the area when Europeans arrived. ❷ Arkansas, Alabama, and Massachusetts were named for the Native American tribes living there.

---

❸ The names of states in the United States often came from geographical features, the names of people in power, or the names of Native American tribes.

Take Notes

When you **take notes**, you write down the important ideas and details of a paragraph, passage, or chapter. A chart or an outline can help you organize your notes to use in the future.

The following passage describes several different types of bodies of water. Use the steps listed below to help you take notes on the passage.

Learn the Skill

Step ❶ Look at the title to find the main topic of the passage.

Step ❷ Identify the main ideas and details of the passage. Then summarize the main idea and details in your notes.

Step ❸ Identify key terms and define them. The term *hydrosphere* is shown in boldface type and underlined; both techniques signal that it is a key term.

Step ❹ In your notes, use abbreviations to save time and space. You can abbreviate words such as *gulf* (g.), *river* (r.), and *lake* (l.), as long as you write the proper name of the body of water with the abbreviation.

Practice the Skill

Making a chart can help you take notes on a passage. The chart at right contains notes from the passage you just read.

Apply the Skill

Turn to Chapter 1, Lesson 1, "The World at Your Fingertips." Read "Learning About the World" and use a chart to take notes on the passage.

❶ **BODIES OF WATER**

❷ All the bodies of water on Earth form what is called ❸ the <u>hydrosphere</u>. The world's ❷ oceans make up the largest part of the hydrosphere. Oceans have smaller regions. ❷ Gulfs such as the Gulf of Tonkin and seas such as the Sea of Japan are extensions of oceans. Land partially encloses these waters.

❷ Oceans and seas contain salt water, but most lakes and rivers contain fresh water. The water in rivers, such as the ❷ Nile River in Africa, flows down a channel in one direction. This movement is the current. Lake water, such as that found in ❷ Lake Victoria in Tanzania, can have currents too, even though the water is surrounded by land. Some lakes feed into rivers, and some rivers supply water to lakes.

❷ Item	Notes
I. ❸ hydrosphere	all water on Earth
a. oceans	salt water; largest part of hydrosphere
b. gulfs and seas	❹ G. of Tonkin; ❹ S. of Japan part of ocean
c. lakes and rivers	usually fresh water; ❹ Nile R. flows; ❹ L. Victoria surrounded by land

Sequence Events

Sequence is the order in which events follow one another. By being able to follow the sequence of events through history, you can get an accurate sense of the relationship among events.

The following passage explains the sequence of events that led to the American Civil War. Use the steps listed below to help you follow the sequence of events.

Learn the Skill

Step ❶ Look for specific dates provided in the text. The dates may not always read from earliest to latest, so be sure to match an event with the date.

Step ❷ Look for clues about time that allow you to order events according to sequence. Words and phrases such as day, week, month, or year may help to sequence the events.

Practice the Skill

Making a timeline can help you sequence events. The timeline below shows the sequence of events in the passage you just read.

Apply the Skill

Turn to Chapter 11, Lesson 2, "Traders, Explorers, and Colonists." Read "Leaders in Exploration" and make a timeline showing the sequence of events in that passage.

THE CIVIL WAR BEGINS

On ❶ December 20, 1860, South Carolina became the first state to secede, or leave the Union. Many other states followed. In ❷ February of the following year, these states united to form the Confederate States of America, also known as the Confederacy. Soon afterward, Confederate soldiers began seizing federal forts. By the time that Lincoln was sworn in as President on ❶ March 4, 1861, only four southern forts remained in Union hands. The most important was Fort Sumter, which was on an island in Charleston harbor.

On the morning of ❶ April 12, Confederate cannons began firing on Fort Sumter. The war between North and South had begun.

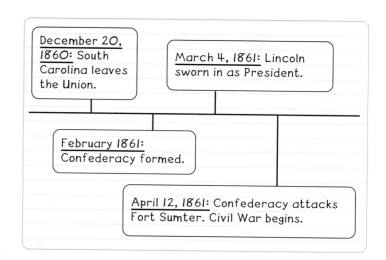

December 20, 1860: South Carolina leaves the Union.

March 4, 1861: Lincoln sworn in as President.

February 1861: Confederacy formed.

April 12, 1861: Confederacy attacks Fort Sumter. Civil War begins.

Find Main Ideas

The **main idea** is a statement that summarizes the subject of a speech, an article, a section of a book, or a paragraph. Main ideas can be stated or unstated. The main idea of a paragraph is often stated in the first or last sentence. If it is the first sentence, it is followed by sentences that support that main idea. If it is the last sentence, the details build up to the main idea. To find an unstated idea, use the details of the paragraph as clues.

The following paragraph provides reasons why Japan and Australia make such good trading partners. Use the steps listed below to help you identify the main idea.

Learn the Skill

Step ❶ Identify what you think may be the stated main idea. Check the first and last sentences of the paragraph to see whether either could be the stated main idea.

Step ❷ Identify details that support the main idea. Some details explain that idea. Others give examples of what is stated in the main idea.

Practice the Skill

Making a chart can help you identify the main idea and details in a passage or paragraph. The chart below identifies the main idea and details in the paragraph you just read.

Apply the Skill

Turn to Chapter 8, Lesson 2, "Economies and Cultures." Read "The Economies" and create a chart that identifies the main idea and the supporting details.

TRADING PARTNERS

Australia is an island. Japan is also an island, though not nearly as large as Australia. Australia is not nearly as densely populated as Japan is. ❷ In Japan, an average of 867 people live in each square mile. In Australia, an average of 6 people live in each square mile. ❷ Australia has wide-open lands available for agriculture, ranching, and mining. ❷ Japan buys wool from Australian ranches, wheat from Australian farms, and iron ore from Australian mines. To provide jobs for its many workers, ❷ Japan has developed industries. Those industries ❷ sell electronics and cars to Australia. ❶ Australia and Japan are major trading partners because each country has something the other needs.

Main Idea: Australia and Japan are good trading partners because each supplies something the other needs.
Detail: Japan's population density is 867 people per square mile; Australia's is 6 per square mile.
Detail: Australia has land, natural resources, and agricultural products.
Detail: Japan buys wool, wheat, and iron from Australia.
Detail: Japan has many industries.
Detail: Australia buys electronics and cars from Japanese industries.

Categorize

To **categorize** is to sort people, objects, ideas, or other information into groups, called categories. Historians categorize information to help them identify and understand patterns in historical events.

The following passage discusses the involvement of various countries in World War II. Use the steps listed below to help you categorize information.

Learn the Skill

Step ❶ First, decide what kind of information needs to be categorized. Decide what the passage is about and how that information can be sorted into categories. For example, look at the different ways countries reacted to World War II.

Step ❷ Then decide what the categories will be. To find how countries reacted to the war, look for clue words such as *in response*, *some*, *other*, and *both*.

Step ❸ Once you have chosen the categories, sort information into them. Which countries were Axis Powers? Which were Allies? What about the ones who were conquered and those who never fought at all?

Practice the Skill

Making a chart can help you categorize information. You should have one more column than you have categories. The chart to the right shows how the information from the passage you just read can be categorized.

Apply the Skill

Turn to Chapter 14, Lesson 4, "Germany." Read "A Divided Germany" and make a chart in which you categorize the changes that took place in Germany after World War II.

WORLD WAR II ALLIANCES

❶ During World War II, most countries around the world had to choose which side to take in the conflict. Some countries were conquered so quickly that they could not join either side.

❷ *Others* chose to remain neutral. ❷ Italy and Japan joined with Germany to form the Axis Powers. In 1939, Germany began the war by invading Poland. ❷ *In response*, Great Britain and France (the first two Allied Powers) declared war on Germany. Germany quickly conquered many countries, including Denmark, Norway, the Netherlands, Belgium, and France. ❷ In 1941, *both* the Soviet Union and the United States entered the war on the Allied side. ❷ Sweden and Switzerland remained neutral during the war.

❸ Name of Alliance	Axis	Allied Powers	Neutral
Countries	• Italy • Japan • Germany	• Great Britain • France • Soviet Union • United States	• Sweden • Switzerland

Make Public Speeches

A speech is a talk given in public to an audience. Some speeches are given to persuade the audience to think or act in a certain way, or to support a cause. You can learn how to **make public speeches** effectively by analyzing great speeches in history.

The following is from a speech that British suffragist Emmeline Pankhurst gave to explain why women were using forceful tactics to gain the right to vote. Use the steps listed below to help you analyze Pankhurst's speech and prepare a speech of your own.

Learn the Skill

Step ❶ Choose one central idea or theme and organize your speech to support it. Pankhurst organized her speech around the idea that a thing worth having is worth fighting for.

Step ❷ Use words or images that will win over your audience. Pankhurst asked her audience to put themselves in a woman's place by using such phrases as "if the situation were reversed."

Step ❸ Repeat words or images to drive home your main point—as if it is the "hook" of a pop song. Pankhurst repeats the phrase *You know perfectly well* to urge male listeners to consider how it would feel to suffer the injustices that women faced.

Practice the Skill

Making an outline like the one to the right will help you create an effective public speech.

Apply the Skill

Turn to Chapter 7, Lesson 2, "Government in Mexico." Read the lesson, especially the quotation from Emiliano Zapata on page 180, and use the quotation as the subject of your speech. First, make an outline like the one to the right to organize your ideas. Then write your speech. Next, practice giving your speech. Make it a three-minute speech.

WHY WE ARE MILITANT

❶ Now, gentlemen, . . . you know perfectly well that there never was a thing worth having that was not worth fighting for. ❸ You know perfectly well that ❷ if the situation were reversed, if you had no constitutional rights and we had all of them, if you had the duty of paying and obeying and trying to look as pleasant, and we were the proud citizens who could decide our fate and yours, because we knew what was good for you better than you knew yourselves, ❸ you know perfectly well ❷ that you wouldn't stand for it a single day, and you would be perfectly justified in rebelling against such intolerable conditions.

Title: Why We Are Militant
  I. Introduce Theme: There never was a thing worth having that was not worth fighting for.
  II. Repeat theme: You know perfectly well that if the situation were reversed, you wouldn't stand for it a single day.
    A. if men had no constitutional rights and women had all of them
    B. if men had to act obedient and pleasant all the time
    C. if women could decide men's fates and had the power to say what was good for them
  III. Conclude: You would be perfectly justified in rebelling against such intolerable conditions.

Analyze Points of View

To **analyze points of view** means to look closely at a person's arguments and understand the reasons behind that person's beliefs. The goal of analyzing a point of view is to recognize different thoughts, opinions, and beliefs about a topic.

The following passage describes the difference between Native American and European attitudes about land use. Use the steps below to help you analyze the points of view.

Learn the Skill

Step ❶ Look for statements that show you a particular point of view on an issue. For example, Native Americans believed land should be preserved for the future. European colonists believed land could be owned and changed as desired.

Step ❷ Think about why different people or groups held a particular point of view. Ask yourself what they valued. What were they trying to gain or to protect? What were they willing to sacrifice?

Step ❸ Write a summary that explains why different groups of people might have taken different positions on this issue.

Practice the Skill

Using a diagram can help you analyze points of view. The diagram to the right analyzes the different points of view of the Native Americans and the European colonists in the passage you just read.

Apply the Skill

Turn to Chapter 5, Lesson 2, "A Constitutional Monarchy." Read "Many Cultures, Many Needs" about the disagreement between separatists and nationalists regarding Quebec's independence. Make a diagram to analyze their different points of view.

LAND USE

Native Americans and Europeans had many conflicts because of differing ideas about land use. ❶ Most Native Americans believed that land must be preserved for future generations. They believed the present generation had the right to use land for hunting and farming. However, no one had the right to buy or sell land. Also, no one should ever damage or destroy land.

In contrast, Europeans had a long history of taming wilderness and owning land. As a result, ❶ Europeans believed that they could buy land, sell it, and alter it. For example, if they wished to mine for gold underground, they could destroy landscape as they dug the mine. ❶ Europeans used land to make money.

❷ **Native Americans**
- preserved land for future
- used land to provide for present needs
- believed no one could buy or sell land and should never damage land

❸ Native Americans wanted to preserve the land. They did so because they valued their heritage. The colonists bought land, sold it, and changed it. They did so because they valued making money.

❷ **European Colonists**
- tradition of taming wilderness and owning land
- bought and sold land, changed and sometimes harmed it
- used land to make money

Compare and Contrast

To **compare** means to look at the similarities and differences between two or more things. To **contrast** means to examine only the differences between them. Historians compare and contrast events, personalities, behaviors, beliefs, and situations in order to understand them.

The following passage describes the Dead Sea in southwest Asia and the Red Sea located between northeast Africa and southwest Asia. Use the steps below to help you compare and contrast these two bodies of water.

Learn the Skill

Step ❶ Look for two aspects of the subject that can be compared and contrasted. This passage compares the Red Sea and the Dead Sea, two extremely salty bodies of water that are close to one another.

Step ❷ To find similarities, look for clue words indicating that two things are alike. Clue words include *both, together,* and *similarly.*

Step ❸ To contrast, look for clue words that show how two things differ. Clue words include *however, but, on the other hand,* and *yet.*

Practice the Skill

Making a Venn diagram will help you identify similarities and differences between two things. In the overlapping area, list characteristics shared by both subjects. Then, in the separate ovals, list the characteristics of each subject not shared by the other. This Venn diagram compares and contrasts the Red Sea and the Dead Sea.

Apply the Skill

Turn to Chapter 6, Lesson 2, "Ancient Latin America." Read "The Aztec" and "The Inca" and make a Venn diagram showing similarities and differences between these two ancient civilizations.

SALTY SEAS

❶ According to the Bible, God parted the Red Sea so Moses could lead his people across it. The Bible also mentions the Dead Sea, calling it the Salt Sea. This is because the Dead Sea is the saltiest body of water in the world. ❷ *Similarly,* the Red Sea also has a high salt content. Many observers argue that the Dead Sea is not really a sea at all. It is more of a lake because it is fed by the River Jordan and is surrounded by land on all four sides. ❸ *On the other hand,* the Indian Ocean feeds the Red Sea. The Red Sea is also the larger of the two seas. It is 174,000 square miles, while the Dead Sea is only 400 square miles. ❷ *Both* bodies of water provide minerals for commercial use, especially salt.

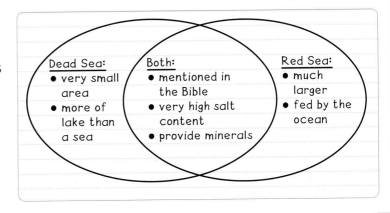

Dead Sea:
- very small area
- more of lake than a sea

Both:
- mentioned in the Bible
- very high salt content
- provide minerals

Red Sea:
- much larger
- fed by the ocean

Analyze Causes; Recognize Effects

A **cause** is an action in history that makes something happen. An **effect** is the historical event that is the result of the cause. A single event may have several causes. It is also possible for one cause to result in several effects. Historians identify cause-and-effect relationships to help them understand why historical events took place.

The following paragraph describes events that caused changes in the way of life of the ancient Maya people of Central America. Use the steps below to help you identify the cause-and-effect relationships.

Learn the Skill

Step ❶ Ask why an action took place. Ask yourself a question about the title and topic sentence, such as, "What caused the Maya civilization to decline?"

Step ❷ Look for effects. Ask yourself, "What happened?" (the effect). Then ask, "Why did it happen?" (the cause). For example, you might ask, "What caused the Maya to abandon their cities?"

Step ❸ Look for clue words that signal causes, such as *cause, contributed,* and *led to.*

Practice the Skill

Using a diagram can help you understand causes and effects. The diagram below shows two causes and an effect for the passage you just read.

Apply the Skill

Turn to Chapter 3, Lesson 2, "Climate and Resources." Read Spotlight on Culture, "The Cajuns: Americans with Canadian Roots," and make a diagram about the causes and effects of the relocation of French Acadians to Louisiana.

---

❶ DECLINE OF THE MAYA CIVILIZATION

❶ The civilization of the Maya went into a mysterious decline around A.D. 900. **❷** Maya cities in the southern lowlands were abandoned, trade ceased, and the huge stone pyramids of the Maya fell into ruin. No one really understands what happened to the Maya, but there are many theories.

❸ Some believe that a change in climate *caused* the decline of Maya civilization. Three long droughts between 810 and 910 meant that there was not enough water for Maya crops. **❷** As a result, the Maya abandoned their cities. **❸** Other researchers believe that additional problems *contributed* to the crisis. They include overpopulation and warfare among the Maya nobility.

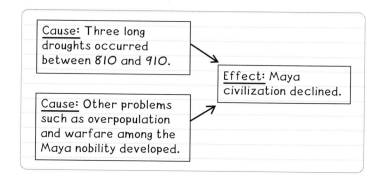

Cause: Three long droughts occurred between 810 and 910.

Cause: Other problems such as overpopulation and warfare among the Maya nobility developed.

Effect: Maya civilization declined.

Make Inferences

Inferences are ideas that the author has not directly stated. To **make inferences** involves reading between the lines to interpret the information you read. You can make inferences by studying what is stated and using your common sense and previous knowledge.

The passage below examines the great pyramids of ancient Egypt. Use the steps below to help you make inferences from the passage.

Learn the Skill

Step ① Read to find statements of facts and ideas. Knowing the facts will give you a good basis for making inferences.

Step ② Use your knowledge, logic, and common sense to make inferences that are based on facts. Ask yourself, "What does the author want me to understand?" For example, from the facts about the pyramids' purpose, you can make the inference that the Egyptians believed in life after death. See other inferences in the chart below.

Practice the Skill

Making a chart will help you organize information and make logical inferences. The chart below organizes information from the passage you just read.

Apply the Skill

Turn to Chapter 10, Lesson 4, "The Middle Ages." Read "Two Medieval Systems" and use a chart like the one to the right to make inferences about the feudal system in medieval Europe.

THE PYRAMIDS OF EGYPT

One reason that ancient Egypt is famous is its giant pyramids. ① The Egyptians built these magnificent monuments for their kings, or pharaohs. Each pyramid was a resting place where an Egyptian pharaoh planned to spend the afterlife. The pharaoh appointed a leader to organize the construction project. ① The leader of the project assembled a staff that managed the workers and tracked the supplies. A single pyramid might contain 92 million cubic feet of stone, enough to fill a large sports stadium. ① Workers built these long-lasting structures with none of the modern cutting tools and machines that we have today.

① Stated Facts and Ideas	② Inferences
Egyptians built their pyramids as resting places for their pharaohs in the afterlife.	Egyptians believed in life after death.
A staff oversaw construction of the project.	Pyramid building was a complicated task that required organization.
The Egyptians built the pyramids without modern equipment.	The Egyptians were skilled engineers and hard workers.

Make Decisions

To **make decisions** you need to choose between two or more options, or courses of action. In most cases, decisions have consequences, or results. Sometimes decisions may lead to new problems. By understanding how historical figures made decisions, you can learn how to improve your own decision-making skills.

The passage below explains the decision British Prime Minister Chamberlain faced when Germany threatened aggression in 1938. Use the steps below to analyze his decision.

Learn the Skill

Step ❶ Identify a decision that needs to be made. Think about what factors make the decision difficult.

Step ❷ Identify possible consequences of the decision. Remember that there can be more than one consequence to a decision.

Step ❸ Identify the decision that was made.

Step ❹ Identify actual consequences that resulted from the decision.

Practice the Skill

A flow chart can help you identify the process of making a decision. The flow chart to the right shows the decision-making process in the passage you just read.

Apply the Skill

Turn to Chapter 13, Lesson 2, "Eastern Europe and Russia." Read "The Breakup of the Soviet Union" and make a flow chart to identify Gorbachev's decision and its consequences as described in the lesson.

PEACE OR WAR?

In 1938, German leader Adolf Hitler demanded a part of Czechoslovakia where mostly Germans lived. ❶ British Prime Minister Neville Chamberlain had to decide how to respond to that aggression. ❷ He could threaten to go to war, but he feared that Britain was not ready. ❷ If he gave Germany the region, he might avoid war, but he would be setting a bad example by giving in to a dictator. ❸ Along with the leader of France, Chamberlain decided to give Germany what it demanded. In exchange, Hitler promised not to take any more land in Europe. ❹ Six months later, Germany took the rest of Czechoslovakia and later invaded Poland.

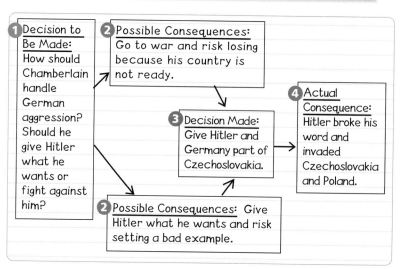

❶ Decision to Be Made: How should Chamberlain handle German aggression? Should he give Hitler what he wants or fight against him?

❷ Possible Consequences: Go to war and risk losing because his country is not ready.

❷ Possible Consequences: Give Hitler what he wants and risk setting a bad example.

❸ Decision Made: Give Hitler and Germany part of Czechoslovakia.

❹ Actual Consequence: Hitler broke his word and invaded Czechoslovakia and Poland.

Recognize Propaganda

Propaganda is communication that aims to influence people's opinions, emotions, or actions. Propaganda is not always factual. Rather, it uses one-sided language or striking symbols to sway people's emotions. Modern advertising often uses propaganda. By thinking critically, you will be able to recognize propaganda and avoid being swayed by it.

The photograph below shows Chinese workers in 1950 celebrating the first anniversary of the founding of the People's Republic of China. Use the steps listed below to help you understand how the photograph works as propaganda.

Learn the Skill

Step ❶ Identify the aim, or purpose, of the photograph. Point out the subject and explain the point of view.

Step ❷ Identify images in the photograph that viewers might respond to emotionally and identify possible emotions.

Step ❸ Think critically about the image. What facts have been ignored or omitted?

Practice the Skill

Making a chart will help you think critically about a piece of propaganda. The chart to the right summarizes the information from the pro-Chinese government photograph.

Apply the Skill

Turn to Chapter 13, Lesson 1, "Eastern Europe Under Communism." Read "Soviet Culture," paying special attention to the photograph on page 357. Use a chart like the one to the right to think critically about the statue shown in the photograph as an example of propaganda.

❶ Identify Purpose	The photograph aims to show that the Chinese people support their ruler Mao Zedong.
❷ Identify Emotions	The image of so many people carrying posters of Mao gives the impression of widespread support for the Chinese leader. The fact that the marchers appear to be workers is meant to demonstrate Mao's popularity among the working class.
❸ Think Critically	The image ignores the fact that China under the Communists was a one-party state that allowed no protests. So one might wonder whether the marchers in the photo truly support Mao or were forced to carry the posters.

Identify Facts and Opinions

Facts are events, dates, statistics, or statements that can be proved to be true. **Opinions** are judgments, beliefs, and feelings. By identifying facts and opinions, you will be able to think critically when a person tries to influence your own opinion.

The following passage tells about a man named John Henry, who became a legend in American folklore. Use the steps listed below to distinguish facts from opinions.

Learn the Skill

Step ① Look for specific information that can be proved or checked for accuracy.

Step ② Look for assertions, claims, and judgments that express opinions. In this case, the author gives a direct opinion about the story told of John Henry.

Step ③ Think about whether statements can be checked for accuracy. Then, identify the facts and opinions in a chart.

Practice the Skill

The chart below analyzes the facts and opinions from the passage above.

Apply the Skill

Turn to Chapter 3, Lesson 2, "Climate and Resources," and read the section titled "Neighbors and Leaders." Make a chart like the one to the right in which you analyze key statements to determine whether they are facts or opinions.

JOHN HENRY: MAN AND MYTH

① John Henry was an African American who worked for the railroads in the late 1800s. His job was to lay down track for the trains. Many famous stories have been written about John Henry, and the most famous is the one about his race against the steam drill. ① The first written version of the story dates from 1900.

According to the tale, John was helping to dig out the Big Bend Tunnel when someone started using a steam-powered drill. John Henry was the strongest man on the job, so he raced the drill to see whether he could dig faster than a machine. John Henry won the race, but he died soon after. ② This legend may be the most interesting story in U.S. history.

Statement	③ Can It Be Proved?	③ Fact or Opinion
John Henry worked for the railroads in the 1800s.	Yes. Check newspapers and other historical documents.	Fact
The first version of the story dates from 1900.	Yes. Check the date of the actual written version of the story.	Fact
The legend of John Henry's race against the steam-powered drill may be the most interesting story in U.S. history.	No. This is the author's opinion; other stories may be just as interesting.	Opinion

Form and Support Opinions

When you **form opinions,** you interpret and judge the importance of events and people in history. You should always **support** your opinions with facts, quotations, and examples.

The following passage describes the impact of apartheid on South Africa. Use the steps listed below to form and support an opinion about the policy.

Learn the Skill

Step ❶ Look for important information about the subject. Information can include facts, quotations, and examples.

Step ❷ Form an opinion on the subject by asking yourself questions about the information. For example, how important was the subject? How does it relate to similar subjects in your own experience?

Step ❸ Support your opinions with facts, quotations, and examples. If the facts do not support the opinion, then rewrite your opinion so that it is supported by the facts.

Practice the Skill

Making a chart can help you organize your opinions and supporting facts. The chart to the right summarizes one possible opinion about the policy of apartheid in South Africa.

Apply the Skill

Turn to Chapter 8, Lesson 4, "Guatemala Today." Read "Guatemala's Government" and form your own opinion about the independent government in Guatemala. Make a chart like the one to the right to summarize your opinion and the supporting facts and examples.

THE POLICY OF APARTHEID

From the mid- to late-twentieth century, South Africa had a policy called apartheid, which separated whites and nonwhites. ❶Nonwhites faced discrimination concerning where they could live, what jobs they could hold, and whether they could attend school. Many were forced to leave their homes and relocate in less desirable regions. Many nonwhites protested these policies, leading to years of conflict. A number of nations also criticized apartheid. ❶In 1985, the United States and Great Britain restricted trade with South Africa. In 1989, F. W. de Klerk became president of South Africa. He opposed apartheid. His efforts helped end the country's policy of segregation.

❷Opinion	The policy of apartheid oppressed many South Africans and hurt the nation's economy.
❸Facts	Nonwhites faced discrimination concerning where they could live, what jobs they could hold, and whether they could attend school. Many nonwhites were forced to relocate in less desirable regions. Nations opposed to apartheid restricted trade with South Africa.

Identify and Solve Problems

To **identify problems** means to find and understand the difficulties faced by a particular group of people during a certain time. To **solve problems** means to understand how people tried to remedy those problems. By studying how people solved problems in the past, you can learn ways to solve problems today.

The following paragraph describes the problems that resulted when women tried to gain equality. Use the steps listed below to learn how women responded.

Learn the Skill

Step ❶ Look for the difficulties or problems caused by the situation.

Step ❷ Consider how the problem affected people or groups with different points of view. For example, the main problem described here is how to increase job opportunities for women.

Step ❸ Look for the solutions that people or groups used to deal with the problem. Think about whether the solution was a good one for people or groups with differing points of view.

Practice the Skill

Making a chart will help you identify and organize information about problems and solutions. The chart to the right shows problems and solutions included in the passage you just read.

Apply the Skill

Turn to Chapter 12, Lesson 1, "European Empires." Read "The Spread of Nationalism." Then make a chart that summarizes the problems faced by the monarchies of Europe and their citizens and the solutions they agreed on.

JOB OPPORTUNITIES FOR WOMEN

❶ In the mid-twentieth century women had limited job opportunities. In 1950, only 30 percent of women worked outside the home. By 1960, that number had risen to about 40 percent. Women working outside the home faced several obstacles.

❷ For example, the jobs traditionally open to women were in areas like clerical work. Such jobs paid poorly and offered few chances to advance. ❷ Many men were unwilling to share power with women. ❸ In the 1970s, women demanded more rights. They began to move into "blue collar" jobs, such as construction work. ❸ Other women gained the education needed to move into professions such as law. By 2000, women were working in every field.

❶ Problem	❷ Differing Points of View	❸ Solution
In the mid-20th century, there were limited job opportunities for women.	Women wanted jobs with better pay and opportunity to advance. Men did not want to share power.	Women demanded rights. Women gained education. In time, women were working in every field.

Evaluate

To **evaluate** is to make a judgment about something. Historians evaluate the actions of people in history. One way to do this is to examine both the positives and the negatives of a historical action, then decide which is stronger—the positive or the negative.

The following passage examines the rule of Mustafa Kemal of Turkey. Use the steps listed below to evaluate the success of his reforms.

Learn the Skill

Step ❶ Before you evaluate a person's actions, first determine what that person was trying to do. In this case, think about what Kemal wanted to accomplish.

Step ❷ Look for statements that show the positive, or successful, results of his actions. For example, did he achieve his goals?

Step ❸ Also look for statements that show the negative, or unsuccessful, results of his actions. Did he fail to achieve something he tried to do?

Step ❹ Write an overall evaluation of the person's actions.

Practice the Skill

Using a diagram can help you evaluate. List the positives and negatives of the historical person's actions and decisions. Then make an overall judgment. The diagram to the right shows how the information from the passage you just read can be diagrammed.

Apply the Skill

Turn to Chapter 4, Lesson 2, "A Constitutional Democracy." Read "Limiting Powers of Government" and make a diagram in which you evaluate the decision to divide power in the United States between federal and state governments.

KEMAL RULES TURKEY

In 1923, Turkey became an independent republic. Mustafa Kemal became Turkey's first president. ❶ Kemal wanted Turkey to resemble European countries rather than its Islamic neighbors. Kemal quickly got rid of Turkey's Islamic government and replaced it with a secular, or nonreligious, system. He also replaced the Arabic alphabet and calendar with Western versions of each. ❸ Kemal's actions drew protests from many traditionalists. ❷ However, Kemal's changes helped modernize Turkey. ❷ They also benefited women, who had lived with many restrictions under Islamic law. Women now had greater social freedom. They also could vote and run for political office.

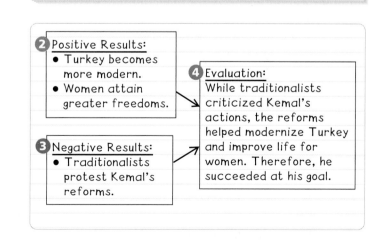

❷ Positive Results:
- Turkey becomes more modern.
- Women attain greater freedoms.

❸ Negative Results:
- Traditionalists protest Kemal's reforms.

❹ Evaluation:
While traditionalists criticized Kemal's actions, the reforms helped modernize Turkey and improve life for women. Therefore, he succeeded at his goal.

Make Generalizations

To **make generalizations** means to make broad judgments based on information. When you make generalizations, you should gather information from several sources.

The following three passages contain ideas on America as a melting pot of different cultures. Use the steps listed below to make a generalization about these ideas.

Learn the Skill

Step ❶ Look for information that the sources have in common. These three sources all look at the relationship of immigrants to the United States.

Step ❷ Form a generalization that describes this relationship in a way that all three sources would agree with. State your generalization in a sentence.

Practice the Skill

Using a chart can help you make generalizations. The chart below shows how the information you just read can be used to generalize about the contributions of immigrants.

Apply the Skill

Turn to Chapter 7, Lesson 1, "The Roots of Modern Mexico." Read "Changes in Mexico," and study the graph on page 172. Also read the biography, "Father Hidalgo," on page 173. Use a chart like the one to the right to make a generalization about the class system in Mexico.

THE MELTING POT

At the turn of the century, ❶ many native-born Americans thought of their country as a melting pot, a mixture of people of different cultures and races who blended together by abandoning their native languages and customs.

—*The Americans*

❶ A nation, like a tree, does not thrive well till it is engrafted with a foreign stock.

—*Journals* (Emerson, 1823)

❶ The United States has often been called a *melting pot.* But in other ways, U.S. society is an example of *cultural pluralism.* That is, large numbers of its people have retained features of the cultures of their ancestors.

—*World Book Encyclopedia*

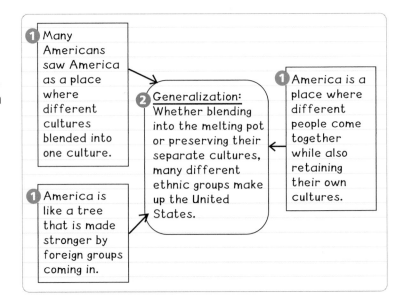

❶ Many Americans saw America as a place where different cultures blended into one culture.

❷ Generalization: Whether blending into the melting pot or preserving their separate cultures, many different ethnic groups make up the United States.

❶ America is a place where different people come together while also retaining their own cultures.

❶ America is like a tree that is made stronger by foreign groups coming in.

Interpret Timelines

A **timeline** is a visual list of events and dates shown in the order in which they occurred. Timelines can be horizontal or vertical. On horizontal timelines, the earliest date is on the left. On vertical timelines, the earliest date is often at the top.

The timeline below lists dates and events associated with the invention of the first systems of writing. Use the steps listed below to help you interpret the information.

Learn the Skill

Step 1 Read the dates at the beginning and end of the timeline. These will show the period of history that is covered. The timeline to the right is a horizontal timeline. It shows the sequence of events from left to right instead of from top to bottom.

Step 2 Read the dates and events in sequential order, beginning with the earliest one. Pay particular attention to how the entries relate to each other. Think about whether earlier events influenced later events.

Step 3 Summarize the focus, or main idea, of the timeline in a few sentences.

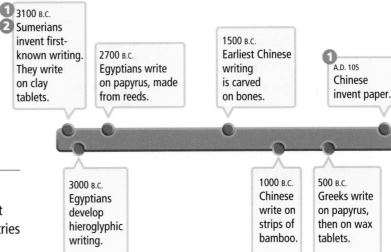

1 3100 B.C.
2 Sumerians invent first-known writing. They write on clay tablets.

2700 B.C. Egyptians write on papyrus, made from reeds.

1500 B.C. Earliest Chinese writing is carved on bones.

1 A.D. 105 Chinese invent paper.

3000 B.C. Egyptians develop hieroglyphic writing.

1000 B.C. Chinese write on strips of bamboo.

500 B.C. Greeks write on papyrus, then on wax tablets.

Practice the Skill

Writing a summary can help you understand information shown on a timeline. The summary to the right states the main idea of the timeline and tells how the events are related.

3 Different groups developed writing at different times, beginning with the Sumerians in 3100 B.C. At first, people used available resources such as clay, papyrus, and bone for writing materials. The paper we use today was invented by the Chinese in A.D. 105.

Apply the Skill

Turn to Chapter 9, page 232, and write a summary of the information shown on the timeline.

Use an Electronic Card Catalog

An **electronic card catalog** is a library's computerized search program that helps you locate books and other materials in the library. You can search the catalog by entering a book title, an author's name, or a subject of interest to you. The electronic card catalog also provides basic information about each book (author, title, publisher, and date of publication). You can use an electronic card catalog to create a bibliography (a list of books) on any topic you want.

The screen shown below is from an electronic search for information about the Congo River. Use the steps listed below to help you use the information on the screen.

Learn the Skill

Step ❶ Begin searching by choosing either subject, title, or author, depending on the topic of your search. For this search, the user chose "Subject" and typed in the words "Congo River."

Step ❷ Once you have selected a book from the results of your search, identify the author, title, city, publisher, and date of publication.

Step ❸ Look for any special features in the book. This book includes a map and four pages of notes.

Step ❹ Locate the call number for the book. The call number indicates the section in the library where you will find the book. The card catalog should indicate whether or not the book is available in the library you are using. If not, it may be in another library in the network.

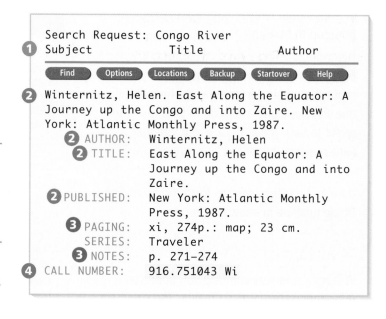

```
    Search Request: Congo River
 ❶  Subject            Title            Author
    ⬡ Find ⬡  ⬡ Options ⬡  ⬡ Locations ⬡  ⬡ Backup ⬡  ⬡ Startover ⬡  ⬡ Help ⬡
 ❷  Winternitz, Helen. East Along the Equator: A
    Journey up the Congo and into Zaire. New
    York: Atlantic Monthly Press, 1987.
       ❷ AUTHOR:     Winternitz, Helen
       ❷ TITLE:      East Along the Equator: A
                     Journey up the Congo and into
                     Zaire.
    ❷ PUBLISHED:     New York: Atlantic Monthly
                     Press, 1987.
       ❸ PAGING:     xi, 274p.: map; 23 cm.
         SERIES:     Traveler
       ❸ NOTES:      p. 271-274
 ❹  CALL NUMBER:     916.751043 Wi
```

Apply the Skill

Turn to Chapter 10, "Western Europe: Land and History," and find a topic that interests you, such as the Gulf Stream, the history of the Roman Republic, or Greek philosophy. Use the SUBJECT search on an electronic card catalog to find books about your topic. Make a bibliography of books about the subject. Be sure to include the author, title, city, publisher, and date of publication for all the books in your bibliography.

Create a Database

A **database** is a collection of data, or information, that is organized so you can find and retrieve information on a specific topic quickly and easily. Once a computerized database is set up, you can search it to find specific information without going through the entire database. The database will provide a list of all information in the database related to your topic. Understanding how to use a database will help you learn how to create one.

The chart below is a database for famous mountains in the Eastern Hemisphere. Use the steps listed below to help you understand and use the database.

Skillbuilder Handbook

Learn the Skill

Step ❶ Identify the topic of the database. The keywords, or most important words, in this title are "Mountains" and "Eastern Hemisphere." These words were used to begin the research for this database.

Step ❷ Identify the kind of data you need to enter in your database. These will be the column headings of your database. The key words "Mountain," "Location," "Height," and "Interesting Facts" were chosen to focus the research.

Step ❸ Identify the entries included under each heading.

Step ❹ Use the database to help you find information quickly. For example, in this database you could search for "Mountains over 28,000 feet" to find a list of famous mountains that are more than 28,000 feet tall.

❶ FAMOUS MOUNTAINS OF THE EASTERN HEMISPHERE			
❷ MOUNTAIN	LOCATION	HEIGHT ABOVE SEA LEVEL (FEET)	INTERESTING FACTS
❸ Dhaulagiri	Nepal	26,810	Name means "White Mountain"
Everest	Border of Nepal and China	❹ 29,035	Tallest mountain in the world
Fuji	Japan	12,388	Considered sacred by many Japanese
K2	Pakistan	❹ 28,250	Second tallest mountain in the world
Khan-Tengri	Border of China and Kyrgyzstan	22,940	Pyramid-shaped mountain known as "Lord of the Sky"
Xixabangma Feng (formerly Gosainthan)	China	26,291	Related to many Hindu myths of Shiva

Apply the Skill

Create a database of Latin American countries that shows the name of each country, its location, its land area, and its population. Use the information on pages 144–147, "Data File," to provide the data. Use a format like the one above for your database.

Use the Internet

The **Internet** is a computer network that connects to universities, libraries, news organizations, government agencies, businesses, and private individuals throughout the world. Each location on the Internet has a website with its own address, or URL (Universal Resource Locator). With a computer connected to the Internet, you can reach the websites of many organizations and services. The international collection of websites, known as the World Wide Web, is a good source of up-to-date information about current events and research on subjects in geography.

The website below shows helpful links for *World Cultures and Geography*. Use the steps listed below to help you understand how to use the website.

Learn the Skill

Step 1 Go to a website. For example, type http://www.eduplace.com/kids/hmss05/ in the box at the top of the screen and press ENTER (or RETURN). The website will appear on your screen. Then click on the link for the student. A new page on the website will appear.

Step 2 Explore the links on the right side of the screen. Click on any one of the links to find out more about a specific subject. These links take you to other pages on this website. Some pages include links to related information that can be found at other places on the Internet.

Step 3 When using the Internet for research, you should confirm the information you find. Websites set up by universities, government agencies, and reputable news sources are more reliable than other sources. You can often find information about the creator of a site by looking for copyright information.

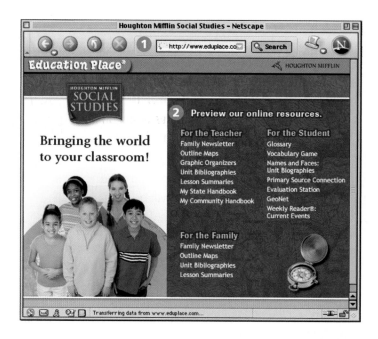

Apply the Skill

Turn to Chapter 6, Lesson 1, "Physical Geography." Read the lesson and make a list of maps you would like to research. If you have Internet access, go to www.eduplace.com/kids/hmss05/. There you will find links that provide more outline maps.

Create a Multimedia Presentation

Movies, CD-ROMs, television, and computer software are different kinds of media. **To create a multimedia presentation,** you need to collect information in different media and organize it into one presentation.

The illustration below shows students using computers to create a multimedia presentation. Use the steps listed below to help you create your own multimedia presentation.

Learn the Skill

Step ❶ Identify the topic of your presentation and decide which media are best for an effective presentation. For example, you may want to use video or photographic images to show the dry character of a desert. Or you may want to use CDs or audiotapes to provide music or to make sounds that go with your presentations, such as the sounds of a camel.

Step ❷ Research the topic in a variety of sources. Images, text, props, and background music should reflect the region and the historical period of your topic.

Step ❸ Write the script for the presentation and then record it using a microphone and an audiotape. You could use a narrator and characters' voices to tell the story. Primary sources are an excellent source for script material.

Step ❹ Videotape the presentation or create it on your computer. Having the presentation as a file on your computer will preserve it for future viewing and allow you to show it to different groups of people. It will also allow you to make changes, if you need to.

Apply the Skill

Turn to Chapter 11, "The Growth of New Ideas." Choose a topic from the chapter and use the steps listed to the left to create a multimedia presentation about it.

Glossary

A

absolute location *n.* the exact spot on Earth where a place is found. (p. 31)

acid rain *n.* rain or snow that carries air pollutants to Earth. (p. 387)

alliance (uh LY uhns) *n.* an agreement among people or nations to unite for a common cause and to help any alliance member that is attacked. (p. 337)

armed neutrality *n.* a policy by which a country maintains military forces but does not take sides in the conflicts of other nations. (p. 386)

B

bilingual *adj.* able to speak two languages. (p. 125)

Bill of Rights *n.* ten amendments to the U.S. Constitution that list specific freedoms guaranteed to every U.S. citizen. (p. 90)

C

capitalism *n.* an economic system in which the factories and businesses that make and sell goods are privately owned and the owners make the decisions about what goods to produce. (p. 318)

cartographer *n.* a person who makes maps. (p. 38)

censorship *n.* the outlawing of materials that contain certain information. (p. 400)

chinampa (chee NAHM pah) *n.* a floating garden on which the Aztec grew crops. (p. 158)

circumnavigate *v.* to sail completely around. (p. 312)

citizen *n.* a legal member of a country. (p. 16)

citizenship *n.* the status of a citizen, which includes certain duties and rights. (p. 87)

city-state *n.* a central city and its surrounding villages, which together follow the same law, have one form of government, and share language, religious beliefs, and ways of life. (p. 276)

climate *n.* the typical weather of a region over a long period. (p. 74)

coalition government *n.* a government formed by political parties joining together. (p. 365)

Cold War *n.* after World War II, a period of political noncooperation between the members of NATO and the Warsaw Pact nations, during which these countries refused to trade or cooperate with each other. (p. 348)

collective farm *n.* a government-owned farm that employs large numbers of workers, often in Communist countries. (p. 347)

colonialism *n.* a system by which a country maintains colonies outside its borders. (p. 332)

Columbian Exchange *n.* the exchange of goods between Europe and its colonies in North and South America. (p. 161)

Communism *n.* an economic and political system in which property is owned collectively and labor is organized in a way that is supposed to benefit all people. (p. 213)

competition *n.* the rivalry among businesses to sell the most goods to consumers and make the greatest profit. (p. 99)

Constitution *n.* the document that is the foundation for all U.S. laws and the framework for the U.S. government. (p. 89)

constitutional amendment *n.* a formal change or addition to the U.S. Constitution. (p. 90)

constitutional monarchy *n.* a government ruled by a king or queen whose power is determined by the nation's constitution and laws. (p. 117)

consumer *n.* a person who uses goods or services. (p. 99)

continent *n.* a landmass above water on Earth. (p. 30)

criollo (kree AW yaw) *n.* a person born in Mexico whose parents were born in Spain. (p. 172)

Crusades *n.* a series of military expeditions led by Western European Christians in the 11th, 12th, and 13th centuries to reclaim control of the Holy Lands from the Muslims. (p. 302)

culture *n.* the beliefs, customs, laws, art, and ways of living that a group of people share. (p. 18)

culture region *n.* an area of the world in which many people share similar beliefs, history, and languages. (p. 19)

currency *n.* money used as a form of exchange. (p. 372)

czar (zahr) *n.* in Russia, an emperor. (p. 321)

D

deforestation *n.* the process of cutting and clearing away trees from a forest. (p. 153)

democracy *n.* a government that receives its power from the people. (p. 87)

departamento (deh pahr tah MEHN taw) *n.* a Guatemalan state. (p. 218)

dependency *n.* a place governed by or closely connected with a country that it is not officially part of. (p. 200)

deposed *v.* removed from power. (p. 358)

détente (day TAHNT) *n.* a relaxing of tensions between nations. (p. 359)

dictator *n.* a person who has complete control over a country's government. (p. 203)

dissident *n.* a person who openly disagrees with a government's policies. (p. 400)

distribution *n.* the process of moving products to their markets. (p. 187)

diversify *v.* to conduct business activities in a variety of industries. (p. 207)

dual monarchy *n.* a form of government in which one ruler governs two nations. (p. 333)

E

economic indicator *n.* a measure that shows how a country's economy is doing. (p. 237)

economics *n.* the study of how resources are managed in the production, exchange, and use of goods and services. (p. 17)

economy *n.* the system by which business owners in a region use productive resources to provide goods and services that satisfy people's wants. (p. 76)

ejido (eh HEE daw) *n.* in Mexico, a community farm owned by the people of a village together. (p. 181)

El Niño (ehl NEE nyaw) *n.* a current in the Pacific Ocean that results from changes in air pressure and that causes changes in weather patterns. (p. 154)

empire *n.* a nation or group of territories ruled by an emperor. (p. 288)

encomienda (ehn kaw MYEHN dah) *n.* a system that the rulers of Spain established in Mexico, under which Spanish men received a Native American village to oversee and gain tribute from. (p. 172)

equal opportunity *n.* a guarantee that government and private institutions will not discriminate against people on the basis of factors such as race, religion, age, gender, or disability. (p. 86)

erosion *n.* the process by which environmental factors, such as wind, rivers, and rain, wear away soil and stone. (p. 67)

ethnic cleansing *n.* the organized killing of members of an ethnic group or groups. (p. 367)

euro *n.* the common unit of currency used by European Union countries. (p. 372)

European Community *n.* an association developed after World War II to promote economic unity among the countries of Western Europe. (p. 390)

European Union (EU) *n.* an economic and political grouping of countries in Western Europe. (p. 371)

export *n.* a product traded with or sold to another country. (p. 122)

factor of production *n.* one of the elements needed for production of goods or services to occur. (p. 97)

fascism (FASH ihz uhm) *n.* a political philosophy that promotes a strong, central government controlled by the military and led by a powerful dictator. (p. 339)

federal government *n.* a national government. (p. 91)

feudalism *n.* in medieval Europe, a political and economic system in which lords gave land to less powerful nobles, called vassals, in return for which the vassals agreed to provide various services to the lords. (p. 294)

fiesta *n.* a holiday celebrated by a village or town, with events such as parades, games, and feasts. (p. 195)

First Nations *n.* in Canada, a group of descendants of the first settlers of North America, who came from Asia. (p. 113)

fjord (fyawrd) *n.* a long, narrow, deep inlet of the sea located between steep cliffs. (p. 271)

Francophone *n.* a French-speaking person. (p. 126)

free enterprise/market economy *n.* an economy that allows business owners to compete in the market with little government interference. (p. 98)

free-trade zone *n.* an area in which goods can move across borders without being taxed. (p. 237)

GDP *n.* gross domestic product, or the total value of the goods and services produced in a country during a given time period. (p. 98)

geography *n.* the study of people, places, and the environment. (p. 15)

glacier *n.* a thick sheet of ice that moves slowly across land. (p. 66)

globalization *n.* the spreading of an idea, product, or technology around the world. (p. 106)

government *n.* the people and groups within a society that have the authority to make laws, to make sure they are carried out, and to settle disagreements about them. (p. 16)

guerrilla warfare *n.* nontraditional military tactics by small groups involving surprise attacks. (p. 249)

guild *n.* a business association created by people working in the same industry to protect their common interests and maintain standards within the industry. (p. 296)

hacienda *n.* in Spanish-speaking countries, a big farm or ranch. (p. 180)

hieroglyph *n.* a picture or symbol used in hieroglyphics. (p. 157)

history *n.* a record of the past. (p. 15)

Holocaust *n.* the organized killing of European Jews and others by the Nazis during World War II. (p. 339)

hydroelectricity *n.* electrical power generated by water. (p. 387)

immigrant *n.* a person who comes to a country to take up residence. (p. 84)

imperialism *n.* the practice of one country controlling the government and economy of another country or territory. (p. 312)

import *n.* a product brought into a country through trade or sale. (p. 122)

impressionism *n.* a style of art that creates an impression of a scene rather than a strictly realistic picture. (p. 391)

Industrial Revolution *n.* a period of change beginning in the late 18th century, during which goods began to be manufactured by power-driven machines. (p. 317)

industry *n.* any area of economic activity. (p. 122)

inflation *n.* a continuing increase in the price of goods and services, or a continuing decrease in the capability of money to buy goods and services. (p. 243)

interdependence *n.* the economic, political, and social dependence of culture regions on one another. (p. 20)

Iron Curtain *n.* a political barrier that isolated the peoples of Eastern Europe after World War II, restricting their ability to travel outside the region. (p. 344)

labor force *n.* a pool of available workers. (p. 317)

ladino (lah DEE noh) *n.* a person of mixed European and Native American ancestry. (p. 201)

landform *n.* a feature of Earth's surface, such as a mountain, valley, or plateau. (p. 66)

latitude *n.* a measure of distance north or south of the equator. (p. 31)

limited government *n.* government in which the powers of the leaders are limited. (p. 90)

longitude *n.* a measure of distance east or west of a line called the prime meridian. (p. 31)

malnutrition *n.* poor nutrition, usually from not eating the right foods, which can result in poor health. (p. 215)

manorialism *n.* a social system in which peasants worked on a lord's land and supplied him with food in exchange for his protection of them. (p. 294)

map projection *n.* one of the different ways of showing Earth's curved surface on a flat map. (p. 39)

maquiladora (mah kee lah DAW rah) *n.* in Mexico, a factory that imports duty-free parts from the United States to make products that it then exports back across the border. (p. 188)

market economy See **free enterprise/market economy.**

medieval (mee dee EE vuhl) *adj.* relating to the period of history between the fall of the Roman Empire and the beginning of the modern world, often dated from 476 to 1453. (p. 292)

mestizo (mehs TEE saw) *n.* a person of mixed European and Native American ancestry. (p. 172)

migrate *v.* to move from one area in order to settle in another. (p. 33)

mulatto (mu LAT oh) *n.* a person of mixed African and European ancestry. (p. 201)

multiculturalism *n.* an acceptance of many cultures instead of just one. (p. 114)

national identity *n.* a sense of belonging to a nation. (p. 125)

nationalism *n.* strong pride in one's nation or ethnic group. (p. 330)

nationalize *v.* to establish government control of a service or industry. (p. 189)

NATO (NAY toh) *n.* the North Atlantic Treaty Organization, a defense alliance formed in 1949, with the countries of Western Europe, Canada, and the United States agreeing to defend one another if attacked. (p. 340)

oasis *n.* a region in a desert that is fertile because it is near a river or spring. (p. 247)

oligarchy (AHL ih gahr kee) *n.* a government in which a few powerful individuals rule. (p. 276)

ombudsman *n.* a Swedish official who protects citizens' rights and ensures that the courts and civil service follow the law. (p. 385)

one-party system *n.* a system in which there is only one political party and only one candidate to choose from for each government position. (p. 345)

P

Pan-American *adj.* relating to all of the Americas. (p. 233)

Parliament *n.* Canada's national lawmaking body. (p. 118)

parliamentary republic *n.* a republic whose head of government, usually a prime minister, is the leader of the political party that has the most members in the parliament. (p. 365)

patrician (puh TRIHSH uhn) *n.* in ancient Rome, a member of a wealthy, landowning family that claimed to be able to trace its roots back to the founding of Rome. (p. 287)

patriotism *n.* love for one's country. (p. 88)

peninsula *n.* a body of land surrounded by water on three sides. (p. 271)

peninsular (peh neen soo LAHR) *n.* a person who was born in Spain but who lived in Mexico after the Spanish took control. (p. 172)

philosopher *n.* a person who studies and thinks about why the world is the way it is. (p. 278)

plain *n.* a large flat area of land that usually does not have many trees. (p. 271)

plebeian (plih BEE uhn) *n.* a common citizen of ancient Rome. (p. 287)

polis *n.* the central city of a city-state. (p. 276)

political process *n.* legal activities through which a citizen influences public policy. (p. 88)

precipitation *n.* moisture that falls to Earth, such as rain or snow. (p. 74)

prime minister *n.* in a parliamentary democracy, the leader of the cabinet and often also of the executive branch. (p. 118)

private property rights *n.* the right of individuals to own land or industry. (p. 357)

privatization *n.* the process of replacing community ownership with individual, or private, ownership. (p. 187)

profit *n.* the money that remains after the costs of producing a product are paid. (p. 99)

propaganda (prahp uh GAN duh) *n.* material designed to spread certain beliefs. (p. 356)

puppet government *n.* a government that is controlled by an outside force. (p. 345)

R

Reformation *n.* a 16th-century movement to change practices within the Roman Catholic Church. (p. 306)

refugee *n.* a person who flees a country because of war, disaster, or persecution. (p. 115)

relative location *n.* the location of one place in relation to other places. (p. 31)

Renaissance *n.* an era of creativity and learning in Western Europe from the 14th century to the 16th century. (p. 303)

republic *n.* a form of government in which people rule through elected representatives. (p. 286)

reunification *n.* the uniting again of parts. (p. 395)

river system *n.* a network that includes a major river and its tributaries. (p. 67)

rural *adj.* of the countryside. (p. 194)

S

scarcity *n.* a word economists use to describe the conflict between people's desires and limited resources. (p. 17)

Scientific Revolution *n.* a period of great scientific change and discovery during the 16th and 17th centuries. (p. 316)

secede *v.* to withdraw from a political union, such as a nation. (p. 382)

Senate *n.* the assembly of elected representatives that was the most powerful ruling body of the Roman Republic. (p. 286)

separatist *n.* a person who wants to separate from a body to which he or she belongs, such as a church or nation. (p. 119)

single-product economy *n.* an economy that depends on just one product for the majority of its income. (p. 206)

skerry *n.* a small island. (p. 387)

socialism *n.* an economic system in which businesses and industries are owned collectively or by the government. (p. 390)

standard of living *n.* a measure of quality of life. (p. 373)

sugar cane *n.* a plant from which sugar is made. (p. 206)

tariff *n.* a fee imposed by a government on imported or exported goods. (p. 372)

technology *n.* tools and equipment made through scientific discoveries. (p. 106)

thematic map *n.* a map that focuses on a specific idea or theme. (p. 40)

tourism *n.* the business of helping people travel on vacations. (p. 189)

transportation barrier *n.* a geographic feature that prevents or slows transportation. (p. 124)

transportation corridor *n.* a path that makes transportation easier. (p. 123)

tributary *n.* a stream or river that flows into a larger river. (p. 153)

Tropical Zone *n.* the region of the world that lies between the latitudes 23°27′ north and 23°27′ south. (p. 154)

unlimited government *n.* a government in which the leaders have almost absolute power. (p. 322)

urban *adj.* of the city. (p. 194)

urbanization *n.* the movement of people from the countryside to cities. (p. 238)

value *n.* a principle or ideal by which people live. (p. 104)

vegetation *n.* plant life, such as trees, plants, and grasses. (p. 74)

weather *n.* the state of Earth's atmosphere at a given time and place. (p. 74)

Spanish Glossary

A

absolute location [ubicación absoluta] *s.* lugar exacto donde se halla un lugar en la Tierra. (pág. 31)

acid rain [lluvia ácida] *s.* lluvia o nieve que lleva sustancias contaminantes a la Tierra. (pág. 387)

alliance [alianza] *s.* acuerdo de unión entre pueblos o naciones por una causa común y de ayuda mutua en caso de que uno sea atacado. (pág. 337)

armed neutrality [neutralidad armada] *s.* política mediante la cual un país mantiene fuerzas armadas pero no participa en conflictos de otras naciones. (pág. 386)

B

bilingual [bilingüe] *adj.* que puede hablar dos idiomas. (pág. 125)

Bill of Rights [Declaración de Derechos] *s.* las diez enmiendas a la Constitución de los Estados Unidos que enumeran libertades específicas garantizadas a todos los ciudadanos estadounidenses. (pág. 90)

C

capitalism [capitalismo] *s.* sistema económico en el cual las empresas y comercios que fabrican y venden productos y mercancías son de propiedad privada; los dueños de dichas empresas y comercios deciden lo que desean producir y vender. (pág. 318)

cartographer [cartógrafo] *s.* persona que hace mapas. (pág. 38)

censorship [censura] *s.* prohibición de materiales que contienen cierta información. (pág. 400)

chinampa *s.* huerta flotante en la que los aztecas sembraban sus cultivos. (pág. 158)

circumnavigate [circunnavegar] *v.* dar la vuelta alrededor de algo en una nave. (pág. 312)

citizen [ciudadano] *s.* habitante legal de un país. (pág. 16)

citizenship [ciudadanía] *s.* estado de un ciudadano que incluye derechos y obligaciones. (pág. 87)

city-state [ciudad-estado] *s.* ciudad central y sus aldeas aledañas que acatan las mismas leyes, tienen una sola forma de gobierno y comparten una lengua, creencias religiosas y estilos de vida. (pág. 276)

climate [clima] *s.* condición típica de la atmósfera en determinada región. (pág. 74)

coalition government [gobierno de coalición] *s.* gobierno formado por la unión de partidos políticos. (pág. 365)

Cold War [Guerra Fría] *s.* período político posterior a la Segunda Guerra Mundial, caracterizado por la falta de cooperación y relaciones comerciales entre los países miembros de la OTAN y las naciones del Pacto de Varsovia. (pág. 348)

collective farm [granja colectiva] *s.* granja que pertenece al gobierno, que emplea a gran número de trabajadores generalmente en países comunistas. (pág. 347)

colonialism [colonialismo] *s.* sistema mediante el cual un país mantiene colonias en otras partes del mundo. (pág. 332)

Columbian Exchange [Intercambio Colombino] *s.* intercambio de mercancías entre Europa y sus colonias en América. (pág. 161)

Communism [Comunismo] *s.* sistema político y económico en el cual la propiedad es colectiva y la actividad laboral es organizada de manera de beneficiar a todos los individuos. (pág. 213)

competition [competencia] *s.* rivalidad entre empresas por vender la mayor cantidad de productos y mercaderías a los consumidores y por obtener el mayor beneficio. (pág. 99)

Constitution [Constitución] *s.* documento que fundamenta todas las leyes del gobierno de Estados Unidos y constituye su marco jurídico. (pág. 89)

constitutional amendment [enmienda constitucional] *s.* cambio formal a la constitución de los Estados Unidos. (pág. 90)

constitutional monarchy [monarquía constitucional] *s.* gobierno encabezado por un rey o reina, cuyo poder está determinado por la constitución y leyes de la nación. (pág. 117)

consumer [consumidor] *s.* persona que usa productos o servicios. (pág. 99)

continent [continente] *s.* masa continental sobre agua en la Tierra. (pág. 30)

criollo s. persona nacida en México cuyos padres provienen de España. (pág. 172)

Crusades [Las Cruzadas] *s.* serie de expediciones militares dirigidas por Cristianos de Europa occidental en los siglos XI, XII y XIII, para apoderarse de nuevo de las Tierras Santas, en poder de los musulmanes. (pág. 302)

culture [cultura] *s.* conjunto de creencias, costumbres, leyes, formas artísticas y de vida compartidas por un grupo de personas. (pág. 18)

culture region [región cultural] *s.* territorio donde muchas personas comparten creencias, historia y lenguas similares. (pág. 19)

currency [moneda] *s.* sistema que sirve para medir el valor de las cosas que se intercambian. (pág. 372)

czar [zar] *s.* emperador ruso. (pág. 321)

deforestation [deforestación] *s.* proceso mediante el cual se cortan árboles y se van eliminando bosques. (pág. 153)

democracy [democracia] *s.* sistema de gobierno mediante el cual los gobernantes reciben el poder del pueblo. (pág. 87)

departamento s. nombre que reciben los estados en Guatemala. (pág. 218)

dependency [territorio dependiente] *s.* lugar gobernado o que está estrechamente conectado con un país del cual no forma parte. (pág. 200)

deposed [depuesto] *v.* removido del poder. (pág. 358)

détente [distensión] *s.* disminución de la tensión entre países. (pág. 359)

dictator [dictador] *s.* persona que tiene el control absoluto del gobierno de un país. (pág. 203)

dissident [disidente] *s.* persona que abiertamente muestra desacuerdo con la política de un gobierno. (pág. 400)

distribution [distribución] *s.* proceso mediante el cual se transporta la mercancía a los mercados. (pág. 187)

diversify [diversificar] *v.* llevar a cabo actividades comerciales en una variedad de industrias. (pág. 207)

dual monarchy [monarquía dual] *s.* gobierno en que un solo jefe gobierna dos naciones. (pág. 333)

economic indicator [indicador económico] *s.* medida que muestra el estado de la economía de un país. (pág. 237)

economics [economía] *s.* estudio del uso de los recursos naturales y del modo de producción, intercambio y utilización de los productos, mercaderías y servicios. (pág. 17)

economy [economía] *s.* sistema de administrar recursos de producción en una región con el fin de proveer productos y servicios que satisfagan las necesidades humanas. (pág. 76)

ejido s. granja comunitaria en México que pertenece colectivamente a los habitantes de un pueblo o localidad. (pág. 181)

El Niño *s.* corriente del Océano Pacífico que surge de los cambios en la presión atmosférica y que causa cambios meteorológicos. (pág. 154)

empire [imperio] *s.* nación o conjunto de territorios gobernados por un emperador. (pág. 288)

encomienda *s.* sistema establecido en México por los gobernantes españoles mediante el cual los españoles controlaban comunidades indígenas y recaudaban tributo. (pág. 172)

equal opportunity [igualdad de oportunidades] *s.* garantía de que el gobierno e instituciones privadas no discriminarán en contra de ciertas personas por motivos de raza, religión, edad o sexo. (pág. 86)

erosion [erosión] *s.* desgaste del terreno y suelo producido por factores ambientales tales como el viento, la lluvia y los ríos. (pág. 67)

ethnic cleansing [limpieza étnica] *s.* matanza sistemática (genocidio) de uno o varios grupos étnicos que conforman una minoría. (pág. 367)

euro [euro] *s.* unidad monetaria de los países miembros de la Unión Europea. (pág. 372)

European Community [Comunidad Europea] *s.* asociación creada después de la Segunda Guerra Mundial para promover la unidad económica entre los países de Europa occidental. (pág. 390)

European Union [Unión Europea] *s.* asociación económica y política de países de Europa occidental. (pág. 371)

export [exportación] *s.* mercadería que se vende a otro país. (pág. 122)

factor of production [factor de producción] *s.* elemento necesario para producir mercaderías y ofrecer servicios. (pág. 97)

fascism [fascismo] *s.* filosofía que promueve un gobierno centralista fuerte, controlado por el ejército y dirigido por un dictador poderoso. (pág. 339)

federal government [gobierno federal] *s.* gobierno nacional. (pág. 91)

feudalism [feudalismo] *s.* sistema político y económico de la Europa medieval en el que los señores feudales repartían tierras a miembros de la nobleza menos poderosos, llamados vasallos, quienes, a cambio de éstas, se comprometían a brindar varios servicios a los señores feudales. (pág. 294)

fiesta *s.* feriado celebrado por una comunidad o pueblo, con desfiles, juegos y banquetes. (pág. 195)

First Nations [Primeras Naciónes] *s.* nombre que reciben en Canadá los descendientes de los primeros pobladores en Norteamérica que provenían de Asia. (pág. 113)

fjord [fiordo] *s.* entrada larga y estrecha del mar formada entre acantilados abruptos. (pág. 271)

Francophone [Francófono] *s.* persona que habla Francés. (pág. 126)

free enterprise/market economy [librecambismo/economía de libre mercado] *s.* economía que permite a empresarios y comerciantes competir en el mercado con poca interferencia del gobierno. (pág. 98)

free-trade zone [zona de libre comercio] *s.* área en la que tanto personas como mercaderías pueden circular más allá de las fronteras sin que esta actividad sea gravada con impuestos. (pág. 237)

GDP [PIB, Producto Interno Bruto] *s.* valor total de los productos y servicios producidos en un país durante un período determinado. (pág. 98)

geography [geografía] *s.* estudio de los pueblos, lugares y el medio ambiente. (pág. 15)

glacier [glaciar] *s.* espesas formaciones de hielo que se mueven lentamente por la tierra. (pág. 66)

globalization [globalización] *s.* difusión de una idea, producto o tecnología por todo el mundo. (pág. 106)

government [gobierno] *s.* los individuos y grupos en una sociedad que tienen la autoridad de crear leyes y hacerlas cumplir, y de resolver desacuerdos que puedan surgir con respecto a ellas. (pág. 16)

guerrilla warfare [guerrilla warfare] *s.* tácticas militares no tradicionales llevadas a cabo por grupos pequeños que realizan ataques sorpresivos. (pág. 249)

guild [gremio] *s.* asociación creada por personas que trabajan en una misma industria, con el fin de proteger sus intereses comunes y mantener ciertos criterios y principios aplicables a la industria. (pág. 296)

hacienda s. en países hispanos, finca o granja de gran tamaño. (pág. 180)

hieroglyph [jeroglífico] *s.* dibujo y símbolo de la escritura jeroglífica. (pág. 157)

history [historia] *s.* un registro de los acontecimientos del pasado. (pág. 15)

Holocaust [Holocausto] *s.* matanza sistemática (genocidio) de los judíos europeos y otros por el Partido Nazi durante la Segunda Guerra Mundial. (pág. 339)

hydroelectricity [electricidad hidráulica] *s.* energía eléctrica producida por el agua. (pág. 387)

immigrant [inmigrante] *s.* persona que llega a un país y allí se establece. (pág. 84)

imperialism [imperialismo] *s.* práctica mediante la cual un país controla el gobierno y la economía de otro país o territorio. (pág. 312)

import [importación] *s.* mercadería y producto que se compra del extranjero. (pág. 122)

impressionism [impresionismo] *s.* estilo de arte que crea una impresión de algo en lugar de una obra con características concretas. (pág. 391)

Industrial Revolution [Revolución Industrial] *s.* período de cambio en el siglo XVIII que dio lugar a la fabricación de productos por máquinas. (pág. 317)

industry [industria] *s.* sector o rama de actividad económica. (pág. 122)

inflation [inflación] *s.* aumento continuo del precio de mercaderías y servicios, o disminución continua de la capacidad de la moneda de comprar mercaderías y servicios. (pág. 243)

interdependence [interdependencia] *s.* dependencia económica, política y social que mantienen las sociedades de diversas regiones culturales. (pág. 20)

Iron Curtain [Cortina de Hierro] *s.* barrera política que aisló los países de Europa del Este luego de la Segunda Guerra Mundial, limitando la capacidad de movimiento y tránsito fuera de esta región. (pág. 344)

labor force [fuerza laboral] *s.* trabajadores disponibles. (pág. 317)

ladino s. persona de descendencia mixta, con sangre europea e indígena. (pág. 201)

landform [accidente geográfico] *s.* característica del suelo o terreno, como montañas, valles y mesetas. (pág. 66)

latitude [latitud] *s.* distancia norte-sur con relación al ecuador, de la superficie terrestre. (pág. 31)

limited government [gobierno limitado] *s.* gobierno en que los gobernantes tienen poderes limitados. (pág. 90)

longitude [longitud] *s.* distancia este-oeste de un punto de la Tierra, a partir de la línea inicial llamada primer meridiano (meridiano de Greenwich). (pág. 31)

malnutrition [desnutrición] *s.* mala nutrición debida a la falta de alimentos nutritivos que puede causar mala salud. (pág. 215)

manorialism [régimen señorial] *s.* sistema social en el que campesinos trabajan las tierras de un señor, a cambio de protección y seguridad. (pág. 294)

map projection [proyección cartográfica] *s.* una de las diversas maneras de mostrar la curvatura de la Tierra en una superficie plana. (pág. 39)

maquiladora s. fábrica en México que importa partes sin arancel aduanero de los Estados Unidos para fabricar productos que luego envía de vuelta a través de la frontera. (pág. 188)

market economy Ver **free enterprise/market economy.**

medieval [medieval] *adj.* que pertenece al período de la historia comprendido entre la caída del Imperio romano y el comienzo del mundo moderno, aproximadamente desde 476 a 1453. (pág. 292)

mestizo s. persona de descendencia mixta, con sangre europea e indígena. (pág. 172)

migrate [migrar] *v.* irse de un área para establecerse en otra. (pág. 33)

mulatto [mulato] *s.* persona con descendencia mixta, de sangre europea y africana. (pág. 201)

multiculturalism [multiculturalismo] *s.* la aceptación de muchas culturas en vez de una solamente. (pág. 114)

national identity [identidad nacional] *s.* sentimiento de pertenencia a una nación. (pág. 125)

nationalism [nacionalismo] *s.* intenso orgullo por el país o grupo étnico propio. (pág. 330)

nationalize [nacionalizar] *v.* pasar al control gubernamental un servicio o industria. (pág. 189)

NATO [OTAN, Organización del Tratado del Atlántico Norte] *s.* alianza de defensa que agrupa a los países de Europa occidental, Canadá y Estados Unidos, que acuerdan la defensa común en caso de ataque. (pág. 340)

oasis [oasis] *s.* región fértil en un desierto que se formó alrededor de un río o manantial. (pág. 247)

oligarchy [oligarquía] *s.* gobierno de sólo unos pocos individuos poderosos. (pág. 276)

ombudsman [defensor del pueblo] *s.* funcionario del gobierno sueco que protege los derechos de los ciudadanos y asegura que los tribunales y la administración pública cumplan con la ley. (pág. 385)

one-party system [sistema monopartidista] *s.* sistema donde sólo se puede votar por un partido político y por un candidato para cada puesto de gobierno. (pág. 345)

Pan-American [Panamericano] *adj.* relativo a todas las Américas. (pág. 233)

Parliament [Parlamento] *s.* cuerpo legislativo nacional de Canadá. (pág. 118)

parliamentary republic [república parlamentaria] *s.* república cuyo jefe de estado, en general un primer ministro, es el líder del partido político que tiene la mayoría de representantes en el parlamento. (pág. 365)

patrician [patricio] *s.* miembro de familia adinerada y hacendada en la antigua Roma, que afirmaba que sus orígenes se remontan a la época de la fundación de Roma. (pág. 287)

patriotism [patriotismo] *s.* amor por el país propio. (pág. 88)

peninsula [península] *s.* territorio rodeado de agua en tres de sus lados. (pág. 271)

peninsular *s.* persona que nació en España pero vivió en México luego de la conquista de los españoles. (pág. 172)

philosopher [filósofo] *s.* persona que estudia y piensa sobre el mundo y su naturaleza. (pág. 278)

plain [llanura] *s.* superficie extensa y plana que suele no tener muchos árboles. (pág. 271)

plebeian [plebeyo] *s.* ciudadano corriente (sin título de nobleza) en la antigua Roma. (pág. 287)

polis [polis] *s.* ciudad central de una ciudad estado. (pág. 276)

political process [proceso político] *s.* actividades permitidas por la ley mediante las cuales el ciudadano influye en las políticas públicas. (pág. 88)

precipitation [precipitación] *s.* humedad como la lluvia o la nieve que cae a la Tierra. (pág. 74)

prime minister [primer ministro] *s.* en una democracia parlamentaria, líder del gabinete y frecuentemente de la administración ejecutiva. (pág. 118)

private property rights [derechos de propiedad privada] *s.* derechos individuales de ser propietario de bienes raíces, campos o industrias. (pág. 357)

privatization [privatización] *s.* proceso mediante el cual la propiedad que pertenece a la comunidad se convierte en propiedad privada o individual. (pág. 187)

profit [ganancia] *s.* dinero que sobra luego de pagar el costo de producir un producto. (pág. 99)

propaganda [propaganda] *s.* material cuyo objetivo es difundir ciertas creencias. (pág. 356)

puppet government [gobierno títere] *s.* gobierno que hace lo que le indica un poder exterior. (pág. 345)

Reformation [Reforma] *s.* movimiento del siglo XVI que se propuso cambiar las prácticas de la Iglesia Católica. (pág. 306)

refugee [refugiado] *s.* persona que huye de un país a raíz de una guerra, catástrofe, o porque es objeto de persecuciones. (pág. 115)

relative location [ubicación relativa] *s.* ubicación de un lugar en relación con otros. (pág. 31)

Renaissance [Renacimiento] *s.* período de creatividad y de aprendizaje en Europa occidental entre los siglos XIV y XVI. (pág. 303)

republic [república] *s.* forma de gobierno controlado por sus cuidadanos a través de representantes elegidos por los cuidadanos. (pág. 286)

reunification [reunificación] *s.* acción de unificar nuevamente las partes. (pág. 395)

river system [sistema fluvial] *s.* red que incluye ríos principales y sus tributarios. (pág. 67)

rural [rural] *adj.* que pertenece al campo. (pág. 194)

scarcity [escasez] *s.* palabra usada por los economistas para describir el conflicto que existe entre el deseo de los seres humanos y los recursos limitados para satisfacerlo. (pág. 17)

Scientific Revolution [Revolución Científica] *s.* período de grandes cambios científicos y descubrimientos durante los siglos XVI y XVII. (pág. 316)

secede [separarse] *v.* independizarse de una unidad política, como una nación. (pág. 382)

Senate [Senado] *s.* asamblea más poderosa de la República romana, cuyos representantes eran elegidos. (pág. 286)

separatist [separatista] *s.* persona que desea separarse del cuerpo al que pertenece, como la iglesia o la nación. (pág. 119)

single-product economy [economía de un solo producto] *s.* economía cuya mayor parte de los ingresos depende de un solo producto. (pág. 206)

skerry [arrecife] *s.* islote. (pág. 387)

socialism [socialismo] *s.* sistema económico en donde algunos negocios e industrias le pertenecen a una cooperativa o al gobierno. (pág. 390)

standard of living [nivel de vida] *s.* forma de medir la calidad de vida. (pág. 373)

sugar cane [caña de azúcar] *s.* planta de la que se extrae el azúcar. (pág. 206)

tariff [arancel aduanero] *s.* tarifa o suma de dinero impuesto por el gobierno en productos que se importan o exportan. (pág. 372)

technology [tecnología] *s.* herramientas o equipos que se crean a partir de ciertos descubrimientos. (pág. 106)

thematic map [mapa temático] *s.* mapa que se centra en una idea o tema particular. (pág. 40)

tourism [turismo] *s.* industria que estimula a la gente a viajar por placer. (pág. 189)

transportation barrier [barrera al transporte] *s.* obstáculo que impede el transporte o lo disminuye. (pág. 124)

transportation corridor [vía de transporte] *s.* camino que facilita el transporte. (pág. 123)

tributary [tributario] *s.* arroyo o río que confluye en otro río de mayor caudal. (pág. 153)

Tropical Zone [Zona Tropical] *s.* región del mundo comprendida entre las latitudes 23°27′ al norte y 23°27′ al sur. (pág. 154)

unlimited government [gobierno ilimitado] *s.* gobierno en el que las autoridades ejercen la mayor parte del poder. (pág. 322)

urban [urbano] *adj.* que pertenece a la ciudad. (pág. 194)

urbanization [urbanización] *s.* movimiento de personas del campo a la ciudad. (pág. 238)

value [valor] *s.* principio e ideal básico de las personas. (pág. 104)

vegetation [vegetación] *s.* conjunto de plantas, arbustos, árboles y hierbas. (pág. 74)

weather [tiempo] *s.* estado atmosférico cercano a la Tierra en un momento y lugar determinados. (pág. 74)

Index

D

Index

Acknowledgments

Unit Opener Quotes

Unit 1: Robert Frost; *The Gift Outright*, by Robert Frost, Henry Holt, 1961. **Unit 2:** Declaration of Independence, 1776. **Unit 3:** Oscar Arias Sanchez; *The New York Times*, December 11, 1987. **Unit 4:** Aristotle.

Text Credits

Chapter 4, page 94: "Coney" from *Subway Swinger* by Virginia Schonborg, copyright © 1970 by Virginia Schonborg. Used by permission of HarperCollins Publishers.

Chapter 4, page 94: "Knoxville, Tennessee" from *Black Feeling, Black Talk, Black Judgment* by Nikki Giovanni. Copyright 1968, 1970 by Nikki Giovanni. Reprinted by permission of HarperCollins Publishers Inc.

Chapter 4, page 95: "Scenic" from *Collected Poems, 1953–1993* by John Updike, copyright © 1993 by John Updike. Used by permission of Alfred A. Knopf, a division of Random House, Inc.

Chapter 9, page 238: "Chilean Earth" from *A Gabriela Mistral Reader*, translation copyright 1993 by Maria Giachetti. Reprinted by permission of White Pine Press.

Chapter 10, page 278: Quote by Herakleitos, translated by Guy Davenport, from *7 Greeks*, copyright © 1995 by Guy Davenport. Reprinted by Sales Territory: U.S./Canadian rights only.

Chapter 12, page 334: "The Giant's Causeway" from *Irish Fairy Tales and Legends* retold by Una Leavy. Copyright © 1996 by The Watts Publishing Group Ltd.

Map Credits

Maps by MAPQUEST.COM

Photography Credits

COVER (Mayan Temple) © Warren Marr/Panoramic Images. (Louvre Museum) © Nik Wheeler/CORBIS. (map) © Steve Gorton/DK Images. (compass) © HMCo./Michael Indresano. (leaves) Brand X Pictures. (Zapotec statuette) Museo Nacional de Antropologia, Mexico City. (spine) Museo Nacional de Antropologia, Mexico City. (backcover statue) © Connie Ricca/CORBIS. (backcover nickel) Courtesy of the United States Mint. **v** (t) © Photodisc/Getty Images. (b) © Angela Coppola/HMCo. **vi** (t) NASA/Roger Ressmeyer/CORBIS. (b) © Austrian Archives/CORBIS. **vii** (t) © Didier Dorval/Masterfile. (m) Terry Wild Studio. (b) © SuperStock. **viii** (t) Michel Zabe/Art Resource, New York. **ix** (t) © Marge George/Spectrum Stock. (b) Staffan Widstrand/CORBIS. **x** (t) Nimatallah/Art Resource, New York. (b) The Pierpont Morgan Library/Art Resource, New York. **xi** (t) Dave Bartruff/CORBIS. (m) © Premium Stock/CORBIS. (b) AFP/CORBIS. **xii** (t) NASA The Everett Collection. (b) © James Schwabel/Panoramic Images. **xiii** © Ken Karp/HMCo. **xiv** NASA. **xvii** Art Resource, New York.

UNIT 1

2-3 NASA. **4** (l) © Owen Franken/Stock Boston/ PictureQuest. (tr) Science Museum/Science and Society Picture Library, London. **12** (l) Thomas Hoepker/Magnum/PictureQuest. (r) Reuters New Media Inc./CORBIS. **13** (l) © Spencer Grant/Photo Edit. (r) Hulton Archive/Getty Images. **15** (l) Oliver Benn/Stone/GettyImages.(m) © Alon Reininger/Contact Press Images.(r) © Alex Farnsworth/The Image Works. **16** (t) Richard Drew/AP/ Wide World Photos. (b) © Jim West. **17** NASA/Roger Ressmeyer. **19** Brian A. Vikander/CORBIS. **21**(l)Dean Conger/CORBIS.(m) Chris Andrews Publications/CORBIS.(r) K. Gilham/Robert Harding Picture Library. **26** Picture Finders/eStock Photography/PictureQuest. **28** (l) NASA. **29** (l) The Mariner's Museum/CORBIS. **32** © Eastcott-Momatiuk/The Image Works. **34** David Muench/Stone/GettyImages. **42** (t) The Granger Collection, New York. (b) The Newberry Library/The Granger Collection, New York. **43** (t) Reproduced with permission of Garmin Corporation. **44** US Geographical Survey. **46** (l) David Muench/Stone/GettyImages. (r) © Owen Franken/Stock Boston/ PictureQuest.

UNIT 2

50-51 © Panoramic Images. **62** (l) © SuperStock. (r) Paul A. Souders/CORBIS. **63** (l) © Getty Images. (r) © Michael S. Yamashita/CORBIS. **64-65** James Randklev/CORBIS. **66** Bettmann/CORBIS. **67** © Paul A. Souders/CORBIS. **68** (l) © Didier Dorval/Masterfile. (r) Paul A. Souders/CORBIS. **70** European Space Agency. **71** European Space Agency. **70-71** NASA The Everett Collection. **72** Michael Melford/The Image Bank/GettyImages. **73** (t) Raymond Gehman/CORBIS. (b) David Reed/AP/Wide World Photos. **74** © Michael S. Yamashita/CORBIS. **76** © Phillip Gould/CORBIS. **78** © Suzanne & Nick Geary/Stone/Getty Images. **80** (l) James Randklev/CORBIS. (r) David Reed/AP/Wide World Photos. **82** (l) Joe Raedle/Newsmakers/Getty Images. **83** (l) Andrea Pistolesi/Getty Images. (r) European Space Agency. **84** The Granger Collection, New York. **87** Reuters NewMedia Inc./CORBIS. **88** AP/Wide World Photos. **90** (l) Art Resource, New York. (r) The Granger Collection, New York. **92** © Topham/The Image Works. **94** (t) Tony Freeman. (b) © Rafael Macia/Photo Researchers. **95** © Jim Corwin/Photo Researchers. **97** (l) Teri Bloom. (m) Digital Vision/Getty Images. (r) Kevin R. Morris/Bohemian Nomad PictureMakers/CORBIS. **98** © Monika Graff/The Image Works. **101** © Danny Lehman. **104** © Bettmann/CORBIS. **105** Terry Wild Studio. **107** © Eddie Adams/CORBIS Sygma. **108** (l) The Granger Collection, New York. (ml) The Granger Collection, New York. (mr) U.S. Treasury Department. (r) Terry Wild Studio. **110** (l) © Bill Brooks/Masterfile. (r) © Bettmann/CORBIS. **111** (l) Michael Melford/The Image Bank/GettyImages. (r) © Paul A. Souders/CORBIS. **112** The Granger Collection, New York. **113** © Kevin R. Morris/CORBIS. **114** Private Collection/Phillips, Fine Art Auctioneers, New York/The Bridgeman Art Library. **115** © James Schwabel/Panoramic Images. **117** © Bill Brooks/Masterfile. **118** © Bettmann/CORBIS. **119** RonPoling/Canadian Press/AP/Wide World Photos. **120** Yves Marcoux/Stone/Getty Images. **121** © Bettmann/CORBIS. **122** Alec Pytlowany/Masterfile. **124** The Granger Collection, New York. **125** © J. A. Kraulis/Masterfile. **126** © Carl & An Purcell/CORBIS. **127** Lee Snider/CORBIS. **128** © Rob Howard/CORBIS. **129** Archivision.com **130-133** Ken Karp/HMCo. **134** © James Schwabel/Panoramic Images. **136** (l) © James Schwabel/Panoramic Images. (ml) © Bill Brooks/Masterfile. (mr) The Granger Collection, New York. (r) © J. A. Kraulis/Masterfile.

UNIT 3

140-141 © Bill Pogue/Stone/GettyImages. **148** (l) Layne Kennedy/CORBIS. (r) Hervé Collart/CORBIS Sygma. **149** (l) © Richard A. Cooke/CORBIS. **150** AFP/CORBIS. **152** (t) Guido A. Rossi/The Image Bank/GettyImages. (b) © Stephen Frink/CORBIS. **153** © Galen Rowell/CORBIS. **157** (t) © Richard A. Cooke/CORBIS. (b) © Craig Lovell/Painet. **159** (t) Werner Forman Archive/Art Resource, New York. (b) Edwin Sulca Lagos. **160** Archivo Iconografico, S.A./ CORBIS. **161** Michel Zabe/Art Resource, New York. **164** © Kevin Schafer/CORBIS. **166** © AFP/CORBIS. **168** (l) Tom Bean/CORBIS. (r) © Danny Lehman/CORBIS. **169** (l) © Corbis Royalty Free. (r) © David Hiser/Stone/GettyImages. **170** (l) Erich Lessing/Art Resource, New York. (r) Cabacete [Helmet] (c. 1480). Private collection. Photograph courtesy of the Cleveland (Ohio) Museum of Art. **171** © David Hiser/Stone/GettyImages. **172** © Schalkwijk/Art Resource, New York. **174** © Greg Probst/CORBIS. **176** Cosmo Condina/Stone/GettyImages. **177** Gary S. Withey/Bruce Coleman/Picture Quest. **178** © Bettmann/CORBIS. **179** (l) The Granger Collection, New York. (r) Bettmann/CORBIS. **180** (l) Bettmann/CORBIS. (m) Bettmann/CORBIS. (r) Hulton Archive/Getty Images. **181** © Tom Bean/CORBIS. **184** © Time Life Pictures/Getty Images. **187** (l) © Robert Frerck/Stone/GettyImages. (r) © Annie Griffiths Belt/CORBIS. **188** (t) Danny Lehman. (b) Jose Welbers/Latin Focus.com. **190** ZSSD/Latin Focus.com. **191** © Robert Frerck/Stone/GettyImages. **192** (t) © Bettmann/CORBIS. (b) Schalkwijk/Art Resource, New York. **193** Peter Menzel/Stock Boston/PictureQuest. **194** © Danny Lehman/CORBIS. **195** Kal Muller/Woodfin Camp/PictureQuest. **196** (l) Schalkwijk/Art Resource, New York. (mr) © Annie Griffiths Belt/CORBIS. (r) © Danny Lehman/CORBIS. **198** (l) Sovfoto/Eastfoto/PictureQuest. (r) © Tim Page/CORBIS. **199** (l) © Gantner/CORBIS Sygma. (r) © Jan Butchofsky-Houser/CORBIS. **200** James Strachan/Stone/GettyImages. **202** (l) Ladino Reuters NewMedia Inc./CORBIS. (m) Ladino Reuters NewMedia Inc./CORBIS. (r) Ladino Martin Rogers/CORBIS. **203** Jeff Greenberg/eStock Photography/PictureQuest. **204** (l) © Bill Gentile/CORBIS. **205** (l) © Bill Ross/CORBIS. (r) Dave G. Houser/CORBIS. **206** © Topham/The Image Works. **208** AFP/CORBIS. **209** Suzanne Murphy-Larronde. **210** © Nik Wheeler/CORBIS. **211** Sovfoto/Eastfoto/PictureQuest. **212** (l) Richard Bickel/CORBIS. (r) Latin Focus.com. **214** (l) Latin Focus.com. (r) © AFP/ CORBIS. **215** © Jose Luis Pelaez/CORBIS. **217** Latin Focus.com. **218-219** © Jan Butchofsky-Houser/CORBIS. **219** (t) Martin Rogers/CORBIS. **220** © Photodisc/Getty Images. **224** © Jan Butchofsky-Houser/CORBIS. **226** (l) © The Image Works. (ml) Suzanne Murphy-Larronde. (mr) Sovfoto/Eastfoto/PictureQuest.(r) © Jan Butchofsky-Houser/CORBIS. **228** (l) © Bettmann/CORBIS. (r) © Eye Ubiquitous/CORBIS. **229** (r) Cory Langley. **230** The Granger Collection, New York. **232** (t) Christie's Images/CORBIS. **233** (t) © Bettmann/CORBIS. (b) © Richard Hamilton Smith/CORBIS. **235** © Yann Arthus-Bertrand/CORBIS. **236** L.B. Bastlan/DDB Stock Photo. **238** © CORBIS. **240-241** Victor Englebert. **241** (t) Tony Morrison/South American Pictures. (b) © HMCo. Archive. **242** © Eye Ubiquitous/CORBIS. **243** Les Stone/The Image Works. **244** David Wolf. **245** © Tony Scarpetta/HMCo. **246** (t) Reuters NewMedia Inc./CORBIS. (b) © Bettmann/CORBIS. **247** Cory Langley. **248** (t) © Charles and Josette Lenars/CORBIS. (b) Richard Hamilton Smith/CORBIS. **249** (l) Victor Engelbert. (r) © Moshe Shal/CORBIS. **250** (t) Staffan Widstrand/CORBIS. (b) Victor Engelbert. **252** © Yann Arthus-Bertrand/CORBIS. **254** (l) Christie's Images/CORBIS. (ml) Victor Engelbert. (mr) David Wolf. (r) Staffan Widstrand/CORBIS.

UNIT 4

258-259 © Stuart Dee/The Image Bank/GettyImages. **268** (l) Arnulf Husmo/Stone/GettyImages. (r) Nimatallah/Art Resource, New York. **269** (l) Erich Lessing/Art Resource, New York. (r) AKG, London. **270** © Bill Ross/CORBIS. **271** Arnulf Husmo/Stone/GettyImages. **272** (l) Walter Bibikow/Index Stock Imagery/PictureQuest. (r) © Eye Ubiquitous/CORBIS. **273** © Jonathan Blair/CORBIS. **274** © Johan Elzenga/Stone/GettyImages. **275** © HorreeZirkzee Produk/CORBIS. **277** Foto Marburg/Art Resource, New York. **278** (t) Sef/Art Resource, New York. (b) Nimatallah/Art Resource, New York. **279** Scala/Art Resource, New York. **280-283** © Ken Karp/HMCo. **285** Sef/Art Resource, New York **286** Erich Lessing/Art Resource, New York. **288** (l) Giraudon/Art Resource, New York. (r) Erich Lessing/Art Resource, New York. **289** © Macduff Everton/The Image Works. **290** (t) © Araldo de Luca/CORBIS. (b) © O. Alamany and E. Vicens/CORBIS. **291** Erich Lessing/Art Resource, New York. **293** (t) Catherine Karnow/CORBIS. (b) Reunion des Musées Nationaux/Art Resource, New York. **294** Jose Fuste Raga/eStockPhotography/PictureQuest. **295** Erich Lessing/Art Resource, New York. **296** (l) AKG, London. (r) Dept. of the Environment, London/The Bridgeman Art Library. **297** The Granger Collection, New York. **298** (l) Walter Bibikow/Index Stock Imagery/PictureQuest. (ml) Sef/Art Resource, New York. (mr) Erich Lessing/Art Resource, New York. (r) Jose Fuste Raga/eStockPhotography/PictureQuest. **300** (l) © CORBIS. (r) North Wind Pictures. **301** (l) The Granger Collection, New York. (r) © Roger Tidman/CORBIS. **302** The Granger Collection, New York. **303** Alinari/Art Resource, New York. **304** (t) Scott Gilchrist/Archivision.com. (b) Palazzo Medici-Riccardi, Florence, Italy/The Bridgeman Art Library. **305** (l) Reunion des Musées Nationaux/Art Resource, New York. (r) Scala/Art Resource, New York. **306** The Pierpont Morgan Library/Art Resource, New York. **307** © CORBIS. **308** © The Bridgeman Art Library/Getty Images. **310** Reunion des Musées Nationaux/Art Resource, New York. **311** Giraudon/Art Resource, New York. **315** © Angela Coppola/HMCo. **316** (l) Scala/Art Resource, New York. (r) NASA. **317** © HMCo. Archive. **318** The Granger Collection, New York. **319** (t) Hulton-Deutsch Collection/CORBIS. (b) Photo Bulloz. **320** Victoria & Albert Museum, London/Art Resource, New York. **321** Scala/Art Resource, New York. **323** (t) Erich Lessing/Art Resource, New York. (b) Chuck Nacke/Woodfin Camp/PictureQuest. **324** © Bettmann/CORBIS. **326** (l) North Wind Pictures. (ml) Alinari/Art Resource, New York. (mr) Hulton-Deutsch Collection/CORBIS. (r) Scala/Art Resource, New York. **328** (l) © Mark Rykoff/Rykoff Collection/CORBIS. **329** (l) © Bettmann/CORBIS. (r) © Dave Bartruff/CORBIS. **330-331**© Bettmann/CORBIS. **332** © Mark Rykoff/Rykoff Collection/CORBIS. **333** © Archivo Iconografico, S.A./CORBIS. **336** © Bettmann/CORBIS. **337** (t) Art Young. (b) Hulton Archive/Getty Images. **339** Hulton Archive/Getty Images **340** © Hulton-Deutsch Collection/CORBIS. **341** © Bettmann/CORBIS. **342-343** Reprinted with the permission of the St. Louis Post Dispatch, 2002. **344** © Ralph White/CORBIS. **345** © Peter Turnley/CORBIS. **346** © Hulton-Deutsch Collection/CORBIS. **347** (t) Hulton Archive/Getty Images. (b) Culver Pictures. **348** Hulton Archive/Getty Images. **349** © Dave Bartruff/CORBIS. **350** (l) © Mark Rykoff/Rykoff Collection/CORBIS. (m) © Hulton-Deutsch Collection/CORBIS. (r) Sovfoto/Eastfoto/PictureQuest. **352** (l) Sovfoto/Eastfoto. (r) © Bettmann/CORBIS. **353** (l) © Hulton-Deutsch Collection/CORBIS. (r) Hoa Qui/Index Stock Imagery/PictureQuest. **355** © Giuliano Bevilacqua/TimePix. **356** © Bryn Colton/CORBIS. **357** Sovfoto/Eastfoto. **358** (t) © Bettmann/CORBIS. (b) AP/Wide World Photos. **360** Sovfoto/Eastfoto/PictureQuest. **364** © David and Peter

Turnley/CORBIS. **366** (t) © Craig Aurness/CORBIS. (b) © Bios (F. Gilson)/Peter Arnold. **368** (l) © Peter Turnley/CORBIS. (r) Peter Turnley/CORBIS. **370** Scala/Art Resource, New York. **371** © Brannhage/Premium/Panoramic Images. **372** Hoa Qui/Index Stock Imagery/PictureQuest. **373** © AFP/CORBIS. **374** S. Bavister/Robert Harding Picture Library. **375** © Malcolm S. Kirk/Peter Arnold. **376** (l) © Bettmann/CORBIS. (m) © David and Peter Turnley/CORBIS. (r) © Premium Stock/CORBIS. **378** (l) © Robert Estall/CORBIS. (r) Art Resource, New York. **379** (l) © AFP/CORBIS. (r) © Bettmann/ CORBIS. **382** © Julian Nieman/Collections. **383** (l) John Launois/Black Star Publishing/PictureQuest. (r) © AFP/CORBIS. **385** Hans T. Dahlskog/Pressens Bild. **386** Alex Farnsworth/The Image Works. **387** © John Noble/CORBIS. **388** © Nik Wheeler/CORBIS. **389** © Wally McNamee/CORBIS. **390** © Robert Estall/CORBIS. **391** Art Resource, New York. **392** © CORBIS/Sygma. **393** © Bettmann/CORBIS. **394** © Kim Sayer/CORBIS. **395** (l) Josef Karl Stieler/Archivo Iconografico, S.A./CORBIS. (l) Erich Lessing/Art Resource, New York. **396** © Carmen Redondo/CORBIS. **397** Chuck Fishman/Contact Press Images/PictureQuest. **399** (l) © Bettmann/CORBIS. (r) Dennis Chamberlain/Black Star Publishing/PictureQuest. **400** © Steven Weinberg/Stone/GettyImages. **401** © Vittoriano Rastelli/CORBIS. **402-403** © Rob Matheson/CORBIS. **403** Michel Bussy/Photo Alto **406** (ml) Alex Farnsworth/The Image Works. (m) Art Resource, New York. (mr) © Carmen Redondo/CORBIS. (r) © Bettmann/CORBIS. **408** Brooklyn Eagle.

Art Credits

Beverly Doyle **22–23**. Nenad Jakesevic **149, 158, 162-3, 166, 381, 406**. Rich McMahon **44–45**. Lyle Miller **130–133**. Gary Overacre **334–345**. Matthew Pippin **222–223, 295**. Craig Spearing **280–283**. Wood Ronsaville Harlin, Inc. **28, 33**. All other artwork created by Publicom, Inc.